RANDY SPRICK'S
safe & civil
SCHOOLS
Practical Solutions, Positive Results!

Administrator's Desk Reference of Behavior Management

Volume I
Leadership Guide

Randall S. Sprick, Ph.D • Lisa Howard • B.J. Wise • Kim Marcum • Mike Haykin

ISBN 1-57035-333-6 (Set)

ISBN 1-57035-132-5 (Volume 1)

Edited by Betty Taylor

Text layout and design by Sherri Rowe

Cover Design by Katherine Getta

Printed in the United States of America
Published and Distributed by:

Pacific
Northwest
Publishing

P.O. Box 50610 • Eugene, OR 97405
(866) 542-1490 • (541) 345-1490
FAX: (541) 345-1507 • www.safeandcivilschools.com

dedication

This work is dedicated to our own children from whom we have learned so much about life, love, and learning:

Matt Sprick

Jessica Sprick

Mike Scott

Kevin Wise

Tristan Marcum

Brynn Marcum

Rachael Haykin

acknowledgments

First and foremost, we are indebted to the effective building principals with whom we have all worked. Nothing facilitates school improvement more than the building principal. It is our hope that this book will assist others to become like the inspirational building leaders who have taught us so much.

We are particularly grateful to Mickey Garrison, Ph.D., who provided extensive and helpful feedback and generously donated her time, ideas, and the tools she has developed for assessing the current condition of a school's policies and practices.

We would also like to acknowledge: Marilyn Sprick for constructive feedback on content; Judy Shinn and Dani Smith for their help and for holding the office together through the entire project; Joyce Maeda for meticulous copyediting; and the entire staff of Sopris West for their hard work, helpful support, and generous spirit of cooperation. In particular, we wish to thank Lynne Timmons, managing editor; Sherri Rowe, layout and design; and Betty Taylor, editor.

Randall S. Sprick, Ph.D., is an educational consultant and teacher trainer in Eugene, Oregon. Each year, Dr. Sprick conducts workshops and classes for over 5,000 teachers and administrators throughout the United States and Canada. Much of his work involves helping teachers set up classrooms that encourage student responsibility and motivation, while humanely and effectively helping misbehaving students learn to behave in more responsible ways.

Dr. Sprick has developed numerous articles, books, audio tapes, and videotapes that assist school personnel in dealing with the issues of discipline and classroom management. Dr. Sprick has been an assistant professor and currently is an adjunct faculty member of the University of Oregon and the Seattle Pacific University. He is a past president of the Association for Direct Instruction.

Lisa M. Howard, B.A., is a former special and general education teacher. She has worked on a number of school-based research projects in California, Oregon, and Washington. Lisa is a co-author on *The Teacher's Encyclopedia of Behavior Management: 100 Problems/500 Plans*, and is co-author with Marilyn Sprick on *Read Well: A Beginning Reading Program*.

B.J. Wise is a practicing principal who has been a teacher at the elementary, junior high, and senior high school levels. She has been honored as a National Distinguished Principal and has received the Washington State Award for Excellence in Education. B.J. has consulted on educational issues throughout the United States and Europe.

Kim Marcum, M.Ed., is a practicing elementary principal in the Central Kitsap School District in the state of Washington. Kim is a longtime educator with an extensive background in special education. She has taught special education at both the elementary and secondary levels. Kim is a highly respected educational leader with a passion for orchestrating success for the most challenging children in our schools. As a presenter, her work in the areas of behavior management, inclusion, and study skills are well known throughout the United States.

Mike Haykin, M.Ed., is a certified mental health counselor and a school counselor in Kitsap County, Washington. Mike has specialized in working with children and adolescents with severe behavioral and emotional difficulties. He has consulted with schools, hospitals, and social service agencies and has been an instructor for Seattle University's Addiction Studies Department. Mike also served as a special education educator in elementary, junior high, and postsecondary settings.

Overview of The Safe & Civil Schools Series

Management, Motivation & Discipline

The Safe and Civil Schools Series is a collection of practical materials designed to help create productive, safe, and respectful learning environments. The goal of the series is to empower school personnel with techniques to help all students behave responsibly and respectfully. The materials are full of specific "how-to" information. Though each resource stands alone, all are designed around five basic beliefs:

All students must be treated with dignity and respect.

Students can and should be taught the skills and behaviors needed for success.

Motivation and responsibility should be encouraged through positive interactions and through building relationships with students.

Student misbehavior provides a teaching opportunity.

Collaboration is critical. All school staff members must work together to help students behave responsibly and to meet student needs.

Other Components of The Safe & Civil Schools Series

Foundations: Establishing Positive Discipline Policies is a three-module CD-ROM program that assists staff in designing a school-wide discipline policy that creates a calm, safe school environment. The goal of the policy is to establish consistency, clear expectations, positive interactions, improve student motivation, and reduce office referrals. Materials provide step-by-step information on how to write, implement, and maintain a policy that guides actual daily practice.

START on Time! Safe Transitions And Reduced Tardies is a multi-media in-service designed for middle and high schools. Your entire staff works together to coordinate hallway supervision, resulting in fewer tardies, increased academic time, safer hallways, and an improved school climate.

Interventions: Collaborative Planning for Students At Risk is both a resource and a process for education professionals. Through consultation and collaboration, staff members learn to share their expertise in developing practical intervention plans for at risk students. An optional 20-cassette audiotape album is available to accompany this resource. The manual explains how to (a) analyze a behavior or motivation problem, (b) select interventions, (c) work with classroom teachers, and (d) follow up and monitor progress. Booklets describe 16 specific interventions that teach individual students how to work successfully in the classroom setting.

CHAMPs: A Proactive and Positive Approach to Classroom Management is a systematic guide for teachers on how to design a classroom management plan that will help them to overtly teach students how to behave responsibly. Classroom teachers develop methods for clearly communicating and teaching students to meet their expectations. This resource will help any teacher increase respectful and civil interactions, maximize student on-task behavior, reduce classroom disruptions, and improve overall classroom climate.

CHAMPs Video In-service Series is a group of ten videotapes with print materials that provide everything necessary to lead a class or study group working through the CHAMPs book. These fast-paced videos bring the CHAMPs book to life and guide groups of teachers in discussion and self-assessment activities.

The Teacher's Encyclopedia of Behavior Management is a comprehensive reference for elementary and middle/junior high school teachers. It provides practical solutions to more than 100 common classroom problems. For each problem covered, there are three to five step-by-step intervention plans that teachers can choose from or modify to fit their particular situations. Alphabetically arranged, with an extensive index, as well as cross-referencing among the problems, the Encyclopedia is an indispensable tool for teachers wishing to help their students learn to be responsible for their own behavior.

ParaPro: Supporting the Instructional Process is a resource book that enables paraprofessionals in your school or district to better assist teachers and students. ParaPro will confirm and extend the behavioral skills of your most productive paraprofessionals and raise the skill level of others.

Bus Discipline is a four-tape video program designed to help bus drivers and classroom teachers improve student behavior on busses. The program also contains information for administrators on how to assess, revise, and implement transportation policies.

Cafeteria Discipline can help you turn your school's lunchroom into a calm, orderly place that staff and students will enjoy. This two-tape video program provides information on how to better prepare students to behave appropriately in the cafeteria, as well as specific strategies for lunchroom supervisors on how to manage behavior more effectively. The program also includes reproducible materials that can be used by staff.

contents

Introduction   1

Purpose 1
Rationale 1
Overview of Contents 3
How to Use This Book 4

chapter one

Leadership Skills—Improving School Climate   5

Task One—Clarify and Promote a Vision 6
Task Two—Build Trust 14
Task Three—Strive to Meet Basic Human Needs 23
Task Four—Use Rituals and Traditions 27

chapter two

Leadership Skills—Effective Decision
Making and Handling Disagreements   39

Making Decisions 39
Handling Disagreements 45
Conclusion 52

chapter three

Practical Guidelines for Behavior Change   53

Changing Behavior—Five Variables to Manipulate 55
Guidelines for Modifying Settings 57
Guidelines for Corrective Consequences 60
Guidelines for Encouraging Responsible Behavior 65
Conclusion 70

chapter four

Understanding Behavioral Theory 71

Section One: Behavioral Theory (A Model and Its
Implications) 72
Section Two: Questions and Misconceptions
Regarding a Behavioral Approach 82

chapter five

A Process for Improving Your Schoolwide Behavior Plan (SBP) 89

Section One: SBP Improvement Activities 90
Section Two: Sample Tools for Doing a "Review" 115

chapter six

Guiding Principles—The Core of Your SBP 139

Section One: Why Have a "Guiding Principles"
Section in your SBP? 140
Section Two: A School Mission Statement 141
Section Three: Statement of Staff Beliefs About
Managing Student Behavior 144
Section Four: Guidelines for Student Success 150
Section Five: Sample Policy Documents 153

chapter seven

Encouragement Procedures—Meeting Students' Basic Needs 159

Section One: Why Have an "Encouragement
Procedures" Section in Your SBP? 161
Section Two: Meeting Students' Basic Needs 166
Section Three: Using Schoolwide Reinforcement
Systems 174
Section Four: Menu of Procedures/Programs to
Encourage Responsible Behavior 179

chapter eight

Disciplinary Procedures—Increasing Consistency and Effectiveness 209

Section One: Planning for Emergency Situations 211
Section Two: Supporting Staff Efforts to Deal With
　　　Student Misbehavior 216

chapter nine

Common Areas—Improving Behavior in Halls, Cafeteria, Playground, and Other Areas 253

Introduction 254
Seven Strategies for Improving a Common Area 255
Supplement One: Evaluating the School Cafeteria
　　　Environment 277
Supplement Two: Model Procedures for Common Areas 292

chapter ten

Classrooms—Assisting Teachers With Behavior and Discipline 315

Section One: Guiding Principles of Classroom
　　　Management 317
Section Two: Guiding Staff in Effective Classroom
　　　Management 341

Resources/References 363

introduction

Purpose

The Administrator's Desk Reference of Behavior Management consists of three volumes designed to assist building principals (and assistant principals) in:

- Ensuring that all school settings are safe and productive.

- Creating a positive school climate with a high expectancy of student success.

- Designing effective policies and procedures for prompting students to be responsible, highly motivated, and actively engaged in school tasks.

- Guiding staff in being

  - Proactive (preventing problems before they begin);

  - Positive (interacting with students in a friendly, inviting way and providing age-appropriate, positive feedback); and

  - Instructional (correcting misbehavior calmly and consistently to teach students to behave more responsibly).

Rationale

Every school has characteristics that distinguish it from other schools. Some are "external" features that are not within the staff's ability to influence—for example, number of students attending, grade levels served, socioeconomic status of students' families, racial and ethnic composition of students and staff, and so on. Other school characteristics are unique and idiosyncratic and evolve over time. They include such things as school climate, the amount and intensity of student misbehavior, the level of student motivation, the consistency of staff in enforcing expectations, and staff treatment of at-risk students. These latter characteristics, when taken together, might be described as the "school culture." Schools that resemble each other exactly on external characteristics (e.g., size, grade levels, etc.) can, and often do, have very different school cultures. It is our belief that the characteristics of a school's culture can be "managed" to create an environment that fosters growth and encourages responsible behavior, and that daily staff actions play a huge role in this process. The following figure demonstrates how a school culture is established, or at the very least influenced, by staff actions.

School 1	School 2
"BE QUIET! I DO NOT WANT TO HEAR ANOTHER WORD OUT OF ANY OF YOU!" could be the motto in this school. As you walk down the hall, the sounds of adult anger and heavy-handed control seem pervasive.	"YOU DID IT! YOU SHOULD BE VERY PROUD OF YOUR ACCOMPLISHMENT!" could be the motto of this school. As you walk down the hall, the sounds of enthusiastic students and supportive adults celebrating student accomplishments seem pervasive.
While sitting in the faculty room, one repeatedly hears comments such as: • "These kids are driving me crazy—what a bunch of little animals." • "That Adam should just be kicked out of school. I don't see why we have to put up with his crap." • "Shawna's mother is just as much of a b—— as Shawna is."	In the faculty room, you regularly hear things like: • "My class is so excited about their projects for the science fair." • "That Adam is a real challenge. We need to have a staffing to set up a plan to help him." • "Shawna's mother seems pretty hostile. We have to figure out some way to get her to work with us."
Consequences for misbehavior are implemented hostilely, inconsistently, and arbitrarily.	Consequences for misbehavior are implemented calmly and consistently. For chronic misbehaviors, consequences are only part of a comprehensive plan for teaching the student to behave more responsibly.
Never is heard an encouraging word— unless a student is a star athlete or an "A" student.	Encouraging words are used frequently and effectively to motivate every student to meet his/her fullest potential.

We also believe that the building administrator has the primary responsibility for guiding and shaping the attitudes and actions that influence his/her school's culture. This book focuses specifically on an administrator's responsibilities related to student motivation and discipline (i.e., behavior management). It addresses those things an administrator can and should do with students, parents, and staff to ensure the kind of effective behavior management practices that create a school culture that encourages responsible and motivated behavior (from students, parents, and staff). Working as a team, administrators, staff, parents, and students can create a dynamic environment that celebrates the unique strengths of every individual and encourages each individual to strive to achieve his/her full potential.

Overview of Contents

Volume I:
Leadership Guide

Every school has a Schoolwide Behavior Plan (SBP)—it is the sum of all current policies and procedures related to improving student behavior and motivation. Although every school has one, some SBPs are better thought out and more carefully constructed than others. Volume I is designed to help you, along with your staff, review and revise your SBP to make it more proactive, positive, and instructional.

The first part of the book delineates the skills and knowledge necessary for you as principal to guide your staff in the development and implementation of a proactive, positive, and instructional SBP. Chapters One and Two focus specifically on the leadership skills you need to enhance your school's climate and to guide your staff in making efficient and effective decisions. The next two chapters provide both the practical and theoretical knowledge of behavior (i.e., how behavior is learned and how behavior can be changed) that will allow you to make informed judgments about which behavior management practices are likely to be effective (and humane) and which may not be.

The second part of Volume I begins with a chapter describing a process for involving staff, students, and parents in developing an effective SBP. It includes detailed suggestions for evaluating your SBP as it is right now. The next five chapters deal with each of the five "content" sections all SBPs should address. They have information, activities, and sample written policies to assist you and your staff in examining and revising your current practices. The five sections are:

- Chapter Six, Guiding Principles—The Core of Your SBP

- Chapter Seven, Encouragement Procedures—Meeting Students' Basic Needs

- Chapter Eight, Disciplinary Procedures—Increasing Consistency and Effectiveness

- Chapter Nine, Common Areas—Improving Behavior in Halls, Cafeterias, Playgrounds, and Other Areas.

- Chapter Ten, Classrooms—Assisting Teachers With Behavior and Discipline

Volume II:
Referrals and Solutions

Volume II begins with general information on how to deal with disciplinary referrals. This section offers suggestions on what to do before you meet with a student who has been referred, what to do and say during the meeting with the student, and what to do after the meeting. Guidelines include when and how to set up proactive plans with individual students to reduce the chance that they will behave in a manner that results in another referral. The bulk of Volume II is a reference source that you can use to look up problems that you, as principal, are often called upon to handle (stealing, fighting, the bully, playground problems, vandalism, absenteeism, and more). For each problem, there are detailed suggestions on what you can do to help solve the problem.

Volume III:
Meaningful Work

This volume describes how to set up a schoolwide plan for assigning jobs around the school as a strategy for improving student behavior and motivation. We have found that giving students "real" responsibilities around the school can significantly reduce behavior problems, in part, because well-designed jobs meet students' needs for attention, recognition, competence, belonging, stimulation, and so on. The information in this volume contains everything you need to get a Meaningful Work program up and running in your school, including more than 100 specific job descriptions (from Advice Column Editor to Zoologist [Fish Tender]).

How to Use This Book

There is no right or wrong way to use this series. You can view it sequentially—working through Volume I first, then Volume II, and eventually implementing a Meaningful Work program (Volume III). Or you could do just the reverse. The best advice is for you to skim through all three volumes, and then decide what makes the most sense for you and your situation. Implementing all the different strategies suggested in these volumes would, realistically, take at least a year, and if you pace things so you don't burn out your staff or yourself, it may be more like several years.

Regardless of where you begin, you should plan fairly early to study Volume I, Chapter Five: A Process for Improving Your Schoolwide Behavior Plan (SBP). This chapter offers detailed advice on how to establish SBP improvement as an ongoing process in which you and your staff review yearly your current SBP, identify its strengths and weaknesses, and revise your procedures to address the weaknesses.

The bad news is that you are never done with the process of improving your SBP. The good news is you have a comprehensive set of resources with practical suggestions for making any needed improvements.

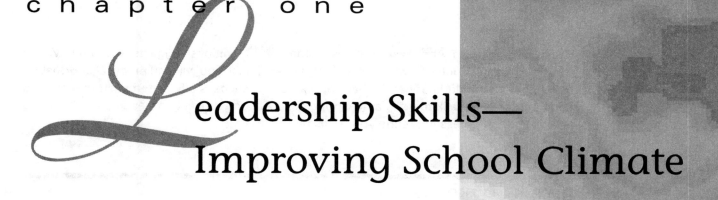

chapter one

Leadership Skills—
Improving School Climate

As unskilled jobs in fields, factories, and farms disappear, the importance of schools on the long-term success of their students is unparalleled. For young people, dropping out of school represents a dead end before they've even begun. Unfortunately, at the same time a good education has become increasingly critical for all students, more students come to school struggling with issues of divorce, neglect, and sometimes abuse. Therefore, schools are being asked to keep more students in school, dealing with greater numbers of students who have significant emotional and behavioral needs. This task is difficult, if not impossible, when schools take an old-fashioned approach to discipline.

One of the most pressing jobs for a principal, therefore, is to direct and coordinate efforts by a school's staff, students, and parents to successfully create a school environment that is safe and productive for all. Whereas in the past effective principals primarily needed to be good managers—that is, people who worked out the logistics of class assignments and bus schedules, handled occasional behavior problems, and dealt with crisis situations—today the effective principal must be for his/her school what all successful organizations need: an effective leader.

This chapter describes four major leadership tasks that serve as important foundations for your efforts to ensure a safe and productive environment at your school. Task One: Clarify and Promote a Vision is about picturing what you want your school to look like, feel like, and accomplish. Along with practical information about why and how to develop a "vision" for your school, is discussion of the many "hats you must wear" to guide staff, students, and parents toward that vision. Task Two: Build Trust provides guidelines for developing and maintaining the trust of your staff, students, and parents so that they will be willing to let you lead them toward the vision. A mental schema for thinking about and addressing the social and psychological needs of staff, students, and parents is presented in Task Three: Strive to Meet

Basic Human Needs. And, Task Four: Use Rituals and Traditions suggests why and how you can make your school a fun and joyful place. For each task you will find practical information on what you should know and what you can do to successfully accomplish that task. In addition, for each task there is at least one Take Action! subsection designed to help you assess and, as necessary, refine your skills on the task.

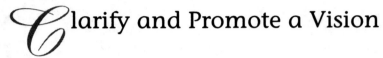

task one
Clarify and Promote a Vision

When you don't know where you want to go, you are likely to end up someplace you don't want to be. This simple truism applies to individuals and organizations alike. Your school will evolve and change whether or not you do anything. The real issue is whether the inevitable changes will benefit your students. As school leader, one of your most important tasks is to see that your school moves in beneficial directions. You can do this by: (1) Identifying a clear picture or vision of your desired "destination" (i.e., a school with a safe and productive environment); (2) Defining that vision in a clear, concise mission statement; and (3) Recognizing and refining the many roles that you, as building leader, must fill to successfully guide staff, students, and parents toward the vision.

Identify Your Destination

Unfortunately, no one can argue that there are bad schools in our nation—schools that fail day after day to meet the needs of their students. Yet, it's important to keep in mind that no one sets out to create a bad school. Most often bad schools happen due to the lack of vision and/or ineffective leadership. That is, when staff do not have a clear picture of what they want their school to be and/or have no one to effectively lead them to the vision they do have, the changes that occur in a school can be disastrous. As your school's leader, it is up to you to create, and then share with your staff, a vision of what your school can and should be.

Our vision for schools is simple—the school environment, in all settings, is safe and productive for both students and staff. Students are responsible, highly motivated, and actively engaged. Staff facilitate positive student behaviors by being proactive, positive, and by teaching effectively.

Additional Reading

For additional reading on the importance of vision and the role of leadership in developing and maintaining that vision, see *Visionary Leadership* by Burt Nanus.

Take Action!

1. If you feel that you have a general sense of what you want your school to be, but cannot articulate the specifics of that vision, identify exemplary schools that serve student populations similar to yours. Arrange to visit these schools. Pay particular attention to how things look and sound. What do the classrooms, office, cafeteria, and other settings look like? What do the various settings sound like? What is the tone of interactions—among staff members? among students? between students and staff members? Do people treat each other respectfully? Do students seem excited about learning? Are students actively engaged in meaningful activities? As you observe, identify specific aspects of the school you like and do not like.

2. Familiarize yourself with the research literature on effective schools. In the past 25 years, researchers have confirmed many common features of effective schools. The Northwest Regional Labs has developed an excellent summary of the research in *Effective Schooling Practices: A Research Synthesis, 1995 Update*, compiled by Kathleen Cotton. This inexpensive resource provides an overview of the major features of effective schools and effective classrooms, and identifies the research studies from which those findings have been drawn. In various chapters throughout this book, you will find relevant excerpts from the synthesis, labeled "What the Research Says." If you would like a copy of the actual document for your school, you can call or write:

Document Reproduction Service
Northwest Regional Educational Laboratory
101 S.W. Main Street, Suite 500
Portland, Oregon 97204
(503) 275-9519

3. Establish priorities annually to translate vision into action.

Operationalize Your Vision in a Clear, Concise Mission Statement

If your school doesn't have a mission statement, you should plan to develop one. To be useful, a mission statement should be consistent with your picture of a safe and productive school. It should, in effect, define the purpose of your school and explain why you, staff, students, and parents bother to work hard. With its definition of a common purpose, a mission statement can make clear the goal of your school and, thereby, serve as an overall guide to everyone's actions.

If your school already has a clear mission statement, ask yourself whether it is functioning as it should. First of all, do most staff, students, and parents know what the mission statement is? If they don't, you need to publicize it. Staff and students should know and understand why they come to school every day. Parents should know and understand why they send their children to school every day.

Mission Statement Example

The following mission statement answers why the school exists by stating, "Horace Mann Middle School's Mission is to provide a compassionate learning environment in which all students experience acceptance and success." This mission statement tells us why our role as a school staff is important. It tells us why we ask for parental support, and explains why students come to our school each day. This particular mission statement comes from Horace Mann Middle School in Amarillo, Texas.

If you have a mission statement that people know, the next question to ask yourself is whether or not it is being used as a basis for making school decisions (e.g., about discipline and motivational procedures). For any given decision, are the alternatives weighed by looking at which option best supports the school's mission? A mission statement should guide both immediate and long-range decision making. For example, when you are faced with the need to respond to severe student misbehavior, you should first ask, "What are my response choices in this situation?" Then you should ask, "Which of these choices best fits the mission of the school?" When the mission statement isn't factored into a school's decisions, the choices made may be based more on expediency or ease of implementation rather than on their potential to help the school achieve its goal.

Take Action!

1. If your school doesn't have a mission statement, plan to develop one. Chapter Six: Guiding Principles—The Core of Your SBP walks you through the development of various written policies, including a mission statement, a statement of staff beliefs about behavior management, and a statement of the school's guidelines for student success. Samples of each of these documents, along with a rationale for each, are provided.

   For some schools, developing a working mission statement and clarifying staff beliefs may be important as a first step in creating a safer and more productive school. For other schools, this task will be secondary to solving more immediately pressing problems such as chaotic hallways, an out-of-control playground, rampant vandalism, or high rates of absenteeism.

2. If your school has a mission statement that is not being fully used, start referencing it overtly and continually. Occasionally begin assemblies, staff meetings, and parent meetings by reviewing the mission statement. Let staff, students, and parents know when their actions support and maintain the mission statement. Remember, it is everyday actions that bring a mission statement to life.

Recognize the Many Roles You Must Play as Building Leader

Movement toward a school's vision does not occur without daily action. As principal, you will have to fill many roles (i.e., wear many hats) in order to successfully lead staff, students, and parents toward your school's vision. What follows are short and generic explanations of these many roles.

Teacher

As building principal, you should think of yourself as your school's "big teacher." In that role, one of your most important jobs is to teach staff, students, and parents to share your vision of what the school should be like. An important key to achieving the school vision is that it be held by all the various members of the school community.

In addition, as big teacher you need to teach and model the behaviors you expect from your staff. If you want staff doing things differently, you must be prepared to teach them different ways of doing things. If you have staff who treat students disrespectfully, you have to teach them how to get what they need while treating students in a respectful manner. When staff are required to learn a new skill or technique (e.g., better classroom management strategies), participate in the training with them—so that you will be able to model the new approaches. This does not mean that you have to do everything perfectly. Actually, it can be very powerful for staff to see that you are willing to try new skills, make mistakes, and learn from those mistakes.

You need to function as big teacher for students and parents as well. When you see a student misbehaving in the hall, you need to step in and correct the student in a way that teaches a more positive alternative. When a parent yells at her child in front of other children in the school, an unskilled principal will lament that parents like this exist. The skilled principal, on the other hand, accepts the parent's limitations, but models alternative ways of behaving. (Obviously this needs to be done skillfully so that the parent feels supported—not alienated or belittled by the experience.)

Coach

You also need to be a coach, as well as teacher, to staff, students, and parents. A coach provides nonthreatening practice opportunities, positive feedback on successful attempts, and corrective feedback when mistakes are made. Think about a basketball coach. She doesn't simply tell her players how to shoot free throws at the beginning of the season and then not address free throws again. She makes sure her players get plenty of practice, repeated instruction, positive and corrective feedback, and then more practice—all of which will result in gradual improvements as the season progresses. A truly great coach accomplishes all this while concurrently structuring things so that team members have a great time, love the sport, and function as a true TEAM in the most positive sense of that word. An effective coach realizes that behavior change takes time. Most teams do not function perfectly on the first day of practice. However, by the last game of the season, the team (and each individual on the team) should be more skilled than they were at the beginning of the season.

Staff, students, and parents need to know that it is all right to make mistakes while learning something new. As coach, you should provide feedback, both positive and corrective, to guide people in the direction of the vision—and you need to create a sense of team spirit. You need to teach the important skills and watch for gradual improvements as the season (school year) progresses.

Preacher

In your role as preacher, your job is to keep people motivated to strive toward the vision. This is especially important when it comes to staff. Working in a school is hard, demanding work. Even as you acknowledge the work they are currently doing, you also have to continually ask your staff to do things more effectively (i.e., move closer to the vision). One way to do this is to always let them know the benefits that will be derived from any specific efforts to achieve the vision. Let them know the point of the various policies and procedures you want them to implement. Nobody wants to do extra work (or learn to do something differently) if there will be no positive results. As various strategies and procedures are introduced in this book, we have tried to include information that can be shared with staff on the positive results that should occur if the strategy or procedure is implemented.

Effective preachers know that just telling people the benefits of doing something is not enough; they know that part of preaching involves making emotional appeals or giving people emotional "jump starts" to help them renew the vision and "recharge their batteries." Effective preachers also realize that emotional appeals cannot be one-time events—even the most religious congregation needs ongoing reminders to keep it motivated to continue moving toward its goal.

Monitor

As building leader, one of your roles is to monitor, or check, that people are following through on what they should be doing. Even when people know what they are supposed to do and are motivated to do it, they often do not follow through without someone monitoring them. Think about it this way. Most drivers know (and agree with) the benefits of coming to a complete stop at a stop sign, yet some still tend to do rolling stops. When a police officer is present, however, most "rolling stoppers" do come to complete stops. In fact even when there is only a reasonable chance that a police officer might be observing a particular intersection, most "rolling stoppers" will come to a complete stop.

Besides increasing follow-through, monitoring has the added benefit of staff knowing that you are aware of their efforts to implement procedures designed to move the school toward the vision. When you take the time to teach, coach, and preach about a specific policy or procedure, most staff will be motivated to implement it; and they will want to know that you see that they are following through. As monitor, you need to be highly visible, so that staff, students, and parents realize that not only do you expect them to do what they are supposed to do, but that you will know whether or not they do.

Nag

Occasionally as you monitor, you may notice things that require you to be a nag. Everyone needs periodic reminders to follow through on tasks that, although seemingly unimportant, must be done. For example, if you have some staff who view attendance procedures as a nuisance, and occasionally "forget" to get the attendance slips filled out and in the proper place on time, you may have to "nag" these staff members to follow through. Varying how you nag can reduce the likelihood that your message will be tuned out. For example, sometimes you might give a gentle reminder to all staff during faculty meetings (without naming names of individuals). Other times you can use humor: "Yesterday, 63% of staff had attendance slips ready on time. Perhaps there is room for improvement. Think of this as my homework assignment to you all." And finally, there will be times when you have to directly tell certain individuals that they must begin to follow through on whatever the expectation is.

Supporter, Follower, Booster

In a school community of highly motivated people, ideas for improvement will come from staff, parents, and students, as well as from you. Whenever you believe that an idea will move your school toward the vision, you need to support that idea and even allow others to take the lead in implementing it. A skilled leader welcomes opportunities for others to get credit for new and more effective ways of doing things. Your willingness to follow the lead of others demonstrates that you have no need to wield power for power's sake. Throwing administrative support behind an idea developed and implemented by staff, students, or parents makes it clear that you support (and will give credit to) all ideas that support the vision. Remember, leadership sometimes involves clearing the road, getting out of the way, or falling in behind other leaders, while supporting and cheering them on.

Gatekeeper

One of your biggest challenges may be avoiding "change for the sake of change." When you believe that a proposal (e.g., for a new curriculum or a new behavior management procedure) will not be beneficial for your school, you need to act as gatekeeper and not allow the proposal to be implemented. Your decision about opening or closing the gate should be based on three criteria. First, does it seem likely that the proposal will move the school toward the vision? If not, keep the gate closed. Second, does the proposal have a sound research base supporting its effectiveness? This is especially critical for major staff development efforts and curricular decisions. Unfortunately, too often the implementation of new school programs resembles a jumping-on-the-band-wagon phenomenon. Popular trends, whether they have research to back them up or not, tend to sweep the country—and everybody starts implementing them. You need to be aware that when a proposal is not supported by the school effectiveness literature, you should be very cautious about opening the gate. (Use the *School Effectiveness Research Synthesis: 1995 Update* cited earlier as a starting point in this investigation.) The third criteria to consider, as your school's gatekeeper, is timing. Is it the right time to pursue a particular proposal given other priorities? Are there people available and willing to carry out the tasks at this time? Will undertaking the new idea put undue stress on people (especially when weighed against the proposal's potential benefits)?

When you believe a proposal reflects your school's vision, is supported by research (or at least does not contradict known research findings), and has been presented at a good time, then shift into your roles of teacher, coach, preacher, supporter, follower, and booster. Visibly get behind the proposal and work to see that it happens.

Evaluator

In the business world, organizations use objective measures such as sales reports, production records, and measures of goal attainment to determine the effectiveness of their operations. One of your jobs as principal, obviously, is to evaluate the performance of your staff members. It's also important for you to assume responsibility for evaluating (or arranging for others to evaluate) the overall effectiveness of your organization and the effectiveness of specific programs—particularly new ones. Most districts have some sort of plan to evaluate their students' academic achievement growth. We believe that you should also have a plan for evaluating the overall quality of your school's behavior management practices. Chapter Five: A Process for Improving Your Schoolwide Behavior Plan (SBP) contains information (including sample instruments) on how to assess staff, student, and parent satisfaction with current behavior management policies and procedures, as well as suggestions for gathering other information (data) to guide your behavior management decisions. The SBP content chapters (Chapters Six through Ten) also include ideas for assessing specific aspects of your current behavior management practices (along with suggestions for making any necessary changes).

Along with an overall evaluation of your behavior management practices, you should always plan on evaluating the effectiveness of any major innovations or new staff development efforts. The questions to ask yourself include: Did this innovation or effort produce the desired result? Is it moving us closer to our vision?

Mediator

Conflicts arise within all organizations. This is especially true in dynamic organizations whose members are actively striving to achieve a common vision. Conflicts can stem from people having different goals, or from people having the same goals but very different ideas about how to achieve those goals, or from people having very different perceptions of events that have taken place. As the school's leader, one of your roles is to mediate those inevitable conflicts so that everyone feels supported, everyone gets their needs met, and the organization progresses toward the vision. Specific strategies for dealing with conflict situations and achieving consensus about decisions are provided in the next chapter.

Take Action!

Think about your varied roles as building leader. Identify four roles that you view as current strengths—those in which you do well. Then identify four or five that you consider to be weaker areas—those in which you need to improve. Reread the descriptions of the roles that are your weaker areas, and come up with ways that you can, in the next couple of days, practice each role. If you think that one of your weaker areas is as coach, identify ways that you can create safe opportunities for staff to practice a new skill or behavior. You might, for example, design a role play activity for a faculty meeting, or establish times for teachers to observe each other (voluntarily), or model a lesson yourself and ask a teacher to give you feedback, then reverse roles.

Your weaker roles can also be useful guides to the kinds of strategies and procedures that will be most beneficial to you. Keep those weaker roles in mind as you read the various suggestions in this book, and specifically seek out tasks that could help you improve in those roles. For example, Chapter Five: A Process for Improving Your Schoolwide Behavior Plan (SBP) presents a number of ideas for keeping people excited about implementing effective behavior management procedures. If you identified the preacher role as one of your stronger areas, you might not find too much useful information in that section. However, if preacher is a weaker area for you, you may wish to study and practice the suggestions we have included.

Identify four or five areas in each category.

Leadership Roles	Strengths	Weaknesses
Teacher		
Coach		
Preacher		
Monitor		
Nag		
Gatekeeper		
Evaluator		
Mediator		

task two
Build Trust

In any organization, the leader needs to have people's trust. As leader of a school, you need to have the trust of your staff, the students, and the students' parents. You will find that while trust comes easily from some people, from others it must be earned and carefully nurtured. Building trust is one of your most important tasks, because mistrust will almost always adversely affect a school. For example, mistrust may cause parents to be angry at you or other school staff for no apparent reason. A student may act out his/her mistrust with angry disruptive behavior. Mistrust might be at the root of a staff member's consistently negative interactions with students. And mistrust is often behind some staff members' efforts to habitually sabotage what you are trying to accomplish.

Trust will be created by what you do. The following 12 guidelines provide practical suggestions for building and maintaining a foundation of trust with staff, students, and parents.

Manage Space and Materials Efficiently

It is very important to make sure that staff members' needs for workspace and materials are met. Although this harkens back to a more traditional view of a principal's job (as building manager), by seeing that workspaces are adequate and basic materials are provided (or at least divided equitably), you show staff that you value them and respect what they do. Even when budget constraints limit what you can actually do, you will earn staff respect by trying to free them from minor logistic concerns. For example, by assuming responsibility for simple administrative decisions you ensure that staff do not waste their time "fighting" over art paper or the use of the copy machine.

Communicate Expectations Clearly

Entire books have been written about effective communication, so we will not presume to try and present everything about this topic in a few short paragraphs. However, because simple misunderstandings can easily lead to loss of trust, we will offer one basic suggestion for clear communication. In short, we believe that clear communication depends, in part, on giving information or directions specifically, descriptively, and redundantly.

When you have expectations of staff, students, or parents, be specific and descriptive when you tell them what those expectations are. That is, describe precisely how you want something to look and/or sound, and provide examples if appropriate. Furthermore, because communication tends to be imprecise, plan on repeating your expectations at least once—at a later date, and if possible, in a different form. For example, if you give staff a direction in a memo, restate it at the next faculty meeting. Repetition reduces the potential mistrust that can arise from missed or misunderstood communication.

Consider the following examples of general versus specific and descriptive messages and statements.

Example Messages and Statements

General	**Specific and Descriptive**
STAFF	**STAFF**

STAFF

Please make a greater effort to arrive at staff meetings on time. Some people have been arriving later and later as the year progresses.

STAFF
3:30 Staff Meetings Will Now Actually Begin at 3:30!

Please make a greater effort to arrive at staff meetings on time so we can begin the first agenda item at exactly 3:30. In the interest of efficiency we will begin and end on time. Arrive before 3:30 with pencil, paper, and your attention (that means no student papers to grade). Thanks!

P.S.   In appreciation of your efforts, we will occasionally have a "Door Prize" drawing for people who arrive on time.

STAFF

Please talk to your students about the playground rules and treating the people on duty more respectfully.

STAFF
Playground Safety

Students have been following most of the playground rules, but have gotten careless about a couple. Please review the following playground rules with your students:

- No rough play (includes wrestling, pushing, grabbing clothing, fighting or martial arts, real or pretend).
- Stay on the playground side of the yellow line between the blacktop and parking lot.
- Treat playground supervisors with respect—they are there to keep the playground safe!

Please emphasize the last item. More students have been overtly rude to the assistants. Let students know that you (teacher) and I (principal) fully expect them to follow directions of playground assistants immediately and politely.

Finally, tell students that everyone has been doing an excellent job of coming in quickly and quietly when the bell rings at the end of recess. Let them know there has been a big improvement in the past month and that we appreciate their efforts.

PARENTS

Please be more careful when you pick up your children. Some people have been going way too fast, and have been picking up children in the bus loading areas.

PARENTS
Remember—for the safety of our kids, please drive slowly and follow our basic safety rules!

We need to work together to make "After School Pickup" safer! Please follow these three important safety procedures:

1. Go no more than 5 miles per hour in the turnaround or parking lot.
2. Pick up your children in the turnaround or parking lot. DO NOT go into the bus loading areas.
3. Keep alert! With 752 middle school students leaving at one time, a student may forget the rules and step out into a traffic area.

Thanks for your cooperation! By working together we can ensure that all of our children stay safe!

Provide Positive Feedback

Positive feedback (praise) is a way of letting people know their actions are productive. When you take the time to acknowledge the efforts of your staff, they do not need to second-guess whether their efforts are making a difference. With positive feedback you can let all staff members, including those who might be feeling insecure, know that their actions are contributing to the well-being of the school. Providing positive feedback to students lets them know they have grown in their academic efforts or in their maturity and sense of responsibility. And positive feedback to parents reminds them that their efforts on behalf of the school and their children are appreciated. Following are guidelines for providing praise (i.e., positive feedback).

- Be accurate. Never praise someone for something they have not done.

- Focus on the individual(s) you are praising. Your purpose should not be to get others to behave better. Although praising one student may result in another student behaving better, your goal is to sincerely acknowledge the first individual's actions.

- Be specific by describing the behavior and/or product. The following statement acknowledges a specific behavior of students and how that behavior contributes to a safe school environment. "Eric and Timothy, thank you for keeping our halls safe by remembering to walk."

  This next statement not only acknowledges a staff member's efforts to recognize student accomplishments, but also shows how good ideas can be shared in a spirit of cooperation with other staff members. "Mrs. Howard, that is one of the most creative ways to display student work I have ever seen. May I have your permission to mention it in the next faculty meeting?"

  Don't forget to acknowledge parental efforts to support the school. A simple comment made in passing may mean as much as or more than some kind of formal recognition. A statement like, "Mrs. Smith, thanks for your help at the popcorn machine. We are halfway to making enough money to buy the new playground equipment," lets a parent know that her presence is noticed and worthwhile.

- Avoid the phrase "I like the way you …," which actually focuses the attention on yourself, rather than on the person and what he/she has done.

- Praise in a style that is comfortable for you. If you are an enthusiastic person, praise enthusiastically. If you tend to be quiet and businesslike, praise in a quiet and businesslike manner. When a businesslike person tries giving praise like a cheerleader, the feedback sounds insincere. The purpose of providing positive feedback is to communicate that you have noticed something important. How you do that should fit your communication style.

Be Genuine

Effective administrators avoid appearing self-important. Most of the time the position of principal brings with it natural respect from parents, students, staff, and community members. Haughty actions, though, tend to put up roadblocks. Talking down to others may, in fact, result in some people placing you on a pedestal, but you cannot lead from "up there."

Genuineness can be demonstrated by displaying a sense of humor, "letting your hair down" occasionally (e.g., sitting in the dunk tank at a school carnival), and being willing to give others credit for accomplishments.

Empathize With Others

Showing an active interest in and empathy for staff, students, and parents is a major way to build trust. The ability to empathize comes, in part, from accepting the fact that you will be working with individuals (staff, students, and parents) who cover the full range of human diversity. This range will include saints and sinners, the smart and not so smart, the caring and not so caring, the racist, the sexist, the creative, and so on. If your vision of your school is a place where everyone enters the door as a hardworking, highly motivated, logical, and kind human being, then your vision is actually a hallucination! Your vision should reflect an environment in which the full range of people are accepted and dealt with productively.

Empathy, or making the effort to understand how another is thinking and feeling, (i.e., trying to "walk a mile in their shoes") will allow you to work more successfully with everyone. Telling a single mom with three children and two jobs, "You know, Ellen, if you would just read to Sammy for half an hour before bed, she would calm down enough to go right to sleep," is likely to cost you that parent's trust. Asking someone who is barely managing to meet her own and her children's basic needs to do one more time-consuming task is unfair.

Empathy for staff is also important, but it cannot and should not cause you to lower your basic expectations of them. A staff member who is dealing with difficult personal issues needs, and deserves, your support. However, if students are suffering due to that individual's personal troubles, you need to look for ways to help him/her cope and still ensure that there are no deleterious effects in the classroom.

It is important to note that empathy is not sympathy. Empathy means trying to view reality from another person's perspective, so that any assistance is realistic and supportive. Empathy builds trust. Feeling sorry for someone, on the other hand, does not build trust.

Treat Everyone With Dignity and Respect

All those with whom you interact in the school setting deserve to be treated with dignity and respect—regardless of their educational level, age, or socioeconomic status. In other words, a school cook, an uneducated parent, and a kindergarten child deserve the same respect from you as you give the superintendent of schools. Regardless of his/her role or position in life, listen actively to anyone who comes to talk to you. When a parent stomps into your office demanding that you expel another child for calling his child a name, listen. When you can recognize that the parent's anger arises from concern, you can show respect for his perspective and needs, even as you let him know that you cannot do as he asks. Staff, students, and parents all need to know that you will invite, listen to, and appreciate suggestions from them.

Ask yourself whether you treat different people differently. While you may want to make adjustments in your vocabulary, the basics of listening, validating, and giving credit should be essentially the same with all people—certified and classified staff, well-educated parents and poorly educated parents, first graders and high school students.

Be Highly Visible

One important way to build trust is to take an active part in everything that goes on in your school. This can be done in a variety of ways. You can schedule regular and frequent visits to classrooms throughout the year. You can volunteer to substitute in individual classrooms for short periods of time, allowing teachers to observe in each other's classrooms. You can read to students or listen to students read. You might occasionally teach a lesson. You can simply be in the common areas (e.g., hallways). Walk the halls. Visit the playground, cafeteria, and bus loading area. Attend extracurricular activities. Wherever you go, talk to students and staff. Drop into the faculty room during breaks and lunches to visit with staff in a less formal setting. Interacting frequently with students, teachers, noncertified staff, and parents clearly indicates your active involvement and interest.

High visibility makes you more approachable and enhances your ability to lead and respond to the needs of your school community. A playground assistant, for example, is more likely to discuss a playground concern with you if he knows that you have been out on the playground. Think of the benefits that can be derived from something as simple as boarding a bus after the majority of the students have loaded. You greet the driver, "Good afternoon, Mrs. Crosset. How are you today? That's good to hear. I know these students are going to have a great ride this afternoon. (To the students) Have a safe ride. You are lucky to have such a responsible and safe driver. (Back to Mrs. Crosset) Mrs. Crosset, drop in and see me if you ever need anything." An interaction like this, which takes about 30 seconds, demonstrates to students that you like and respect the driver, that you are concerned about their safety, and that you will support the driver's efforts to maintain a safe bus ride. Further, you show the driver that you appreciate what she does, support her efforts to enforce the rules, and recognize that her primary responsibility is to safely transport your students. These are powerful messages to convey (and, in a very short period of time).

Respect Confidentiality

Effective leaders are careful to respect everyone's confidentiality. Even a minor violation of confidential information can quickly destroy trust. For example, consider the following scenario.

During a classroom observation, you see a student quietly inform Mr. Goetz, the science teacher, that his zipper is partway down. Mr. Goetz laughs as he discreetly zips up, and continues with the excellent lesson. That afternoon when chatting with another staff member, you laughingly describe the situation. Because that staff member, Ms. Ruiz, is a friend you feel confident that she will not mention the incident to any other staff members or even to Mr. Goetz. The fact is though, this seemingly innocent scenario might very well lead to a loss of trust in you by Ms. Ruiz. At some level (perhaps even unconsciously), she will have to worry about whether you talk about her to other staff members.

As principal you have no peers in the building. And, while building trusting relationships with staff is an important and worthwhile goal, you are still "the boss." No matter how friendly you may be with individual staff members, you will undermine trust if you make some staff privy to confidential information about others. Being principal may mean that you have to be "lonely at the top," but sharing confidential information will invariably damage the trust people have in you and diminish your effectiveness as the school's leader.

Treat Professional Staff As Professionals

Maintaining high expectations of professional staff is very important and requires a delicate balance. The goal is to encourage your staff to exercise professional judgment, yet simultaneously require them to meet your expectations. Chapter Ten: Classrooms—Assisting Teachers With Behavior and Discipline recommends you require each teacher to keep a classroom management plan on file in the office. It also suggests that you allow for differences in teachers' styles by encouraging professional latitude in designing the plans. However, you cannot allow so much latitude that any individual teacher's plan violates the school's guiding principles related to behavior management. That is, all the management plans should be primarily positive and proactive in nature—no teacher should be allowed to have a management plan that includes only punishment of misbehavior.

Some teachers mistakenly think that being a professional means that no one can tell them what to do. This is certainly not the case for members of other professions. Lawyers, physicians, and architects all must work within clear and specific legal expectations, as well as the expectations of the organizations for which they work. Being a professional actually means operating within specified parameters and making professional judgments within those parameters.

Make a Special Effort to Involve Classified Staff

When you are careful to treat everyone with respect and dignity, you set the tone for valuing your classified staff members. However, you also need to make the effort to specifically include these staff members in problem-solving and decision-making activities that affect their roles in the school. For example, if because of serious problems in the cafeteria you are setting up a task force to study the problems and propose solutions, you should make a point of including a custodian, a cafeteria worker, and a lunchroom supervisor on the task force. If it is difficult to hold meetings during the classified staff members' workday, explore extra pay options. If it just isn't feasible for classified staff to participate on a task force, at least arrange for them to review and comment on all recommendations before they go to the full staff.

Whenever possible, include your classified staff in staff development activities. In some districts, assistants are never invited to participate in workshops or other training opportunities. If budget constraints are an issue, a second-best option is to let your classified staff know they are welcome, but not required, to attend inservice opportunities.

Classified personnel should be overtly included in rituals and traditions. For example, if you and the counselor traditionally cook a breakfast for staff, *all staff* should be invited. Although not including classified staff may have simply been an omission (nobody thought to invite them), a sense of belonging is violated when any members of the staff are excluded.

Finally, always be sure to inform your classified staff of all policy and procedural issues that affect them. Take the time to develop lines of communication that ensure that no one in the school community is left out when changes occur.

Acknowledge Past Efforts Prior to Suggesting Changes

Enthusiasm for something new can sometimes be perceived as criticism of what has been. Particularly if you are new to a building, you want to avoid seeming overly critical of things that are currently in place. Nothing creates more immediate distrust than a disregard for past work. This does not mean that you have to live with everything as it is, just that you want to initiate any changes thoughtfully and respectfully.

As you guide staff, students, and parents in purposeful change, try preceding suggestions for change with activities that acknowledge past work. For example, if the focus of a staff meeting is going to be how to improve parent participation, you might first have staff break into groups and take three minutes to brainstorm things they currently do to involve parents. As the various groups share the many things staff are already doing to include parents, past efforts are affirmed, staff learn from one another, and a productive groundwork is laid for working on a plan to improve parent participation.

Build Trust With Parents

Successfully educating students requires that parents and school personnel work together cooperatively. A key to making this happen is for parents to know, first and foremost, that their children are safe and respected at school and that the unique educational needs of their children are being met. As principal, you have an extraordinary opportunity to foster the kind of parent-school relationships that can provide long-lasting benefits to your students.

Some of your interactions with parents will occur when a student is having behavioral or academic difficulties. In these cases, it is important to actively engage the parents in solving the problem. If you have established a trusting relationship with parents in advance, they are more likely to be willing to work with you when problems arise. There will, of course, be occasions when you will be faced with parents who are defensive and angry before they have even met with you or other staff members. It may help to remember that some of these parents may have had difficult (or even painful) experiences when they were in school—which is all the more reason for you to work at building trust with parents whenever the opportunity presents itself. The following strategies can be useful in building trust with parents:

- Go out of your way to greet parents. Recognize that some parents may not feel comfortable enough to initiate an interaction, but will feel rejected if you fail to do so.

- As soon as possible (given your memory abilities) call parent(s) by name.

- Refer to a parent's child frequently. ("Hi, Mrs. Keisling. Nice to see you. I saw Kendal's school picture. She has a beautiful smile.)

- Use gently self-deprecating humor. ("I don't know how Kendal does it. My own pictures make me look like the Bride of Frankenstein.")

- Ask for advice. ("What do you think we ought to do about ...")

- Listen actively. Parents should feel they are valued partners who are listened to and respected.

- Accept parents unconditionally. The school can create a sense of belonging for both students and parents, and become a place where families feel accepted, needed, and useful.

- Accept parents' feelings. When there is a problem and a parent is upset, honestly acknowledge the emotion and make it clear that it is natural for them to feel anger, frustration, or fear. Accepting and acknowledging their feelings communicates to parents your "permission" for them to have emotions, which can be the beginning of successfully solving problems together.

- Accept and validate concerns or complaints in a nondefensive manner. For parents who expect to be treated with a bureaucratic shuffle, it is a pleasant surprise when someone listens, understands their concerns, and tries to respond with a plan that will meet everyone's needs.

- Make a special effort to acknowledge those parents who contribute to the school. Giving parents appreciation awards, acknowledging parental assistance in the school newsletter, taking parents to lunch, writing parents thank-you notes, acknowledging an individual parent's help around other parents or staff, and/or taking the time to simply chat with parents are all wonderful ways to let them know that their contributions are valued.

- Finally, when possible make your school a resource for helping high-risk parents gain access to academic assistance, health care, mental health, and social services. You cannot, nor should you try to be everything to all people, but making the effort to connect needy parents with appropriate community assistance programs can significantly increase the chances for some of your students to thrive in the school setting.

Take Action!

Take the 12 guidelines for building trust listed on the chart below and rank order them. Number 1 should be the one in which you consider yourself the strongest and Number 12 the one in which you consider yourself the weakest. Write your 12th ranked guideline on your planning calendar. For about two weeks, try to focus being more effective at that one trait. After two weeks, write your 11th ranked guideline on your calendar. Focus on it for two weeks. Continue working on the guidelines in descending order until you have specifically practiced each of the guidelines you want to improve.

Leadership Traits That Engender Trust

_____ Manage space and materials efficiently.

_____ Communicate expectations clearly.

_____ Provide positive feedback.

_____ Be genuine.

_____ Empathize with others.

_____ Treat everyone with dignity and respect.

_____ Be highly visible.

_____ Respect confidentiality.

_____ Treat professional staff like professionals.

_____ Make a special effort to include noncertificated staff.

_____ Acknowledge past efforts prior to suggesting changes.

_____ Build trust with parents.

task three
Strive to Meet Basic Human Needs

The concept of basic needs is found in many different theories of human behavior. The gist of the concept is that getting or not getting some basic needs met can affect people's ability and/or willingness to work toward common goals. In fact, some people's behavior becomes erratic, negative, unproductive, or hostile when their basic needs are not met. We have found that we can work more effectively with (i.e., lead) staff, students, and parents when we keep the idea of meeting their basic needs in mind. The following framework of eight basic needs has proven to be a simple, yet effective means of doing this. The specific needs included in this framework are: acknowledgment, nurturing, competence, attention, belonging, purpose, and stimulation and change. (**Note:** This framework represents only one way of looking at basic needs—and the real issue here is not how you define the specific needs, but *that you recognize the importance of meeting the emotional and social needs of your staff, students, and parents*.) Additional information on how staff can positively meet basic needs of students can be found in Chapter Seven: Encouragement Procedures—Meeting Students' Basic Needs.

The Need for Recognition

People have a basic need to have their accomplishments recognized—particularly when they are trying something new or working especially hard. If a person who is learning something new receives only corrective feedback regarding his unsuccessful efforts (but no recognition of his successes), he is likely to become discouraged. On the other hand, a person who has her accomplishments recognized will generally be more motivated to keep trying. Providing recognition when people are first learning a new task helps them learn to do that task better.

Recognition can take a variety of forms, from praise or positive feedback to more structured forms of recognition—as in the case of a diploma, a paycheck, or a "1,000 Hour" volunteer pin given by a charitable organization.

The Need for Acknowledgment

Human beings have a fundamental need to be acknowledged—simply because they exist, not for what they do or who they are. This need in people encompasses knowing that their presence, feelings, and thoughts are recognized—and it can be met through friendly greetings and interactions. Asking simple questions like, "How do you feel about ...?" "What do you think about ...?" helps meet a person's need for acknowledgment. So does smiling, making eye contact , saying hello, and talking to people. The key is that the interactions should not be contingent upon anything and that every person should receive this kind of acknowledgment every day.

As principal, simple acknowledgments from you tend to be highly valued. Conversely, your failure to provide an acknowledgment can be misinterpreted. If you fail to greet a parent in the hall, for example, that parent may assume you don't feel she is worth noticing. Or, if by omission, you consistently fail to ask a staff member's opinion on key school issues, that staff member may think you do not value his opinion.

William James, in *The Principles of Psychology* stated, "No more fiendish punishment could be desired, were such a thing physically possible, than that one be turned loose in society and remain absolutely unnoticed by all the members thereof." By attending to the basic need of acknowledgment, you can help ensure that no individual in your school community goes unnoticed.

The Need for Attention

Each person has a need for attention (i.e., interactions with and/or responses from other human beings). This need for attention is one of quantity rather than quality. When a person's need for attention is high, you may find yourself dealing with someone who engages in behaviors (positive and/or negative) that generate attention.

For example, there may be a staff member or parent who frequently seeks you out to discuss seemingly trivial issues or questions. While it may seem as though the person's behavior is simply designed to annoy you, it is more likely that he/she just wants attention. Students with a high need for attention often find (unconsciously perhaps) that disruptive behavior is the best way to get the focused attention they need, while teachers tend to feel that the purpose of such behavior is to get them angry. Regardless of age, when a person's need for attention is not being met, the kind of attention sought may not matter. That is, annoyance may be better than no attention, and anger may be the best of all because of the intensity of the attention.

When you are able to give individuals some of the attention they need, they are less likely to demand it at inconvenient times and in unproductive ways. Generally, you can meet an adult's need for attention by going out of your way to find opportunities for short, positive interactions with the individual several times a day. Because many students have high needs for attention and because this need often results in behavior problems, you will find many suggestions for providing positive attention to students throughout this book.

The Need for Belonging

Being a part of something bigger than oneself (e.g., a family, church, social group, club, or company) is important to most people. Since the school, for those who work at or attend it, occupies such a large portion of their days, they need to feel that it's a place where they belong. That sense of belonging, or affiliation, can be fostered by creating school spirit and promoting the idea that every staff member, student, and parent has an important role to play at your school.

You can promote a sense of belonging for staff by making sure they all have opportunities to contribute positively, and by letting them know that their efforts contribute significantly to the overall well-being of the whole school. If your custodian creates a program that gets students to keep the lunchroom neater, you might write up the procedures and results in a staff bulletin. By making a public statement that his actions increased student responsibility, you give the custodian deserved recognition and let him know that he plays an important role in teaching students to be responsible—and, in the process, you enhance his sense of belonging.

The use of rituals and traditions also fosters the sense of belonging to a school community. The next section in this chapter, Task Four: Use Rituals and Traditions, includes many suggestions for developing and maintaining a rich school community atmosphere that helps meet people's need for belonging.

The Need for Competence

Enjoyment of an activity or task is greatly influenced by one's competence or success at it. It is human nature for people to seek out tasks that they do well. Thus, when people are successful at tasks, their motivation to do these tasks tends to be high. Conversely, people often dislike tasks that they do poorly, and so they may tend to withdraw from these tasks completely and/or engage in alternative behaviors or activities to avoid doing them.

The implication for you is that you need to make sure that staff and students feel competent and are competent in the activities that are required of them at school. For staff, this means being able to do their jobs successfully. If they cannot succeed due to a lack of materials, skills, or knowledge, it is up to you to see that they get what they need. Staff development efforts should focus on helping both certified and classified staff to complete their jobs with greater competence. For students, competence originates with knowing that expectations of them are high and with being given the skills, knowledge, and practice opportunities necessary to succeed—at both academic and behavioral tasks.

Part of meeting people's need for competence requires that you both recognize their successes and provide corrective feedback when needed. Motivation to make improvements is increased when people know their successes will be recognized. For example, if you think that a volunteer parent coordinator needs assistance in writing clear notices, he is more likely to appreciate such assistance if you first let him know that he is doing a fine job as coordinator. When someone has gotten little or no positive feedback, any corrective feedback is likely to cause discouragement. Thus, if a teacher needs help from colleagues with a child who has severe misbehaviors, she will probably be more likely to seek and accept that help if she has gotten positive feedback for her successful efforts when working with other students.

The Need for Nurturing

Akin to the need for acknowledgment is the need to be nurtured—to be shown through actions, as well as words, that one is cared about and supported. This need is met by receiving frequent expressions of warmth, security, and protection—provided in a way that makes it clear they will never go away, even in times of crisis or anger. Most people get the majority of their nurturing needs met in their home environments. Unfortunately, however, you may have some staff members, students, and parents who do not.

While you cannot be all things to all people, you can make the effort to let those with whom you work know that you have unconditional positive regard for them, and that you care about their growth and development within the organization. This kind of ongoing nurturing helps people develop self-confidence and independence.

The Need for Purpose

All people have a need to know that what they do has a reason, a purpose. Staff members, students, and parents should never feel as though they are simply putting in time. They should have a sense of energy and excitement about the fact that what they do makes a difference. Staff must believe that the hard work they do educating students is worthwhile. Students must believe that the hard work they do to learn is worthwhile. And parents need to believe that the hard work they do parenting and forging a partnership with a school is worthwhile.

Ideally, a school's mission statement clarifies for staff, students, and parents that the purpose of the school is to help students prepare for life. Working together to help students learn the skills to work and grow in independence and responsibility is a mission that needs to be reviewed and celebrated frequently.

The Need for Stimulation/Change

The old adage, "Variety is the spice of life" captures the essence of this basic need. People need variety in what they do to remain interested in and enthusiastic about it. When each day is exactly like the one before, people lose energy and their daily lives can start to feel like drudgery. By increasing their stimulation and variety, you increase their energy and enthusiasm.

For students, this can be done through providing engaging and challenging instruction, having assemblies that offer variety, and by holding special events such as project fairs. For staff, variety comes from learning new and worthwhile professional skills and in doing things for fun. It might involve observing someone else teaching for a period. Or it can be derived from something like having the principal and counselor prepare and serve a special dessert during a staff meeting. (Besides, food is always nurturing!) Little changes in routine like these can result in renewed energy on everyone's part.

Take Action!

Identify one staff member and one parent whose behavior is somewhat problematic (e.g., a parent who seems hostile to school staff and a staff member who complains a lot at faculty meetings). Now, think about which of the eight basic needs are not being met for these individuals. For each person, develop an informal plan to make an effort to address one of that person's basic needs. Remember, a little purposeful behavior on your part can go miles in helping others become stronger emotionally and socially. If you see changes in behavior within a couple of weeks, you will know that your actions are making a difference.

Chapter Seven: Encouragement Procedures discusses a structured approach to determining whether your school is implementing procedures that meet students' basic needs.

---

task four
$\mathcal{U}$se Rituals and Traditions

A joyful school community goes hand in hand with developing positive school behaviors. When students have their accomplishments celebrated, they are more likely to honor school guidelines and engage in school programs. When teachers feel valued, they are more likely to put energy into creating and maintaining school programs. When parents witness a nurturing atmosphere for their children, they are more likely to support and take pride in the school—even when problems need to be addressed. And, effective use of rituals and traditions helps meet everyone's need for belonging.

Rituals and traditions have a long history in every culture. They can be filled with pomp and circumstance as in the swearing in of a new president, or reflect a simple family tradition as in using Grandma's china for birthdays. Whatever their basis, rituals and traditions make a statement about what is important to a particular community.

Rituals and traditions should play a significant role in a school community. And, as principal, you are in a unique position to create and maintain a fun-loving atmosphere at your school—one in which the successes of both staff and students are systematically celebrated. Events that recognize student accomplishments, staff efforts, and parent support create the kind of memories that last across the years. When you start with a foundation of trust, the rituals and traditions you foster will help build a sense of ownership and pride in your school.

School rituals and traditions can be formal or informal, simple or elaborate. While each school should develop rituals and traditions that best fit the members of its community, the following samples of school-based rituals and traditions (some for staff and some for students) may help you add breadth to your current rituals and traditions.

Examples of School-Based Rituals and Traditions for Staff

First Day of School

Set a positive tone for a new school year by gathering the staff together at the end of the first day of school to toast the great beginning to a wonderful year. It goes without saying that alcohol never belongs in the school workplace; however, a sparkling cider toast is a delightful and appropriate way to celebrate. Use the library (or a courtyard, if feasible) and prepare a table complete with fancy tablecloth, stemware (from your prop collection) filled with sparkling cider, flowers, and snacks. Although you may want to start the proceedings yourself with a toast that speaks to the school's quality staff and the promise of a wonderful year, don't hesitate to invite other staff members to join in the toasting. A lively staff can turn this into a memorable event by exchanging humorous toasts to their colleagues.

Last Day of School

The last day of school also provides an excellent opportunity to celebrate. It can be used to acknowledge a successful school year and recognize staff members who are relocating or retiring. A parade with departing staff members wearing banners and crowns can be lots of fun. You might also want to decorate the office chairs of retiring staff members like floats and wheel them (people included) down the hall with the music playing. For more outlandish fun, follow the parade with a staff line dance—the more challenging the year, the livelier the dance!

Educational Degrees

Honor a staff member who completes a higher education degree by holding a formal cap and gown ceremony during a staff meeting. While playing a tape of "Pomp and Circumstance," present the gowned staff member with a rosette in the colors of his/her school. Have the rest of the staff join in a standing ovation. Other ideas include placing a congratulatory message on the school reader board or in the school newsletter.

Staff Retirements—The Formal Ceremony

Retiring staff members should be recognized by the entire school community. During an assembly, stage a short, formal, and dignified ceremony that includes past and present students taught by the staff member. You might begin with a trumpet fanfare to announce the staff member, followed by you (the principal) making a short speech about the staff member's accomplishments, the school chorus or band doing a musical number, and ending with the staff member giving a brief farewell speech.

For a particularly touching conclusion, consider a student flower presentation to end the ceremony. Have students representing every grade line both sides of a red carpet (made of red butcher paper), each holding a single flower. As the entire audience sings a farewell song, the retiring staff member walks down the carpet, collecting the flowers from the children. With this type of tribute, you can be sure that there won't be a dry eye in the room.

Staff Marriages

A staff member's wedding provides a perfect opportunity to celebrate and acknowledge an important life event in which the entire staff might not otherwise get to share. During a staff meeting, you might deck a bride out in a veil (made from an old curtain attached to a crown of paper flowers) and a plastic flower bouquet, while a groom could be dressed in a top hat and a plastic or paper boutonniere. The more gaudy the props the better! Get the staff to sing a chorus of *My Fair Lady's* "He's Getting Married in the Morning," and if appropriate present a gift. It can also be fun to let staff members take turns offering the newlywed choice bits of advice.

Improved School Test Scores

Good test scores reflect the efforts of an entire staff working together to ensure well-prepared and competent students. These efforts should always be recognized and reinforced! You might hang a banner in the staff room that congratulates everyone on a job well done. Or, you can give each staff member a flower or thank-you card, and/or take yet another opportunity for a sparkling cider toast.

Valentine's Day

Valentine's Day is a perfect time to let your staff know that you care about them. You might, for example, decorate the staff room table with hearts and flowers and provide a valentine fruit or vegetable tray. Staff members may especially appreciate a personalized valentine in their mailbox. It can be as simple as a note of appreciation on a heart-shaped piece of paper or as involved as an individualized rhyming poem. Or, you can hang a large valentine with a written poem about the staff in the staff room.

Income Tax Day

Income tax day is a good excuse for a staff party at the principal's home. You and/or the social committee can plan a soup kitchen menu and provide prizes for a staff drawing. Anyone who has had to pay an additional income tax can be encouraged to wear black, or you can make black armbands available at the party. Sometime during the evening have a drawing to give out prizes to the tax-paying group, (e.g., a sack of potatoes or flour, cans of beans, piggy banks, and calendars with April 15 circled in red).

PTA Meetings

Skits are a great way to make PTA meetings humorous while highlighting a goal. You can begin the first PTA meeting of the year with a lighthearted skit, involving both staff and parents, that emphasizes the PTA's goals. One possibility for skits is to pick cartoon characters and then set them up in a plot that makes your point. For example, you might have a skit in which the character "Snidely Whiplash" refuses to join the PTA. Various "townspeople" can then attempt to change the villain's mind by pointing out the merits of the school's PTA. Western and circus themes also make good subject matter for skits.

Special Honors

Publicly acknowledge and celebrate any and all professional accomplishments by staff—service awards, Fulbright Scholarships, National Science Foundation Awards, and so on.

Easter

A traditional "Easter egg hunt" can become an annual event that all staff enjoy. Each day for a week, hide a large plastic egg filled with several slips of paper. The first thing each morning, provide a clue to the egg's whereabouts. (Reading the clue promptly at the start of the workday encourages staff members to be on time to school.) Staff members then search throughout the day, individually, until they find the egg. Once a person finds the egg, he/she opens it, writes his/her name and the time on one of the pieces of paper, puts the paper back in the egg, and closes it. At the end of the day, you remove the papers, fill the egg with blank slips of paper, and hide the egg in a new location for the next day. Run the hunt for five days. On the last day, determine the winners—those with the best combined times for the five days. Prizes can include: a certificate for the winner and a friend to have lunch with their classrooms; having the winner's position covered for a period by you or a learning specialist; a special Easter basket filled with goodies, certificates for release time, and/or Easter flowers. You might also have students make small paper baskets that you fill with candies so that all participants get a prize.

Important: The members of any school community generally have diverse religious beliefs. Thus, holiday celebrations need to be handled in a sensitive manner. While the Easter celebration described above is clearly secular in nature, rituals like this should not be implemented if they might offend anyone in your school community. Rituals should pull people together, not drive them apart.

Special Note

Because classified staff members often work a shorter day, they may not always be available for staff meetings. This can make it difficult for you to acknowledge special occasions. Look for times when all staff members, both certified and classified, are available to celebrate their successes. For example, a bus driver who wins a state driver's competition can be honored at a staff luncheon. He or she would also probably be delighted to see a notice about his/her award posted on the school reader board.

Examples of Student-Based Rituals and Traditions for Students

The key to rituals and traditions for students is to mark significant events without disrupting the educational focus of the school. The purpose is to create activities that are fun and increase the students' sense of belonging to a special place. Use your mission statement to guide your selection of rituals. For example, if your mission is to "provide a compassionate learning environment in which all students experience acceptance and success," then you need to make sure your rituals express compassion, emphasize learning, and increase students' sense of acceptance and success.

Kindergarten Orientation

Kindergarten orientation typically occurs just before school begins in the fall or on the first day of school. Orientation offers an ideal opportunity for you (the principal) to meet new parents and students, and to reassure the parents that their children will be nurtured and valued by the school. It is also a chance for you to introduce these new students to the first of many traditions to come. For example, while the kindergarten teachers share their expectations and answer questions from parents, you can take the students on a tour of the building "to look for the gingerbread man." At the last "stop" on the tour, there can be a tray of gingerbread men waiting. Arranging for your fifth or sixth graders to make the gingerbread men is a great way to reinforce the idea of community service in your older students at the same time as you are developing a sense of fun and affiliation with your new kindergartners and their parents.

First Day Greeting

On the first day of school, muster nonclassroom staff, parents, and community volunteers to greet and help students locate their classrooms. Give your volunteer greeters copies of class lists and maps of the school. Remind them to welcome the students enthusiastically with words of encouragement for a great year. If possible, arrange for the school band to be playing outside as students arrive.

Middle School Orientation

The anxiety that often accompanies entering middle school can be alleviated by beginning the year with an activity (e.g., a carnival) for the incoming class that is staged by the student body officers, staff members, and selected upper classmen.

At a carnival, for example, you can put the incoming class into teams, by homeroom or teacher, and have the teams play games designed to foster team building. In "Jail Break," the teams try to get their members over a string without any form of verbal communication. In a "shoe relay," all students put one of their shoes in a giant pile in the center of the room. The relay starts with one member from each team trying to find his/her shoe in the pile. Once he/she has the shoe, he/she runs back and tags the next team member, who goes to look for his/her shoe, and so on.

The important components of a successful activity are: (1) Selecting events that promote team building; (2) Carefully choosing and training upper classmen to run the events and welcome the new students; (3) Making sure that all students have fun; and (4) Emphasizing that the staff and upper classmen are glad to have the new students on board.

Class Pictures

Many schools hang each year's classroom pictures in the hallway. This fine tradition keeps parents returning to the school for years to look at the photos. Remember though, once the photos have been hung, the community will expect them to remain there forever!

Birthdays

Having an all-school birthday bulletin board is an effective yet simple way to incorporate ritual and tradition in your school. (Plus, posting birthdays on the calendar can be a perfect job for students doing Meaningful Work.) Every month, you can recognize student birthdays for that month by putting each student's name on some kind of symbol (e.g., a snowman for January, a heart for February) and placing the symbols on the appropriate day of the calendar. During the last week of school, you can have a special bulletin board display that lists the names of all students with summer birthdays.

Some principals use birthdays as occasions to provide special greetings to individual students. Some even give students a small gift, such as a pencil, along with their wishes for a happy birthday.

Fifth Grade Chairs

Many schools allow their fifth graders (or their highest grade students) to sit in chairs at school assemblies while the rest of the students sit on the floor. This tradition can be enhanced by having the current year's fourth graders bring chairs to the last assembly of the year. They can be presented as the next fifth grade class and the new role models for the upcoming year.

Special Academic Projects

It's always nice to have rituals that incorporate an academic component. For example, as culmination to a traditional fifth grade project of working all term on a report about a famous American, you can have an assembly at which the fifth grade students give speeches as the individuals they reported on—in costume, without notes. Those invited to the assembly could include third and fourth graders, as well as the parents and grandparents of the fifth grade students. At the conclusion of all the speeches, you or one of the fifth grade teachers might say something like, "Let's give another round of applause to the fifth grade students. You third and fourth graders need to know that it took courage for these students to give their speeches. Part of what made it possible for them was knowing how much support they had from everyone in the room. When you are in fifth grade and give your speech, you will also be giving it to people who care about and support you and each other."

Traditional Field Trips

Field trips that mark significant events can easily become part of a school's rituals. For example, a traffic patrol's end-of-the-year trip to an amusement park may become an anticipated tradition. Graduation parties at the skating rink, class dinners at a fine restaurant, or grade level trips to a community beach all can become memorable occasions that each incoming group of students looks forward to experiencing.

Halloween Parade

Although some schools have eliminated Halloween celebrations because of religious objections, others observe the holiday—but invite parents with religious objections to plan an alternative event. If appropriate for your school community, a traditional Halloween parade can create delightful memories. The parade might include just the primary students dressed in their costumes, or it can involve the whole school. The parade might begin in the gym with a colorful narration provided by staff members. If intermediate students are not participating, the parade can move on a predetermined route through the intermediate hallways with the older students sitting along the parade route. When the parade will involve all students, you can start it in one classroom and have it move from one classroom to the next. As the parade moves through each classroom, the students in that classroom join the parade.

Field Day/Talent Show

Many schools hold a school field day during the last week or two of school. The traditional games and events for teams and individuals can be expanded to include a school talent show. Kids love to show off their talents and parents are often available to help when their children are performing. Including a staff talent number can be a great addition to the festivities.

School Play

An annual school play offers yet another way to involve parents, students, and staff in a joyous activity that promotes positive connections between the school and community. An old-fashioned melodrama that features the principal as the villain is always a surefire hit.

An annual school variety show can also pull people together for a little fun. A holiday variety show by staff can be a great gift from staff to students and parents. Have staff members dance and sing, or even bring their pets for stupid pet tricks. Schools with these kinds of activities soon develop reputations as places where children learn and have great fun!

The School Dance

As elementary principals know, intermediate students are always asking if they can have a dance. For many of us, the idea of promoting girl-boy relationships at a young age does not seem appropriate. One alternative is to hold a theme dance (e.g., a barn dance or fifties dance) to which people of all ages are invited to come dressed in appropriate attire. This can be a perfect family event and a good answer to an age-old dilemma.

Elementary and Middle School Graduation

Graduation from elementary and/or middle school becomes an all-school tradition when the entire school is invited to a ceremony on the last day of school. For the graduating students, the ceremony puts closure on their elementary school (or middle school) experiences and accomplishments. And, witnessing an elegant ceremony helps younger students realize the importance of scholarship, responsibility, and goal setting.

The key is to have a simple and short ceremony—a musical presentation and a few important awards (e.g., Presidential Fitness Awards or the Principal's Award). All other awards should be given in the individual classrooms. End the ceremony by asking the graduating class to stand and presenting them as "The (School Name) Class of (year they graduate)." When you involve the graduating students and their parents in the planning and execution of the ceremony, it promotes ownership of the event. Parents, for example, can help with decorations and by preparing a reception to follow the ceremony.

The Last Day of School

The last day of school offers a natural celebration for students and staff—a time to celebrate hard work and a sense of community. Have the entire staff and all the students assemble at the busses. Let students know they will be missed, and wish them a happy summer. As the busses pull out and walkers start on down the road, everyone (staff and students) waves joyously and blows kisses to each other.

Take Action!

Guidelines and Suggestions for Creating School Rituals and Traditions

1. Determine significant events that can and should be recognized (e.g., first day of school, staff retirements, staff marriages, births, holidays, the last day of school, the completion of higher education degrees, and improved performance on standardized tests). The idea is to have ritual celebrations at regularly scheduled times and on special occasions.

2. Develop a system for finding out when important events will occur. Ask the school secretary or someone who has access to your calendar to make note of these events for you.

3. Keep an eye out for props and small gifts that can be used as part of your celebrations. Items that can come in handy include punch bowls, stemwear, old trophies and rosettes (that can be relabeled with staff accomplishments), and graduation caps and gowns (for ceremonies celebrating the completion of advanced degrees).

4. Remember the basic rule for orchestrating a celebration: *Keep it simple, short, sweet, and sincere*. While a short, heartfelt, and dignified toast is generally always appreciated, long events tend not to be viewed as reinforcing, but rather as uncomfortable and annoying wastes of time.

5. Seize the moment! Timing is everything. Tie celebrations to existing events where everyone is already expected to be in attendance. Incorporating short celebrations into your staff meetings is perfect because everyone has already planned to give up the time and is not likely to begrudge a brief diversion.

Conclusion

The job of the principal has changed. Today's principal, in addition to being a building manager, must also be an effective building leader with a crystal clear picture of what his/her school can and should be. In this chapter, we described four major leadership tasks in which you should engage to successfully guide your staff, students, and parents toward the ideal vision of your school. Those tasks include: (1) Clarifying and promoting your vision of the school; (2) Building trust with staff, students, and parents; (3) Striving to meet the basic human needs of the members of your school community; and (4) Using rituals and traditions to increase staff members', students', and parents' sense of belonging to and pride in your school. Working on these major tasks—in your own style and at your own speed—will increase the probability that you, together with your staff, students, and parents, can create the school of your vision.

In the next chapter, we offer specific suggestions regarding two other important leadership tasks—making decisions and resolving conflicts.

What the Research Says About Leaders in Effective Schools

Strong Leadership Guides the Instructional Program

Andrews and Soder (1987); Bamburg and Andrews (1991); Berman and McLauglin (1979); Biester et al. (1984); Bossert (1988); Brookover (1979b, 1981); Brookover and Lezotte (1979); Brundage (1979); Cawelti (1987); Cohen, S.A. (1994); Cohen S.A. (1994); Corbett et al (1984); Crisci et al. (1988); DeBevoise (1984); Druian and Butler (1987); Eberts and Stone (1988); Edmonds (1979a); Emrick (1977); Evertson et al. (1986); Fullan (1993); Glasman (1984); Good and Brophy (1986); Hallinger, Bickman, and Davis (1989); Hawley et al. (1984); Heck (1992); High and Achilles (1986); Krug (1992); Larsen (1987); Leithwood and Montgomery (1982, 1985); Levine and Lezotte (1990); Little (1982); Louis and Miles (1989); Madden, Lawson, and Sweet (1976); Ogawa and Hart (1985); Pavan and Reid (1991, 1994); Purkey and Smith (1983); Rosenholtz (1985, 1989a,b); Sammons, Hillman, and Mortimore (1994); Schmitt, (1990); Venezky and Winfield (1979); Weber (1971)

Leaders Undertake School Restructuring Efforts as Needed to Attain Agreed Upon Goals for Students

Fortune, Williams, and White (1992); Fullan (1993); Lee and Smith (1993); Leithwood (1994); Lewis (1989); McCarthy and Still (1993); Murphy and Hallinger (1993); Prestine (1993); Prestine and Bowen (1993)

Administrators Communicate High Expectations for Teachers' Performance

Boyd (1992); Brookover and Lezotte (1979); DeBevoise (1984); Edmonds (1979a); Evertson (1986); Gaddy (1988); Gall and Renchler (1985); Good and Brophy (1986); Hallinger and Murphy (1985); Hord (1992a); Keedy (1992); Leithwood and Montgomery (1982, 1985); Levine (1990); Louis and King (1993); Madden, Lawson, and Sweet (1976); Murphy and Hallinger (1985, 1988); Pavan and Reid (1991, 1994); Porter and Brophy (1988); Rosenholtz (1985, 1989a,b); Sparks (1983, 1986); Stevens (1985); Stringfield and Teddlie (1988); Tracz and Gibson (1986); Wade (1985)

(continued)

What the Research Says About Leaders in Effective Schools (continued)

Administrators and Other Leaders Provide Incentives, Recognition, and Rewards to Build Strong Staff Motivation

Anderson, C.S. (1985); Armor et al. (1976); Block (1983); Boyd (1992); Brookover (1979); Brookover and Lezotte (1979); Fullan (1990, 1991); Good and Brophy (1986); Hawley et al. (1984); Levine and Eubanks (1989); Levine and Lezotte (1990); Little (1982); Louis and Miles (1990); Mortimore et al. (1988); Oakes (1989); Purkey and Smith (1983); Rosenholtz (1985, 1989a,b); Vincenzi and Ayrer (1985); Wade (1985); Wilson and Corcoran (1988)

Administrators and Teachers Establish and Enforce Clear, Consistent Discipline Policies

Bain, H.P. and Jacobs (1990); Block (1983); Boyd (1992); Brookover and Lezotte (1979); Cantrell and Cantrell (1993); Corcoran (1985); Cotton (1990b); Doyle (1989); Duke (1989); Edmonds (1979a,b,1982); Edmonds and Frederiksen (1979); Fenley et al. (1993); Good and Brophy (1986); Gottfredson, D.C. (1987); Gottfredson, D.C., Gottfredson, and Hybl (1993); Hawley et. al. (1984); Lasley and Wayson (1982); Leach and Byrne (1986); Leming (1993); Levine and Eubanks (1989); Levine and Lezotte (1990); Madden, Lawson, and Sweet (1976); Render, Padilla, and Krank (1989); Rutter et al. (1979); Sammons, Hillman, and Mortimore (1994); Short (1988); Staub (1990); Wayson and Lasley (1984); Weber (1971); Wilson and Corcoran (1988); Wilson-Brewer et al. (1991)

The above material is reprinted with permission from *Effective Schooling Practices: A Research Synthesis, 1995 Update*. This excellent summary of school and teacher effectiveness literature was compiled by Kathleen Cotton. To order copies of this resource, call or write:

Document Reproduction Service
Northwest Regional Educational Laboratory
101 S.W. Main Street, Suite 500
Portland, Oregon 97204
(503) 275-9519

Leadership Skills—Effective Decision Making and Handling Disagreements

Creating and maintaining a safe and productive school environment requires focused leadership in an evolving school culture. This, in turn, requires making ongoing decisions efficiently and in a manner that results in "buy in" from the people most affected by any given decision. As various decisions are considered and made, there will, inevitably, be disagreements. This chapter discusses another two important leadership tasks—effective decision making and handling disagreements.

Making Decisions

Hundreds of decisions are made in a school each day. Some decisions can or must be made immediately; others require research and a careful weighing and balancing of options first. Some decisions should be made unilaterally by you (the principal). For example, if there is a change in federal law regarding special education service delivery, you are required to see that this change is carried out, regardless of how staff may feel about it—so getting their input would actually be a waste of your time and theirs.

Other decisions should be made by you, but with input from others. Suppose the superintendent issued a districtwide directive such as, "Each building will take steps to improve communication and coordination among the elementary, middle, and high school levels." While you may want to get staff input on how they think this directive should be carried out on your campus, ultimately the decision about how to interpret and implement the directive will be yours. Finally, some decisions should be group decisions, made by you and your staff together. This is a particularly powerful way of making schoolwide decisions about such things as behavior management procedures because including stakeholders in the decisions tends to increase their sense of ownership of and cooperation with them.

Given this range of "types" of school decisions, one of your most important tasks, as building principal, is to designate *who* should be responsible for the various decisions and *how* they should be made. The following guidelines may help:

1. **Before a decision is made, decide what type of decision it will be (i.e., unilateral, unilateral with staff input, or full staff)—and let staff know.**

    Determining which decisions you should make unilaterally and which should involve staff (either to give input or as co-decision makers) requires balancing issues of efficiency and ownership. While unilateral decisions are the quickest and most efficient, morale tends to plummet when staff have no say in matters that affect their ability to support and instruct students. On the other hand, when management is overly participatory, staff members can quickly tire of endless committee meetings and/or may resent having to make decisions about the minute details of running the school.

    Once you have decided what type a decision is, you need to be clear with your staff about who is responsible for the decision and why. If the decision will be yours alone, wait until you have decided and then explain the issue, your decision, and why you made the decision yourself. Staff members generally appreciate it when they are asked to participate in decisions that truly need collaboration and consensus.

    If a decision is to be made by you with staff input, make sure staff understand from the outset that you will be making the final decision. Never give people the impression that they can change a decision that has already been made. By the same token, if you ask for staff input, be sure to use that input in reaching your decision. Staff will become resentful if they spend time working on recommendations that are ignored. "Our principal makes us serve on all these committees and then does what he was going to do anyway. It's a huge waste of time!"

    Finally, when you have a decision that will be made by the entire staff, make sure to use decision-making procedures that are fair and clearly understood by everyone. And, once a full-staff decision has been made, remember that you need to honor and support that decision—even if you disagree with it.

2. **Use efficient strategies for getting staff input.**

    For decisions that are yours but on which you want staff input, you need specific strategies for efficiently and fairly soliciting suggestions, opinions, and concerns. Descriptions of three such strategies follow:

    *   *Faculty Meeting Agenda*—Put the issue on the agenda for a staff meeting. First, describe the issue and tell staff that you will be making the final decision. Then explain the solutions that you have already considered, keeping your opinions about them to yourself. Next ask staff to give you their thoughts on the pros and cons of each solution you have identified and ask them if they have other possible solutions. Limit the discussion to the time indicated on the agenda. Thank the staff for their input and tell them when you expect to make your decision. Once you

have made your decision, be sure to inform staff of both the decision and your rationale for it.

- *Written Comments*—An alternative strategy for getting staff input, one that allows them more time, is to solicit written comments. Introduce the issue at a faculty meeting and tell staff that you would appreciate their written comments on it over the course of the next week. Place a large piece of poster paper in the faculty room so that people can jot down their ideas or opinions. Before making your decision, carefully review the written comments. Again, let staff know of your decision and how you arrived at that decision.

- *Staff Meeting Plus Written Comments*—For complex or controversial issues, it can be beneficial to let staff voice their opinions both during a staff meeting and through the option of writing their comments and suggestions down. As in all cases, once you've made your decision, let staff know what it is and how you took their opinions and comments into account.

3. **Use effective strategies for reaching full-staff decisions.**

Prior to having the full staff decide an issue, consider forming a task force of three to seven people who will be charged with gathering information and making recommendations about the issue to the staff. Exploring difficult questions and hashing out opposing perspectives is often more effectively done during small committee meetings than during full-staff meetings. Therefore, on complex issues, we recommend that full-staff decisions occur only after the issue has been considered by an ad hoc committee or task force—made up of people with diverse views on the subject being studied. (**Note:** When you use this option, avoid stacking the committee with supporters of your goals. Group diversity is necessary if you want to develop and promote a strong and productive working relationship with all staff members). Have the task force present its recommendations and reasoning to the total faculty, and then proceed with a final decision.

Once a proposal has been presented to the staff, effective decision making requires the use of agreed upon procedures for arriving at consensus. Although many schools use a "majority rules" approach to staff-based decisions, we have found that this approach can result in disgruntled staff members and less than adequate implementation of the final decision. That is, when 30%-45% of a staff end up having to use a procedure that they voted against, the chances are greater that the procedure will be implemented halfheartedly—if at all. Following are two consensual decision-making procedures that allow a greater voice to the concerns of the minority and tend to increase staff members' sense of involvement in decisions.

- *"Fist of Five"*—True consensus means that any given decision has at least the passive approval of every stakeholder. This particular decision-making procedure involves having stakeholders indicate their degree of support for a decision with the fingers of one hand. Raising five fingers indicates a full commitment and willingness to be a leader in implementing the proposal. Four fingers means the staff member wholeheartedly supports the decision, but is not willing to act as a leader in implementing it. Three fingers indicates moderate support. Two fingers indicates a moderately negative feeling about the proposal, but an agreement to support its implementation at least passively. One finger indicates dissatisfaction with the decision, but a pledge not to undermine its implementation. Finally, a closed fist—zero fingers—indicates total disagreement with the proposal. Staff members are informed in advance that a vote of zero, one or two (which will roadblock implementation of the issue being decided), carries with it the responsibility of sharing one's concerns about a particular proposal and working to find an alternative solution.

To have consensus on any given decision, all staff members must support a proposal with at least a three-finger response. When there have been staff members who raised a closed fist, one finger, or two fingers, they explain their objections and the group negotiates whether to adjust or eliminate the unacceptable elements of the proposal. While, at first glance, this procedure may seem overly responsive to the negative views of a few staff members, it is actually a proactive attempt to resolve concerns. Not only are staff members asked to make honest and public responses about important decisions, but those staff who are concerned about a particular decision are also required to help make it acceptable. Actively working to resolve differences helps everyone ultimately become part of the solution, rather than a part of the problem.

Note: You and your staff may wish to modify the criteria for consensus to better fit your staff. For example, you may decide that consensus is achieved as long as no one votes zero or one, and no more than five people vote two fingers. The important point is that you and your staff agree to the definition of consensus that assures minority opinion is not squelched, but that balances a need for efficiency in making decisions.

- *"Red, Yellow, Green"*—This procedure is similar to "Fist of Five," but it provides a more rapid visual check of staff members' positions. It is particularly useful when staff are reviewing a series of recommendations that are fairly straightforward. Each staff member is issued a red card, a green card, and a yellow card. After a recommendation is explained, staff members vote on it by raising one of their cards. The green card indicates full support, the yellow card indicates neutral acceptance, and the red card indicates no support. Recommendations that are universally supported (i.e., primarily green cards, and no red cards) are "passed." Recommendations that do not receive full support can be negotiated at that time, returned to committee for further study, or rescheduled for a full-staff discussion during a later staff meeting. The advantage of this procedure is that it allows quick resolution for issues on which all staff basically agree and negotiation for those issues that need additional work for full support.

Both of these procedures, in contrast to a majority rules approach, assure that everyone's voice is heard. They not only encourage, but rely on full-staff participation, and they overtly recognize the importance of working through differences so that all staff members feel comfortable with important decisions.

Example of Effective Full-Staff Decision Making

A "School Improvement Team" has been working on strategies for dealing with student behavior problems after school—in bus waiting areas, halls, and on the busses. The team recommends that all teachers walk their classes to a dismissal area in front of the school at the end of each day. A "Fist of Five" vote shows that there are a few teachers who strongly disagree with the recommendation. When, as part of the "Fist of Five" process, these teachers are asked to explain their objections, they indicate that they have told students that they will always be available to answer questions and help with problems after school. They feel they will not be available for students if they have to walk students to the bus. Staff members discuss the benefits of walking their students to the bus—calmer students for the ride home, safer bus rides, the opportunity for casual conversations with the children, a positive end to the day, and so on. Finally someone suggests that all teachers escort their students to the dismissal area during the first week of school and for the week following each major vacation—to establish a pattern of appropriate behavior. At all other times, escorting students will be optional. Another vote is taken, and this time everyone votes with three or more fingers. With a simple majority vote, the concerns of the few teachers may not have been explained, and they would have ended up having to follow a procedure they resented.

4. **Use an agenda, in which the purpose of each item of business is clear, for staff meetings.**

   Achieving decisions during staff meetings is more likely to occur when staff members have been given a written agenda in advance. We suggest that you organize the agenda items by major activity heading (e.g., "information dissemination, "brainstorming," "input," and "decision making") and give each item a time designation. The activity headings will help define expectations for participation, and the time parameters will help you avoid prolonged discussions and unnecessary debates. A sample agenda is shown along with a brief explanation of our sample agenda item headings.

   - *Information Dissemination*—This heading indicates that information will be reported to the staff by you or someone else (e.g., another staff member). For each item, the information is given and a brief time for clarification is allowed. Should issues be raised that require more discussion time, they are noted and the issue is rescheduled for another meeting.

Sample Agenda

Staff Agenda, September 20, 1996

7:45 - 8:00 Optional coffee and socializing

8:00 - 8:05 Information Dissemination

- Welcome and introduction to new playground assistant, Toni Ward
- Field Day announcements
- Revised "Attendance Reports" required by district

8:05 - 8:15 Input

- Playground Problems—Fighting is on the increase. What can we do?

8:15 - 8:25 Brainstorming

- Suggestions for use of $500.00 Rotary Club gift

8:25 - 8:30 Decision Making

- Decide how to use Rotary Club gift.

- *Input*—The "input" heading is used for items that will involve discussion, suggested solutions, and the exploration of pros and cons. These items do not require final decisions. Staff members are invited to engage in a lively debate during a designated time limit; but there is no expectation of closure. Unlike brainstorming, the details of issues or alternatives should be discussed.

- *Brainstorming*—With brainstorming items, any staff member can make suggestions concerning the item without lobbying for or against it. Brainstorming should be used with those items that will benefit from staff creativity and the opportunity for all staff to offer suggestions on an issue. The rule for brainstorming is to get as many ideas as possible, without having any particular idea evaluated or discussed.

- *Decision Making*—Items listed under the "decision making" heading are those on which staff should be ready to make a final decision. For each item, the issue should be reviewed first, and the possible solutions summarized. Then, after a brief discussion period, a proposal should be offered (possibly in the form of a motion) and a consensual vote taken.

5. **Communicate the outcome of decisions to all people affected.**

Regardless of what type of decision has been made, it is critical that all members of the school community (staff, students, parents) be informed of any decision that affects them. For example, when the school board makes a decision, you may need to communicate that decision to staff, students, and parents. Or, when a full-staff decision is made during a faculty meeting, staff members who were not at the meeting should be informed. Even when a decision has been made by a small committee (or you), everyone who will be affected by that decision needs to know what it is. To avoid future misunderstandings, make sure you present decisions verbally and in writing.

6. **Accept responsibility for poor decisions.**

   No matter who makes a decision, as building leader you must be prepared to accept responsibility for poor decisions. Some administrators use site-based decision making as a thinly veiled attempt to distribute blame for bad decisions. ("Don't blame me, it is what the staff decided!") As building principal, you are responsible for determining who makes decisions and for guiding how decisions are made. Therefore, you bear the ultimate responsibility for every decision regardless of the procedure used to arrive at that decision.

Handling Disagreements

Disagreements are part of any human enterprise involving more than one person. Disagreements are not necessarily bad. In fact, when handled well, disagreements can contribute to the dynamic and cooperative nature of a school's culture by allowing people to learn from different perspectives and gather new ideas. Disagreements can foster progress and growth within an organization because they permit current thinking to be challenged (e.g., "I think there is a better way to organize the lunch schedule to reduce cafeteria crowding"). When unresolved, however, disagreements can lead to ongoing conflicts and hostility between people within a school, which in turn can undermine the organization. In this section, we look at having staff "rules" for disagreeing with others, ideas for how to deal with people who are angry, and suggestions for conducting a caring confrontation when, as principal, you must address someone regarding a particularly uncomfortable situation (e.g., you have a staff member who may have a drinking problem).

1. **Establish staff operating procedures, (i.e., rules of engagement) for resolving disagreements.**

   Getting staff to identify, in advance, what constitutes acceptable behavior in conflict situations increases the probability that staff will work through their disagreements productively and respectfully.

   A set of sample operating procedures follows. You may find it useful to share these as you and your staff develop your own operating procedures for resolving disagreements.

   Once they have been developed, you will need to distribute and regularly review your school's operating procedures for resolving disagreements. Publishing them in a format that allows them to be displayed on a staff member's desk is one way to encourage the daily use of these principles.

2. **Prepare yourself (and your staff) to interact productively with people who are angry.**

   It would be ideal if all situations could be resolved through rational and thoughtful problem solving. However, there will be times, in the school setting, when you will have to interact with people who are very angry. Learning to "de-escalate" anger is an important skill for all school-based personnel. We have found the following steps to be helpful:

Sample Operating Procedures for Disagreeing With Others

1. I solve problems by dealing directly and honestly with people with whom I disagree.

2. Before discussing an issue with others, I first make sure the person who is responsible for the decision or situation knows why I am concerned.

3. I recognize that disagreement is not disloyalty. Disagreement fosters productive change and is a healthy way to help our school grow.

4. I treat all people with respect, even when I disagree with their positions.

5. I strive to create win/win situations and always seek to avoid anyone having to lose.

- Acknowledge the person's anger. This is not the time to play down the seriousness of a concern. A simple statement such as "I can see that you are very angry" both acknowledges the person's feelings and gives him a reason to believe that you may understand his concerns.

- Match his/her tone of rising anger, but with a caring statement. Surprisingly, using a quiet, calm voice with a person who is shouting can actually escalate the hostile behavior. A calm voice in response to anger is often perceived as patronizing. An authoritarian response to the anger—"Mrs. Jones, if you don't calm down I'm going to have you removed," is also likely to escalate the hostility. The best alternative is to match the angry tone, but with a caring statement. "Mrs. Jones, I want Jennifer to feel safe at this school. I am willing to do whatever it takes to make that happen." This type of statement, voiced assertively, can be very effective. It tells the person that you heard her concerns and are willing to respond.

- Show a willingness to help. Immediately offer to talk about the problem. This can be accomplished by inviting the person into your office. "Mrs. Jones, I'm very concerned about Jennifer's safety on the playground. Why don't you come into my office so that I can hear the details and take care of this situation?"

- Arrange the conference setting to facilitate a calm discussion. Quickly arrange chairs so that you can talk face to face with the person. Sitting behind your desk will make you appear to be more authoritarian. At a time of intense conflict, this may accelerate or aggravate an already difficult situation.

- Arrange the conference setting with safety considerations in mind. Unfortunately, an angry person can become a dangerous person. Allow ample space between you and the person to reduce the possibility of physical contact. Put your chair near the door so that you can quickly exit the office if needed—without being blocked by the other person. Leave your door slightly ajar so that office staff can monitor your safety. At the beginning of every year, develop a signal that will be used to let staff know that an emergency situation has developed and it is necessary to call 911.

- Listen actively. Any angry person wants to be heard. Therefore, as the person shares his/her concerns, take notes and ask for clarification when the facts are unclear. Indicate your understanding by paraphrasing what you have heard, and check to see if you have clearly captured the person's concerns.

- Address the person's desired outcome (i.e., what it would take for the person to feel the situation has been resolved). Present that outcome in general rather than specific terms. For example, if you are working with a parent who is angry that her child was hit by another child, you might say, "Mrs. Jones, it sounds to me as though you would like assurance that Jenny will be safe at school, that the child who hit Jenny will be dealt with, and that the child will stop hitting others." This type of statement leaves the power of discipline in your hands. If the parent wishes to know specifically how the child will be disciplined, you can say, "I would never let another parent know how I planned to discipline Jennifer if she were in trouble. That information would be between you, me, and Jennifer. I can assure you that this child will be dealt with in a way that ensures he will quit hitting others and that his parents will be contacted." Taking a general approach to outcomes gives you flexibility and options, whereas addressing an angry person's specific demands ("Mrs. Jones, you want me to suspend the child that hit Jenny") is likely to box you into a lose-lose situation. Restating what you cannot or will not do actually has the potential of heightening a conflict.

- Close the discussion by commending the person for coming to you with his/her concerns and by guaranteeing that you will do your best to resolve the issue. Remind the person of any mutually held objectives. For example, if a parent is upset, you might remind the parent that each of you has the student's well-being in school as your goal.

3. **Deal immediately and directly with situations or problems requiring administrative intervention.**

   At one time or another, every principal faces uncomfortable situations involving parents or staff. Examples include a staff member or parent who is abrasive and hurtful to others during meetings, a staff member whose personal problems are negatively impacting his/her classroom, or a parent who publicly treats a teacher or his/her own child disrespectfully.

   Such situations need to be handled promptly, with honesty and courage. There is a natural tendency to ignore problems, to hope they will go away. However, ignoring and delaying often result in a problem getting worse—and, in some cases, actually lead to crisis situations that might have been averted.

   As building leader, it is your responsibility to deal directly with difficult issues and to offer help and support as a problem is brought out into the open. When you have to address a difficult situation, keep the notion of "caring confrontation" in mind. With caring confrontation, you respond to a problem directly, but in a way that conveys support and reassurance, rather than an adversarial or arbitrarily authoritarian manner. The steps below summarize caring confrontation.

- Schedule an appointment to discuss the issue with the individual. Do not try to address a serious problem in a casual hallway conversation. A special appointment highlights the importance of the issue, ensures a degree of privacy, and gives both parties time to think and respond to one another.

- Open the discussion by gently introducing the problem as you see it and by letting the person know that you are addressing the problem because you value her and her role in the school too much to allow the problem to continue.

- Ask the person whether your perception of the problem is accurate or whether you need more information.

- Specify what needs to happen. Be clear and direct. For example, you may say something like, "Janice, I know this is a difficult time for you at home. I would like to support you at work in any way I can. One of the ways I can help is to let you know when your problems are taking over here at school. I know that you are a caring teacher and staff member, yet lately I've heard you yelling at students and belittling other staff members. Let's talk about ways to help you deal with the stress levels you are currently experiencing. You know that I can't allow you to take things out on your students—and I don't think you want to either."

- Help the person explore possible solutions to the problem. Encourage the staff member to identify ways she can work on clearing up the problem. Take care to keep the discussion focused on the immediate problem and the possible steps that can be taken to solve the problem. When someone is upset, a myriad of concerns can be brought up that distract from the actual problem.

- Establish a plan for achieving the needed outcome. Set up a time line and schedule a follow-up appointment to discuss the degree to which the required outcome has been achieved.

- End the discussion by conveying confidence that the problem can be solved. Let the person know you will provide support in any way you can and that she can ask you for assistance at any time.

Example of Caring Confrontation

John teaches third grade. A successful teacher for over fifteen years, he has a community reputation as a fine teacher and is often requested by parents. Over the last several months, however, the principal, Mrs. Gaven, has noticed a gradual change in John. He seems to be more short-tempered with his students and often comes to school late and leaves as soon as possible each afternoon. Office referrals from him have steadily increased, and Mrs. Gaven has had two parental complaints about the way John treats their children. Mrs. Gaven is sure something is very wrong, but doesn't know what. When she speaks to John, he makes excuses about his behavior, saying that he just needs time to get a particularly difficult class under control.

A month passes and Mrs. Gaven notices little improvement in John's behavior. Finally, two of John's fellow grade level teachers ask to talk with Mrs. Gaven privately. They express their concern about John and their belief that he may have developed a drinking problem. The teachers are sure that John doesn't drink during the school day, but believe that he binges in the evenings and on weekends. John's colleagues note that he is so short-tempered that he is beginning to destroy the self-confidence of many of his students. His team members are worried because they see a wonderful teacher destroying himself, as well as causing problems for his students. They aren't sure what can be done, but feel Mrs. Gaven should know.

Mrs. Gaven's first reaction is, "Why me? Why, after fifteen years, should John have a breakdown on my watch?" Yet, Mrs. Gaven knows that she needs to act quickly.

Before talking directly with John, Mrs. Gaven decides to first explore the kinds of support she can offer to John. With guidance from the human services director, Mrs. Gaven finds out that a substitute can be hired and that the district will provide referral services to John. Insurance will cover the cost of any treatment required.

Mrs. Gaven then makes an appointment with John—when both can talk without time constraints. She begins the conference by telling John why he is a valued staff member. "John, you know that you are a wonderful teacher. I can't tell you how many parents have let me know that your teaching has made a positive difference for their children. Mrs. Smith was just in and she mentioned that Toby was having a great experience in middle school. She attributes his success to Toby having been in your room."

Next, Mrs. Gaven addresses the problem. "John, this year seems to be different." John interrupts explaining that he has one student who keeps everyone off balance and that the whole class is a difficult group. At this point, Mrs. Gaven reminds John that he has always been able to work well with children who have problems. Then Mrs. Gaven tells John that she is concerned that he may have a drinking problem. John reacts by not reacting. When Mrs. Gaven asks John if her suspicions could be true, John denies that there is a problem. Mrs. Gaven continues, "John, what you do after work is normally a private issue—and something I would not ask you to share with me. However, what we are talking about now is something that affects your students—not just this year, but possibly in the future as well." Next, Mrs. Gaven asks John how much he drank on Monday, on Tuesday, and so on. Although John continues

(continued)

to deny that there is a problem, Mrs. Gaven recognizes that they need to continue to work on a resolution to the problem.

As this initial discussion ends, Mrs. Gaven tells John that she is planning on hiring a substitute for the next day, and that she wants John to talk with the district personnel officer to set up a plan. Mrs. Gaven lets John know that there are many options they can work with and that he has all of her support in this very difficult situation. As John leaves, Mrs. Gaven tells him she knows that they can work out something to help him get back on track. John says very little. Mrs. Gaven is unsure how things will turn out but sadly recognizes that they cannot allow students to be adversely affected. No one will win if this situation goes unattended, but there is the possibility that everyone will win with this caring confrontation.

Take Action!

Use the chart below to evaluate how effective you are at decision making and managing conflict. Circle a "1" if you have a lot of room for improvement and a "5" if you are highly skilled. Reread the sections of this chapter that cover any areas in which you feel you need to improve. Then, identify specific ways you can work on these areas. Practice one skill actively for a couple of weeks. Then add another skill or strategy to practice.

	SKILL LEVEL				
	Needs Improvement				**Highly Skilled**

1. Make decisions efficiently:

• Are you clear with staff regarding which decisions are yours and which decisions will be participatory?	1	2	3	4	5
• For decisions that are yours, do you have an efficient strategy for seeking input from staff on decisions that will affect them?	1	2	3	4	5
• For decisions that will be made by staff (or student council, or parent advisory committee, and so on) do you have a consistent process for achieving consensus?	1	2	3	4	5
• Do you clarify the purpose of each agenda item during staff meetings (e.g., brainstorming, input, decision making)?	1	2	3	4	5
• Do you communicate the outcome of all decisions clearly?	1	2	3	4	5
• Do you accept responsibility for poor decisions?	1	2	3	4	5

2. Deal effectively with conflict:

• Do you have agreed upon rules for dealing with disagreements?	1	2	3	4	5
• Do you have strategies for interacting productively with people who are angry?	1	2	3	4	5
• Do you deal immediately and directly with conflicts or problems requiring administrative intervention?	1	2	3	4	5

Conclusion

Being a building principal has grown more and more complex over the years. When schools could focus their efforts on teaching the best and the brightest, it was acceptable to expel some students and encourage other students to drop out and get a job. Now that schools need to educate everyone, increased building leadership is essential in guiding decision making and conflict resolution. Part of this leadership includes involving the entire staff in designing and implementing procedures for successfully reaching all students. In addition, it means establishing procedures for making decisions effectively and handling disagreements humanely and productively. In this chapter we have explored efficient mechanisms for making decisions and effective strategies for dealing with disagreements and problems that may arise.

chapter three

Practical Guidelines for Behavior Change

Along with basic skills and knowledge in effective school leadership (see Chapters One and Two), you should have a solid understanding of some basic principles of effective behavior change. This knowledge will allow you to work more successfully with staff, students, and parents as you guide your building's efforts to ensure a safe and productive school environment for all.

The principles of behavior change are grounded in the assumption that people are constantly engaged in learning, and that every experience adds to a person's knowledge base and influences her choices—both conscious and unconscious. For example, someone who has submitted scores of résumés but hasn't gotten any job interviews might decide to write a new résumé. If the new résumé leads to multiple interviews, the person is more likely to use it in the future rather than the old résumé. Or, when someone goes to a movie based on a friend's recommendation, but finds it to be a poor movie and a waste of her money, she isn't likely to take that friend's movie recommendations as seriously in the future. Scenarios such as these are repeated in each individual's life many times per day—in uncountable, interwoven combinations—to create a rich fabric of experiences and learning. Simply put, a person's behavior is influenced by events and conditions experienced, some that encourage the person to engage in certain behaviors and others that discourage the person from engaging in certain behaviors. The following graphic representation shows the three main variables that affect behavior.

Three Main Variables That Affect Behavior

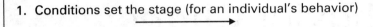

1. Conditions set the stage (for an individual's behavior)

2. Pleasant consequences result in behavior increasing in the future

3. Unpleasant consequences result in behavior decreasing in future

Those with behavioral training will recognize this graphic representation as a model of behavioral theory—expressed in common sense and pragmatic terms. We believe that this model provides a useful structure to successfully change behavior. Unfortunately, the language associated with behavioral theory is often misunderstood and/or misused. Therefore, in this chapter we present the principles of school-based behavior change using examples and commonsense advice, rather than the more emotionally charged technical vocabulary. Basically, the model suggests that to change behaviors one needs to focus on: (1) What is prompting a behavior (desirable or undesirable); (2) What is encouraging or sustaining that behavior; and (3) What might discourage that behavior from occurring in the future.

The purpose of this chapter is to provide general guidelines about how to effectively implement the behavior management procedures for doing those things that are recommended in the remainder of this book. The chapter is organized into four main sections. The first section describes five main categories of actions that can be taken when attempting to change behavior (of either an individual or a group). The second section presents guidelines for procedures related to "setting the stage" for (or prompting) behaviors—specifically, how to analyze and modify the various settings in your school to reduce the probability of behavior problems and increase the probability of responsible student behavior. Section three covers guidelines for implementing corrective consequences (i.e., procedures designed to reduce future occurrences of misbehavior) more effectively. The fourth section offers guidelines for how to effectively use encouragement procedures (e.g., praise) to increase responsible behavior.

The information in this chapter is based on a large and comprehensive body of research findings. In an attempt to keep things brief and pragmatic, however, only information most useful to you is included. Thus, like most commonsense advice, the chapter reflects a simple understanding of complex principles. Perhaps the following slightly crude analogy will clarify this. Someone given the advice, "Don't spit into the wind," will find it sound advice whether or not they like the advice, or like to spit, or like the wind (or have any other opinions or subjective perceptions). They do not need a complex and technical explanation involving biology, meteorology, and physics to understand or apply the advice. The guidelines presented in this chapter are intended to reduce the chance that your efforts to implement any of these behavior management suggestions will be like "spitting in the wind."

Note: For a more detailed discussion of behavioral theory and/or for suggested responses to common concerns about that theory (e.g., "I think students should work for intrinsic motivation, not for rewards"), see Chapter Four: Understanding Behavioral Theory.

Changing Behavior—Five Variables to Manipulate

One of the most important concepts for school staff to grasp is that *any behavior that occurs repeatedly is serving some function for the individual exhibiting the behavior*. It's also important to understand that this is as true for behaviors that are negative or destructive as it is for behaviors that are positive and productive. Staff may find it difficult to understand an individual student's behavior when the consequences of that behavior seem so unpleasant. For example, consider a seventh grade student who is chronically argumentative with staff (and has been since he entered the middle school). This student may continually be sent out of class, be assigned detention, have his parents called, and have school staff angry and frustrated with him. Yet, as unpleasant as these consequences appear to be, staff have to realize that the student is getting some positive benefit from his behavior or he would change it.

In some cases an irresponsible behavior functions to create positive consequences for the individual. The student who argues, for example, may be getting lots of attention (direct and angry engagement) from adults—which gives him a sense of power. Or, he may be getting lots of attention from peers (for appearing strong and powerful enough to "fight" with teachers). In other cases, a behavior functions as a way to avoid unpleasant results that come from exhibiting responsible behavior. For example, a student with academic problems who is compliant ends up having to work on assignments that she is incapable of doing. However, if she argues and gets thrown out of class, she avoids having to publicly demonstrate her lack of academic ability.

This concept (that any chronic behavior serves a function) is essential to keep in mind as you and your staff strive to teach students to behave responsibly. Fundamentally it means that you may have to do more than just "correct" irresponsible behavior and "encourage" responsible behavior. The following five categories represent the main types of actions that school personnel can take to influence student behavior. (The specific procedures included for each category are those that might be part of an intervention effort for our hypothetical argumentative student.)

1. **Modify a setting (organization, schedule, physical structure, and so on) to prompt responsible behavior.**

    *   Give the student a high-status job (to be performed daily) that will increase his sense of power and purpose in the school.

    *   Arrange for the student to privately receive tutorial assistance in his most difficult subjects.

    *   Make sure staff give the student very clear directions.

    *   Remind staff to avoid power struggles with the student.

2. **Remove any aversive aspects of exhibiting responsible behavior.**

   • Modify academic assignments so that the student can succeed.

   • Preteach particularly difficult assignments to the student.

   • Prearrange times during the day when the student can privately ask teachers questions and/or get assistance so he does not have to do so in front of his peers.

   • Remind staff to avoid publicly praising the student for following directions.

3. **Implement procedures designed to encourage responsible behavior.**

   • Ask staff to give the student frequent adult attention.

   • Remind staff to privately praise the student when he follows directions without arguing.

4. **Remove any positive aspects of exhibiting irresponsible behavior.**

   • Train staff to NOT engage in arguing.

   • Train staff to maintain instructional momentum so the student does not get lots of attention from peers when he attempts to argue.

5. **Implement procedures designed to correct irresponsible behavior. Inform staff to:**

   • Give the student a warning when he begins to argue.

   • Calmly implement a corrective consequence if the student continues to argue after the warning.

   • Ignore any further attempts by the student to engage in arguing.

Developing and implementing intervention plans that include procedures in some or all of these five categories increases the probability that staff efforts to help students learn to behave more responsibly will be successful. The sample plan described above, for example, might not be effective if staff did nothing to remove positive aspects of exhibiting the irresponsible behavior (e.g., training teachers NOT to engage in arguing). That is, the student's behavior would not improve if the benefits of getting peer and teacher attention outweighed all the other steps taken.

The remainder of this chapter delineates basic guidelines for you to keep in mind with respect to modifying a setting, correcting irresponsible behavior, and encouraging responsible behavior. Although not addressed specifically, you should remember that it may also be necessary to remove or reduce the positive aspects of engaging in an irresponsible behavior and/or reduce or eliminate any negative aspects of exhibiting responsible behavior.

Guidelines for Modifying Settings

In the school setting, as in all aspects of life, the physical and social environments constantly provide information to an individual's senses. Much of this information sets the stage for or influences how an individual will behave. A basic principle of school-based behavior change is that to change student behavior, one of the first things to do is examine the extent to which the physical and social conditions in the various settings are prompting responsible and/or irresponsible behavior. For example:

- A cafeteria where students have to stand in lunch lines for up to twenty minutes each day may be setting the stage for frustrated, restless, and angry student behavior. Shortening their time spent in lines is likely to lessen this undesirable student behavior.

- Hallways where adults are never present have a greater probability of students running in them. Having adults monitor those hallways will lessen that probability.

- Listening to a boring teacher may prompt students to engage in distracted and off-task behavior, whereas listening to a dynamic and interesting teacher will prompt attentive behavior.

As principal you need to continually monitor the physical and social conditions of all your school's settings to determine whether students are being prompted to behave responsibly or irresponsibly. You should also help your staff learn to conduct this same sort of analysis for the settings they supervise. A chronic pattern of misbehavior in any setting should prompt a reevaluation of the conditions in that setting.

Following are general guidelines to help you improve how well the stage is set to prompt desired behavior in all your school's settings. (**Note:** In Chapters Nine and Ten we provide information on specific procedures for the school's common areas and individual class-rooms, respectively.)

1. **Develop clear expectations and see that they are taught to all students.**

   When the expectations for student behavior in a specific school setting are clear, consistent, and have been directly taught to students, the behavior in that setting will, in general, be more responsible than if the expectations were not clear and/or had not been communicated well. Students cannot be expected to behave responsibly if they have not been taught exactly what responsible behavior consists of and/or how to demonstrate it. A teacher who has and teaches clear classroom behavioral expectations will have fewer problems with student behavior and motivation than the teacher who does not. The teacher effectiveness literature overwhelmingly shows that effective teachers are clear about precisely how they expect students to behave during each daily activity (instructional activities and transitions) and that they teach students their expectations during the first two weeks of school—providing sufficient practice for students to reach mastery.

   In many schools, the behavioral expectations for common areas (playground, halls, restrooms, and so on) are not clear, to either staff or students. In these schools, common area supervisors tend to be inconsistent in their expectations for student behavior and in how they correct inappropriate behaviors. Thus, in a school that has ongoing problems in the halls, you are more likely to find that only some staff members bother to stop students from running in the halls; the rest do not. You are also more likely to find that students have not had lessons on the importance of walking instead of running in the halls, and that classified staff are not sure whether they are even supposed to intervene when they see students running in the halls.

It is essential to get your staff to come to agreement on their expectations for student behavior in the common areas and then—once those expectations have been established—to clearly communicate them to students.

2. **See that the organizational and structural features of all settings prompt success.**

In schools, as in many institutions, procedures tend to become (no surprise here) institutionalized. A school may have two recesses each day simply because there have always been two recesses and/or because all the other elementary schools in the district have two recesses. Or, the reason a school's recesses are unstructured is just because they have always been that way. But, there is no universal rule that says a school has to have two (or none or one or three) recesses or that recesses have to be unstructured. In fact, when playground misbehavior is frequent, it may be because there are too many recesses each day, or that the recesses are too long, or that the students do not have enough to do. The students may need to be taught rules for specific games or activities and/or required to participate in one of several supervised games or activities. Possibly they need to learn a structured conflict resolution strategy. Or, perhaps there are just too many students on the playground at one time or the particular mix of ages is problematic. The types of common area organizational and structural features that should be evaluated, and modified as necessary, include the physical setting, student proximity to adults, the traffic patterns, scheduling issues, how long students have to wait in lines (e.g., lunch lines or lines to come in from recess), crowding, and routines. Classroom features to address include scheduling issues, quality of instruction, clarity of expectations, frequency of positive feedback, and so on.

3. **Ensure adequate adult supervision.**

Most adults tend to drive with more care and closer to the speed limits when a police officer is in view than when one is not present. Students in school are no different than adults on the highway. Most will behave more responsibly when a supervisor is present than when there is no supervision. Think about each of the common areas in your school. Does it have adequate supervision? Do students believe there is a good chance they will get caught if they behave inappropriately? If they don't, teaching them what corrective consequences will be used for various misbehaviors is a joke. Knowing that "If you get caught running in the halls, you have to go back and walk" means nothing if you also know that there is hardly ever an adult in the halls to catch you running.

The most effective classroom teachers are highly skilled at proximity management and scanning. They move unpredictably throughout their rooms, and no matter where they are or what they are doing, they visually scan the entire room frequently. They know what is going on in all parts of the room at all times. These teachers generally have far fewer behavior problems than a teacher who stays in one place (e.g., behind the desk) and/or whose attention gets so fixed (e.g., on the student she is talking to at the moment, or on grading papers) that she does not keep track of the rest of the class. When misbehavior is occurring because of inadequate supervision, improving the use of encouragement procedures or corrective consequences is not likely to significantly improve student behavior.

Whenever there are patterns of misbehavior exhibited by many different students in a particular setting, these three critical considerations need to be reviewed: (1) Student knowledge of the behavioral expectations for that setting; (2) The setting's organizational and structural features; and (3) The adequacy of the supervision in that setting.

Take Action!

As a preview to the sort of analysis and tasks that will be presented in Chapter Nine, identify a common area setting (halls, cafeteria, bus waiting areas, busses, playground) in your school that has the most frequent behavior and discipline problems, and ask yourself the following questions:

- Are the expectations for student behavior in that setting clear and explicit?

- Do all staff who supervise that setting know what the expectations are?

- Have those expectations been taught to students?

- Are the expectations reviewed with students on a reasonably regular basis?

- Is the area structured and organized in a way that prompts behavioral success?

- Is there adequate supervision?

If your answers to any or all of these questions suggest there is room for improvement, make some preliminary notes regarding what might be done. Then read Chapter Nine: Common Areas—Improving Behavior in Halls, Cafeteria, Playground, and Other Areas to develop a systematic plan for improving how the stage is set for that area.

Next, identify a teacher who is having difficulty with behavior management and discipline, and ask yourself the following questions:

- Does the teacher have clear and consistent expectations for student behavior in all classroom activities?

- Have these expectations been taught directly to students?

- Does the teacher have a schedule that keeps students occupied with meaningful, relevant tasks?

- Are transitions between tasks smooth and efficient?

- Does the teacher have consistent routines for attendance, handing papers out, turning papers in, correcting papers in class, and so on?

- Is the teacher's classroom supervision, in terms of proximity management and visual scanning, adequate?

If the answers to any or all of these questions suggest there is room for improvement, make some preliminary notes regarding what might be done to help this teacher. Then read Chapter Ten: Classrooms—Assisting Teachers With Behavior and Discipline to develop a systematic plan for helping the teacher improve.

Guidelines for Corrective Consequences

No matter how effectively you set the stage at your school to prompt responsible student behavior, there will still be misbehavior. And, how staff respond to that misbehavior will significantly influence whether it occurs more or less often in the future. Staff responses to misbehavior also have a huge impact on your school's climate. Not surprisingly, when staff are overly harsh or consistently negative, a negative and adversarial tone is set in the school. The following quote captures this notion succinctly and powerfully:

> *I've come to a frightening conclusion that I am the decisive element in the classroom. It's my personal approach that creates the climate. It's my daily mood that makes the weather. As a teacher, I possess a tremendous power to make a child's life miserable or joyous. I can be a tool of torture or an instrument of inspiration. I can humiliate or humor, hurt or heal. In all situations, it is my response that decides whether a crisis will be escalated or de-escalated and a child humanized or dehumanized.*
>
> — Haim Ginott

The following guidelines for effectively implementing corrective consequences apply to schoolwide practices and to working with individual children, and they are applicable regardless of the type of misbehavior or the setting (e.g., classrooms, busses, playgrounds). They should be kept in mind whenever you or your staff are using any of the corrective consequences recommended in the remainder of this book.

1. **View misbehavior as a teaching opportunity.**

    When you understand that the ultimate purpose of behavior management is to help students learn to behave responsibly, then it makes sense that the goal of using corrective consequences in response to a student's misbehavior is to help that student learn not to behave that way in the future. The purpose is not to make the student *pay* for what he did or make him feel guilty about his behavior, but rather to increase the chance that if faced with the same situation in the future, the student will choose to behave more responsibly.

    A direct corollary of this goal is that when a student has misbehaved because he does not know how to behave responsibly in a given context, the corrective consequence must include teaching the student what and how to behave appropriately. For example, if the reason a student consistently reacts negatively to having errors in his work pointed out by the teacher is that he does not know how to react differently, at least part of the corrective consequence should involve providing the student with information and/or practice on ways of reacting positively to corrective feedback.

    Another corollary is that when a student knows how to behave responsibly in a given context, but chooses not to, the corrective consequence should have a logical association to the misbehavior. Making a student who has been rude to a guest speaker pick up trash in the halls, for example, will probably do little to teach the student anything. On the other hand, requiring the student to write a letter of apology and/or personally call the speaker to apologize may help the student learn that he must try to repair damage to social relationships by reestablishing positive contact with the other person involved.

2. **Use only humane corrective consequences for misbehavior.**

    Humiliation and ridicule have no place in the school. Although corrective conse-
    quences that belittle or attack a student may change his/her behavior (i.e., decrease
    the future occurrence of the undesired behavior), they tend to be so destructive to an
    individual student's self-image and to the overall school climate that any benefits that
    come from reducing the misbehavior are far outweighed by the damage done. Most
    adults can remember a time as children when they were embarrassed by a teacher,
    parent, or some other adult for having made an error. The very fact that such events
    are remembered (often with shame or resentment) into adulthood is testimony to the
    destructive power of ridicule and belittlement. Effective corrective consequences for
    student misbehavior reduce the future occurrence of the misbehavior—but in ways
    that avoid alienating or humiliating students.

3. **Implement corrective consequences for misbehavior calmly.**

    A calm response to misbehavior is more likely than an emotional one to effectively
    teach a student not to behave that way again in the future. In fact, for some students
    angry and emotional responses from adults are actually reinforcing (i.e., they increase
    the probability that the student will misbehave that way in the future). For students like
    this, being able to make an adult angry satisfies a need for influence and power. When
    the adult stays calm, on the other hand, the possibility that the misbehavior will be
    reinforced is reduced.

    A calm response to misbehavior also helps communicate a more appropriate message.
    If a teacher calmly explains to a student who was overtly defiant to a cafeteria
    supervisor that she must write (and hand deliver) a letter of apology to the supervisor,
    the student is more likely to get the message that it's important to try and repair the
    damage her original misbehavior caused. However, if the teacher is angry or hostile
    when assigning the corrective consequence, the student may perceive that because
    she made the teacher mad, the teacher is now making her write a letter.

    Finally, staying calm reduces the chance that, in the heat of anger, a staff member will
    say something that will humiliate or hurt the student, or be impossible to follow through
    on. "You are such a horrible little brat, I am going to take away your recess for the rest
    of the month!"

4. **Use as mild a corrective consequence as reasonably fits the infraction.**

    One of the most common errors when responding to misbehavior is to use as harsh
    a corrective consequence as possible. This has several drawbacks. First, harsh proce-
    dures often create avoidance situations. In an effort to reduce speeding, for example,
    the Oregon legislature passed a law that significantly increased the monetary penalties
    for speeding. The law changed some people's behavior all right—they invested in radar
    detectors. In other words, otherwise honest people became more sneaky. Another
    outcome was that many people came to view the police in a more negative light. Finally,
    it made it much more difficult for the police to be consistent. Because the penalties
    were severe enough that going 76 mph in a 55 zone could bankrupt a low-income
    family, the police ended up giving out lots more warnings and far fewer tickets. The
    severe penalties just did not work. After a year and a half, when it was determined that

average speeds had actually increased, the legislature changed the penalties back to those more in line with other states.

For school personnel, the same kind of situation can arise. Imagine a teacher who, in a moment of frustration, states that any student who disrupts the class from now on will be removed from the classroom and have his/her parents contacted. What does the teacher do if a student is tapping his pencil? Does she follow through on the stated corrective consequence? If she does, how will she justify the extreme nature of that response to the administration, student, and his parents? On the other hand, if she doesn't follow through, her students get the message that she doesn't really mean what she says.

Harsh corrective consequences can also be destructive to student motivation. They may cause some students to fear coming to school. Other students may come to school but avoid interacting with adults because they are afraid of them. Still other students will just stop trying to do their best on tasks or expectations assigned by someone they perceive to have been mean to them or one of their peers.

5. **Implement corrective consequences consistently.**

Not only are inconsistently implemented corrective consequences highly unlikely to change students' irresponsible behaviors, they also increase the probability of confusion and resentment on the part of students. Consistent implementation is essential for several reasons. First of all, it is an issue of fairness. When it has been stated that a particular misbehavior will result in a certain corrective consequence, but some students who engage in the misbehavior receive the corrective consequence while others do not, students will perceive this as unfair—because it is, in fact, unfair. The net result is likely to be hostility and resentment toward staff for "not being fair."

Consistency is also important for clear communication. If a corrective consequence has been established for a particular misbehavior, but an individual student only receives the corrective consequence some of the times she engages in that misbehavior, that student gets a mixed message. Staff say that the behavior is unacceptable, but their actions imply that sometimes it is permissible to behave that way. The student may conclude that staff really are not seriously concerned about that particular behavior. If staff do not believe the misbehavior is serious enough to implement the corrective consequence consistently, why should the student think that the misbehavior is serious.

A final reason that consistency is important is that whenever a designated corrective consequence is not applied, a student may very well feel a sense of satisfaction at getting away with the misbehavior—which may reinforce the student for misbehaving, and increase rather than decrease the probability that the student exhibit that behavior in the future.

6. **Chronic misbehavior by any individual student should prompt the development of a proactive individualized plan.**

Whenever a particular student's misbehavior appears to be chronic, and efforts to address it with simple encouragement and corrective consequences have been ineffective, a comprehensive intervention plan to help the student learn to be more responsible is generally required. If the encouragement and corrective consequences alone were going to work, they would have worked already. Providing more and harsher corrective consequences is likely to be equally as ineffective. Staff need to do a comprehensive examination of the situation in order to develop an intervention plan that will effectively help the student change his behavior. Information on developing and implementing individualized behavior management plans is provided in Chapter Five: A Process for Improving Your Schoolwide Behavior Plan (SBP).

Take Action!

Each of the guidelines for effectively implementing corrective consequences is listed on the grid below. For each, determine whether you are already sufficiently skilled in your use of it (mark "S" for skilled) or whether you need to improve your use of it (mark "I" for improvement). Then, for two weeks keep those corrective consequence guidelines on which you need improvement in mind as you respond to student misbehavior.

Also, consider the collective skill level of your staff in the use of each guideline. Mark an "S" or an "I" to indicate the guidelines that most staff—on average—are currently skilled at using, and those on which most need to improve. Prepare (or ask some highly skilled staff members to prepare) a series of five- to ten-minute faculty meeting presentations on these guidelines. Begin by reviewing the guidelines staff use skillfully. Be sure to include congratulations and encouragement to keep up the good work. Then address the guidelines (one or two each week) on which staff need improvement. Lead a discussion about why each of the guidelines is useful and how it can be applied to procedures used in classroom and nonclassroom settings.

Circle "S" for skilled or "I" for improvement.

Guideline	SELF Evaluation		STAFF Evaluation	
1. Misbehavior should be viewed as a teaching opportunity.	S	I	S	I
2. Corrective procedures for misbehavior must be implemented humanely.	S	I	S	I
3. Corrective procedures for misbehavior should be implemented calmly.	S	I	S	I
4. Use as mild a corrective procedure as reasonably fits the infraction.	S	I	S	I
5. Corrective procedures should be implemented consistently.	S	I	S	I
6. Patterns of chronic misbehavior by any individual student should prompt staff to develop a proactive individualized plan.	S	I	S	I

Guidelines for Encouraging Responsible Behavior

An essential part of effective behavior management is providing students with meaningful, relevant, and age-appropriate feedback when they are behaving responsibly. Although corny, the old adage, "You can catch more flies with honey than with vinegar," is true. Another of the basic principles of behavior change is that encouragement procedures actually have more power to shape behavior than corrective consequences. Unless implemented appropriately, however, encouragement procedures can be ineffective or even destructive. The following guidelines should help you and your staff effectively implement encouragement procedures, so that you are increasing the probability that your students will engage in responsible behavior. The guidelines are applicable to all the encouragement procedures presented in the remainder of this book.

1. **Use positive recognition (praise and/or structured rewards), which should be contingent upon student behavior.**

   Contingency means that you only give the praise or reward if students meet the conditions previously identified. For example, if a student is on a point contract (i.e., is earning points) for demonstrating self-control on the playground, she should only get points on days that she meets the prespecified criteria for demonstrating self-control. If she gets points on a day that she has not earned them, she will soon learn that the points really have no value—she gets them whether she successfully demonstrates self-control or not. It does not take long for a student in this situation to cease being motivated to even try to earn the points.

   Contingency also means that the behavior being reinforced must be of some importance. Most people find it insulting to have someone gush over a behavior they know is no big deal. For example, imagine driving into the parking lot of your school and having the assistant superintendent say to you, "Great right turn into the parking lot. You didn't hit a post or a child or anything. You are such a wonderful person. Nice work. I am so proud of you." Compare that with how you would feel if you have led a task force to develop a gang prevention plan for your district and the assistant superintendent says to you, after reviewing your report, "The recommendations within this report are clear and practical. I believe that implementing these procedures will really make a difference in this community."

2. **Use acknowledgment and nurturing of students, which should *not* be contingent upon appropriate behavior.**

   Regardless of how any student behaves, each and every student at your school should be welcomed and made to feel like valued members of the school community. If the only adult attention a student receives is in the form of praise or structured rewards, that student may come to feel that she only has value when she does what adults want her to do. That is why you and your staff must make a conscious effort to give all students unconditional attention and nurturing on a regular basis—in addition to using contingent praise and structured rewards for particular behaviors. Every student who enters the building in the morning should have at least one adult who says hello and welcomes them to school—not because they are (or are not) following the school rules, but just because they are important. All students should have teachers who check to see that they understand new concepts, just because the teachers want all students to achieve mastery of important objectives. When students appear lonely or sad, there should be adults who check to see if they need assistance. A student who has been absent should hear, "You were absent yesterday and we missed you," from at least one adult. None of these interactions should be contingent on a student's behavior—staff should do them to show they truly care about and value every student.

3. **Use praise that is specific and descriptive, but *not* evaluative.**

Praising a student's behavior is more likely to increase the chances that the student will engage in that behavior again if the praise itself provides the student with information about exactly what he did that was important. "Good job!"; "Fantastic!"; and "That was terrific!" are all examples of praise that is too general. None of them gives any information about what the student did that was "praiseworthy." Contrast those comments with the following praise statements:

- "Shondra, your essay provided many powerful examples of the use of figurative language."

- "Zachary, our guest speaker was very pleased and appreciative of the way you welcomed her to our classroom and introduced her to the class. She asked me to thank you."

- "Vera, while presenting your project you spoke loudly, clearly, and confidently. Even the students in the back of the room had no difficulty hearing your presentation."

- "Allen, you are showing great self-control. You have remembered to raise your hand when you want to speak, and you have been respecting other students' space."

It's also important to avoid evaluative praise. Each of the preceding praise comments would be weakened if they included things like: "You are so great," or "It is such a pleasure to have you in my class," or "What a fantastic student you are." Evaluative elements like that may imply that if a student did not exhibit the positive behaviors then she would not be "great," or that having trouble will make the teacher think that she is not "a pleasure to have in class," or that making a mistake means she's not a "fantastic student." Effective praise describes exactly what a student has done, but does not pass judgment.

When giving praise, avoid making oneself the center of attention. Comments such as: "I like the way you …" or "I am so proud of you," take the focus away from the student and put it on the fact that the student has pleased the praise giver. The ultimate goal of using praise is for students to become personally responsible for their behavior—doing things not because they please someone, but because they are personally satisfying.

4. **Use praise that is age-appropriate.**

Praising a primary age student with language that's too sophisticated is unlikely to be effective because the student will not understand. Likewise, praising an adolescent publicly and/or with unsophisticated language may embarrass the student. If students do not seem to respond when they are praised (i.e., they do not seem to exhibit the behaviors being praised more frequently), the manner in which the praise is delivered should be modified. For example, the sophistication of the vocabulary can be changed, or whether the praise is given publicly or privately. Other ways to modify how praise is delivered include experimenting with being closer or farther away from students when you praise and modifying your tone of voice to sound more or less excited about what the student has done.

5. **Give praise sincerely—in a manner that fits one's style.**

When students are praised, they need to know that the adult praising them views the behavior being praised as important. There is no right or wrong way to do this. For some people it means interacting with students in a businesslike manner, and for others it means interacting in a very friendly manner. Both approaches can effectively motivate students. Staff should not feel that they must praise in a certain style. In fact, if a businesslike person tries to praise in a more friendly and excited way than he/she is actually comfortable doing, students will probably sense that staff member's discomfort, and may even feel that the staff member is being dishonest in his/her praise or is trying to manipulate the students. Thus, while praise should be specific and descriptive and should avoid embarrassing students, it can be effectively delivered in any style.

6. **Periodically use "celebrations of success" (intermittent rewards) as an encouragement procedure.**

In an effective school, the adults look for and make use of opportunities to celebrate the growth and accomplishments of students. If a particular student's essay demonstrates significant improvement, a teacher might ask the student's permission to share it with the class. If a student with a history of disrupting the class demonstrates improved self-control, a teacher might send the student to the principal's office for congratulations and perhaps a certificate of some sort. If the members of a class significantly improve their rates of work completion, they might get an extra-long recess. When an entire student body has worked at something like reducing waste at lunch and improving the school's recycling efforts, the money saved might be donated to a charity and press releases about the students' efforts sent to local papers and news channels. Then the publicity could be shared with students. Intermittent (after-the-fact) rewards are a way of highlighting the importance of students' accomplishments without turning everything into a "If you do this, here is what you earn" system.

7. **Use structured reward systems sparingly.**

Structured reinforcement systems (such as individual contracts and schoolwide reward systems) are time-consuming to manage. Thus, before establishing any kind of a structured system, efforts should be made to motivate students with effective praise, noncontingent attention and nurturing, and intermittent celebrations of progress. The fact is that whenever student motivation can be maintained without a structured system, there is more time for important instructional activities. It is only when less intrusive reinforcement efforts repeatedly fail to motivate students to meet behavioral and academic expectations that staff should consider setting up reward systems.

8. **When using schoolwide structured reward systems, make sure they have great flexibility.**

    Effective schoolwide reward systems are those in which staff members can reinforce individual students for behaviors that are important to those students. For example, in an effective system, staff can reinforce a student who always behaves responsibly for "being so independent and cooperative for the past week," as well as reinforcing a student who frequently misbehaves for "demonstrating self-control for the entire morning."

    Systems that have the exact same criteria for everyone (everyone who does not get his/her name on the board for misbehaving, gets to see the film on Friday), tend to end up rewarding students who do not really need it (they would have behaved appropriately anyway), and not rewarding the students who actually need the additional motivation (because the criteria is too high, and they never receive the reward). Examples of different types of schoolwide systems and the pros and cons will be provided in Chapter Seven: Encouragement Procedures—Meeting Students' Basic Needs.

9. **When using structured reward systems with individuals, avoid implementing time limits.**

    Probably the most frequent use of structured reward systems in schools involves placing individual students on "contracts" to help them manage their own behavior. (**Note:** a classroom teacher should not be expected to manage more than one or two individualized contracts). A major problem with many contracts is that they include an arbitrary time limit. For example, consider a student who has a contract to earn points for demonstrating "self-control." The student can use the points to "buy" independent time on a computer in the office—something he really wants. The contract is set up so that he earns one point for each successful recess and one point for each successful half day within his classroom—a possibility of five points per day. There are three major disadvantages to setting up a system with time limits (e.g., if the students earns 21 points by Friday, he receives 45 minutes on the computer). First, the student could earn his 21 points by the first recess on Friday morning and then behave miserably the rest of the day—but he would still get his computer time. Or, he might try really hard (for him), but only have 19 points by Friday afternoon—not enough to earn his reward. The next week, when he has to start all over, he may feel as if it just isn't worth it to try. Finally, if the student has a bad time at the beginning of the week, he may realize he has no chance of earning the reward, no matter how well he does the remainder of the week. A stronger system is one in which, as soon as the student earns 21 points, he receives his 45 minutes on the computer. It may take him until Friday or it may take him until the following Wednesday—but the reinforcement immediately follows goal attainment. Information on setting up individualized contracts is provided in Volume II: Referrals and Solutions.

Take Action!

The guidelines for effectively implementing encouragement procedures are listed on the grid below. For each, determine whether you are sufficiently skilled in using it (mark "S" for skilled) or whether you need to improve your use of it (mark "I" for improvement). Then, for two weeks keep in mind the guidelines that you are trying to improve on as you encourage responsible behavior from staff and students.

Also, think about the collective skill level of your staff in applying these guidelines—on average. Mark an "S" or an "I" to indicate the guidelines on which most staff are skilled and the guidelines on which most staff need improvement, respectively. Prepare (or ask some skilled staff members to prepare) a five- to ten-minute presentation on the guidelines for the next faculty meeting. Start with the guidelines staff currently implement skillfully. Congratulate them and encourage them to keep up the good work. Next, identify the guidelines on which staff need improvement. Lead a discussion about why each guideline is useful and how it can be applied to encouragement procedures in both classroom and nonclassroom settings.

Circle "S" for skilled or "I" for improvement.

Guideline	SELF Evaluation		STAFF Evaluation	
1. Praise and/or structured rewards should be contingent upon student behavior.	S	I	S	I
2. Attention and nurturing should not be contingent on appropriate behavior.	S	I	S	I
3. Praise should be specific and descriptive, but not be evaluative.	S	I	S	I
4. Praise is more likely to be a reinforcing consequence if it is age-appropriate.	S	I	S	I
5. Praise should be sincere—given in a manner that fits the adult's style.	S	I	S	I
6. Implement periodic celebrations of success (intermittent rewards).	S	I	S	I
7. Use structured reward systems sparingly.	S	I	S	I
8. If using structured rewards on a schoolwide basis, implement strategies that allow great flexibility.	S	I	S	I
9. If implementing a structured reward system with an individual, avoid systems with time limits.	S	I	S	I

Conclusion

When you want to change student behavior (both individual students or whole groups of students), use the behavioral model to guide your intervention efforts. First look at the big picture—in particular, determine whether there are things about the setting in which a problematic behavior occurs that may be prompting it. Remember if you limit your efforts to encouragement and corrective consequences only, your intervention efforts are not likely to be successful. For example, for a student who exhibits frequent angry outbursts, it is not enough to focus only on correcting the outbursts when they occur and recognizing and encouraging the student when he demonstrates self-control. You also need to consider what might be precipitating the student's outbursts—whether he is being asked to do academic tasks too far beyond his current skill level, whether there is any possibility that he is a victim of abuse, or whether he is abusing drugs. If conditions such as these are prompting a student's outbursts and your intervention doesn't include some attempt to modify those conditions (in addition to implementing corrective consequences and encouragement procedures), you might actually be training the student to tolerate an unreasonable situation.

When you do implement encouragement procedures and corrective consequences, remember the commonsense implementation guidelines. They will increase the chances that the procedures will have the desired effect (i.e., either reducing or increasing a particular behavior). If a particular procedure is not working (e.g., praise is not increasing responsible behavior), analyze how the procedure is being implemented in light of the guidelines provided in this section and make appropriate modifications.

chapter four

Understanding Behavioral Theory

Note: This chapter extends the practical guidelines provided in the preceding chapter by providing:

- A more detailed explanation of behavioral theory, specifically the ABC (antecedent/behavior/consequence) model of how behavior is learned.

- Responses to common concerns and misconceptions about behavioral theory.

While the concepts and techniques suggested in this book are eclectic (drawn from a variety of sources and the experiences of the authors), fundamentally the book rests on a behavioral approach. By using a model that explains how most behavior is learned, as well as by using empirically validated principles of behavior management that have been derived from that model, the behavioral approach offers an extremely effective structure for analyzing situations and identifying procedures that will prevent and/or remedy problem behaviors. The previous chapter presented practical guidelines for behavioral change. The purpose of this chapter is to present a more in-depth consideration of behavioral theory. The information is intended to help you understand the more technical aspects of behavioral theory, to clarify specific vocabulary, and to address common concerns regarding a behavioral approach.

Section One deals primarily with the ABC model of behavioral theory and contains information that will help you: (1) Realize that behavior is not mystical, but can be logically explained; (2) Develop a consistent vocabulary for discussing behavioral issues; (3) Understand more about why people behave the way they do; and (4) Increase your knowledge about how to change behavior. Then, since the behavioral model can be controversial

("I just don't like that Stimulus/Response stuff"), Section Two of the chapter directly examines some of the most common criticisms leveled at behavioral theory. If you or your staff have concerns about the validity, efficacy, and/or ethics of a behavioral approach, these explanations may be useful in alleviating those concerns.

Note: Those with a strong background in behavioral theory and the school-based application of that theory may prefer to skip or merely skim this chapter. For those who would like an even more detailed treatment than is provided here, the following books are recommended:

- Kerr, M.M. & Nelson, C.M. (1989). *Strategies for managing behavior problems in the classroom* (2nd ed.). New York: Macmillan.

- Wolery, M.R., Bailey, D.B., & Sugai, G.M. (1988). *Effective teaching: Principles and procedures of applied behavior analysis with exceptional students*. Boston: Allyn and Bacon.

---

section one
*B*ehavioral Theory (A Model and Its Implications)

The essence of behavioral theory is that humans are constantly engaged in learning and that one learns based on one's experiences. Each experience a person has influences the way that person will behave in the future (i.e., the choices, conscious or unconscious, that he/she will make).

In technical terms the model states that in the presence of certain events/conditions (antecedents) a person engages in certain actions (behaviors). Events or conditions (consequences) that occur after that particular behavior then serve to either increase the likelihood that the individual will again engage in the behavior in the presence of those antecedent conditions (reinforcing consequences) or decrease the likelihood that the individual will engage in the behavior in the presence of those antecedent conditions (punishing consequences).

This simple, but elegant model (known as the antecedent/behavior/consequence or ABC model) explains learning. Basically, its functional use for an educator is its implication that when you want to change someone's behavior (e.g., eliminate a problem behavior and/or promote appropriate behavior), you need to focus your intervention efforts in three main areas: the events or conditions that prompt the behavior, and/or the events or conditions that reinforce the behavior, and/or the events or conditions that punish the behavior.

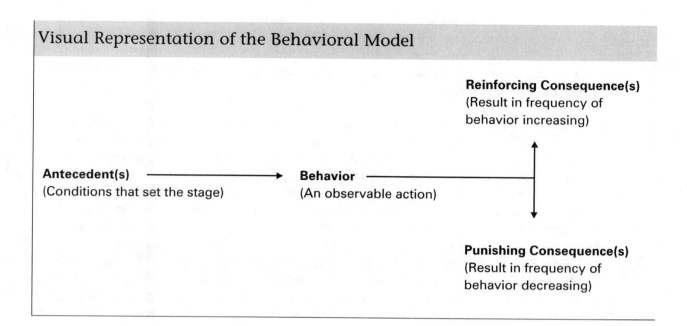

Functional Definitions of Essential Vocabulary

Before going any further, we need to define certain terms that will be used in this chapter. We will start with each of the terms in the ABC model, and then follow with additional terms that are necessary in order to fully understand the model.

Behaviors

"Behaviors" are defined as observable actions, or actions that can be seen or heard. The model focuses on observable actions because cognitive processes, such as feeling or thinking, cannot be known for sure—they can only be inferred. And, they are inferred from actions that an individual exhibits. For example, while we may conclude (i.e., infer) that a person has a negative self-image, we base this conclusion on specific things we have observed (e.g., the way the person stands, her facial expression, how she deals with stressful situations). Similarly, when we observe a person exhibiting certain behaviors, we may conclude that the person is feeling sad, but we can only know for sure that he is crying, verbally expressing sorrow, and so on.

Focusing on observable actions allows for more precision and accuracy when discussing, planning for, and evaluating whatever situations we would like to change. Consider a hypothetical situation in which a school is trying to improve its playground. If staff members identify as the goal of their intervention efforts reducing some nonobservable behavior(s) (e.g., meanness and/or aggression), they are likely to have a hard time knowing whether their efforts have been successful. In fact, it's questionable whether they can even claim with certainty that what they have identified as a problem is actually the problem. On the other hand, if they define the problem and frame their intervention goal in terms of observable actions (e.g., amount of hitting, pushing, fighting, and name-calling), they can not only clearly describe the nature and extent of a problematic situation, but they can also objectively document the effect of their intervention efforts on that situation. For example, they would be able to state that the amount of hitting was reduced by 80%. And, this level of precision in describing what has actually occurred makes it more reasonable for them to conclude that their intervention has reduced meanness and aggression, and that the playground is a better, safer place for students.

Another advantage to focusing on observable behaviors, as opposed to conclusions based on behavior, is that communication tends to be less value-laden. Imagine meeting with a student and his parents regarding problems that student has been having on the playground. If you start the meeting by saying something like, "We have asked for this meeting because Bryan is mean and aggressive on the playground," the parents and student may conclude that you just do not like the student. Or, based on that description, the parents may envision that their son is simply being assertive, defending himself, and sticking up for his rights. In addition, hearing the principal say that he is "mean and aggressive" may lead the student to start viewing himself as a mean and aggressive person. Presenting the situation in terms of observable behavior, however, lessens the potential for misunderstanding. "The reason we are meeting is because last week during recess, Bryan was observed (and given consequences for) calling other kids names four times, hitting other children twice, pushing in line twice, and fighting once."

Clarity of communication can also be important when dealing with staff. Think about confronting a staff member who has been somewhat remiss in his duties. If you describe a specific behavior, the individual is less likely to misunderstand your point or take it personally. "Paul, this is the third day in a row that you have been late for playground duty. The safety of the students requires that you be on the playground before the students start coming outside." Contrast that with a statement of conclusion based on behavior. "Paul, you are being irresponsible and undependable. The safety of the students requires that you fulfill your duties."

The basic rule is that if a word or phrase describes something that cannot be observed (seen or heard), then it is probably a conclusion about behavior rather than an actual behavior. Words that describe conclusions include: discouraged, happy, responsible, furious, trouble-maker, Attention Deficit Disordered, independent, euphoric. Words that describe specific behaviors include: walking, crying, turning in assignments, arriving on time, verbally participating, pushing, writing.

Note: We are not saying that one should never use terms that are conclusions based on behaviors—only that when you do use such a term (e.g., "responsibility"), you need to clarify the precise behaviors that the term encompasses. For example, throughout this book, we frequently use the term "responsible student behavior." It is precisely because this term reflects a broad goal, rather than an observable action or actions, that we emphasize the need for a school staff to clarify exactly what specific behaviors constitute responsible student behavior in their school. It is only by focusing on those observable behaviors that a staff will be able to accurately conclude whether their students are, in fact, behaving responsibly.

Antecedents

"Antecedents" are events or conditions that set the stage for a particular behavior (or set of behaviors) to occur. For example, seeing a stop sign usually prompts drivers to engage in the behaviors of braking and bringing their vehicles to a stop. Sitting in a stadium with thousands of others and watching a favorite team score a touchdown may prompt a person to exhibit behaviors that he/she never exhibits at any other time or place—yelling, jumping, back slapping, hooting, shaking fists in the air, and so on. The idea is that when present, the antecedents for a specific behavior prompt that behavior, and when the antecedents are not present, the behavior is not likely to occur.

Consequences

"Consequences" are events or conditions that follow a behavior and influence whether that behavior is likely to occur more or less often in the future when the same antecedents are present. Reinforcing consequences increase the probability that the behavior will occur in the future, and punishing consequences decrease the probability of its future occurrence. Although this definition seems simple and straightforward, the concept of consequences is actually complicated by several factors. Because your effectiveness at behavior management will, in part, depend on your ability to use reinforcing and punishing consequences appropriately, it's important that you understand these terms precisely—what they mean and what they *do not* mean.

1.   **Consequences (i.e., actions or events) are defined as reinforcing or punishing based on what *actually* happens to the target behavior.**

     This means that you cannot know for sure whether something will be a reinforcing consequence or a punishing consequence for a particular behavior until you try it and see how it affects the future occurrence of that behavior. Understanding this after-the-fact nature of reinforcing and punishing consequences is terribly important because often what a certain action is intended to accomplish (e.g., to punish or decrease the future occurrence of a behavior) may not be what actually happens. For example, imagine a student who attempts to participate in class by raising her hand (which is one of the teacher's rules). However, whenever she raises her hand she does not get called on. The student then tries blurting out when she has something to say. Although the teacher usually responds by initially reminding the student that she should raise her hand (a gentle attempt to punish the blurting out behavior), she also usually goes on to comment on the content of what the student blurted out. "Carla, you should raise your hand, but the point you raise is correct in that …" The result is that, although the blurting out seems to exasperate the teacher, the student blurts out more and raises her hand less as time goes on. This is a classic example of a teacher thinking that she is punishing the blurting out behavior by gently reprimanding the student when she is actually reinforcing the behavior (evidenced by the fact that the behavior is occurring more often). The point here is that whether someone intends an action or event to be a reinforcing consequence or a punishing consequence doesn't matter—it's what happens to the target behavior that determines whether the action/event is reinforcing or punishing.

Another feature of this after-the-fact nature of consequences is that an event or condition that serves as a reinforcing consequence for one individual may be a punishing consequence for another individual—and vice versa. Consider a teacher who responds to classroom disruptions by harshly and loudly telling the disruptive students that their behavior is totally unacceptable (not a procedure we recommend by the way!). The teacher uses the procedure twice in September with both Rico and Andrew. Rico does not disrupt again in either October or November, but Andrew gets one to two reprimands a week in October for disrupting and several a day in November.

It is clear that the same action (i.e., the teacher's harsh and loud verbal response to a disruption) functioned as a punishing consequence for Rico's disruptive behavior, but as a reinforcing consequence for Andrew's behavior. Again, it doesn't matter that in both cases the teacher's intent was to provide a punishing consequence—the fact is, at some level Andrew enjoyed having the teacher reprimand him.

This should also make it clear that there are no actions or events that serve as punishing consequences for all people, and none that function as reinforcing consequences for all people. The only way to know for certain whether a procedure will be reinforcing or punishing for a target behavior is to try it and see what happens to future occurrences of that behavior. And finally, this should make it clear that *any behavior that occurs repeatedly is getting reinforced in some manner*. Often an individual's behavior is difficult to understand because, from our perspective, the consequences of that behavior seem so unpleasant. Yet, the behavior has to be resulting in some kind of reinforcing consequence (i.e., serving some function) for that individual—and this is as true for behaviors that are negative or destructive as it is for behaviors that are positive and productive.

2. **The labels "reinforcing consequence" and "punishing consequence" are value-free.**

    That is, there is no implication of good or bad, right or wrong, ethical or unethical. The labels are simply applied, after the fact, to explain how an action or event affected the future occurrence of a target behavior. If the behavior has decreased, the event or action is considered to have been a punishing consequence. If the frequency of the behavior increases, then the event or action was a reinforcing consequence.

Example

Consider the following:

- Kylie is disruptive in class. Her teacher, Ms. Iturri, comes over and quietly states, "Kylie, making noise during quiet work time disturbs others. Please work quietly." When Kylie disrupts again the next day, Ms. Iturri quietly reprimands her again. Thereafter Kylie no longer exhibits disruptive behavior in class.

- Sara is also disruptive in her class. Her teacher, Ms. Paulson, responds by loudly announcing from the front of the room, "Sara, you are a fifth grader. Stop acting like you are in preschool. Babies don't belong in the fifth grade. Grow up!" The following day Sara is disruptive again, and Ms. Paulson again corrects her in a loud and belittling manner. Sara does not disrupt class again.

Both of these teachers' actions would be defined as punishing consequences, because in both cases the future occurrence of the behavior they followed was reduced. The fact that both actions would be considered punishing consequences shows the straightforward and value-free nature of that label. It is simply an explanation of events that occurred. The fact that one teacher's action was more humane than the other's (or that one of the actions should be an acceptable practice in a school and the other should not) does not change the fact that both functioned as punishing consequences. The idea that educators should implement procedures that are ethical, humane, just, and compassionate is one that we strongly support—but it is a separate issue from the concept of punishing consequences.

3. **The terms "reinforcing consequences" and punishing consequences" are often misunderstood, and they tend to generate emotionally charged reactions.**

Although the language of behavioral theory is technically value-free, some people who lack a thorough understanding of the behavioral approach have viewed the term "punishing" to mean being vindictive, aggressive, judgmental, and hostile, and/or the term "consequences" to mean being fair, assertive, nonjudgmental, and logical. Similarly, some people believe that "reinforcement" involves being manipulative, controlling, and bribing students, whereas "encouragement" is seen as being intrinsically motivating and promoting of self-control. When accurately using behavioral language, however, a hostile, vindictive, aggressive way of responding to a behavior may be neutral, reinforcing, or punishing—depending only on what happens to the future occurrence of the targeted behavior. Likewise, a person's fair, assertive, nonjudgmental, and/or logical response to a behavior may be a neutral, reinforcing, or punishing consequence—again depending on what happens to the future occurrence of the targeted behavior. Remember, in behavioral theory the terms "reinforcing consequence" and "punishing consequence" are value-free, after-the-fact labels for what has occurred.

One of the most common errors people make when using behavioral terminology is to describe a procedure that they haven't yet implemented, but plan to, as being either reinforcing or punishing. "I am going to reinforce Ike for completing his work by giving him tickets for extra time in the computer lab." The truth is, you cannot know whether extra time in the computer lab will be reinforcing to Ike until you see if his future rate of work completion increases. You also hear people say, "I tried positive reinforcement with Wes, but it doesn't work." In point of fact, the person tried something that they thought would be, but did not prove to be, a reinforcing consequence for Wes.

In an effort to be more precise and to avoid the possibility of emotional reactions, we use the term "encouragement procedure" to describe an event or action that is *intended* to reinforce or increase the future occurrence of a desired behavior. (Remember you can't know for sure whether it's reinforcing until you see what happens to the behavior.) So, in Chapter Nine: Common Areas—Improving Behavior in Halls, Cafeteria, Playground, and Other Areas, for example, you may find a statement like "Providing specific information to students about their appropriate hallway behavior is a potentially effective *encouragement procedure*—one that may increase the students' desire to demonstrate continued responsibility in the halls." For the same reasons, the term "corrective consequence" is used to describe an action or event that is intended to reduce the future occurrence of (or punish, in the nonvalue sense of the term) a nondesired behavior: "It can be useful to implement an in-class time-out as a corrective consequence when a student exhibits disruptive behavior." For the remainder of this book, the terms "reinforcing consequence" and "punishing consequence" will refer only to actual after-the-fact explanations of events or actions. For example, "Even though the teacher thought she was implementing a corrective consequence, the fact that the student's behavior increased over time means that the teacher's response was actually a reinforcing consequence," and, "Even though the teacher thought he was using an encouragement procedure, the fact that the student's class participation decreased indicates that providing public praise was, in fact, a punishing consequence for this student."

To avoid problems that may arise from people's preconceived notions about the words "consequences," "reinforcement," and "punishment," you might want to develop a consistent vocabulary (perhaps like that described above) that can be used by you and your staff.

The Difference Between "Positive" and "Negative" Reinforcement

The following information IS NOT essential. If you are completely comfortable with the concepts of reinforcing consequences and punishing consequences, you may find it interesting. However, if you are in any way confused about the concept of consequences, skip this section.

In the interests of technical accuracy, we should explain that there are two types of reinforcing consequences, positive and negative.

Positive reinforcement is defined as the "*presentation* of something desirable" that increases the future occurrence of a behavior.

Negative reinforcement is defined as the "*removal* of something aversive" that increases the future occurrence of a behavior.

Both positive and negative reinforcement are *reinforcing consequences*—and both increase the frequency of the behavior they follow. The difference is why: by providing something desired or taking away something not desired. An example of negative reinforcement involves the ringing of the telephone. You may pick it up, even if you really don't particularly want to talk to anyone, just to get the darned thing to stop ringing. Thus, answering the phone removes an aversive stimulus (the ringing). If the outcome of stopping the noise was pleasant enough that it results in your answering the phone in the future (even when you don't want to talk to someone), then answering the phone and stopping the noise constitutes a negative reinforcer.

Most examples of reinforcing consequences involve positive reinforcement. The main reason for even bringing up this distinction is to help you avoid making a mistake made by many people—treating negative reinforcement as the equivalent of punishing consequences. Remember, both *positive and negative reinforcement* increase the future occurrence of the behavior they follow. Since, in practice, negative reinforcement occurs so infrequently compared to positive reinforcement, we only use the term "reinforcing consequences" to refer to an action or event that has led to an increase in a particular behavior.

4. **Humans do not have to directly experience consequences to learn.**

    People can and do learn a great deal about reinforcing and punishing consequences vicariously, through language and/or by observing others. For example, children do not have to be hit by cars to learn not to run in the street—their parents can teach them this important lesson by pointing out the danger. Similarly, a student who likes adult attention can learn about the beneficial (reinforcing) consequences of behaving responsibly by observing that students who behave responsibly tend to get more and better teacher attention than those who behave inappropriately.

    This idea that people can "learn" through language or observation is one main reason we urge school personnel to identify and then teach the behaviors they expect from students. It is also the reason that we recommend that students be informed about the corrective consequences that will be used (e.g., an hour of cleaning halls for littering) in advance. Actually, the need for school staff to implement corrective consequences in response to misbehavior is generally reduced when students are taught (at the beginning of the school year) exactly what is expected of them and what corrective consequences will be implemented for not following those expectations.

5. **Reinforcing consequences may be immediate and/or delayed, and people vary in the degree to which they understand the benefits of delayed vs. immediate reinforcement.**

    In a simplistic view of the behavioral model, the implication seems to be that people will seek the most immediate and powerful reinforcers possible. However, for any behavior there are usually multiple pleasant outcomes and multiple unpleasant outcomes. And, with both pleasant and unpleasant outcomes, some will be immediate and some will be delayed. Often when people are consciously or unconsciously having difficulty making a decision, it is because they are making guesses about the pleasant versus unpleasant outcomes of a given action and weighing the immediate versus long-term outcomes of engaging in that behavior. "Should I eat that pie? It would taste so good, and I am really hungry, and no one is around to see me pig out, and it does have some fruit in it. BUT, if I eat it all, I'll feel guilty, and I'll gain weight, and my roommate will be upset because I ate it, and it will probably contribute to clogging my arteries so that twenty years from now I will have a heart attack. BUT, maybe I could just eat one piece, and ..."

    Some people seem to have little trouble making the decision to act in a way that reduces immediate pleasure when they believe that their action will have more important long-term benefits. For example, a college student who foregoes a party to study for a test is rejecting an immediate reinforcement (the enjoyment of the party) for a more delayed gratification (the pleasure and benefits [e.g., graduating] that will come from doing well on the test). Other people, though, tend to consistently leap before they look (i.e., behaving in ways that are immediately gratifying, either without thinking of or disregarding the long-range outcomes resulting from their behavior).

    The idea of immediate and delayed gratification can be very important when you are trying to help an individual change a behavior that currently provides him/her with immediate pleasant outcomes. For these individuals, it may be necessary to use more immediate corrective consequences (in response to instances of misbehavior), and/or more immediate encouragement procedures (in response to instances of desired behavior), and/or to specifically teach the individual about the benefits that come with more delayed gratification (e.g., using role play or having the person imagine the short-term versus long-term benefits of different behaviors).

As you work with individuals (staff, students, or parents) to help them improve their behaviors, remember to assess and experiment with the immediacy of the encouragement procedures. For example, if an intervention plan isn't working, you may want to consider whether implementing the encouragement procedures more immediately will increase the probability that they will actually reinforce the desired behavior.

To summarize the ABC model on which the behavioral approach is based:

- Antecedents prompt certain behaviors. These same behaviors are less likely to occur if the antecedents are not present.

- Consequences are defined as reinforcing or punishing based on what actually happens to the target behavior (i.e., whether it increases or decreases).

- The technical labels of "reinforcing consequence" and "punishing consequence" are value-free; there is no implication of good or bad, right or wrong, ethical or unethical.

- The terms "reinforcing consequence" and "punishing consequence" may be misunderstood and emotionally charged, and should be used cautiously.

- Humans do not have to directly experience consequences to learn (i.e., to have those consequences affect their behavior).

- People vary in the degree to which they have learned the benefits of delayed versus immediate reinforcement.

An Interesting Debate—Nature vs. Nurture

Although most behavior is learned, it's true that behavior can also be affected by physiological factors. For example, most people would acknowledge that they behave differently when they are running a fever than when they are feeling well. And most parents would probably agree that some personality traits of children seem to be there from birth. The ongoing debate about which has more influence—physiological or environmental factors (i.e., the old "nature versus nurture" debate) is largely irrelevant to this book, however.

While we believe that behavior is unquestionably influenced by physiological factors, we also believe that educators need to focus their efforts on those factors that they can reasonably influence—which more often than not exclude physiological factors. Educators can and should see that a hungry child gets fed, or that a child who exhibits certain symptoms is evaluated by a physician to rule out the possibility of diabetes and the need for insulin injections. However, in most situations, educators will affect behavior by modifying environmental conditions (antecedents and consequences). We cannot control a student's physiology or her past. So while nature/nurture debates may be interesting in principle, educators will most frequently be working on the nurture factors by modifying the environment to prompt and encourage responsible student behavior.

Take Action!

During the next week or so, spend some time thinking about various positive and negative behaviors exhibited by yourself, members of your staff, students, and/or parents. For each specific behavior, try to identify the antecedents that prompt it and the consequences that seem to reinforce and/or punish it. Think about what possible actions you might take if you wanted to change one of those behaviors (e.g., behavior that is not helping the person who exhibits it). Would you attempt to modify antecedents that prompt it, or remove current reinforcing or punishing consequences, or apply new procedures in the hopes of encouraging more responsible behavior or correcting irresponsible behavior? Examples of types of behavior patterns you might wish to analyze could include:

- You always complete a particular report form at the last minute, and it is always frantic right before the form is due at the district office.

- You are in the front hall every morning greeting staff, students, and parents.

- A student is consistently rude to all staff members, but is never rude to one paraprofessional on staff.

- A teacher frequently brings treats or decorations that brighten up the staff room.

section two
Questions and Misconceptions Regarding a Behavioral Approach

In this section, we identify and respond to some common concerns and objections about a behavioral approach. The information in this section may not only deepen your own understanding of the approach taken in this book, but also help you to respond to others who question procedures and techniques recommended in this book.

"This behavioral stuff is just not my philosophy. It is too mechanistic."

Some people object to the "philosophy" of behavioral theory as too mechanistic, too limiting. Keep in mind that the antecedent/behavior/consequence (ABC) model is simply an after-the-fact explanation of events that have occurred. This model states that any behavior that is happening more frequently in the presence of certain antecedents has been reinforced, and any behavior that is happening less frequently in the presence of certain antecedents has been punished. This is not a philosophy—it is not imposed by belief. It's a factual statement that everyone's behavior is influenced by events that happen. Furthermore, its implication is not that humans are mechanistic, but rather that we are smart—that we do the things that bring us satisfaction and avoid the things that lead to unpleasant circumstances. Whether or not staff members or parents specifically use the ABC analysis, they are unavoidably engaged in implementing reinforcing and punishing consequences. The question is whether they do it thoughtfully and effectively, or without thought and probably ineffectively.

"I just don't like this stimulus/response stuff—people are not Pavlov's dogs!"

A comment like this indicates that a person does not really understand behavioral theory. Stimulus/response is associated with classical conditioning—which is only a minute fraction of behavioral theory, a fraction in fact that has very little to do with teaching or parenting. Classical conditioning basically deals with instinctual physiological responses such as salivating, sweating, dilating pupils, and so on. In his famous experiment, Pavlov discovered (by accident) that a neutral stimulus—something that would not normally illicit a physiological response—could be made to do so. Pavlov had noticed that a dog would salivate when presented with meat powder. Meat powder—then salivation. Meat powder—then salivation. He also found that by repeatedly presenting a neutral stimulus (in this case a bell ringing) immediately before presenting the actual stimulus (meat powder), the physiological response (salivation) could eventually be prompted by the neutral stimulus (bell) alone—without the actual stimulus (meat powder). Thus, he *conditioned* a dog to respond to a bell by salivating.

Most behavioral theory deals with *operant conditioning*, which states that in the presence of certain antecedents behavior will decrease if followed by punishing consequences and increase if followed by reinforcing consequences. It is operant conditioning that describes learning, and operant conditioning that is the basis for behavioral theory as it is applied to schools. Although it would be possible for school staff to *condition* students to salivate to a bell, there would be little point. The goal of schools is to help students become more responsible, more academically able, and so on. Behavioral theory, and operant conditioning in particular, gives school staff technical tools to help them accomplish those goals.

"People are much more complicated than just their observable behaviors—why all this emphasis on dealing only with that which is observable?"

Dealing with observable behavior, rather than conclusions based on behavior, allows for a clear and objective discussion about, planning for, and evaluation of interventions. It is in no way a denial that people are more than the sum of their behaviors (strict behaviorists may argue this, but that is the position of these authors). Although mind, soul, conscience, ego, and so on may be very real, they are impossible to measure or even discuss with accuracy. Remember also, the behavioral model provides no information about which behaviors ought to be encouraged and which should be discouraged, and no information about how humans ought to be treated. It is simply a value-free explanation of events. Schools, however are not value-free. You and your staff must decide what your goals for student behavior are and what procedures you will use to achieve those goals. The behavioral model will mainly help you determine and assess ways to achieve those goals.

"But a behavioral explanation is just too simplistic—I do many things without getting immediately reinforced."

While the basic ABC model itself is very simple, in operation, it is very complex. First of all, for any given behavior, there are many antecedents and many consequences. And then there's the fact that people learn through language and through observing others.

Take some aspect of your own behavior. First identify what the reinforcing and punishing aspects of engaging in that behavior are. Then determine the antecedents. For example, consider the behavior of having a phone in your home. This behavior has a number of potentially reinforcing (positive) aspects and a number of potentially punishing (negative) aspects. (See the "Owning a Phone" figure that follows.)

Owning a Phone

Positive (Potentially Reinforcing) Aspects of Owning a Phone	Negative (Potentially Punishing) Aspects of Owning a Phone
• Important in an emergency	• Expense
• Allows talking to friends	• Sales calls
• Convenient	• Interruptions
• Maintains contact with distant family	• Crank calls
• Gives your teenager something to do	• Sometimes you don't want to talk
	• The annoying ring
	• The teenager is always on the phone
	• Some people talk too long

Despite the complexity of the preceding analysis, we can conclude that for those who (right now) choose to have a phone in their homes, the reinforcing aspects of owning a phone must outweigh the punishing aspects. And, for those who choose not to have phones in their homes, the punishing aspects of having a phone must outweigh the reinforcing aspects. We can also conclude that whether or not a person has a phone right now, his/her choice represents smart behavior given that person's learning history (the reinforcing and punishing consequences for that specific behavior).

The ABC analysis provides a structure for looking at and then changing behavior. Thus, while it's true that a person's current behavior is smart behavior for that individual, it is also true that by changing the antecedents and consequences of that behavior, it is possible to teach the person even smarter ways to behave.

"This behavioral approach is just too controlling. Who are we to be forcing these kids to change their behavior."

On its face, this concern may sound legitimate. However, if you ask yourself why we even bother to have schools, the most basic answer probably is that as a society we want our children to be able to engage in behaviors that they might not be able to do if we did not have schools. Most parents (and other community members) would not be happy if the goal of schools was, "At the end of 13 years in a K-12 system, a child will behave (academically and socially) in exactly the same way he/she would have if he/she had not spent six hours a day, five days a week in that system, or if the billions of dollars spent on schools every year had not been spent." On the contrary, most parents (and others) want our schools to teach students to behave in increasingly competent and responsible ways. That is, they want and expect students to leave the school system being able to read, compute, reason, analyze, question, function independently, work cooperatively, be self-motivated, and so on.

In other words, the whole purpose of schools is to change students' behaviors. And, the act of teaching is, by it's very nature, a controlling act. Now, teachers may not know for sure whether their students read when not in school, but if the teachers have taught the students how to read and helped them experience the joy and broadened horizons that come from reading, they (the teachers) can be fairly certain that the students will be more likely to read than had they not been taught. The really important ethical or moral question isn't whether or not schools should be trying to change students' behaviors—that is, teach—but rather what they choose to teach. Schools can choose to teach students to blindly obey, or to cooperate with, yet question, authority. They can teach students to be aggressive or passive or assertive. It is for this reason that we believe the staff for each school need to clearly identify the attitudes, behaviors, and traits they hope to foster in their students. (See Chapter Six: Guiding Principles—The Core of Your SBP for more details on how to do this.)

"I think students should work for intrinsic motivation— not because of reinforcing or punishing consequences."

One of the major criticisms of a behavioral approach is that it overly depends on extrinsic reinforcement (i.e., overtly rewarding desired behaviors and penalizing undesired behaviors). To respond to this concern, we have to first define intrinsic and extrinsic reinforcement. A behavior is generally said to be maintained by intrinsic reinforcement when there are no external factors present that appear to reinforce the behavior. For example, a person reads every night before bed simply because he finds the act of reading enjoyable and relaxing. Or, a person collects stamps, not for any potential monetary benefit, but because the act of researching, organizing, and caring for the collection is satisfying in and of itself. Extrinsic reinforcement, on the other hand, is any reinforcement that is not intrinsically part of the task. Praise, a diploma, a paycheck—all of these are examples of extrinsic reinforcement.

However, the distinction between intrinsic and extrinsic reinforcement in any given situation is not always completely clear. For example, getting a paycheck for working is clearly extrinsic reinforcement, but if the person also loves the work she does, then she is getting intrinsic reinforcement as well. Similarly, the person who reads every evening for the enjoyment of it may also find that what he learns from reading allows him to converse knowledgeably about a variety of subjects and, as a result, get positive feedback from people about how well informed he is. That feedback could be considered extrinsic reinforcement.

The goal of all educators is to have students who are intrinsically motivated to do what it takes to learn. Yet, it's a simple fact that there are students who are not intrinsically motivated. Teachers may wish those students were, but they actually have little control over whether or not an individual will find a task intrinsically motivating. For example, a fifth grade student who reads at the second grade level probably won't find reading intrinsically reinforcing. The fifth grade reading material will be too difficult and the second grade reading material may be uninteresting and/or a source of embarrassment in front of peers. To help this student learn to read well may very well involve motivating him to work on improving his reading skills. And, motivating him to work hard on what for him is a difficult task may require the use of extrinsic reinforcement as encouragement. The idea, of course, is that as he learns to read more and more fluently (which could take several years of effective remedial instruction), the act of reading itself will become intrinsically reinforcing for him and extrinsic rewards won't be needed to get him to practice.

It's also true that some people make the mistake of giving extrinsic rewards to students who are already intrinsically motivated, which can, in fact, result in the students no longer being intrinsically motivated. That is why we urge school staff to be cautious in their use of motivational systems, especially when less intrusive methods will maintain student motivation.

"I hate all this positive reinforcement because I don't think we should be bribing students."

Is a paycheck bribery? Is a diploma bribery? Is a thank-you letter bribery? Probably not by most definitions. Although dictionaries often have several definitions of bribery, one of those definitions usually will be something similar to, "the inducement, usually monetary, to do something illegal or unethical." Bribery is the inducement to do something wrong—such as illegally paying a politician to vote a certain way. Appropriately used, extrinsic reward systems (as in the case of individual contracts) are used to induce a student to learn to do something positive such as to complete work or demonstrate increased self-control. This is not bribery—it is the act of making the benefits of a particular behavior more overt and immediate for a student who is not currently intrinsically motivated to exhibit that behavior.

"But can't a school do too much positive reinforcement? Can't you do it wrong?"

Yes! If staff depend too much on high-powered tangible rewards—giving students tokens and food and trinkets, students can develop a "Why should I do that unless you offer to give me something" attitude. The goal of schools should be to use methods of encouraging responsible behavior that are as close to intrinsic reinforcement as possible. For example, it's a mistake to give a student who is an avid reader rewards—or even very much praise—for reading. A better approach is for staff members to show an interest in what the student has read, suggest other books the student might find interesting, and create challenging but fun assignments that allow the student to read for even deeper meaning. In addition, reading instruction for this student should be as interesting, fun, and relevant as possible. When a student is not intrinsically motivated to read, however, extrinsic reinforcement may be a useful and appropriate step in helping her to eventually develop that intrinsic motivation.

Another key to the appropriate use of extrinsic reinforcement (whether praise or a structured reward system) is to focus on what a student does, not what the student will get. The comment, "Wow! You earned five points. When you add that to your total you have 53. Fantastic!" emphasizes the wrong thing. A better response would be, "This morning was a very positive example of how much you can accomplish when you keep your attention focused on your work. You earn one point for each completed assignment—five points. This brings your total to 53."

"Okay, but I still don't buy it. Nobody gets all this praise and positive feedback on a job."

Actually, this may be more an indictment of the workplace than a legitimate reason why schools should not provide praise and positive feedback. (In fact, an important part of your job as principal is to ensure that your employees—i.e., staff—receive meaningful and relevant positive feedback about their efforts.) Furthermore, there is an aspect of being a student that makes it like no job that has ever or will ever exist. That is, every time a student masters some aspect of his/her job, the job description changes and the student is required to learn a whole new set of skills. In a well-run classroom, students are continually challenged with new and difficult expectations. And, because they need feedback on how well they are doing with the new skills (academic or behavioral) they are learning, the rates of praise and positive feedback necessarily have to be higher than what is provided on most jobs.

Think about when you are learning a new sport—say skiing. At first, you need your instructor to tell you (give you feedback on) what you are doing right and what you need to do differently. As you become more proficient, you no longer need feedback on the basics, but you do need continual information about how well you are carrying out the more advanced skills. Finally, when you are an expert, you do not need feedback from anyone. For students learning new skills, it's the same thing. They need frequent feedback on their efforts, and much of this feedback should involve reinforcing them or letting them know what they are doing correctly.

A Process for Improving Your Schoolwide Behavior Plan (SBP)

Among the most important things that you, as a principal, can do to improve your school's environment are to: (1) Arrange for and guide your staff in a structured process to "update" (i.e., improve) your current SBP; and (2) Establish an ongoing cycle of SBP improvement activities. The purpose of this chapter is to give you practical information and strategies for doing so.

The chapter begins with a discussion of why and how to involve a representative staff team in the management and coordination of your SBP improvement activities. Next, it outlines a four-phase improvement cycle—review, revise, adopt, implement/maintain. As part of that process, specific information is offered on why and how to make "informed" decisions about your SBP improvement activities and why and how to employ a systematic approach when making necessary SBP revisions (i.e., additions, deletions, or modifications). Efficient procedures for having staff develop revision proposals are described, as are procedures for staff adoption of those proposals. As the final part of the ongoing process, we explain how to effectively implement and maintain your SBP. The ongoing nature of the cycle is made clear in the sample calendar offered at the end of the chapter, which models how the improvement process might look across a typical school year. Finally, Section Two contains sample staff, student, and parent surveys; suggestions for using existing data sources; suggestions for conducting observations in different settings; and a checklist for identifying important aspects of a comprehensive SBP. We have found these tools to be useful for a school doing a general review of its current SBP.

Note: This chapter focuses on a *process* for improving an SBP; it does not contain suggestions about SBP content—the specific policies and procedures themselves. Content considerations and recommendations for each of the five major areas that should be covered in a comprehensive SBP (i.e., Guiding Principles, Encouragement Procedures, Disciplinary Procedures, Common Areas, and Classrooms are covered in the five chapters that follow this one.

What the Research Says About Effective Schools

A School-Based Management Team Makes Many of the Decisions Regarding School Operations.

Arterbury and Hord (1991); Bachus (1992); Caldwell and Wood (1988); Cistone, Fernandez, and Tornillo (1989); Conley and Bacharach (1990); David (1989); Hord (1992b); Jackson and Crawford (1991); Levine (1982); Levine and Eubanks (1992); Louis and King (1993); Malen, Ogawa, and Kranz (1990a,b); Mojkowski and Fleming (1988); Odden and Wohlstetter (1995); Short and Greer (1993); Taylor and Levine (1991); White (1989); Wohlstetter, Smyer, and Mohrman (1994).

The above material is reprinted with permission from *Effective Schooling Practices: A Research Synthesis, 1995 Update*. This excellent summary of school and teacher effectiveness literature was compiled by Kathleen Cotton. To order copies of this resource, call or write:

Document Reproduction Service
Northwest Regional Educational Laboratory
101 S.W. Main Street, Suite 500
Portland, Oregon 97204
(503) 275-9519

section one
SBP Improvement Activities

A Staff Team Should Guide SBP Improvement Activities

Directing SBP improvement activities (whether during the initial update effort or as part of the ongoing cycle) is a big task. That is one reason we recommend that you have a site-based team help you. Another reason has to do with the potential problems of relying on just one person to see that all the activities occur. If you alone are responsible for coordinating and managing the SBP improvement activities, and you get swamped with work or for some reason leave the school, they may not happen at all. Last, but not least, involving a site-based team in the management of the SBP improvement activities can increase the kind of staff "buy in" necessary if SBP policies and procedures are going to be effective. Staff are the people most responsible for actually implementing your behavior management policies and procedures. The more "ownership" they feel for the SBP, the greater the commitment they are likely to have for using its policies and procedures and for making those policies and procedures work.

Your team can be an existing leadership team or site council. Or, if you have one, your school's discipline committee might be the most logical group to assist you with the tasks and responsibilities suggested in this chapter. It's also possible that you will want or need to set up a new team specifically for this purpose. Your decision about this will depend, to some extent, on the size of your school and how many responsibilities currently existing teams already have, as well as your personal preference. Whatever you decide, we suggest that you call this group something other than the "discipline" committee/team. For many people the word "discipline" connotes only punitive action (e.g., setting rules and consequences), but an important function of this group will be to ensure that your SBP includes sufficient and effective motivational procedures as well. For the remainder of this book, we will use the term "Responsibility Team" when referring to the group that will be helping you direct your SBP improvement efforts.

If you will be assembling a Responsibility Team (as opposed to using an existing team or committee), you should first make some "command decisions" about team composition and size, how team members will be selected, and how team members will be rotated. The following information may be useful in making those decisions.

Team Composition and Size

A Responsibility Team should include representatives from all the various subgroups of a school's staff (e.g., primary classroom teachers, intermediate classroom teachers, support staff, remedial/special education teachers, classified staff, etc.). Remember, effective school-wide behavior management requires a commitment from and a sense of ownership by all staff members. At the same time, however, you may have to balance the goal of comprehensive representation with the need to keep team size reasonable. That is, having more than seven people on a team tends to decrease team efficiency and effectiveness.

You (the principal) must be a member of this team. Many of the issues the team is likely to consider overlap directly with administrative decisions. For example, you may have to identify issues that cannot be decided by the team ("What you are referring to is covered by Board policy. Changing it would require a formal proposal to the School Board"), as well as those that can ("There's no reason we can't explore the idea of adding one more lunch shift to reduce crowding. Let's examine the pros and cons").

You should also consider whether or not to include student and/or parent representatives on your team. While student/parent involvement is not necessary (or even appropriate) for all SBP improvement activities, getting their input on certain of the policies and procedures is very important. Many schools have found that it makes most sense to simply solicit student/parent feedback on any relevant policies and procedures during the revision and/or adoption phases of the process. On the other hand, if you already have a well-established working relationship with students and/or parents, you may want representatives from one or both of these groups on your team.

Team Member Selection and Rotation

Another command decision regarding the team involves how initial team members will be selected, and how new members will be rotated in. If your school has an established committee selection method, you'll probably want to use that. Or, you can handpick your team—choosing those individuals you know to be thoughtful and hardworking. The problem with handpicking the team, though, is that it may lead to resentment or passive/aggressive resistance on the part of other staff members. The best option might be to have each subgroup that you want represented on the team choose their own representative—using whatever selection method they want (e.g., electing someone, letting someone volunteer, randomly drawing from all members, randomly drawing from interested volunteers). For example, if you have decided that one of the team members should be a sixth grade teacher, simply explain to the sixth grade teaching team what the Responsibility Team will be doing (including the likely responsibilities and time commitment that will be required of team members) and ask them to select their own representative.

You should also give some thought to how and when team members will rotate off and be replaced. You want to avoid a situation in which the team functions for a couple of years and then everybody wants off the team at the same time. We recommend having one third of the team rotate off each year, which means each member serves a three-year term. Regardless of how you choose to deal with team member rotation and replacement, keep in mind that your goal is to maintain representative team membership (i.e., a primary level staff person should be replaced by another primary level person), while balancing the advantages of continuity with the benefits of bringing in new ideas and energy.

Compensation for Team Members

For a number of reasons, participating on the Responsibility Team may mean that some team members end up putting in more work time than is contractually required of them. You might want to consider compensating them in some way. Possibilities include:

- Holding team meetings during regular work hours and hiring substitutes/replacements for team members.

- Holding team meetings outside regular work hours and providing extra-duty pay to team members.

- Giving team members extra preparation time by periodically supervising their classes for them (or arranging for someone else to do so).

- Relieving team members of some or all of their other duties (e.g., bus duty).

Note: Even if you are not able to provide minute-for-minute compensation, this type of gesture is generally appreciated.

Decide if Your SBP Will Be a Written Document

One of the first decisions you and the Responsibility Team should make is whether all or part of your SBP will be documented in writing. A written SBP (such as might be found in a staff handbook) is basically an outline of the major behavior management policies and/or procedures that staff have agreed to operate from and implement. We believe there are several advantages to having written SBP. They include:

- **Clarity**—A written document provides an "official" version of policies and procedures to which staff (or students or parents) can go for clarification when there are differences of opinion. A written document also tends to make it easier for new staff members to learn the details of your building's unique policies and procedures (e.g., What are the responsibilities of staff when they have playground supervision?).

- **Consistency**—Having your discipline and motivation procedures (e.g., when and how to use disciplinary referral, hallway supervision responsibilities) in writing increases the probability that everyone will know what is expected of him/her and how to meet those expectations. This, in turn, should increase the consistency with which policies and procedures are implemented—and, therefore, their effectiveness.

- **Continuity**—Procedures that are not written down may have a greater likelihood of getting "lost." For example, say a school has an effective "School Buddies" program for providing adult nurturing to some of its most at-risk students (see Chapter Seven: Encouragement Procedures for a program description). If even as few as three staff members from that building retire or transfer during the same summer, the chances are significantly decreased that someone will bring up doing the program the following fall (due to the hectic beginning of the school year rush). A worthwhile program may go by the wayside, not because anyone wanted to get rid of it, but just because it was not written down and so people were not reminded to take the actions necessary to start it up again.

It is true that some schools manage to implement very effective SBPs without having their policies or procedures written down. Such schools tend to have principals with particularly clear visions of their behavior management goals and exceptional skill in guiding staff toward their visions. Yet without a written document that clearly describes their behavior management policies and procedures, even these schools run the risk of having effective aspects of their SBP lost should their principals retire or transfer to a different building. School staff generally consider and decide on a number of behavior management proposals each year. If those decisions are not summarized in writing, people may forget what they decided from one year to the next. "Didn't we work on that problem last year? What did we decide to do?" Incorporating staff decisions into a written document is one of the best ways to increase the probability that the policies and procedures that have been agreed to will be implemented. (**Note:** Chapters Six through Ten include sample language that could be used in an actual document, such as a staff handbook.)

The Four-Phase SBP Improvement Cycle

In some schools, the policies and procedures that make up the SBP have been carefully developed in an effort to achieve a specific goal (e.g., making sure that the school environment is safe and productive). In other schools, policies and procedures have arisen primarily in response to specific circumstances or needs (e.g., a system for disciplinary referrals comes about because of incidents of student fighting) with little thought given to whether they are coordinated or comprehensive. However your SBP has developed, and whatever shape it is in, we recommend that you make a systematic effort to update it.

One of the most effective ways to successfully update (as well as ensure ongoing improvements in) your school's SBP is through the use of a four-phase cycle.

Four-Phase Cycle

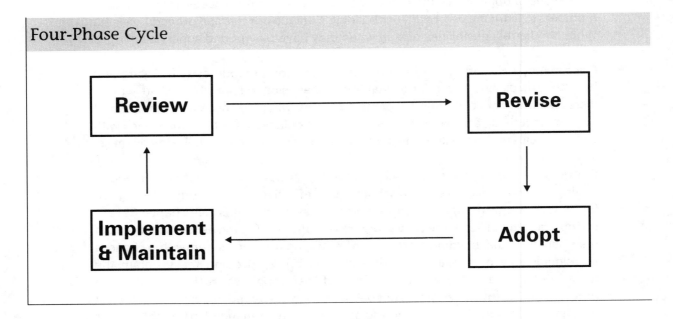

- **Phase One**—The cycle begins with a review—collecting and evaluating information about: (1) The adequacy of policies and procedures that are currently in place; (2) Staff, student, and parent awareness of and satisfaction with those policies and procedures; (3) The degree to which those policies and procedures are being implemented; and (4) The effectiveness of the policies and procedures.

- **Phase Two**—The second phase of the process is to revise (i.e., add to, delete, and/or modify) any part(s) of your SBP that the review indicates could be improved. When many things need to be improved, you and your team will have to make decisions about where to start and how fast to move in making improvements.

- **Phase Three**—The third phase consists of having staff formally adopt revised policies and/or procedures.

- **Phase Four**—The fourth phase in the cycle involves activities to ensure the successful implementation of newly adopted policies or procedures and the maintenance of those currently in place.

Another way to think about this cycle is that making the most of one's SBP is somewhat analogous to making the most of one's home. It requires that you periodically evaluate whether and how your home is or is not meeting your needs and that you regularly maintain it. If, for example, family members conclude after careful review that their home is not meeting their needs, they generally consider making some kind of change. That change may involve a minor modification (e.g., adding shelving in closets, replacing the old water heater), a major modification (e.g., moving walls, installing additional windows, or adding a room), or something as significant as moving to another house. The decision about what change to make will be made by balancing budget, time, and inconvenience considerations with the level of concern about the house as it currently is.

On the other hand, when the house is both functionally and aesthetically meeting the family's needs, changes aren't necessary ("If it ain't broke, don't fix it!")—members just maintain the status quo. Home maintenance, however, is not static. It involves regular upkeep (e.g., cleaning, painting, and "tightening nuts and bolts") and reminding family members to "take care of the house" (e.g., not leaving faucets dripping, locking doors at night, etc.). Both the upkeep and the reminders are necessary if the house is to retain its functionality and livability.

In practice, the SBP improvement process will look different from school to school. For one school, updating their SBP may be as simple as just documenting the policies and procedures that are currently in place and working effectively. For another school, the review process might suggest that the hallway procedures need to be improved but that most things are fine as they are. For still other schools, the review may reveal massive dissatisfaction and problems with all aspects of existing policies and procedures. For a school like this, the improvement process may entail starting from scratch—developing all new policies and procedures. This could be a significant undertaking that takes one or two full years. Because of this variability in school situations, the four-phase process is designed so that it can fit both schools that need to fine tune and schools that need to make major revisions. The remainder of the chapter provides tips on implementing each phase of the cycle.

Phase One—Review

Tips to Implement Phase One

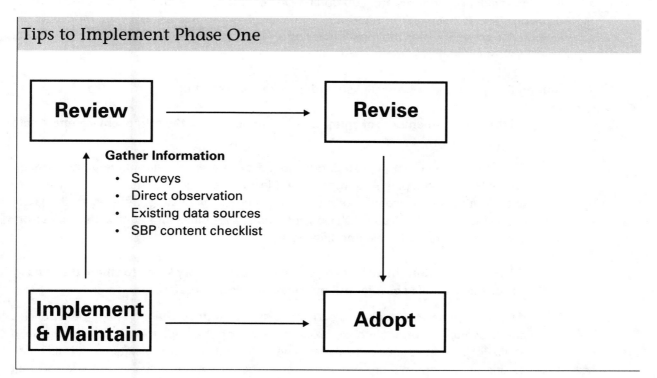

The initial phase in an SBP improvement effort involves gathering information and doing a thorough review of current SBP practices and needs. That is, you start the process by taking stock—trying to get an accurate sense of what behavior management areas you are currently handling well and what areas you are not handling well. During this phase, you should also try to get a preliminary sense of why things are working well and why they are not.

There are two main points to make here. One has to do with the importance of determining where you want to go before you start out and the other has to do with the importance of using "sound" (i.e., accurate) information to make decisions about your SBP improvement activities. Chapter One: Leadership: Improving School Climate points out the importance of developing and sharing a common vision of what your school should be like. The concept here is similar. By starting off your SBP improvement process with a review of what you have and what you need, you will develop a clearer picture of what you want/need to accomplish with your updating efforts. This in turn will make your efforts more focused, efficient, and ultimately successful.

In order to make good decisions about what to add, delete, or modify in your SBP (i.e., decisions that will benefit your students), you also need accurate information about the current behavior management situation at your school. Without accurate information, you may abandon procedures that are working well and maintain procedures that are nonproductive (or possibly even destructive). Without accurate information, you may not realize that the reason a potentially effective procedure is not working well is because staff members do not really understand or agree with it. When you run into the inevitable disagreements about particular procedures and you don't have accurate information on their effectiveness, decisions about keeping or replacing those procedures are as likely to be based on speculation or who wields the most power as on whether or not they are making the school environment safer and/or more productive.

Among the questions your review should help you answer are:

1. **Do the various members of your school community find the school environment safe and productive?**

   This may be the most important question. If even a small percentage of students do not feel safe on the playground, for example, you need to do something. Or, if staff do not feel that they receive the support they need for dealing with severe behavior problems, you need to seriously consider making modifications, with active input from staff on the nature of those modifications.

2. **What do the various members of your school community know (or think they know) about the school's specific SBP policies and procedures?**

   If staff, students, and/or parents do not know what your behavior management policies and procedures are, then those procedures will not be implemented appropriately, if at all. For example, your school may have an excellent mission statement, but if staff, students, and parents are not aware of it, then it cannot serve as a guide for their actions. Or, you may have designed an excellent system for dealing with disciplinary referrals, but if staff do not know what the system is, they cannot possibly implement their part of it appropriately or consistently.

3. **How do the various members of your school community feel about your behavior management policies and procedures?**

    How people feel about what they are supposed to do often has a direct impact on whether or not, and how well, they actually do it. For example, if you found that a significant number of parents are not satisfied with your school's overall approach to behavior management, it would be worth finding out why so you could make a decision about whether to revise certain procedures.

4. **Are your behavior management policies and procedures, as they are currently being used, effective?**

    People may know what a procedure is and may like the procedure, but that does not necessarily mean that the procedure is effective. For example, middle school teachers may be using their after-school detention program appropriately, as a corrective consequence, and may express satisfaction with it. However, if it turns out that the same 20 students are in detention week after week, then the program is not effective in improving student behavior, at least not for those 20 students. (**Note:** The fact that the procedure is ineffective in changing behavior in this example does not necessarily mean that the school should abandon the procedure. But it does indicate that staff need to do a more careful review and analysis of this aspect of their SBP.)

A well-designed review (which need not be excessively time/effort intensive) will provide you with information to answer these questions. You can then use that information to help you make decisions about what and how to improve your SBP. Some general guidelines on tools that can be used in such a review follow:

Surveys—The best way to get information about what people think they know and how they feel about your school's current SBP (Questions 1–3) is to ask them. Surveys or questionnaires offer an efficient and effective means of doing so. Questionnaires allow you to get general information about the big picture from a lot of people. The supplement to this chapter contains sample surveys for staff, students, and parents—which can provide a major source of information for an annual review.

Direct Observations—Another way to get information about your current behavior management situation is to actually observe what is going on in various school settings. A general, nonevaluative observation in a setting can give you a fundamental sense of whether or not your behavior management practices are effective (Question 4). It can also give you some basic information about why or why not. As principal, you should be doing informal and ongoing observations throughout each school year. If you ask yourself the following simple questions each time you are in a setting, you will get information that can be used in your SBP review:

*   Is this setting safe and productive?

*   Are students responsible, engaged, and motivated?

*   Are staff being proactive, positive, and instructional?

Later, when staff are developing revision proposals for various portions of the SBP, there may be a need to conduct additional observations to answer more specific questions. For example, if you have found that your SBP procedures related to the playground need revising, you may need to determine whether the playground supervisors are arriving on the playground before students are out there. Or, if your surveys indicate that primary grade students do not feel safe in the halls, you might want to determine whether there is an adequate number of adults supervising the hallways. The only way to answer these questions and others (e.g., Are teachers implementing agreed upon behavior management strategies in their classes? Are students using the playground equipment the way it was intended to be used? Do students treat adults respectfully?) with any degree of objectivity is to observe.

The supplement to this chapter includes suggestions for how you (building administrator) can screen classrooms and common area settings for safety and/or productivity. Information on how to do more detailed observations of classrooms and common area settings (as part of the revision phase) can be found in Chapters Ten and Nine.

Existing Data—As noted earlier, even when you find out that staff and students know what they need to know, feel good about the way things are, and are doing what they need to be doing, you still don't necessarily know whether your behavior management practices are effective (i.e., accomplishing what you hoped they would). For example, your staff may have implemented a conflict resolution program that they report they like and that students report they enjoy. However, if there are as many (or more) fights occurring on the playground after the program has been implemented as there were before, then the effectiveness of that program has to be questioned.

Although there are many ways to evaluate the effectiveness of your behavior management policies and procedures, you probably already have access to some extremely useful information. By making year-to-year comparisons of suspensions, expulsions, absenteeism, tardiness, special education referrals, and so on, you can get a pretty good picture of your overall progress in accomplishing your behavior management goals—and some direction for your SBP improvement efforts. For example, if you have 30% more suspensions in the current year than in years past, you need to ask why. Year-to-year comparisons of this type are simple enough that details on how to do them are not provided in this book. However, don't forget about this valuable source of information as you are making decisions about what is working and what may need improvement.

Another very important source of information is the records of your current year's disciplinary referrals (office referrals and other disciplinary referrals, such as to a problem-solving room or after-school detention). These records can easily be summarized and used not only to provide information on the effectiveness of current procedures, but also as a guide for staff development activities. Among the specific questions your referral records should help you answer are:

- What behavior results in the most frequent referrals?

- Do we have fewer problems with vandalism this year than last year?

- What setting has the most referrals?

- What day of the week has the highest percentage of referrals?

- What time of day/class period has the most referrals?

- Do we have fewer problems with disrespect toward staff since we have been teaching students how to treat others with respect?

In the supplement at the end of this chapter, information is provided on how to set up a Disciplinary Records Database that will allow you to answer these and many other questions by using information from referral records.

The "Schoolwide Behavior Plan Content" Checklist—Finally, in the chapter supplement, you will also find a checklist of critical features that a comprehensive SBP should have. Working through this checklist each year can be an efficient and effective means for you and your Responsibility Team to identify which of those critical features you have in place and which you might need to add. The checklist also contains information to guide you to the appropriate chapters in this volume that will help you develop those sections of your SBP.

Phase Two—Revise (As Necessary)

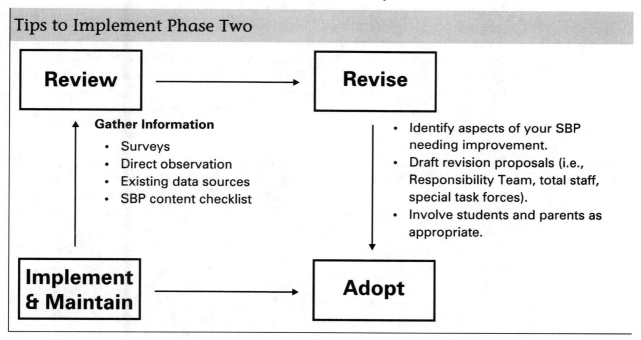

During the review phase of the improvement cycle, you identify the aspects of your current SBP that need improvement (i.e., what needs to be added, deleted, and/or modified). Then, once you know what needs to be improved, you and your Responsibility Team should establish a systematic process for seeing that those necessary revisions are made. It's important to realize that revising behavior management practices (particularly those that are demonstrably ineffective or that people don't like) can be a time-consuming process. And too many teachers have experienced situations in which they have been asked to participate in protracted discussions about discipline issues involving such things as hats or gum chewing. Your goal is to come up with a process for developing revision proposals that is time efficient and politically acceptable to the vast majority of staff. The process you use should address:

1. Who will develop the various revision proposals;

2. How the proposals should be developed; and

3. To what extent will students and/or parents be involved in the revision process.

In most cases, having the staff as a whole do an in-depth review and revision of every section of an SBP is neither efficient nor effective. Following are descriptions of three different approaches to proposal development. Obviously, the alternative you and your team choose should fit the unique needs of your school.

-   **Responsibility Team Approach**—In this approach, the Responsibility Team itself assumes responsibility for developing the proposals for each addition, deletion, and/or modification to the SBP's policies and procedures.

    This approach has the advantage of efficiency. Only a few staff members (i.e., those that are on the Responsibility Team) are involved in designing proposals. The disadvantage, though, is that the rest of the staff may come to view the Responsibility Team members as experts and/or nags who keep telling everyone what to do. This approach tends to work best at a school where staff are generally "committeed out" and would appreciate (rather than resent) having a Responsibility Team do the lion's share of the revision tasks, or in a situation in which there are not many revisions necessary to the SBP.

-   **Total Staff Approach**—With this approach, the Responsibility Team identifies that several major sections of the SBP (e.g., guiding principles, procedures for common areas, and use of disciplinary procedures) need revising and establishes separate committees to develop revision proposals for each section. Every staff member is required to sign up for one of the established committees. The individual committees then develop the proposals for any additions, deletions, and/or modifications to their particular sections.

    This approach involves all staff members in actually developing some part of the school's SBP, which can increase their sense of ownership of the policies and procedures, and yet it avoids the problems associated with trying to have all staff develop proposals for all changes. The disadvantage, of course, is that every staff member has yet another committee on which he/she needs to serve. If your school logistics are such that the majority of the revision cycle work can be done on inservice or early release days (so that the time demands on staff members do not exceed their regular work days), this can be a very effective process.

-   **Task Force Approach**—In this approach, the Responsibility Team finds that one or more of the SBP areas that need revising (entire sections or individual issues) are particularly difficult or emotionally charged. For each of these areas, it sets up a separate "task force" and then solicits interested volunteers for each task force. For example, if a review showed significant staff concern about when and how to use office referrals for disciplinary reasons, as well as across-the-board (i.e., staff, student, and parental) concern about increased behavior problems in the halls, the Responsibility Team would set up two task forces—one to look at hallway procedures and the other to consider office referral procedures. In addition to the volunteering staff members, each task force would also include a person from the Responsibility Team to serve as a liaison. Meanwhile, the Responsibility Team would work on the revision proposals for the remaining (and less complicated or potentially divisive) parts of the SBP.

An approach like this allows individual staff members who want to work on a particular issue or problem to do so, but does not require that everyone be involved in proposal development. Its disadvantage is that some staff may end up not being involved in any part of the proposal development. Nonetheless, it can be a good compromise between the Responsibility Team Approach and the total staff approach.

Regardless of who will be developing the revision proposals, this phase of the improvement process consists largely of three potentially time-consuming tasks—collecting and reviewing information about the particular part of the SBP being revised, carefully considering the issues (logistic, as well as the pros and cons) related to it, and preparing a proposal to be presented to the staff as a whole. Consider the following example. In its initial review, an elementary school staff found that the use of disciplinary referrals was the issue that needed to be improved most urgently. A special task force was established. The task force collected more information about when and how people were using disciplinary referrals (using the suggestions in Chapter Eight: Disciplinary Procedures of this book). From this, they identified four major aspects of disciplinary referral procedures that seemed, in some way, problematic: (1) Inconsistencies among staff in their understanding of what behaviors warranted disciplinary referrals; (2) The fact that there were three different versions of "Referral Forms" that staff were using; (3) Staff resentment over rarely finding out what corrective consequence, if any, the principal implemented in response to their referrals; and (4) Concerns about the amount of adult attention a referred student received while waiting to see the principal. For each of the four major aspects, task force members carefully considered a number of possible solutions and eventually (sometimes after much debate!) developed proposals to address them. Their next step is to present their proposals to the entire faculty.

The question of student and/or parental involvement is, in many ways, a political one—a balance between the value of their active involvement and maximal efficiency. Some schools include students and parents on the developing committees for guiding principles and common areas (or for specific procedures/issues related to either of these two sections). Other schools prefer to have their developing committees composed of staff alone. We recommend that minimally you find some way for students and/or parents to review (and make suggestions on) the proposals for the guiding principles and common areas sections before they are formally adopted by the whole staff.

Phase Three—Adopt

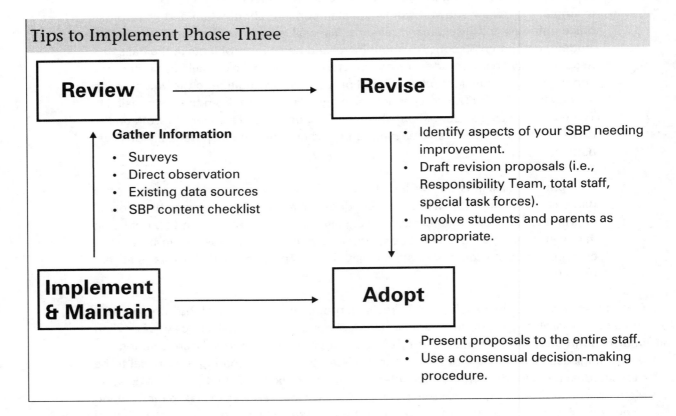

Tips to Implement Phase Three

Review → **Revise**

Gather Information
- Surveys
- Direct observation
- Existing data sources
- SBP content checklist

- Identify aspects of your SBP needing improvement.
- Draft revision proposals (i.e., Responsibility Team, total staff, special task forces).
- Involve students and parents as appropriate.

Implement & Maintain → **Adopt**

- Present proposals to the entire staff.
- Use a consensual decision-making procedure.

After revision proposals have been developed for any part of your SBP, those proposals need to be presented to the entire staff to be adopted or rejected. Therefore, to prepare for this stage you have two issues to decide: (1) How the total staff will be given the chance to provide feedback on the proposals; and (2) How the proposals will be adopted by staff and formally incorporated into the SBP.

All revision proposals should be presented to the entire staff (and, where appropriate, to students and parents) for discussion and feedback because you don't want any one person or subgroup (Responsibility Team or special task force) to have all the say in finished policy. Giving all staff the opportunity to voice support for or express concerns and raise questions about revision proposals increases the probability of their "buy in" to and use of any new policies or procedures.

You can provide an opportunity for staff input by having each developing committee present its proposals at a full-faculty meeting scheduled for that purpose. In addition to the proposals themselves, the committee should also present a summary of the issues considered when developing the proposals. Then there should be a timed discussion period (usually ten minutes) during which all staff are invited to ask questions and voice their opinions about the proposals. (**Note:** Limiting the time for these discussions is essential. If even only a few people on both sides of a given issue feel strongly, a largely unproductive discussion can be maintained for hours. Ten minutes is generally ample time for the main issues and concerns to be raised.)

We also believe that using a consensual decision-making procedure (e.g., "Fist of Five"—see the figure below) for adopting proposals is important. Especially when all staff have not had a say in the initial development of a particular proposal, you can increase their buy-in by giving them a significant voice in whether the proposal is actually adopted or not.

Fist of Five

True consensus means that any given decision has at least the passive approval of every stakeholder. This particular decision-making procedure involves having stakeholders indicate their degree of support for a decision with the fingers of one hand.

- Five fingers indicates a full commitment and willingness to be a leader in implementing the proposal.
- Four fingers means wholehearted support, but the staff member is not willing to act as an implementation leader.
- Three fingers indicates moderate support.
- Two fingers indicates a moderately negative feeling about the proposal, but an agreement to support its implementation at least passively.
- One finger indicates dissatisfaction with the decision, but a pledge not to undermine its implementation.
- A closed fist—zero fingers—indicates total disagreement with the proposal.

Staff members are informed in advance that a vote of zero, one, or two (which can roadblock implementation of the proposal) carries with it the responsibility of sharing their concerns about the particular proposal and working to find an alternative solution.

Consensus on a decision is achieved when all staff members support the proposal with at least a three-finger response. If any staff members raise less than three fingers, they explain their objections and the group negotiates whether to adjust or eliminate the unacceptable elements of the proposal. (**Note:** You and your staff may wish to modify the criteria for consensus to better fit your situation. For example, you may decide that consensus is achieved as long as no one votes "zero" or "one" and no more than five people vote "two." The important point is that you and your staff agree on a definition of consensus that assures that minority opinion is not squelched— yet takes into account the need for efficiency in making decisions.)

Once consensus has been achieved on a particular proposal, something should be done to make the decision official—as a signal to all staff that they must now implement the agreed upon policies and/or procedures. This can be accomplished in a variety of ways. First, follow the consensual vote with a summary of what was agreed to by the staff. "To sum up, we have all agreed that we will be out in the halls during at least two of the six passing periods between classes, and that each wing will work it out so that there are at least two adults in each hall at every passing period." Include the summary statement in the minutes of the faculty meeting. In addition, as principal, you need to demonstrate active support for the decision with some kind of a public statement—even if you are not thrilled with what was decided. (**Note:** If you strongly disagree with a proposal, the time to indicate that is during the discussion and consensual vote. If you are not sure you can live with what your staff might decide about a certain issue, do not allow it to be put to a consensual vote. Once you allow a consensual decision to be reached, it's important that you not go back on it, even passively.)

If consensus is not achieved on a proposal, it should be returned to the developing committee with instructions for them to make revisions that address the concerns that were raised. The proposal should then be re-presented to the staff for another discussion and consensual vote.

If your staff regularly has trouble reaching consensus, you may need to actively encourage compromise. This needs to be done skillfully and carefully—you don't want to squash minority opinion on any particular issue, but you do want to get across the point that everyone should be willing to compromise on some things, some times. The following excerpt from a speech by Benjamin Franklin might help you establish the foundation for ethical compromise:

> I confess that there are several parts of this Constitution which I do not at present approve, but I am not sure I shall never approve them; for having lived long, I have experienced many instances of being obliged, by better information or fuller consideration, to change opinions even on important subjects which I once though right, but found to be otherwise.
>
> The opinions I have had of its (the Constitution's) errors I sacrifice to the public good.
>
> On the whole, Sir, I cannot help expressing a wish that every member of the convention who may still have objections to it would, with me on this occasion, doubt a little of his own infallibility, and, to make manifest our unanimity, put his name to this instrument.

—Benjamin Franklin
Last speech to the Constitutional Convention
September 17, 1787

You can also remind your staff that no portion of the SBP is written in stone. For example, if a proposal that you think is worthwhile seems to be defying compromise, you might suggest implementing it on an experimental basis for one month. Arrange for the proposal to be evaluated (i.e., objectively assessed) after the month is up and schedule a follow-up discussion.

This process of presenting proposals to staff for limited discussion, revising the proposals (if necessary) based on input, and formal adoption continues until consensus is achieved on all proposals. A major advantage is that no issue—even a highly contentious one—is likely to take more than three or four ten-minute discussion periods (spread out across several weeks) on the part of the total staff. Most issues, in fact, will be settled on the first or second presentation. If the total staff had to hammer out the details of every proposal, much more time would be involved.

Phase Four—Implement and Maintain

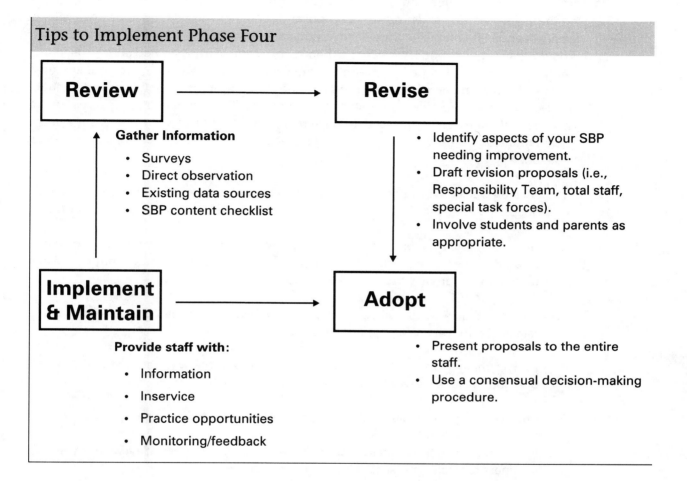

Tips to Implement Phase Four

Review → **Revise**

Gather Information
- Surveys
- Direct observation
- Existing data sources
- SBP content checklist

Revise
- Identify aspects of your SBP needing improvement.
- Draft revision proposals (i.e., Responsibility Team, total staff, special task forces).
- Involve students and parents as appropriate.

Implement & Maintain → **Adopt**

Provide staff with:
- Information
- Inservice
- Practice opportunities
- Monitoring/feedback

Adopt
- Present proposals to the entire staff.
- Use a consensual decision-making procedure.

School improvement projects are too often launched with enthusiasm, only to die slow and quiet deaths. No matter how careful you have been in reviewing and revising your School-wide Behavior Plan, if your policies and procedures are not implemented well initially or maintained adequately over time, your efforts will have been a time-consuming but pointless exercise. You need to bring the same energy, enthusiasm, and attention to implementing and maintaining your SBP policies and procedures that you give to its review and revision.

It's important to remember that implementing new policies or procedures requires staff to learn something new and/or change their behavior—both of which can be difficult and potentially stressful. Therefore, whenever you revise your SBP you need to make sure that staff get sufficient and specific information about what they are expected to do and how they are to do it. This might include providing them with practical suggestions and tools for implementing any new policies or procedures, modeling how a new procedure should "look and sound," and arranging opportunities for positive practice (especially for difficult skills). In addition, you should plan on monitoring staff implementation efforts and giving them periodic reminders regarding both your expectations and the benefits that will be derived if everyone implements a particular procedure.

The ongoing maintenance of behavior management policies and procedures can be the most difficult part of the entire improvement process. You have to keep staff excited and focused on the vision of a safe and productive school and keep them committed to being proactive, positive, and instructional in their behavior management efforts. As staff get busy and into a day-to-day survival mode, it is easy for them to lose sight of using agreed upon procedures. The process of keeping people informed, motivated, and growing requires training time. What follows is a menu of possible inservice and staff development activities that might be used to inform and motivate your staff to implement SBP policies and procedures (or any other school improvement project). Keep in mind that the following suggestions may need to be modified in order to meet the union, district, and state guidelines applicable to your situation.

1.   Hold after-school inservices on a regular basis, and personalize them to your school's needs.

2.   Hire substitutes for one grade level each week, on a six-week rotation, so that all teachers have the opportunity to work with an expert, observe one another, and plan together to improve skills every six weeks.

3.   Use substitutes for a half-day every three weeks so that each grade level team is released for inservice and planning together.

4.   Add 15 minutes to the school schedule four days of the week so that you can have one hour a week early-release time designated for school improvement.

5.   Create a summer institute centered around curriculum or management improvement.

6.   With another school that has common goals, cosponsor a series of evening or weekend seminars for staff on assessment and instruction issues.

7.   Arrange for weekly literature circles where staff can discuss a professional book.

8.   Establish a "professional growth fund" to pay teachers to attend inservices during school days.

9.   Dedicate district professional days to instruction and assessment.

10. Arrange for regional inservices to be offered on an after-school basis for staff at schools throughout the area.

11. Encourage staff to take on an all-school project that requires them to use essential learning and assessment strategies and, thereby, makes group inservices meaningful to everyone.

12. Formulate building goals based on staff improving their skills in the use of essential learnings and performance-based assessment; then plan a schoolwide inservice.

13. Get the curriculum committee to select articles that are jigsawed into weekly staff meetings.

14. Choose staff members who have the expertise to lead planning and inservice efforts.

15. Have your building improvement team focus upon needed skills, gather ideas from their constituents, and suggest areas of inservice for the coming year.

16. Explore several areas for possible inservices and then give staff a list of suggestions from which they can choose the option they like best.

17. Propose that staff make a year-long service contract with an expert—and use that person to give small inservices, do classroom demonstrations, and fit instruction to staff needs.

18. Try to get a district committee, made up of representatives from every school, to assess needs and offer districtwide inservices after school, on weekends, professional days, or release days.

19. Have each staff member create a personalized action plan for gaining skill in areas that he/she has identified as personal growth needs. Staff members should include commercial workshops, as well as building, district, and state offerings.

20. Work at the district level to create a cadre of experts in a "trainer-of-trainers" model, so that each building has someone with expertise who is expected to guide the building improvement effort.

21. Train principals to provide inservice to their staffs on curriculum issues.

22. Establish building mentors for every first year teacher with the expectation that the mentors will help new teachers integrate essential learnings and create good assessments.

23. As part of your ongoing inservices, once a quarter require staff to share a success they have achieved.

24. When new goals are recommended, have staff do a self-assessment on "how are we already doing this?"—so that you build on prior success as you try new innovations.

25. Have staff prioritize their training issues and eliminate those that don't focus upon meeting building goals.

26. Arrange for an August staff retreat (before school starts) at which staff can receive inservice training and focus upon the school improvement effort.

27. Set aside learning time at every staff meeting. Consider the possibility of providing a stipend to each staff member who researches and presents information on an area of current interest to everyone.

28. Train each member of a core team to take responsibility for training one other person. Each trainee then trains someone else. This is repeated until everyone is trained.

29. Arrange for staff members to visit one another's rooms to see innovations in action.

30. Require staff who are approved for out-of-building workshops or visits to do a short article for the staff newsletter or present a summary at a staff meeting.

31. Form study groups around different topics of interest and then have each group plan events to present its topics to the rest of the staff.

32. Schedule a series of inservice dinners at which staff are given a nice dinner and listen to a guest speaker present a topic of common interest.

33. Get a local business to fund a staff pizza party once a month. Have staff stay after school for training, then share a meal together.

34. Arrange for staff to receive college credit or clock hours for a series of inservice activities held throughout the year. Include after-school, professional day, and occasional weekend activities.

35. Form a "sister school" relationship with another school so that staff from the two schools can share expertise and ideas. Provide subs to allow visits between sites and have each staff present to the other prior to, or during, the visit.

36. As a staff, hold a workshop for other educators at which you present innovations you have been using.

37. Get your district to hold an innovation fair on a district professional day. Teachers are encouraged to present their efforts in areas such as curriculum integration, assessment, and "How We Do Student-Led Conferences."

38. Bring in someone to speak on reform issues for district days prior to the start of school.

39. Form a study group to work through a set of quality videotapes (e.g., Playground Discipline, Sprick, 1991). Require teachers to try the recommended approaches and share their successes and frustrations each time the group meets.

40. See if the district will negotiate extra days solely for dealing with reform issues.

41. Arrange a series of "learning lunches" with catered food, 15 minutes of presentation, and 15 minutes of discussion. (Have educational assistants take students to and return them from lunch so that teachers have a full 30 minutes to participate.)

42. Fund individual staff members' self-study projects, allowing them to thoroughly explore reform issues. They share their findings with the entire staff in the form of a report or project.

Dealing With a "Reluctant Employee"

Implementing a schoolwide behavior plan successfully depends on all staff members assuming responsibility for teaching (and, as necessary, reteaching) students expected behaviors, and for providing both positive feedback when students behave appropriately and corrective consequences when they do not. Buildings in which staff have taken the time to carefully craft behavior management policies and procedures using a consensus model (to address individual staff concerns) are more likely to have staff follow-through than buildings that use a simple majority decision-making model. In a simple majority decision-making model, it is possible that ten percent or more of the staff members will not be committed to the SBP. It follows that these staff members may fail to support the plan, either by attending to the policies and procedures in a superficial manner or by ignoring them altogether. If the students of even a few staff members have not been taught the behavioral expectations, the whole program can fail. That is why you must reach consensus, and address the concerns of every staff member, on all your behavior management policies and procedures.

In a perfect world, every staff member who had agreed to your SBP policies and procedures would remain focused and committed to using them throughout the year. Unfortunately, in the real world this is not the case. Even a well-intentioned teacher, when faced with the challenges of the classroom, may revert to his/her degree of original learning and resort to old, familiar practices—whether or not those strategies have been successful in the past. In a few cases, a teacher may not have believed in some of the policies and procedures originally, but did not have the courage to share her views with colleagues. If your SBP is going to be effective, you will have to work with staff members who are reluctant, for whatever reason, in a manner that will ensure lasting change.

Addressing a reluctant staff member can involve steps that range from mild reminders and cues to more intrusive problem-solving strategies. We believe that avoiding a lose-lose confrontation is just as important with an adult staff member as it is with a student. That is, "ordering" a staff member to follow your directions is as likely to create hostility and a passive resistant response from that person as it is to result in full compliance. Similarly, although resorting to discipline when a staff member is not following through on SBP policies and procedures is always an option, it is not a recommended strategy unless every other avenue has proved to be a dead-end. Your goal should always be to look for positive and collaborative ways to encourage your reluctant staff member. The following steps (which increase in intrusiveness) may be useful for motivating a reluctant staff member to become an active participant in your SBP.

- **Step 1**—Remind all staff members of the agreed upon commitments.

  If you remind *all* staff that it is time to teach or reteach a specific behavioral expectation (with a brief message in the weekly staff meeting, daily bulletin, and/or through e-mail), you can present the information you want a particular staff member to get without singling out that individual.

- **Step 2**—Arrange for staff sharing sessions.

  Periodically set time aside for staff members to share what is working well for them as they implement the behavior management policies and procedures. Be sure to give them advance notice to come prepared and ready to share. This will not only promote quality sharing, but can also serve as a cue for a staff member who has not begun to implement the plan.

- **Step 3**—Model the desired behavior.

  Another strategy that can be helpful when dealing with a reluctant staff member is for you to model those behaviors you expect from staff. For example, you might begin all assemblies with a quick lesson on some or all of the school behavioral expectations. Or, you might arrange to go to each classroom and teach lunchroom behavior. Your willingness to "walk the walk and talk the talk" can be a powerful motivator for even reluctant staff members. If your school is fortunate enough to have a video broadcasting system, you have a perfect tool for efficiently modeling how to teach behaviors. On snow days, for example, you could broadcast a "snow behavior" lesson first thing in the morning—not only setting the stage for successful snow play, but also modeling good instructional techniques.

- **Step 4**—Reinforce successive approximations.

  Sometimes staff members who are not consistently implementing *all* of the SBP's policies and procedures will be implementing one or two. Thus, while they may not yet be at an acceptable level of compliance, they are making an attempt to comply. Providing specific praise for what they have accomplished may be just the encouragement they need to take the next step. For example, you might write a positive note or make a comment in person. "Jean, I noticed what a great job you were doing of teaching hallway behaviors to your students on the way to P.E. yesterday. That is exactly the kind of teaching I had hoped to see with our new behavior plan. Your teaching really seemed to pay off in great hallway behaviors."

- **Step 5**—Assign a peer coach.

  As you begin your SBP improvement activities, you might think about asking staff to support each other by using a peer coaching model. Train a team of coaches and assign one coach to each staff member. Arrange the schedule to facilitate observation times for the coaches. If you are serious about using this strategy, you should be willing to cover classrooms when necessary, so that the coaches are free to observe.

- **Step 6**—Conduct a staff observation.

  Asking a staff member to include a behavior lesson when you will be observing in his/her room is a more formal way to encourage staff compliance. Let the person know that you believe the SBP is so important that you want be able to observe a behavior lesson and make suggestions for refining it. Be sure the individual understands that this is an informal observation that is not a part of his/her yearly evaluation and that you want it to be a risk-free learning opportunity.

- **Step 7**—Schedule a conference with the reluctant employee.

  If, after several intervention attempts, a staff member continues not to use SBP policies and procedures, you should consider having a personal conference with that individual. The conference should include:

  – Giving the staff member an opportunity to share what he believes he has accomplished.

  – Your making a point of acknowledging the progress that the staff member has made.

  – Your sharing very clearly what your expectations are.

  – The two of you discussing honestly what seems to be getting in the way of the staff member's compliance.

  – Using a problem-solving approach in which you ask how you can help the staff member comply and what resources are needed to accomplish this goal. This problem-solving session should result in a specific plan to help the staff member implement SBP policies and procedures consistently. A good plan will include a time line for accomplishing that goal, along with a designated time to meet again and review the staff member's progress.

If you want to successfully motivate your staff members and promote the successful implementation of your school's SBP, you must intervene with the reluctant employee in a caring and respectful manner. Using good communication skills will help you foster a climate in which there is a high degree of genuineness, trust, and empathy.

Make SBP Improvement an Ongoing Cycle

The first time you use the four-phase cycle to update your SBP, you may improve a little or a lot of it. As those improvements are adopted and implemented, however, it is essential that you begin viewing the four phases in terms of an ongoing (i.e., never ending) cycle. On the one hand, it may seem somewhat discouraging to realize that you and your staff will never be done with this task. On the other hand, though, you need to keep in mind that maintaining and improving your SBP on a continual basis (just as maintaining and improving your home) will result in your school always being a great place to "live."

Establishing an ongoing SBP improvement cycle tends to be easier when you schedule the fundamental activities ahead of time. The calendar that follows represents one possible schedule. You might want to review it with your Responsibility Team, and then together develop a schedule that fits your school's unique situation. Remember, if it's been several years since your school has done any kind of thorough review and revision of your SBP, or if you have never done it, the first time through the cycle (the SBP update) is likely to be more involved and take more time.

April	Administer staff and student surveys (and every second or third year, parent surveys) to determine current overall perceptions about the environment at the school (i.e., do people feel that all school settings are safe and productive?). Also survey staff/student understanding of and satisfaction with current policies and procedures. Summarize results.
	Summarize the information from your (the principal's) informal observations—conducted over the course of the school year.
	Summarize the information from existing behavior management related documents (e.g., disciplinary referrals, attendance/tardy records, etc.). Compare it with the data from the previous school year. Look for obvious patterns.
	Have the Responsibility Team review survey results, observation summaries, and existing document information, as well as all written behavior management policies and procedures to determine and prioritize revisions needed and maintenance tasks that would be beneficial.
May/June	Set up a system for accomplishing revision tasks (i.e., for how needed changes to SBP will be made).
	Have team(s) develop proposals for changes, get feedback from staff on proposals (and where appropriate, from students and parents), incorporate feedback into revised proposals, and make arrangements for proposals to be formally adopted (using a consensual approval procedure).
August	**First Staff Meeting**: Review with all staff the schoolwide behavioral expectations for students.
	Orient any new teachers to the SBP.
	Review with classroom teachers their responsibilities for teaching behavioral expectations. Provide time for grade level teams to plan "expected behaviors" lessons. Also, remind teachers that their classroom management plans must be on file in the office prior to the first day of school.
	Review with appropriate staff (i.e., classified and/or certified) the rules of and supervisor expectations for nonclassroom settings (i.e., common areas). Focus specifically on new procedures agreed to the previous June.

Train new paraprofessionals on relevant common area expectations and procedures. Use experienced assistants to help with this training.

September   Make informal administrative visits to the cafeteria and playground at least once a week. Summarize your findings, and provide feedback and additional information to supervisors. Give the student body feedback (positive and corrective) on overall student behavior (with an announcement over the intercom, perhaps).

Second Staff Meeting: Provide classroom teachers with copies of a letter to parents/students that defines the school's mission, behavioral expectations for students, and major beliefs about behavior management. With staff, develop strategies for getting the letters home, signed, and returned to school.

Third Staff Meeting: Hold a discussion about how things are going in the common areas (share the findings from your observations). Consider whether or not students need more direct teaching of what the behavioral expectations are and how to meet them.

October   Set aside one staff meeting to review the agreed upon approaches to classroom management.

November   Make another round of administrative visits to cafeteria, playground, halls, bus waiting areas, and so on. Again, summarize your findings, and provide feedback and information to supervisors. Check with custodians regarding students' treatment of property (level of vandalism, messes in restrooms, messes in cafeteria, and so on). Provide student body with feedback on overall student behavior (use bulletin boards and school newsletter).

January   Remind classroom teachers to reteach common area expectations. Also, remind them of the importance of emotionally recharging their students to work hard and behave responsibly.

February   Have the Responsibility Team do a midyear review of office referrals, referrals to after-school detention, and special education referrals; have them look for trends—time of day, day of week, location, type of offense. Then, arrange for them to give a staff inservice based on their analysis.

March   Do another round of nonclassroom setting observations. Summarize your results, and give feedback and information to supervisors. Have fifth grade classes conduct a "School Pride" assembly to review the "Guidelines for Student Success" and to remind younger students of the importance of following the school rules, treating each other respectfully, and so on.

April	Readminister surveys. Review surveys, principal observations, and existing data results and evaluate current policies and procedures. Share findings with staff.
June	Work on revisions of policy to be implemented next year.

Conclusion

This chapter explains why and how you can improve your school's SBP—by arranging for and guiding a structured effort to update your current SBP and by establishing an ongoing cycle of SBP improvement activities. We suggest that you (the principal) have a representative team of staff members (Responsibility Team) help you coordinate and direct these efforts. In both the initial updating effort and the ongoing improvement activities, the first step is a general review of your school's current behavior management situation (i.e., its practices and needs). The information gained through staff and student surveys (and possibly parent surveys), informal observations of the school's common areas conducted by the principal throughout the year, and an analysis of existing behavior management related documents (e.g., summaries of referrals and year-to-year comparisons of suspensions) can be combined with a thoughtful consideration of any currently written behavior management policies/procedures to determine which, if any, parts of your SBP need revising and what kind of maintenance tasks would be beneficial. You and your Responsibility Team can then prioritize the revision tasks and establish a systematic process—one that ensures appropriate staff, student, and parent involvement—for seeing that those tasks are accomplished. Finally, after arranging for all agreed upon SBP changes (additions, deletions, modifications) to be formally ratified by the entire staff, you and your team should establish an ongoing cycle of improvement activities so that continual SBP improvement is a regular part of your school year.

section two
*S*ample Tools for Doing a "Review"

This section includes information on and samples of evaluation tools—specifically, staff, student, and parent surveys; a form for doing a general screening observation; a suggested organization for setting up a disciplinary records database; and a comprehensive checklist of SBP content. These tools can be used (as is, in modified form, or simply for ideas) during the review phase of an SBP improvement effort. In addition to the tools themselves, we have included general guidelines for how to implement and interpret them where appropriate. (**Note:** Specific instruments designed to get detailed information on issues pertaining to the individual sections of an SBP are included in the various SBP content chapters. Instruments for getting accurate information about individual students are included in Volume II: Referrals and Solutions.)

Surveys

Surveys provide perhaps the most efficient way to get general information from a lot of people. There are four sample surveys in this supplement—one for staff members, one for students in intermediate/middle school grades, one for students in primary grades, and one for parents. Basically, these surveys are intended to find out how individuals in these different groups perceive the school's overall environment and what they think about the situation in various school settings, what they know about the school's behavior plan (policies and procedures), and how they feel about the school's behavior management policies and procedures.

Administration and interpretation information follows each survey. In general, it is recommended that you administer staff surveys first, then student surveys, and then parent surveys. Surveys should be administered within two to four weeks of each other and no surveys should be administered within the first six weeks or the last six weeks of school.

Staff Surveys

One of the most important keys to getting good information from staff surveys is to make sure that you give surveys to and get them from all your staff—classified and certified, full-and part-time, regular and itinerant, etc. Although making your surveys anonymous will invite honesty, for analysis purposes, you will want to know the characteristics of the respondents. That is, you may want to compare how safe primary level teachers feel the playground is versus how safe intermediate teachers view the playground. Or, it may be useful to see whether there is a difference between certified staff members and classified staff members in the degree to which they feel their behavior management efforts are supported. Therefore, be sure your surveys have some way of distinguishing these categories.

Getting surveys returned from all staff can be tricky. We have found two useful ways of doing so. One way is to set aside a staff meeting specifically for the purpose of administering your surveys. Be sure all staff are invited, explain why you are asking them to complete the surveys, and then pass the surveys out. Give staff members an allotted amount of time to complete the surveys (approximately 20-30 minutes) and encourage them to answer every question. Position one of your team members at the door where the meeting is being held to collect completed surveys.

Another effective way of ensuring a good return rate is to distribute the surveys during a staff meeting and tell staff that they have two days to respond. With this method, you'll want to write the due date and time on the surveys themselves (in *big red letters* at the top of the first page). Then place a large envelope for completed surveys in a central location, such as in a basket next to the staff mailboxes. On the outside of the envelope, put a list with each staff person's name on it, and ask staff to initial it when they have returned their surveys. This way, you can prompt those individuals who may be a little slow in finishing.

Scoring/Interpretation

- To make use of survey results, you first need to calculate a total staff *mean score* for each item (and for each item for each staff category of interest—primary staff, intermediate staff, office staff, etc.). To calculate a mean score, simply multiply the number of respondents who chose a particular answer by the numeric value of that answer and then divide by the total number of responses for that item.

Scoring Example

If you had 22 people answer a question in the following way:

6 people answered with a "1" (i.e., "Not Much")	=	6 x 1 = 6	**To score:**
5 people answered with a "2"	=	5 x 2 = 10	
7 people answered with a "3"	=	7 x 3 = 21	Divide 54 by 22
3 people answered with a "4"	=	3 x 4 = 12	(people surveyed) = **2.45**
1 person answered with a "5"	=	5 x 1 = 5	
Total		**54**	

- To determine what the mean score for an item signifies, use the following rubric:

   1.0–1.9 = A crisis situation
   2.0–2.9 = Conditions/procedures are inadequate
   3.0–3.8 = Conditions/procedures are adequate
   3.9–4.5 = Conditions/procedures are effective
   4.6–5.0 = Conditions/procedures are very effective

- Next, look for patterns among answers to common items (e.g., items 1, 10, 23, and 28 all concern staff knowledge of policies and procedures) and between answers to single items given by different groups (e.g., was there a difference between how certified staff and classified staff answered item 1). You are also going to want to compare staff responses to general categories of questions (e.g., safety) with student, and perhaps parent, responses to similar items.

- Finally, if you find any particularly disturbing or confusing results—such as everyone thinks student behavior during assemblies is very bad (mean score = 1)—you might want to pursue the issue by doing brief interviews with a random sample of your staff. While a survey is good for getting general information from a lot of people, you'll need some kind of face-to-face conversation with people to get details.

Note: If you enter your survey results into a database or spreadsheet program on your computer, these calculations and comparisons will be easy to do. This will also allow you to compare survey results from year to year.

Staff Survey

Date _____

Dear Staff Member:

As part of our effort to improve our behavior management practices and make our school environment one that is safe and productive for all, we would appreciate your responses to the following questions. Your name is not required on this form; however, for analyses purposes we do ask that you indicate your primary area of responsibility in this school.

Please complete and return to _____ by _____

Thank you!

Primary area of responsibility (circle all that apply):

Certified Staff: ○ K-3 ○ 4-6 ○ 7-8 ○ Specialist ○ Full-time ○ Part-time ○ Itinerant

Classified Staff: ○ Office ○ Playground ○ Custodial ○ Cafeteria ○ Classrooms ○ Bus

	Not Much				Very Much
1. Do you understand our school's approach to discipline?	1	2	3	4	5
2. Do you think our school's behavior plan (i.e., its policies and procedures) promotes student self-dignity, self-worth, and responsibility?	1	2	3	4	5
3. To what extent do you think our students are given adequate instruction on our school's behavioral expectations?	1	2	3	4	5
4. To what extent do you think our students know and understand our school's behavioral expectations for them?	1	2	3	4	5
5. To what extent do you think parents are given adequate information about our school's behavioral expectations for students?	1	2	3	4	5
6. To what extent do you think parents understand our school's behavioral expectations for students?	1	2	3	4	5
7. To what extent do you think staff members in our school implement a consistent approach to discipline?	1	2	3	4	5
8. To what extent do you think staff members in our school are positive and encouraging to students? . .	1	2	3	4	5
9. To what extent do you think our behavior management policies and procedures are applied to students fairly and consistently?	1	2	3	4	5

		Not Much				Very Much
10.	To what extent do you have a clear understanding of the appropriate use of disciplinary referrals in our building?	1	2	3	4	5
11.	To what extent do you, as an individual staff member, feel that there is good communication and support from the administration at this school on issues related to student discipline and motivation?	1	2	3	4	5
12.	To what extent do you feel that we have effective systems in place to help individual staff members implement our school's behavior management plan?	1	2	3	4	5
13.	To what extent do you feel that we have effective systems in place to help individual staff members work with challenging students?	1	2	3	4	5
14.	To what extent do you think student behavior in our classrooms is responsible, engaged, and motivated?	1	2	3	4	5
15.	To what extent do you think student behavior in our hallways is responsible?	1	2	3	4	5
16.	To what extent do you think student behavior in our restrooms is responsible?	1	2	3	4	5
17.	To what extent do you think student behavior during lunch is responsible and engaged?	1	2	3	4	5
18.	To what extent do you think student behavior during recess is responsible, engaged, and motivated? . . .	1	2	3	4	5
19.	To what extent do you think student behavior on school property before and after school is responsible?	1	2	3	4	5
20.	To what extent do you think student behavior in our bus waiting areas on school property is responsible?	1	2	3	4	5
21.	To what extent do you think student behavior during assemblies is responsible and engaged?	1	2	3	4	5
22.	To what extent do you think staff members in our school are kind to students?	1	2	3	4	5
23.	To what extent do you think our school's behavior management policies and procedures are clearly communicated to continuing staff?	1	2	3	4	5
24.	To what extent do you think staff members in our school accept responsibility for managing the behavior of all students in the school?	1	2	3	4	5
25.	To what extent do you think our school climate is friendly and welcoming?	1	2	3	4	5

	Not Much				Very Much
26. To what extent do you think that students in our school are reinforced for demonstrating positive social skills?	1	2	3	4	5
27. To what extent does student behavior contribute to a safe physical environment at our school?	1	2	3	4	5
28. To what extent do you think our school's behavior management policies and procedures are clearly communicated to new staff?	1	2	3	4	5
29. To what extent do you think that staff members in our school are helpful to students?	1	2	3	4	5
30. When faced with a student who has behavior problems, to what extent do you get the administrative support you need?	1	2	3	4	5
31. To what extent do you think students know what appropriate behavior is in conflict situations?	1	2	3	4	5
32. To what extent do you think students who violate behavioral expectations are treated in an understanding and supportive manner?	1	2	3	4	5

Thank you for your time and dedication!

Adapted with permission from Education Support Services (1993).

Student Surveys

Probably the biggest issue with student surveys is their administration. That is, many students may not be familiar with how to respond to a survey. Therefore, you will need to preplan your procedures very carefully. We recommend that students complete the surveys in their classrooms, and that in addition to the time estimated to complete the surveys, you allow five to ten minutes of time to teach students how to fill them out. (In the case of primary students, both the teaching and completion times will be longer.) If possible, have two or three adults in the room—one person to read each item aloud (which we recommend regardless of grade level) and one or two people to monitor the students and answer any questions.

Start by explaining to the students that staff are working on a project to make their school an even better place than it is—and, to help with that, staff want to know what the students think about various aspects of the school. Tell students that they can help by answering some survey questions as honestly as they can. (**Note:** Be sure to tell students that they will **not** be asked to put their names on the surveys, but that they should indicate whether they are a boy or a girl and what grade they are in.) Next, have students practice responding to at least three sample items (that you have placed on the board, for example) so that they will be clear about the different answer categories. Use simple questions for these samples—for example:

- **How much do you like to watch TV?**

1	2	3	4	5
Not Much	A Little	So/So	Mostly	A Lot

- **How much do you like school?**

1	2	3	4	5
Not Much	A Little	So/So	Mostly	A Lot

Once you are certain students understand the response format, direct them to follow along on their surveys as an adult reads each question and the possible answers. Again, regardless of grade level, one adult should read each item aloud while the other(s) circulates among the students encouraging honest answers (and discouraging them from simply responding with a 1 or a 5). It's okay to let students ask questions about survey items throughout the administration time; however, you will probably want to tell them you cannot go back to previous items (this could take you all day!). Collect the surveys from students individually so that you can check to see that they have indicated their gender and grade level.

Scoring/Intrepretation

Use the same scoring method with student surveys that you use with the staff surveys. That is, calculate a *mean score* for each item for the entire group and calculate mean scores for any student categories of interest (e.g., boys/girls, primary/intermediate, individual grade levels). As with the staff surveys, you want to look for patterns:

- Which items were ranked very high (indicating conditions/procedures are working well)?

- Which items were ranked very low (indicating areas of concern)?

- What are the similarities and differences among the various groups of interest?

- How do student perceptions of specific school settings (e.g., the cafeteria) and overall issues involving climate (e.g., fairness of procedures, helpfulness of staff) compare with staff perceptions on those same issues?

Also as suggested with the staff surveys, if you find any particularly disturbing or confusing results, you may want to follow up on the surveys using interviews—with a random sample of students (e.g., two boys and two girls from each grade).

Note: The first of the following sample student surveys is appropriate for students in grades fourth through eighth. The second could be used (or modified for use) with students in grades second through third. For kindergarten and first grade students, you should determine whether or not surveys would be appropriate. One alternative for young students is to do interviews with randomly selected students.

Student Survey

Date _____

O Boy   O Girl   Grade _____

Dear Student:

As part of our continuing effort to make our school environment one that is safe and productive for all, we would appreciate your responses to the following questions. Your name is not required on this form; however, we do need you to indicate whether you are a boy or a girl and what grade you are in. **Your input is very important to us!**

Thank you!

	Not Much	A Little	So/So	Mostly	A Lot
1. How much do you understand our school rules and expectations for behavior?	1	2	3	4	5
2. How much do you think that the adults in our school treat students with kindness and respect?	1	2	3	4	5
3. How much do you think that the adults in our school treat students fairly?	1	2	3	4	5
4. How much do you think that the students in our school treat each other with respect?	1	2	3	4	5
5. How much do you feel safe in your classroom(s)? . .	1	2	3	4	5
6. How much do you feel safe in the halls?	1	2	3	4	5
7. How much do you feel safe in the restrooms?	1	2	3	4	5
8. How much do you feel safe in the cafeteria/lunchroom?	1	2	3	4	5
9. How much do you feel safe on the playground (at recess)?	1	2	3	4	5
10. How much do you feel safe in the bus waiting area at school?	1	2	3	4	5
11. How much do you feel safe on the school grounds before and after school?	1	2	3	4	5
12. How much do the adults in our school make you feel as if you want to do your best?	1	2	3	4	5
13. How much do you think that the students in our school encourage one another?	1	2	3	4	5
14. How much do you think that other students understand our school's rules?	1	2	3	4	5
15. How much do you think that your parents understand our school's rules?	1	2	3	4	5
16. How much do you think that students in our school treat other students **politely**?	1	2	3	4	5

	Not Much	A Little	So/So	Mostly	A Lot
17. How much do you think that students in our school treat other students **fairly**?	1	2	3	4	5
18. How much do you think that students in our school treat other students **in a friendly way**?	1	2	3	4	5
19. How much do you think that students in our school treat other students **in a helpful way**?	1	2	3	4	5
20. How much do you think that students in our school treat other students **with kindness**?	1	2	3	4	5
21. How much do you think that the adults in our school understand the school rules?	1	2	3	4	5
22. How much do you think that the adults in our school are helpful to students?	1	2	3	4	5
23. How much do you think that the adults in our school teach students the school rules?	1	2	3	4	5
24. How much do you think that the adults in our school are friendly to students?	1	2	3	4	5
25. How much do the adults in our school make you want to come to school?	1	2	3	4	5
26. How much do you think that our school rules are the same everywhere in the school?	1	2	3	4	5
27. How much do you believe that the adults in our school care about you?	1	2	3	4	5
28. How much do the adults in our school help make this a nice place to be?	1	2	3	4	5
29. How much do the adults in our school help make this a friendly place to be?	1	2	3	4	5
30. How much do you know how you are supposed to behave on the playground?	1	2	3	4	5
31. How much do you know how you are supposed to behave in your classroom?	1	2	3	4	5
32. How much do you know how you are supposed to behave on the bus?	1	2	3	4	5
33. How much do you know how you are supposed to behave in the cafeteria/lunchroom?	1	2	3	4	5
34. How much do you think that the students in our school help each other to behave?	1	2	3	4	5

Thank you for your help!

Adapted with permission from Education Support Services (1993).

Student Survey

Date _____

○ Boy   ○ Girl   Grade _____

Dear Student:

As part of our continuing effort to make our school environment one that is safe and productive for all, we would appreciate your responses to the following questions. Your name is not required on this form; however, we do need you to indicate whether you are a boy or a girl and what grade you are in. **Your input is very important to us!**

Thank you!

	Not Much	A Little	So/So	Mostly	A Lot
1. How much do you understand our school rules and expectations for behavior?	☹	:|	:|	☺	☺
2. How much do you think that the adults in our school treat students with kindness and respect? . .	☹	:|	:|	☺	☺
3. How much do you think that the adults in our school treat students fairly?	☹	:|	:|	☺	☺
4. How much do you think that the students in our school treat each other with respect?	☹	:|	:|	☺	☺
5. How much do you feel safe in your classroom(s)? . .	☹	:|	:|	☺	☺
6. How much do you feel safe in the halls?	☹	:|	:|	☺	☺
7. How much do you feel safe in the restrooms?	☹	:|	:|	☺	☺
8. How much do you feel safe in the cafeteria/lunchroom?	☹	:|	:|	☺	☺
9. How much do you feel safe on the playground (at recess)?	☹	:|	:|	☺	☺
10. How much do you feel safe in the bus waiting area at school?	☹	:|	:|	☺	☺
11. How much do you feel safe on the school grounds before and after school?	☹	:|	:|	☺	☺
12. How much do the adults in our school make you feel as if you want to do your best?	☹	:|	:|	☺	☺
13. How much do you think that the students in our school encourage one another?	☹	:|	:|	☺	☺
14. How much do you think that other students understand our school's rules?	☹	:|	:|	☺	☺
15. How much do you think that your parents understand our school's rules?	☹	:|	:|	☺	☺

	Not Much	A Little	So/So	Mostly	A Lot
16. How much do you think that students in our school treat other students **politely**?					
17. How much do you think that students in our school treat other students **fairly**?					
18. How much do you think that students in our school treat other students **in a friendly way**?					
19. How much do you think that students in our school treat other students **in a helpful way**?					
20. How much do you think that students in our school treat other students **with kindness**?					
21. How much do you think that the adults in our school understand the school rules?					
22. How much do you think that the adults in our school are helpful to students?					
23. How much do you think that the adults in our school teach students the school rules?					
24. How much do you think that the adults in our school are friendly to students?					
25. How much do the adults in our school make you want to come to school?					
26. How much do you think that our school rules are the same everywhere in the school?					
27. How much do you believe that the adults in our school care about you?					
28. How much do the adults in our school help make this a nice place to be?					
29. How much do the adults in our school help make this a friendly place to be?					
30. How much do you know how you are supposed to behave on the playground?					
31. How much do you know how you are supposed to behave in your classroom?					
32. How much do you know how you are supposed to behave on the bus?					
33. How much do you know how you are supposed to behave in the cafeteria/lunchroom?					
34. How much do you think that the students in our school help each other to behave?					

Thank you for your help!
Adapted with permission from Education Support Services (1993).

Parent Surveys

With parent surveys, there can be problems both with distributing the surveys and getting them back in an efficient manner that does not involve excessive cost (e.g., in postage and/or your time). One method is to hand out surveys when many parents are at the school, for example, during an open house or parent/teacher conference. The problem with this is that the surveys will go primarily to parents who are involved enough to come to school in the first place, and therefore you may not get a true representation of how all parents feel. Still, this is a relatively cost-free way to distribute surveys. If you use this method, you may want to include a self-addressed envelope and ask the parents to return completed surveys with their students (you could have each teacher collect them and/or have a box in the office). You could also put stamps on the envelopes and ask parents to mail their surveys back.

Another distribution method is do a mass mailing of surveys—to ensure that every household with a student or students in your school gets one. Again, you can either ask parents to send completed surveys back with students or include stamped return envelopes. In both cases, we would urge you to calculate the percentage of parents who actually complete surveys so you will be able to evaluate the results more precisely. For example, if you only have 10%–20% of your total households returning surveys and these indicate that parents are very aware of school rules, you have to be very careful about assuming that all parents are aware of school rules. On the other hand, if you have an 85% (of households) return and a majority indicate that they do not think that your discipline procedures are being implemented fairly, you should probably take it to heart.

Scoring/Interpretation

Summarizing the first page of the parent surveys would be done in the same way as the staff surveys. That is, you calculate mean scores; then look at the consistency (or lack of) among similar items and compare answers across categories of parents. The categories of interest may be individual grade levels, but you would probably be as well off simply separating respondents into "parents of primary students" and "parents of intermediate students." (Again, you will also want to compare parent answers as a whole with student answers, and to a lesser extent with staff answers.)

To make use of the information on the second page of the parent surveys requires a somewhat greater investment of time and energy. Someone will have to read through all the written responses and try to summarize them. The idea is to get a general sense of whether lots of people have similar ideas on what is working well and what could be done better—and not pay undue attention to single or isolated suggestions. For example, if a majority of parents indicate that one of the things they like is the way parent/teacher conferences are set up, but one or two parents complain about it, you have to put the complaints in perspective. (You might, however, want to address the complaints in a general fashion in something like the school newsletter—so that the people who have taken the time to respond know that their input was considered.)

Parent Survey

Date _____

Dear Parent:

As part of our continuing effort to make our school environment one that is safe and productive for all, we would appreciate your responses to the following questions. Your name is not required on this form; however, for analyses purposes we do ask that you indicate your student's gender and grade. **Your input is vital!** Please return this completed form by sending it to school with your child or by mailing it in the attached envelope.

Thank you!

I have a student(s) in the following grade(s). Please check all that apply:

Female: ○ K   ○ 1   ○ 2   ○ 3   ○ 4   ○ 5   ○ 6   ○ 7   ○ 8

Male: ○ K   ○ 1   ○ 2   ○ 3   ○ 4   ○ 5   ○ 6   ○ 7   ○ 8

		Not Much				Very Much
1.	To what extent do you think our school's rules and expectations for behavior are clear?	1	2	3	4	5
2.	To what extent do you think that our school's current behavior policies and procedures are fair?	1	2	3	4	5
3.	To what extent do you think staff members at our school treat students with kindness and respect? . .	1	2	3	4	5
4.	To what extent do you think students at our school treat each other with respect?	1	2	3	4	5
5.	To what extent do you think your child feels safe in his/her classroom?	1	2	3	4	5
6.	To what extent do you think your child feels safe in the halls at our school?	1	2	3	4	5
7.	To what extent do you think your child feels safe in the restrooms at our school?	1	2	3	4	5
8.	To what extent do you think your child feels safe in the cafeteria/lunchroom at our school?	1	2	3	4	5
9.	To what extent do you think your child feels safe on the playground during recess at our school?	1	2	3	4	5
10.	To what extent do you think your child feels safe on our school grounds before and after school?	1	2	3	4	5
11.	To what extent do you think your child feels safe in the bus waiting areas at our school?	1	2	3	4	5

		Not Much				Very Much
12.	To what extent do you feel that staff members at our school encourage your child to do his/her best? . .	1	2	3	4	5

13. In your opinion, what are we doing at our school that is working well?

_____

_____

_____

_____

_____

_____

14. In your opinion, what could we be doing better at our school?

_____

_____

_____

_____

_____

_____

Thanks so much for your time and assistance!

Adapted with permission from Education Support Services (1993).

Screening Observations

The observation form on page 131 has been derived from the basic "Safe and Productive" graphic that follows. It is probably most appropriately used by a principal when doing informal observations of the school's various common area settings (e.g., playground, cafeteria, etc.) and contexts (e.g., assemblies). We recommend that the principal do observations like this frequently throughout the year. The form itself can be used as a prompt each time an observation is done and/or it can be used to summarize the findings from several observations on one particular setting/context. It is important to remember that the purpose of these observations is for the principal to get a general sense about the safety and productivity of a setting—they are not intended to be and should not be used for staff evaluation purposes.

If you find that a particular setting/context is **not** safe and productive and/or that student behavior is **not** as responsible as you would like it to be, use the information in Chapter Nine: Common Areas to guide a staff team (or special task force) in a review and revision of your procedures for that setting/context.

Is the Setting Safe and Productive?

Is student behavior:

Responsible?
Are students behaving in a manner you would want the school superintendent to see?

Yes   No

Engaged?
Are students actively involved in a meaningful activity?

Yes   No

Motivated?
Are students interested and enthusiastic about the activities they are engaged in?

Yes   No

If "Yes" to all of the questions:

> If it isn't broken, don't fix it!

If "No" to any of the questions, analyze if staff are:

Proactive?
Are staff preventing problems by scanning the setting and circulating among students. Has the setting been structured to prompt safe and productive behavior?

Positive?
Are staff interacting often and in a friendly manner with all students?

Instructional?
Have expectations been taught? Are staff providing age-appropriate positive feedback and correcting behavioral errors calmly and consistently?

Continue to analyze and modify these three staff variables until student behavior is responsible, engaged, and motivated.

Note: If the behavior of a small number of students (e.g., five percent) is irresponsible, it may be necessary to set up individualized plans for these students.

Observation Form

Observation of _____ on _____
                                      (setting)   (date)

at _____ by _____
           (time)   (observer)

Is This Setting Safe and Productive?

Yes or No   **Are most students (95%+) behaving responsibly** (i.e., behaving in a manner that I would want the superintendent of schools to see)?
Notes: _____

_____

_____

Yes or No   **Do most students (95%+) seem engaged** (i.e., actively involved in some kind of meaningful activity)?
Notes: _____

_____

_____

Yes or No   **Do most students (95%+) seem motivated** (i.e., interested and enthusiastic about the activities in which they are engaged)?
Notes: _____

_____

_____

If "No" to any of the above questions, check staff actions.

- **Are staff proactive?** (Do staff prevent problems by scanning the setting and circulating among students?) (**Note:** Also ask, has the setting been structured to prompt active, safe, and productive behavior?)

- **Are staff positive?** (Do staff interact frequently and in a friendly manner with all students?)

- **Are staff instructional?** (Do staff provide age-appropriate positive feedback? Do staff correct misbehavior calmly and consistently?) (**Note:** Also ask, have students been taught the behavioral expectations?)

Disciplinary Records Database

Useful information for SBP improvement efforts can be gained through a careful examination of your disciplinary records—both office referrals and referrals to other disciplinary action (e.g., time-out rooms, in-school suspensions, noon or after-school detentions, and so on). By identifying patterns in these records, you can answer important questions about your behavior management situation. For example, you should be able to use your disciplinary records to determine:

- Whether staff efforts to encourage student responsibility are making a difference;

- What types of social skills should be taught to students and reinforced by staff;

- Which staff members need additional help with behavior management techniques;

- Whether differential consequences are applied to students based on any sort of racial bias;

- What type of misbehavior is most frequently referred;

- Which month of the year has the most behavior problems;

- Which day of the week has the most behavior problems;

- Which hour of the day (or class period) has the most behavior problems; and

- Which setting in the school has the most behavior problems.

Once you have answers to questions like these, you and your staff can work collaboratively to design procedures to buttress against any identified problem areas. At the most general level, you can compare year-to-year rates of referrals to get an indication of the degree to which you are successfully getting students to behave more responsibly. For example, if staff assign 30% fewer schoolwide consequences (e.g., referrals to the office or after-school detentions) in one school year than they did during the previous school year, it is reasonable to assume that they have improved their efforts to handle problems within their own rooms and/or that students are becoming more responsible.

For more specific questions (e.g., which day of the week has the most behavior problems), though, you need to be able to examine the individual aspects of referrals across all the specific referrals that have occurred. Unfortunately, this is often not easy to do when the information is only on the individual referral forms that have been filed in students' folders. A simple and effective solution is to create some kind of computer database (using any basic database or spreadsheet program) into which you or one of your office staff can efficiently enter pertinent information from each individual referral at the time it occurs. **Note:** If you are not yet familiar with how to set up and use a computerized database or spreadsheet program, get assistance from one of the "computer whizzes"—either staff or student—on your campus.

We have found the following categories to be useful as separate fields in a disciplinary records database: date, day of the week, time or class period, setting, referral type, referring staff person, student name, student gender, specific infraction, and consequence assigned. The following figure shows how such a database might appear on your computer screen.

Sample Database

Date	Day/ Week	Class or Time	Setting	Ref. Type	Ref. Staff	Stud. Name	Stud. Gender	Infrac- tion	Conse- quence

For each field, then, you create codes for the various possible information entries into that field. Code consistency is essential in order to do any sort of analysis. For example, if you have used consistent codes to indicate the type of misbehavior (i.e., the specific infraction) and the type of disciplinary action (e.g., office referral or after-school detention), you can then use your program to create a chart that shows the percentage of each misbehavior that resulted in an office referral and the percentage that resulted in an after-school detention. The following sample codes (for setting, infraction, consequence, and referral type) may help you come up with codes of your own.

Sample Codes

Setting	Infraction	Consequence	Type of Referral
C = Classroom	FT = Fighting	ASD = After-school detention	ASD = After-school detention
L = Lunchroom	AS = Assault	ISS = In-school suspension	DR = Disciplinary referral to office
O = Outside of building	PO = Possession of controlled subst.	OSS = Out of school suspension	
H = Hall	DF = Defiance	JA = Juvenile authorities or police contacted	
A = Assembly	HW = Homework		
R = Restroom	CW = Classwork	WA = Warning	
B = Bus	DS = Disruption	CS = Community service	
O = Other	DR = Disrespect	REST. = Restitution	
	UEA = Unexcused absence	O = Other	
	TD = Tardy (3 or more)		
	O = Other		

Note: The information from your disciplinary records can also be used to help you identify topics for staff development activities. For example, if you find that there are significantly more referrals on Mondays than on other days, you and your staff might decide to structure Monday activities more tightly and develop procedures for helping students reorient to school after the weekend. Or, if you determine that 40% of the referrals in the Fall term were for fighting, you might arrange to teach all students a conflict resolution strategy during the Winter term.

SBP Content Checklist

The following checklist can be used to assess the content and implementation of your current Schoolwide Behavior Plan (SBP) with the recommendations made in this book. Each of the main sections on the checklist correlates with one of the chapters in the book. When there is an item for which your answer is "no," you should have your team (or special task force) reexamine the recommendations in the chapter relevant to that item in order to develop proposals that can be discussed and eventually adopted by the entire faculty. Work through this checklist once a year.

	Yes	No	N/A
The Ongoing Process of SBP Improvement (See Chapter Five)			
1. We have a team that meets on a regular basis to guide an ongoing process of reviewing, revising, adopting, implementing/maintaining the policies and procedures of our SBP.			
2. The team adequately represents the entire staff (i.e., every staff member feels he/she has input to the team).			
3. The team is organized so that each year a few members rotate off, but at least 2/3 of the team stays the same.			
4. The entire staff feel they have an active voice in reviewing and revising the SBP.			
5. When proposed SBP policies and procedures are discussed, most of the nuts-and-bolts problem solving is conducted in a way that does not usurp large amounts of time from the entire faculty.			
6. We have a consensual decision-making process that is respectful of minority opinion, yet maintains time efficiency.			
7. We have varied staff development activities to inform and motivate staff to implement current and new aspects of our SBP.			
8. We provide opportunities for students and parents to participate in the review and revision process of SBP improvement.			
Guiding Principles (See Chapter Six)			
9. We have a school mission statement that reflects the importance of meeting the educational needs of all students.			
10. Staff, students, and parents know the mission statement.			
11. Staff have worked together to clarify basic beliefs about behavior management, which include but are not limited to: a) b) c)			
12. Staff, students, and parents have had input into our "Guidelines for Success" that define the vision of what successful students strive to do.			
13. Our "Guidelines for Success" are positively stated and reflect important expectations based on the long-term needs of students.			
14. Our "Guidelines for Success" reflect the best interests of students rather than adults (i.e., they are not merely compliance oriented).			

	Yes	No	N/A
15. Our "Guidelines for Success" are posted throughout the building.			
16. Our "Guidelines for Success" are regularly used (talked about, celebrated, taught, reinforced, corrected) by staff when interacting with students.			
17. Our school mission statement, staff beliefs about behavior management, and "Guidelines for Success" are written in a SBP staff handbook and in a student handbook (or at least included in the beginning of the year orientation packet for parents).			
Encouragement Procedures (See Chapter Seven)			
18. All our staff understand the concept of meeting students' basic needs.			
19. We have a varied menu of procedures and programs designed to ensure that students' basic needs are being met.			
20. This menu is written into the SBP staff handbook.			
21. Our students receive frequent feedback regarding their progress in meeting expectations for schoolwide behavior.			
22. Our staff maintain a high ratio of attention for positive behavior (recognition and acknowledgment) to attention for negative behavior (reprimands, corrections, consequences).			
23. Our building climate reflects a positive orientation toward students.			
24. Our students feel a sense of pride and belonging toward this school.			
Disciplinary Referrals (See Chapter Eight)			
25. We have clearly defined guidelines regarding when (and when not) to use disciplinary referral—and staff are aware of them.			
26. Staff can make the administrator aware of behavior that does not necessarily warrant disciplinary referral, but is of concern via an "administrator notification" process.			
27. Records are kept of disciplinary referrals, administrator notifications, and any other schoolwide consequences such as after-school detention or referral to a problem-solving room. These records are used as part of the yearly SBP review process to identify staff development activities and to guide SBP improvements.			
28. We have procedures in place to flag students who demonstrate at-risk conditions (e.g., excessive referrals, failing grades, excessive absenteeism, and so on) that indicate the need for collaborative intervention planning.			

	Yes	No	N/A
29. A variety of collaborative resources are available to any staff member who wants assistance in meeting the behavioral or academic needs of a student or group.			
30. We have office procedures in place to ensure a clear chain of command when the principal is out of the building.			
31. Adequate and effective emergency procedures (and back-up procedures) have been designed to ensure physical safety and staff support in the event of emergency behavior situations (e.g., a student is out of control).			
32. Our emergency situation procedures have been documented in writing.			
33. Our staff are consistent in implementing the emergency situation procedures as they are written.			

	Playground	Cafeteria	Halls	Bus Loading Area	Restrooms	Assemblies	Substitutes
Common Areas (See Chapter Nine)							
34. For each of our common areas, we have a written SBP document that includes:							
• The goal for the setting/context							
• Specific behavioral expectations (rules) for student behavior within the setting/context							
• Corrective consequences to be used to respond to student misbehavior in the setting/context							
• Procedures to encourage responsible student behavior in the setting/context							
• Supervision responsibilities of staff in the setting/context							
• Teaching responsibilities of staff related to the expectations for the setting/context							

		Yes	No	N/A
35.	Our staff consistently implement the recommended procedures for each common area (e.g., teaching expectations, providing adequate supervision, interacting positively with students, and so on).			
36.	Student behavior within each common area is, for the most part, safe and productive.			
37.	At the beginning of each school year students are directly taught the behavioral expectations for every school common area setting and context.			
38.	New students who arrive at the school are directly taught the behavioral expectations for every school common area setting and context.			
Classrooms (See Chapter Nine)				
39.	Certified staff have developed a statement that summarizes our agreements about classroom management and have agreed to a template for a Classroom Behavior Plan (CBP) that all teachers will follow.			
40.	Our CBP template includes the categories of:			
	• Classroom rules			
	• Guidelines for success			
	• Encouragement procedures			
	• Corrective consequences			
	• Monitoring procedures			
	• Teaching procedures			
41.	The summary statement of beliefs and the CBP template are included as a written part of our SBP.			
42.	All our certified teachers have their individual CBPs on file in the office.			

chapter six

Guiding Principles—The Core of Your SBP

This chapter contains information and suggestions for reviewing, revising, or developing content for that section of a Schoolwide Behavior Plan (SBP) that addresses the guiding principles (or fundamental policies) that underly a school's behavior management practices. Specifically, this section of an SBP should consist of three policy documents: (1) A school mission statement; (2) A summary statement of staff beliefs about managing student behavior; and (3) a set of "guidelines for student success." Together, these documents should describe what the purpose of a school is, what its staff believe about managing student behavior, and what attitudes, behaviors, and traits the school will be trying to foster in students.

The chapter begins with a brief introduction that explains why a section on "Guiding Principles" is an important component of an SBP. The bulk of the chapter, then, is structured around a series of questions designed to guide efforts to review, revise, or develop the documents that should comprise this section of an SBP. The chapter ends with sample policy documents (that can be used as models) and with a reproducible "Assessment and Evaluation Worksheet." The worksheet, which correlates directly with the content covered in the chapter, is intended to provide a structured tool that can be used by whomever (e.g., yourself, a Responsibility Team, a task force) may be responsible for working on proposals to improve this section of your SBP. You may also find it useful to keep a copy of the worksheet handy as you read through the chapter, and to take notes and/or jot down ideas on it.

Note: For some schools, this section of the SBP represents the logical starting point for their improvement efforts—so that the policy documents can guide subsequent decisions regarding specific procedures. However, when a school has a severe problem with some specific behavior management situation (e.g., the playground is out of control or staff are angry because they feel they are not supported in dealing with severe misbehavior), it may make more sense to address the crisis situation(s) before working on the guiding principles. Because this section tends to be more philosophical than procedural, attending to it may seem like "fiddling while Rome burns" if pressing problems have not yet been addressed. Whenever you choose to work on this section, though, we think you will find that the process itself will help to unify and strengthen the procedures that make up your SBP.

section one
*W*hy Have a "Guiding Principles" Section in Your SBP?

One of the major premises of this book is that the goal of a school's behavior management practices should be to create a safe and productive school environment in which all students behave responsibly and exhibit high levels of motivation while actively engaged in meaningful activities. Another premise is that this goal can best be achieved by implementing behavior management procedures that are proactive, positive, and instructional. These and the rest of our basic premises represent the principles that guided the development of this book—and affected everything from its overall organizational structure to choices about which specific procedures to recommend and which to discourage. Without these guiding principles, the task would have been much more difficult—because it would have been less clear exactly what needed to be accomplished, and a consistent basis for making decisions about what to include would be lacking. As it was, we began the book with a "destination" in mind (i.e., helping principals guide their schools in the creation of safe and productive school environments) and the means to evaluate what we would use to get there (e.g., will this chapter/procedure/concept help a principal achieve a safe and productive school environment? Does it reflect a proactive, positive, and/or instructional approach to behavior management?).

Just as guiding principles served as important foundations for this book, your school's guiding principles should serve as important foundations to your Schoolwide Behavior Plan (SBP). In fact, the process of specifying these principles can be particularly important when staff are not sure what their beliefs are, or when major differences exist among staff members about such things as the purpose of behavior management or the respective value of spending time/effort to encourage responsible behavior versus spending time/effort to correct misbehavior. Without staff awareness of and/or consensus on guiding principles, it can be difficult, if not impossible, to get staff to agree on the use of any specific behavior management procedures.

For example, consider a middle school at which a major schism has developed between the sixth grade teachers and the seventh and eighth grade teachers. Almost every discussion about behavior management (e.g., how to handle misbehavior in hallways) breaks down into an argument, and occasionally even borders on name-calling. "You sixth grade teachers just want to coddle the kids. The reason we have these problems is that students learn they can get away with murder during the year they spend with you. By the time they get to us, they are already impossible to control." And on the other side, "Why does everything you recommend involve 'nailing' kids when they misbehave? Don't you people like kids? You are so negative you turn the students into enemies." Until both sides realize that they are operating from some very different basic beliefs, even a seemingly simple component of their school's behavior plan (e.g., managing hallway behavior) may be impossible to resolve. Discussing and working out viable compromises on their beliefs—and then summarizing them in basic policy documents—would leave this staff better equipped to work out the specific procedures of their SBP.

We have identified three policy documents that we believe serve as important foundations to a school's behavior management practices. The first, a School Mission Statement, describes the school's purpose or reason for existence. The second is a Statement of Staff Beliefs About Managing Student Behavior—a summary of what's important, what works, etc. such as might be found in a staff handbook. The third policy document, which we recommend be called something like "Guidelines for Student Success," is a specification of the attitudes, traits, and behaviors that the school will be trying to foster in its students (i.e., those attitudes, traits, and behaviors students should have in order to succeed in school and in life). The remainder of this chapter deals with each of these documents in turn.

---

section two

 ## School Mission Statement

Do you have some kind of a written statement (e.g., a school "mission statement") that succinctly summarizes your school's purpose and its broad-based goals?

In the business world, successful organizations take the time and effort to clearly articulate the reasons for their existence. These organizations then use their mission statements to help them focus on important goals, identify directions for change, and coordinate the efforts of all their members. A school's mission statement should serve a similar function—for its staff, students, and parents (and even members of the community at large).

For staff, a mission statement should articulate the primary reason for their collective efforts (e.g., "The goal of _____ Elementary School is for all students to learn the academic and social skills necessary to be successful—in school and in life"). As such, it will not only help meet individual staff members' basic needs for "purpose," but also provide staff, individually and as a whole, with a framework and a filter for making both long-range and daily decisions. For students and parents, a mission statement should represent a kind of contract—a promise that helping students is the most important work of the school and its staff. At a practical level, the mission statement should also give students and parents a basis for understanding staff actions (e.g., "Mr. and Mrs. Chard, I am calling because Zach has been having some behavioral problems. Since our mission here is to help Zach, and all students, learn the academic and social skills necessary to be successful, I would like for us to figure out a plan to …"). A mission statement is an important foundation to an SBP because all of a school's behavior management procedures should complement and support its stated purpose.

Is your school's mission statement "user friendly" and comprehensive?

If your school already has a mission statement, it's important to review its quality and how effectively it is being used. We believe that the ideal school mission statement is a short, simple, and positive statement of the school's overall purpose—one that describes the school's responsibility for students' academic and social growth, and that emphasizes the importance of including all students, regardless of home background or past history.

Short and Simple

A short and simple statement makes it easier for the school's purpose to be understood and remembered by all the members of the school community. When a statement is too long, people are more likely to have trouble remembering the important ideas. And, if it is too complicated, some (e.g., younger students, less-educated parents) may not understand it at all. In both of these situations, an important reason for having a mission statement (i.e., to have a readily accessible sense of purpose that can be used by all) is lost.

Positive

The idea of a mission statement is to provide an overarching goal that everyone in the organization (i.e., school community) can strive to achieve. A negatively stated goal is not only uninspiring, but in many cases, it can also be a logical absurdity. For example, a mission statement that says something like "… students will never engage in misbehavior …" puts staff in the position of having to "pump students up" to not misbehave; students in the position of trying to get excited about "not misbehaving"; and parents in the position of feeling proud that their children "didn't misbehave." The best mission statements provide positive goals that everyone in an organization can strive to achieve.

Academic and Social Focus

Success, whether in school, a career, or in life requires both academic and social competence. A school that focuses on only one, but not the other, of these areas cannot fully prepare students to meet the challenges they will face once they leave the school. A mission that emphasizes only academic development does not take into account the fact that some students need to be taught the social and behavioral skills necessary to be successful in school, on a job, and/or in relationships with other people. On the other hand, a mission in which the sole emphasis is on students' social/behavioral growth neglects the reality that students who are not academically competent have severely limited chances of subsequent success. Your mission statement should communicate the importance of students achieving both academic and social/behavioral competence.

Inclusive

In the past, when education was less critical to an individual's success in life, educators could afford the luxury of not being effective with all students. In fact, schools basically only took responsibility for educating those students who were easiest to teach. Students who lagged behind their peers were encouraged to leave the educational system, and students whose behavior did not easily fit the norm for the school dropped out or were suspended or expelled. Today, when the prospects for an individual without a high school diploma are so much more dismal, educators must rethink this approach. In fact, we would argue that a student's failure to thrive in the educational system should be considered a life-threatening problem for both the student and for society. That is why we believe a school's mission statement should reflect its staff members' commitment to the belief that every child is worth the time and effort required to teach them the academic and social/behavioral skills needed to be successful in school and in life.

Take Action!

1. If your school does not have a mission statement, develop one. While some general guidelines are offered regarding the content of such a document, a specific process for developing a mission statement is beyond the scope of this book. The following sources, however, may be helpful:

   - Block, P. (1987). *The empowered manager: Positive political skills at work*. San Francisco: Jossey Bass.

   - Nanus, B. (1992). *Visionary leadership*. San Francisco: Jossey Bass.

2. A school mission statement can only be effective if it is known by the school's staff, students, and parents (i.e., a mission statement that is not known is nothing more than words on a paper or a document in a file cabinet). Therefore, it is important to ensure that your mission statement is familiar, in spirit if not literally, to everyone in your school community. A visitor to your school should be able to ask ten staff members, ten students, and ten parents, "What is the mission of this school—what is the point?"—and hear from most of them a reasonable description of the school's purpose. If this would not happen, you need to find ways to incorporate your mission statement into school activities on a more frequent basis. For example, the statement might be posted throughout the school, and/or reviewed during the openings of assemblies, and/or used as the theme for events such as "Back-to-School Night." New students can be introduced to the mission statement as part of their orientation to the school. Teachers can incorporate it into class discussions about behavior and motivation, and all staff members can refer to it when they are encouraging/motivating responsible student behavior and/or responding to irresponsible student behavior.

section three
Statement of Staff Beliefs About Managing Student Behavior

Do your staff share basic beliefs regarding behavior management?

It is not enough for a school's staff members just to know what behavior management procedures they are supposed to follow—they should be aware of and, ideally, in basic agreement with the fundamental beliefs that underlie those procedures. This is important for several reasons.

First of all, taking the time to clarify and/or reach consensus about their behavior management beliefs increases the probability that individual staff members will feel more committed to and therefore more likely to use the specific behavior management procedures that are adopted. Second, understanding why a particular procedure has been adopted tends to make people more consistent in using that procedure.

A succinct set of clarified beliefs gives staff a framework for making both immediate and long-term behavior management decisions. ("How should I respond to this situation with Brandon?" "Does the proposed change in our SBP hallway procedures support our agreed upon beliefs?") In addition, clarified beliefs can make the task of managing student behavior, especially responding to misbehavior, much less stressful. Dealing with unmotivated, disruptive, and disrespectful students is difficult. When staff understand ahead of time how they should respond to student misbehavior, and why that response makes sense, they are much less likely to have their egos threatened and/or to lose their cool. Finally, this set of behavior management beliefs can serve as an efficient and effective filter when hiring new staff (e.g., is the prospective staff member willing and able to manage student behavior according to agreed upon beliefs).

A simple set of staff beliefs about managing student behavior can be generated by answering the following three questions:

1.   Who is responsible for managing student behavior at a school?

2.   What are the goals of a school's behavior management efforts?

3.   How can a school's behavior management goals best be achieved?

What follows are answers to these questions—statements that reflect the authors' beliefs, along with brief explanations of why the authors believe as they do.

Question 1
Who is responsible for managing student behavior?

• **A school's adults (i.e., the staff) must assume ultimate responsibility for managing student behavior.**

A safe and productive school environment, in which students are expected to behave responsibly and be actively engaged and highly motivated, requires staff to be proactive (setting up environments to maximize student success), positive (interacting with students in friendly and optimistic ways), and instructional (teaching expectations, providing positive feedback and using calm and consistent corrections). This focus on adult responsibility in no way means that students should not be held accountable or taught to take responsibility for their own actions. It simply means that staff realize and accept that the first steps—implementing a proactive, positive, and instructional approach to behavior management—are theirs. It also means that staff understand the need for thoughtful responses to student misbehavior, especially in cases of repeated problems.

• **The responsibility for managing student behavior must be shared by all staff members—with classroom teachers taking the lead roles.**

Effectively reaching students (especially misbehaving students) requires the coordinated efforts of all school personnel, both certified and classified. An administrator, no matter how competent, cannot cure misbehavior by himself/ herself. The only way all students will learn to behave responsibly is for every staff person to thoughtfully and conscientiously implement the behavior management procedures that are part of the schoolwide plan. Thus, all staff members should help with the management of student behavior in common areas—by correcting misbehavior when they see it (e.g., running in the hall) and by providing students with attention and positive feedback—and teachers should have the primary responsibility for managing student behavior in their own classrooms. The building administrator needs to help staff deal with severe and chronic misbehavior and ensure that the school's SBP is continually updated and improved. Specialists such as the counselor, social worker, school psychologist, and district behavior specialist should be available to all staff for help in establishing individualized management plans.

Question 2
What are the goals of a school's behavior management efforts?

• **One major behavior management goal should be to create a "productive" school environment for students and staff.**

The ultimate goal of behavior management practices is to ensure that more learning (and joy in learning) takes place in a school than would occur if the practices were not being implemented. In fact, if the only result of your efforts is a school that is quieter and more orderly, but in which no more learning is taking place, then your behavior management practices are not all they should be. That is, it's important to help students learn to behave responsibly and be highly motivated while engaged in meaningful activities. This focus on learning does not imply that misbehaving students should be removed from their classrooms. The fact is, a student who is repeatedly removed from his/her classroom will not have a chance to learn. The best behavior management practices are those that reduce the deleterious effects of one student's misbehavior on the learning of other students, while concurrently maximizing the learning of the misbehaving student by helping that student learn to behave more responsibly in the future.

- **A second major behavior management goal should be to create a "safe" (physical and emotional) school environment for students and staff.**

    – *Physical Safety*

    When students do not feel physically safe, learning will not take place. Abraham Maslow, in his hierarchy of needs, suggests that a person who is afraid of physical injury will not be motivated to engage in higher order or noble purposes (e.g., satisfying the need to know and learn). Thus, a student who has been stuffed into a locker by bullies, a student who has been sexually molested in a restroom, and a student who has been shoved around at recess will all have one thing in common—their major motivation during a school day will be figuring out ways to keep physically safe rather than learning, belonging, or growing.

    This can be a difficult concept for staff to understand, particularly when they themselves feel safe. Staff may assume that since they feel physically safe, then students must as well. Unfortunately, however, there is increasing evidence that a distressing number of students do not feel physically safe while at school.

    – *Emotional Safety*

    In the same way that people are not motivated to higher purposes when they fear for their physical safety, they are also not motivated when they fear emotional trauma. For example, a student who has been publicly ridiculed by his/her teacher is not likely to try to excel in that teacher's classroom. At best, the student may attempt to "keep a low profile" so as not to be ridiculed again. At worst, he/she may seek revenge against the teacher—by setting up an ongoing battle of wills or, at the extreme, resorting to violence. It is critical that staff understand that ridiculing, humiliating, or belittling students in any way is not appropriate and cannot be tolerated.

    Students should also be reasonably safe from emotional victimization by other students. Although it may not be possible to completely eliminate teasing, cliques, put-downs, ganging up, and so on, staff can and should make every effort to see that the probability of any student being victimized by other students, verbally or nonverbally, is very low.

Question 3
How can a school's behavior management goals best be achieved?

The answer to this question will obviously depend on what the goals are. The sample answers that follow assume the agreed upon goals are a "safe and productive school."

- **Behavior management practices should be designed to meet students' basic needs.**

  Students, like all of us, have basic needs. Trying to meet students' basic needs is not only a fundamentally humane thing to do, it is also practical. Students who are not getting their needs met sometimes engage in misbehavior to get them met. For example, a student who is not getting the attention she needs, might misbehave because she has discovered that adults pay attention to someone who breaks the rules. Or, a student who is not having his need for belonging and purpose met may be tempted to join a destructive clique or gang.

- **Behavior management practices should be proactive.**

  One of the most effective means of ensuring a safe and productive school environment is to *set things up* in ways that increase the likelihood of students behaving responsibly. This includes actually teaching students how they are expected to behave, making sure that the structural and organizational features of the various school settings do more to prompt responsible rather than irresponsible student behavior, ensuring adequate adult supervision for all school settings, and giving staff members sufficient information and support regarding the behavior management policies and procedures they are expected to implement. Students will behave more responsibly in smoothly run schools where the adults know their roles and feel competent and supported, and in schools where everyone is upbeat and encouraging, than they will in disorganized schools where staff members don't know what other staff are doing and where people are generally depressed and negative.

- **Behavior management practices should be positive.**

  Staff should interact with each other, with students, and with parents in a manner that is positive, respectful, and optimistic. Positive interactions and attitudes breed positive behavior and attitudes in others, and it is the responsibility of staff to set this kind of tone in the school. Staff also need to understand that there is tremendous power in interacting frequently with individual students when they are not engaged in misbehavior. They can do this by acknowledging students when they behave responsibly, by giving students noncontingent attention (e.g., simply greeting and showing an interest in them), and by providing highly interactive forms of instruction. Students who have frequent and positive interactions with staff members when they are behaving responsibly learn that staff are genuinely interested in them as people and in their successes as students. On the other hand, when students have predominantly negative interactions with staff members, what they are most likely to learn is that staff simply want to control their behaviors and/or that it is easier to get attention by misbehaving than by behaving responsibly.

- **Behavior management practices should be instructional.**

Students should not have to guess about the behavior expected of them. If staff expect students to behave responsibly, then staff have to teach the students what responsible behavior is—in each school setting. If staff expect students to be motivated and engaged in meaningful activities, then staff have to create meaningful activities, communicate the value of those activities to students, and directly teach students how to be engaged and motivated.

In addition, staff need to give students frequent positive feedback when they are meeting the expectations. This serves two functions. First, it lets students know when they are doing things right. This is not as silly as it sounds. Some students actually do not realize when they are behaving responsibly unless they are "caught" and given information that communicates the importance of what they are doing. This kind of feedback eventually leads to self-motivated individuals who know what it takes to be responsible. Second, positive feedback lets the students know that staff notice and are pleased when they try to meet the positive expectations. When staff want and expect students to behave responsibly and be actively engaged, then staff must take the time and make the effort to communicate to students that they are aware of and appreciate the students' effort.

Finally, staff need to remember that their main purpose when responding to student misbehavior should be to teach students how to behave more responsibly. This means that when a misbehaving student does not know what the behavioral expectations are or does not know how to meet the expectations, the staff response should include giving the student information and/or having the student practice the appropriate behavior. It also means that when a student misbehaves despite knowing what is expected, staff response should involve the unemotional implementation of an appropriate consequence—to help the student learn that there are logical costs to one's actions.

Take Action!

1. If your staff has not already done so, help them to clarify and agree upon a set of beliefs about managing student behavior. This requires time and skilled leadership. One useful way is to have staff discuss the three questions presented above, and then summarize their answers as a series of belief statements. (**Note:** Although your staff may not agree with these beliefs, the answers to the questions may be useful as discussion starters. The sample statement of staff beliefs found at the end of this chapter may also prompt productive discussion).

    This process (i.e., having staff discuss and answer these questions) is ideally done as a half-day inservice activity. When this is an option, you can start by having staff get into small groups to discuss the first question. After a reasonable amount of time (e.g., 15-20 minutes), reconvene them into a single group, compile all the responses into one list, discuss the various responses, and then reach a consensual answer (using a decision-making procedure such as "Fist of Five" [see Chapter One]). Repeat the process for questions two and three. If a half-day inservice is not an option, your Responsibility Team (or another leadership group or special task force) can develop proposed answers to present to the entire faculty for feedback, revision, and eventual adoption.

2. If your staff have clarified and agreed upon their behavior management beliefs, make sure they are summarized in a written form that can be given to all staff members and made available to other interested members of the school community.

section four
Guidelines for Student Success

Have you identified the specific attitudes, behaviors, and traits your students need to have/demonstrate in order to be successful in school (and/or in life)?

Students should have clear information about what they need to do in order to be successful in school (and/or perhaps even more broadly, as life-long learners). Not only should such information give students something to strive for (helping to meet their need for purpose), but it should also give them the means of achieving their goals (helping to meet their need for competence). As Richard Stiggins (1990), a noted assessment expert, says, "Students can hit any achievement target they can see and that will sit still for them."

Develop behavioral "guidelines," which, if followed by students, will help them succeed. These guidelines for student success (which are better framed as goals rather than rules) should reflect those attitudes, behaviors, or traits that staff believe will help students succeed—attitudes, behaviors, and traits that students can learn at deeper and deeper levels as they progress through school. The guidelines should overview and complement the school's expectations for daily student behavior, and they should be used to give students feedback about their school performance, to develop behavioral lessons for students, and as part of the school's rituals and traditions.

Too many school staff do not realize that some students enter school believing their own success is impossible. For example, there really are students who believe that success in school requires that one be "smart or rich or white or have two parents at home." Other students may have simply never thought about the fact that their success or failure in school rests on what they do and how they act. Having identified guidelines for student success gives staff a base from which they can coach students about the possibility of their own success (literally "pump students up") and communicate to students that their success is based on what they do (i.e., as they strive to follow the guidelines, they greatly increase their chances of success).

Since part of the reason for having guidelines for student success is so that they will be widely used by staff and students (and parents), it's important to get as much input and "buy in" as possible from staff, students, and parents. The following scenario describes how one school managed to do this:

> The staff at Franklin Middle School first presented the concept of guidelines for student success to parents at a "Back-to-School Night." During the presentation, staff representatives asked parents to think about the kinds of attitudes, work habits, and so on that they (the parents) wanted the school to instill in their children (i.e., what they hoped their children would learn about being successful in school, career, hobbies, and/or relationships). Then they gave the parents a sheet of paper that

contained a brief description of why the school wanted to develop guidelines for student success and a place to put down their ideas. Finally, the representatives asked the parents to talk to their children, jot down a couple of ideas, and return the form to school within three days.

A similar presentation was made to students the following day during their advisory period. Students were also given an assignment—to discuss the issue with their parents and/or think about it themselves, and to be prepared to brainstorm ideas in their classes two days later.

After the brainstorming sessions, all the lists were compiled by the student council, and redundancies were eliminated. The compiled list was then redistributed to advisory teachers, who conducted discussions and held votes on the list with their classes. Each student voted for the five guidelines that seemed most important to him/her. The student council again tallied the results and developed a "Top 15" list. This time the list was distributed to students, staff, and parents. Parents and students were encouraged to discuss the pros and cons of each item on the list.

For the final selection, parents were given ballots on which they could vote for the five guidelines they felt were the most important. Students and staff voted at school. The student council posted the "Top 15" in the cafeteria. Advisory teachers brought their classes to the cafeteria, where each student was given five dots with sticky backs and told to place one dot next to each of the five guidelines they wanted to vote for. Staff members also used dots to vote. The school results were combined with the parental ballot results, and the new official "Guidelines for Success" were announced by the student council at the next assembly.

Over the next several years, the staff used many activities to highlight the guidelines. For example, they had students make posters depicting the guidelines, they conducted assemblies about the guidelines, they established monthly themes that revolved around the guidelines, and they developed integrated assignments that addressed the guidelines. Each year, the eighth grade class prepared an assembly for the new sixth grade class about the guidelines. Classroom teachers taught the guidelines in their classes, and all staff members were encouraged to use them when giving students positive feedback about appropriate behavior and when correcting inappropriate behavior.

Take Action!

1. If you do not have guidelines for student success, come up with a plan for how you and your staff (with input from students and parents) can develop them.

2. When students and parents are exposed to and understand the principles contained in your mission statement and your guidelines for student success, they are more likely to work with staff for a common purpose. Therefore, you need to share these policy documents with students and parents at least once a year.

   This can be accomplished with students through any number of activities, including those described in the preceding scenario. Sharing the information with parents, however, may require a little more creativity. One way is to include the documents in a letter that is sent to all parents at the beginning of the year. Some schools even ask parents to sign and return the letter. For example, you could send the letter home with students—and encourage them to have their parents read and sign it, and then bring it back to school. In the case of the inevitable unreturned letters, you could have someone make a phone call and/or send a follow-up letter (via the mail) and/or visit the home. If you choose to use something like a letter, be sure that its tone implies that everyone will be working together to help every child have a productive and safe school experience (see sample letter to students and parents at the end of this chapter).

Sample Policy Documents

Sample Mission Statement

We, the staff of Lincoln Elementary, are committed to providing all students with the behavioral and academic skills necessary to reach their fullest potential and to become responsible life-long learners.

Sample Statement of Staff Beliefs

All staff members contribute to Lincoln Elementary School's friendly, inviting environment. We set the tone through our actions and attitudes. We will demonstrate our continuous support and encouragement of students in four important ways.

1. We will teach students the expectations for responsible behavior in all school environments by relating student actions to our guidelines for success. That is, we will encourage students to be responsible, to always try, to do their best, to cooperate with others, and to treat everyone with dignity and respect.

2. We will provide positive feedback to students when they are meeting expectations and following the guidelines for success.

3. We will view minor misbehaviors as teaching opportunities, and respond calmly and consistently with corrections or consequences.

4. We will work collaboratively to solve behavior problems that are chronic or severe in nature.

Sample Guidelines for Student Success

1. Be responsible.

2. Always try.

3. Do your best.

4. Cooperate with others.

5. Treat everyone with respect (including yourself).

Sample Letter to Parents

Dear Parent(s)/Guardian(s):

We want your child to be happy and successful at school. We believe you as parent(s) have a major role in your child's education. Your continual interest in your child's progress and success is vital.

We hope to create an environment where courtesy and kindness prevail. We want your child to work on five school guidelines. These guidelines are explained in the attached letter. Please discuss our guidelines with your child. Have your child sign the attached letter. Sign the letter with your child and return it to his/her classroom teacher.

We believe that communication between parents, students, and teachers is critical. If problems arise, we will work with you to find solutions.

If you have questions or concerns, please feel free to contact your child's teacher or our principal. We look forward to working with you and your child.

Sincerely,

The Lincoln Elementary School Staff

Sample Letter to Students

Dear Lincoln Elementary School Students:

Each of you is very special to us. We want you to be happy at school and to learn all that you possibly can. We have identified five guidelines that will help us all be successful.

Guideline One: Be responsible.

All through your life you must decide how you will act. Therefore, we expect you to do what is right whether anyone is watching you or not. This is called "being responsible." It isn't always easy to make responsible choices, especially if someone else is not being responsible. It is important for you to remember that you are in charge of yourself. You can do what is right!

Guideline Two: Always try.

The best way to learn something new is to practice until you can do it. If you are unwilling to try, you cannot practice. When you first try to do something, it is often difficult, but if you keep trying, it gets easier and easier.

Guideline Three: Do your best.

When you do a job or an assignment, do your very best. While you are working on something, ask yourself, "Is this the best I can do?" If you give a job your best, you learn more and feel more responsible than if you just slide through the job. If you make mistakes, but did your best, your teacher can help you learn from your mistakes.

Guideline Four: Cooperate with others.

Cooperation includes being polite, treating people with respect, accepting differences between people, dealing with disagreements through STP (Stop, Think, Plan), and encouraging others to do their best.

Guideline Five: Treat everyone with dignity and respect.

Everyone must know that Lincoln Elementary is a safe and supportive place to be. Any behavior that could hurt someone else will not be allowed. Treating people with dignity and respect includes such behaviors as being polite, listening to others, following directions, and not engaging in name-calling or teasing.

The staff at Lincoln Elementary will help you achieve success at school. We will do this by helping you solve problems and by protecting your right to learn. We look forward to a good year and are happy to have an opportunity to work with you.

Enjoy a good year!

We have discussed these guidelines.

_____   _____
Student Signature   Parent/Guardian Signature

Assessment and Evaluation Worksheet
(For the "Guiding Principles" section of an SBP)

Note: Use this worksheet for taking notes and identifying implementation ideas as you read this chapter.

1. Do we have some kind of a written statement (e.g., a school mission statement) that succinctly summarizes our school's purpose and its broad-based goals?

   Yes   No

   If **no**, what will be done to see that one is developed? _____

   _____

   _____

   If **yes**, is our mission statement:

User friendly?	Yes	No
Short and simple?	Yes	No
Positive?	Yes	No
Academic and social in focus?	Yes	No
Inclusive?	Yes	No

   If **no** to any of the above, what will be done? _____

   _____

   _____

   What do we do and/or what should we do to ensure that our mission statement is familiar to all staff, students, and parents?

2. Have our staff clarified and agreed upon their beliefs regarding managing student behavior?

   Yes   No

   If **no**, when and how can this be done? _____

   _____

   _____

   If **yes**, how do we answer the following questions:

   Who is responsible for student behavior in our school? _____

   What are the goals of our behavior management efforts? _____

   _____

How can our behavior management goals best be achieved? (What behavior management principles will be most effective in helping us achieve our goals?) _____

_____

What do we do and/or what should we do to ensure that all staff members are aware of our staff beliefs about managing student behavior?

_____

_____

3. Have we, as a school community, identified those attitudes, behaviors, and traits that we believe students should have/demonstrate in order to succeed in school (and/or in life)?

   Yes   No

   If **no**, when and how can this be done? (And how will we ensure parent/student input?) _____

   _____

   _____

   If **yes**, have these attitudes, behaviors, and traits been:

Framed as goals rather than rules?	Yes	No
Summarized in writing (e.g., as guidelines for student success)?	Yes	No

   If **no** to any of the above, what should/can we do? _____

   _____

   _____

   _____

   What do we do and/or what should we do to ensure that these important attitudes, behaviors, and traits are taught to and known by students and parents?

   _____

   _____

   _____

   What do we do and/or what should we do to ensure that these important attitudes, behaviors, and traits are used frequently by staff to provide feedback to students?

   _____

   _____

   _____

chapter seven

Encouragement Procedures—Meeting Students' Basic Needs

This chapter contains information and suggestions for reviewing, revising, and/or developing content for that section of a School-wide Behavior Plan (SBP) pertaining to the positive and proactive procedures that will be used to encourage students to behave responsibly and to be motivated about and engaged in learning activities (e.g., staying on task, completing work, enjoying learning, etc.). This section of an SBP should clearly identify and describe those procedures your staff have agreed to implement to facilitate and reinforce these positive behavioral goals. If your SBP already includes some kind of guidelines for success for students (see the preceding chapter), this section of the SBP should specifically explain how staff will prompt students to strive toward those guidelines and recognize students when they make progress in these efforts. If you have not yet developed guidelines for success, consider doing so prior to, or concurrent with, your work on encouragement procedures.

Section One of this chapter is an explanation of why having an SBP section on encouragement procedures is important. It includes cautions about not implementing positive programs without careful consideration of your particular situation and the particular program. We also recommend that as part of your review of this section of your SBP, you start by listing and evaluating the effectiveness of any encouragement procedures you currently use.

Section Two of the chapter discusses the concept of basic human needs (which was briefly presented in Chapter One: Leadership Skills—Improving School Climate) and makes the case that this section of your SBP should include procedures that address these needs for all students. When a student's basic needs are not met, he/she is less likely to try, academically or socially, at school. Conversely, students whose basic needs are being met are much more likely to strive for success in school. Included in this part of the chapter are tasks that will help you, your Responsibility Team, or a special task force determine whether or not your current procedures/programs are sufficiently meeting the basic needs of your students.

Section Three of this chapter provides information and suggestions on when (and when not) to use schoolwide structured reinforcement systems as part of your SBP encouragement procedures. It includes a series of questions designed to help you systematically evaluate the effectiveness and adequacy of any structured systems you are currently using and/or to guide you in the development of any new schoolwide systems you may be contemplating.

Finally, Section Four consists of a menu of proven procedures/programs for encouraging responsible student behavior. The intent in providing this menu is not to imply that you should use all of the procedures it includes, but to give you a range of possibilities from which you might select those that would be appropriate for your school. The menu items can also be used simply as prompts to help you create your own procedures/programs.

This chapter should be viewed as a structured tool that can be used by whoever (e.g., yourself, a Responsibility Team, or a task force) is responsible for working on proposals to improve this section of your SBP.

Note: For some schools, the Encouragement Procedures section represents a logical starting point for their SBP improvement efforts—particularly if staff have concerns about apathetic and/or unmotivated student behavior and/or about the overall school climate (e.g., many students seem to have little energy and enthusiasm about school and learning). However, when a school has a severe problem with some specific behavior management situation (e.g., restrooms are frequently vandalized, halls seem out of control, staff are angry because they do not feel supported when dealing with severe misbehavior), it probably makes more sense to address the problem(s) before working on encouragement procedures. For example, if your staff do not understand and/or agree on the importance of actively encouraging and motivating students to work hard and behave responsibly, you may first want to clarify your guiding principles (see Chapter Six). Whenever you address this section of your SBP, though, we think you will find that you can improve staff efforts to meet the basic needs of all students and increase your students' levels of motivation, engagement, and responsibility.

section one
Why Have an "Encouragement Procedures" Section in Your SBP?

One major cornerstone of effective behavior management is the use of positive and proactive practices to increase responsible student behavior. (**Note:** By "responsible student behavior," we mean both academic behavior [e.g., staying on task, following directions, working hard, being organized, listening, etc.] and social behavior [e.g., cooperation, managing anger, and treating others with respect].) In order to successfully implement effective behavior management in your building, your staff must not only recognize the need to move away from a predominately punitive approach to discipline, but also understand why and how to actively encourage and motivate students to behave appropriately, independently, and in a manner that leads to academic success. That is why we feel it is essential to have a section in your SBP that clearly identifies and describes those procedures/programs that your staff can and should use to encourage responsible student behavior.

As you begin to review and revise your SBP encouragement procedures, we would like to remind you that in a positive and productive school, staff members actively work to see that every child—regardless of gender, academic ability, or level of maturity: (1) Engages in meaningful activities; (2) Experiences success with those activities; and (3) Receives constructive feedback about his/her social, behavioral, and academic progress. To ensure that your staff efforts will be successful, you need policies/procedures that have been specifically designed to help staff meet students' basic needs. Students whose basic needs are being met are much more likely to be excited about coming to school, excited about learning, and inclined to behave responsibly.

Successfully encouraging and motivating responsible student behavior is not simple, and implementation efforts should not be undertaken mindlessly. The truth is that poorly designed procedures/programs are likely to result in lots of work for staff, but very little benefit in terms of improved student behavior. And, all too often when a school sets up a simple reinforcement system, staff have a tendency to assume that the system is all that's necessary to encourage their students to behave appropriately. Unfortunately, this assumption—that because a procedure is mainly reinforcing it must be good—is naive at best, and at worst is potentially quite damaging.

Consider, for example, a school that establishes a program in which every classroom is to identify a "Student of the Week" to acknowledge students who behave responsibly. Unless staff clearly understand the purpose of the program and have been given sufficient instructions and guidelines for implementing it, several problems could arise. For one thing, some staff may think that because of the program, they do not need to provide any other form of positive feedback or reinforcement. Yet, a program in which only one student per class per week is acknowledged is not likely to motivate many students, particularly the most needy, to behave differently than they otherwise would.

Another potential problem has to do with staff inconsistency. For example, some teachers might award the "Student of the Week" to the same seven or eight students throughout the year—leaving the rest of the students in their classes to soon realize that no matter what they do they will never get to be "Student of the Week"—hardly encouraging or motivating. Other teachers might decide that every student should get to be "Student of the Week" sometime during the year, regardless of whether or not he/she has earned it. As the year progresses, the "Student of the Week" award may actually become a symbol for being irresponsible. Think about the unspoken message conveyed to the last student to receive the award— "Eddie, because we have one week of school left and because you are the only one who has not been 'Student of the Week,' we will now celebrate you as the most responsible student—only because there are no other students left in the room who are less responsible than you!"

This is not to say that using something like a "Student of the Week" program is bad or wrong. In fact, we include one as part of the menu in Section Four of this chapter. We propose, however, that the program's purpose be to acknowledge and celebrate the uniqueness of every student in each class. When the "Student of the Week" award is not contingent upon anything, then everyone will get one and the order will be entirely random. Our message here is that even positive procedures/programs need to be thought through and implemented carefully if they are to accomplish what you intend them to accomplish.

What the Research Says About Encouragement Procedures

Administrators and Teachers Communicate High Expectations to Students and Recognize Excellent Performance on a Schoolwide Basis.

Administrators and Teachers

- Communicate warmth and caring to all students by learning their names and something about their strengths, interests, and needs.

- Exhibit warmth and caring for each other in the presence of students to provide a model for them.

- Communicate to students that they are important and valued through providing activities to develop good health habits and self-esteem, as well as prevention activities regarding dropping out, pregnancy, drugs, and violence.

- Recognize and reward excellence in achievement and behavior. They ensure that requirements for awards are clear, that explicit procedures are used, and that evaluations are based on standards rather than comparisons with peers.

- Provide opportunities for all students to excel in their areas of strength and receive recognition.

- Match incentives and rewards to student developmental levels, ensuring that they are meaningful to recipients and structured to build persistence of effort and intrinsic motivation.

- Allow older students considerable opportunity to manage their own learning and provide input into school policies and operations.

Amabile, Hennessy, and Grossman (1987); Anderson, C.S. (1985); Bain and Jacobs (1990); Boyd (1992); Cantrell and Cantrell (1993); Cotton (1989c, 1990a, 1991b); DeBevoise (1984); Dryfoos (1990); Duke (1989); Fenley, et al. (1993); Gottfredson, D.C., and Gottfredson (1989); Gottfredson, D.C., Gottfredson, and Hybl (1993); Gottfried and Gottfried (1991); Kearns (1988); Keedy (1992); Levine and Eubanks (1989); Murphy and Hallinger (1985); Paredes and Frazer (1992); Sammons, Hillman, and Mortimore (1994); Shann (1990); Stiller and Ryan (1992); Wilson-Brewer, et al. (1991); Woods (1995).

The above material is reprinted with permission from *Effective Schooling Practices: A Research Synthesis, 1995 Update*. This excellent summary of school and teacher effectiveness literature was compiled by Kathleen Cotton. To order copies of this resource, call or write:

Document Reproduction Service
Northwest Regional Educational Laboratory
101 S.W. Main Street, Suite 500
Portland, Oregon 97204
(503) 275-9519

Take Action!

Determine whether your school's current positive practices are purposeful and effective in encouraging and motivating students.

Start by listing all the procedures/programs you currently use in your school to foster responsible and motivated student behavior. (In our example, we have included Student of the Week, Foster Grandparents, and Positive Recognition assemblies.) For each procedure/program that you list, determine whether it is effective in encouraging responsible and motivated student behavior and then make implementation recommendations for it (e.g., "maintain as is," "eliminate it," "modify it," or "expand it"). You may be surprised to find that one or more of your procedures, even those that have been in place for many years, do not have a clear purpose and/or are not really working effectively. It is strongly recommended that unless a procedure/program has some clear benefit, you consider modifying or eliminating it. (**Note:** If any of your procedures is a schoolwide structured reinforcement system, you should also consider how well it meets the guidelines for such systems, which are outlined in Section Three of this chapter.)

Sample:

Name of Practice	Does it Effectively Encourage Responsibility or Motivation?	Recommendations
Student of the Week (good behavior)	Not really. Mainly used with students who tend to already be motivated to behave well.	Maybe modify, so it's not contingent. Purpose would be to meet attention and belonging needs of all students.
Foster Grandparents	Very effective for at-risk students.	**Wish we could expand it!**
Positive Recognition assemblies	Seems to be effective for most students.	May need to spice them up a bit—they're getting pretty routine.

Worksheet 1
Evaluation of Current Encouragement Procedures

Name of Practice	Does it Effectively Encourage Responsibility or Motivation?	Recommendations

section two
Meeting Students' Basic Needs

Chapter One: Leadership Skills—Improving School Climate stated the belief that students (as all of us) have certain basic psychological/social needs, and that effective behavior management practices will take those basic needs into account. The reason, in addition to the fact that meeting students' basic needs is a fundamentally humane thing to do, is fairly simple: When the needs of any individual student are not being met, there is a higher probability that the student will engage in misbehavior to get those needs met. For example, a student who is not getting the attention she needs may engage in misbehavior because she has discovered that when she breaks the rules adults pay attention to her. On the other hand, when a school strives to meet its students' basic needs, there is a greater likelihood that its students will strive to behave responsibly and be motivated to do their very best. Therefore, we suggest that your policies/procedures for encouraging responsible behavior be designed so that they address the basic needs of your students.

In the remainder of this section, we identify and explain several important basic needs. We have also included information on why and how each need can be met. In addition, at the very end of the chapter is a six-page reproducible worksheet that provides a structure for analyzing the degree to which your school's procedures and programs meet the various needs of all students. Make a copy of the worksheet for each person working on this basic needs evaluation (e.g., the members of the Responsibility Team or the task force assigned to this topic) and encourage them to keep the worksheet in front of them as they work through the remainder of Section Two of this chapter.

The purpose of taking such a close look at your efforts to meet students' basic needs is to help you more accurately identify both what you are doing well and what you need to do better. For example, you may think that you are doing a good job of meeting students' needs for recognition; however, upon closer consideration, you realize that although the academically high-performing and academically low-performing students are regularly recognized for their academic achievements, the academically average-performing students get little recognition for their academic performance, and that neither well-behaving nor misbehaving students receive sufficient recognition for their behavioral achievements.

Before beginning your examination of the degree to which students' basic needs are being met in your school, identify individual students who represent specified categories. The following table (which is included on the reproducible worksheet at the end of the chapter) should be filled out with the names of 12 specific students. Each member of the group doing this analysis can have different students in mind. Thus a primary teacher will put in the names of primary students he knows, while an intermediate teacher will be thinking about the students that she knows.

Sample Basic Needs Analysis Worksheet

Students I think about while conducting the analysis:

	Academically High-Performing Students	Academically Average-Performing Students	Academically Low-Performing Students
Students who consistently behave responsibly	Male: Jeff Miller Female: Mary Fernandez	Male: Adam Wright Female: Linda Davenport	Male: Mike Howard Female: Anna Sanders
Students who have trouble behaving responsibly	Male: John Fredrickson Female: Tina Ryan	Male: Peter Douglas Female: Kim Roberts	Male: Aaron Baker Female: Dana Matthews

As you work through the rest of the basic needs worksheet, you can consider whether each basic need is being met for each representative student you have identified. If you find that there is nothing in place for addressing one or more of these needs for any of your representative students, then you should come up with recommendations for how staff might meet that need. (**Note:** To help you with this, for each basic need, we have identified relevant procedures and/or programs from the menu in Section Four of this chapter that you may wish to review.)

The Need for Recognition

Note: As you read this section, be sure to have a copy of the Basic Needs Analysis Worksheet (at the end of this chapter) on hand.

Students have a basic need to have their accomplishments, both academic and social, recognized. When a student who is learning something new (again, either academic or behavioral) only receives correction on her unsuccessful efforts, but no recognition of her successes, she is likely to become discouraged. On the other hand, a student who is recognized for her accomplishments will generally be more motivated to keep trying. In addition, when you provide a student with information about what she is doing right, as well as what she is doing wrong, you help her *learn* to do whatever task she is trying to do better.

For your school to successfully motivate students to behave responsibly, you need to make sure that every student receives meaningful positive feedback about his/her academic performance *and* the behaviors that facilitate his/her academic and social growth. In order to ensure that all children, from the most able to the least able and from the most responsible to the least responsible, receive recognition for their efforts to learn and grow, you will probably need to have a variety of procedures in place.

Let's look at academic recognition first. In most schools, the highest performing students receive lots of recognition (or reinforcement) for their academic achievements—getting teacher praise (verbally and as notes on their work), getting good grades, being on the honor roll, having their work submitted to science fairs and writing contests, enjoying parental acknowledgment, etc. Because it is important for schools to foster and celebrate academic excellence, your school should have structured activities, such as an honor roll, Olympics of the Mind, science fairs, spelling bees, mental math competitions, and so on, which allow your academic stars to shine. Unfortunately, the downside to things such as honor rolls and district spelling bees is that they immediately exclude about 90% of your student population. Thus, for the majority of students, who know they will never be on the honor roll or get the chance to go to a district spelling bee, these programs tend not to be motivating. This does not mean that you shouldn't use them, just that they are insufficient to motivate all your students.

Most schools need to take special care to ensure that their academically average- and low-performing students receive sufficient positive feedback on their accomplishments. Although these less able students actually do many things successfully, because their efforts do not yield the outstanding results achieved by their more able peers, they often go unrecognized. Think carefully about whether you are adequately motivating students of average and below average academic ability to do their best and encouraging them to take pride in the progress they are making. If you are not, you may want to consider adopting specific policies/procedures for recognizing the academic progress of average- and low-performing students.

It is also possible for a somewhat reverse pattern to be present. That is, sometimes a school can go overboard recognizing the achievements of its lowest students, leaving the average and highest performing students without adequate positive feedback on their efforts. Both of these distribution patterns are problematic. As a staff, you want to make sure every student receives recognition for his/her academic progress and accomplishments—keeping in mind that the students' levels of need for recognition will not necessarily be equal. Some students (usually those most secure and independent) do fine with infrequent recognition, while others (usually lower-performing and/or insecure students) tend to quickly become unmotivated if they do not receive recognition frequently enough. And you need to make sure that the needs of your academically average students are being met, because it's easy for these students to just fade into the woodwork.

Recognizing students' behavioral achievements can present similar dilemmas. For example, it is not uncommon for school staff to find that they do not regularly acknowledge the ongoing motivation and responsibility of their students who are consistently well behaved. Yet, even the student who never misbehaves needs to have someone at school occasionally look him in the eye and sincerely say something like, "Bryan, you are such a hard worker and are so responsible. You are truly a model for the other students." Your goal should be to ensure that every child who consistently behaves well receives information (occasionally) from staff members that his/her responsibility is noticed.

At the other end of the spectrum are the students who frequently have trouble behaving responsibly. What often happens to these students is that they don't get any recognition when they *do* make an effort to manage their behavior. If you are going to effectively motivate students who occasionally (or frequently) misbehave to do better, it is essential that those students receive recognition when they behave responsibly. If your "behavior problem" students are going to learn that behaving responsibly feels good, all staff members will have to make a concerted effort to increase the number of times they "catch" and recognize these students when they are engaged in responsible social (and academic) behavior.

As you consider procedures/programs for meeting students' basic needs for recognition, the key is to focus on all students. Every student should have his/her behavioral and academic accomplishments recognized in a variety of ways.

The Need for Acknowledgment

Note: As you read this section, be sure to have a copy of the Basic Needs Analysis Worksheet (at the end of this chapter) on hand.

All students have a fundamental need to be acknowledged—simply because they exist—not for what they do or who they are. This need, which involves individuals knowing that their presence, their feelings, and their thoughts are important to others, can be met through friendly greetings, simple interactions, and asking questions like, "How do you feel about …?" "What do you think about …?" Unlike recognition, your acknowledgment of students should not be contingent upon any specific accomplishments. Whether a student had a good or bad day on Monday, he/she should be greeted warmly and acknowledged as a center of staff interest on Tuesday (and every day).

When the adults in a school show interest in each individual student by smiling at, making eye contact with, saying hello to, and just talking to that student, they are meeting the student's need for acknowledgment. Consider the message that is conveyed to a student when a teacher walks with her down the hall and asks her about her interests and/or shares information about what he (the teacher) was interested in at the same age. The key here is that the interactions should not be contingent upon anything and that every student should receive some kind of adult acknowledgment at school every day.

Think about the difference for students in the following two hypothetical schools. School A has a plethora of fabulous rewards and certificates that students can earn (recognition), but the adults rarely say hello to, smile at, or otherwise interact informally with students. In School B, along with having their academic and behavioral accomplishments recognized, all the children who enter the school in the morning have contact with at least one or two adults who smile and say hello to them as they head toward their classrooms. As they enter their classrooms their teachers say things like, "Rachel, good morning. How did your team do in that soccer game last week?" In the cafeteria, a lunchroom supervisor might say, "John, you were absent yesterday. We missed you. Are you feeling better?"

William James, in *The Principles of Psychology* states that, "No more fiendish punishment could be desired, were such a thing physically possible, than that one be turned loose in society and remain absolutely unnoticed by all the members thereof." You need to make sure that your staff is committed to seeing that no individual child remains unnoticed.

The Need for Attention

Note: As you read this section, be sure to have a copy of the Basic Needs Analysis Worksheet (at the end of this chapter) on hand.

Students need adult attention (i.e., interactions with and/or responses from the adults in the school). This need for attention is one of quantity rather than quality, and although for most students it is met through recognition and acknowledgment, for some students it is also met through reprimands, scolding, arguing, and so on. A student with a high need for attention who is not receiving frequent enough recognition and acknowledgment may engage in misbehavior to force adults to *pay attention* to her. What staff need to understand is that their minute-by-minute interactions with students are extremely important in meeting students' basic need for attention. They also need to realize that while acknowledgment and recognition will meet most students' basic needs for attention, the truly needy student may have learned that it is easier to get his attention needs met by misbehaving than by behaving responsibly.

One particular group of students who may not be getting its needs for attention met includes students who typically have trouble behaving responsibly. These are often the students who most need attention, but the attention they get from adults tends to be in response to their misbehavior rather than as noncontingent and friendly interactions and contingent recognition. Think about it from their perspective: If they don't get any attention from adults when they're not engaged in misbehavior, why not misbehave—being in trouble is better than not being noticed at all. Many times in these cases, staff are actually reinforcing the students for misbehaving, albeit inadvertently.

What's important is that each student's sum total of positive interactions (recognition and acknowledgment) should be far greater than his/her total of negative interactions (i.e., staff actions in response to his/her misbehavior). Ensuring that all students have more positive than negative interactions with adults demonstrates to students, especially those starved for attention, that it is easier to get attention with responsible behavior than with misbehavior.

The Need for Belonging

Note: As you read this section, be sure to have a copy of the Basic Needs Analysis Worksheet (at the end of this chapter) on hand.

Being a part of something bigger than oneself (e.g., belonging to a family, church, social group, club, or company) is as important to students as it is to adults. Because students spend such a significant number of hours in school, they need to feel that they "belong" at their school. If they feel alienated in their school setting because of peer rejection, shyness, poor social skills, having changed schools frequently, or even because of parents who relate negatively to the school, they are likely to be less motivated to try at school. Some may become overtly antagonistic. And some, unfortunately, may even turn to gangs in a desperate attempt to belong somewhere.

You need to consider whether all of your students feel as if they are a part of the school. If you have high-performing students who are ostracized as "geeks and nerds," lower-performing students who feel categorized as "dummies," chronically misbehaving students who constantly act as if they are at war with the school, and/or students who seem to be "outcasts," then you need to do something.

One way to meet students' needs for belonging is to build school spirit. For example, to create the sense that every individual (student, staff member, and parent) is an important part of an important place—your school. Rituals and traditions can be very effective in fostering a strong sense of community (see Chapter One: Leadership Skills—Improving School Climate). In addition, you should make sure that all students have opportunities to contribute positively to the school. A program like the one explained in Volume III: Meaningful Work provides an excellent means of involving students in their school community. Middle school students might also be encouraged to participate in some sort of community service.

The Need for Competence

Note: As you read this section, be sure to have a copy of the Basic Needs Analysis Worksheet (at the end of this chapter) on hand.

It's human nature to seek out tasks and activities that we enjoy and avoid activities that we do not enjoy. One big factor influencing how much we enjoy something is our competence at it. Therefore, most of us tend to enjoy, and seek out, those things at which we are good. In school, where academic growth is a priority, students have little choice about engaging in academic tasks (and we do not mean to imply that they should). However, if a teaching staff is not providing instruction that leads to competence for all students, some children may constantly face tasks that seem impossible. These students, like anyone who is consistently required to perform tasks that lead to frustration and failure, will eventually grow discouraged. Some will withdraw and others will engage in (mis)behavior that helps them avoid those tasks at which they continually fail. Part of your staff's efforts to encourage and motivate students to behave responsibly must include using effective instructional strategies that lead to student competence.

Most affected in terms of this basic need are probably your academically low-performing students. If you have students who regularly fail to experience competence on the tasks they are asked to perform (e.g., they cannot read), you need to make arrangements to remediate their academic deficits and/or make adaptations in their assignments to increase their success rates. Another group for whom not having their competence needs met can lead to behavioral problems are the very gifted students. When these students are not sufficiently challenged (i.e., they do not feel as if they accomplish anything at school), they may become bored and seek other ways to find excitement.

The Need for Nurturing

Note: As you read this section, be sure to have a copy of the Basic Needs Analysis Worksheet (at the end of this chapter) on hand.

Nurturing is not one single event. Ideally it consists of unconditional love given to an individual from birth until death. Ideally it is communicated by daily expressions of warmth, affection, security, and protection that a person knows will never go away—even in times of crises or anger. A nurturing relationship has been described, metaphorically, as "an anchor in the storm," a "safe harbor," and as "the wind beneath one's wings." Children require a great deal of nurturing, and ongoing nurturing helps children develop self-confidence and independence.

Most students will get the majority of their nurturing needs met in their home environments. For these students, the need for nurturing at school can be met with friendly interactions from a caring and inviting staff. However, as sad as it may seem, nearly all schools today have at least some (and maybe many) students who do not get sufficient nurturing at home. These children have no "anchor in the storm," no "safe harbor," and no "wind beneath their wings"—and their behavior often appears chaotic. For example, a student might fly into rages for no apparent reason or become withdrawn despite repeated efforts to include her.

A school can never fully compensate for the lack of a nurturing home environment; however, you should have procedures in place for trying to meet the needs of such students to the extent that you can. (**Note:** This does not mean you should lower your behavioral expectations, or enable such students to continue their chaotic behavior. On the contrary, schools must maintain high expectations for the behavior of all children—even those whose home environments are lacking. It does, however, mean that your staff should be on the watch for children who need nurturing, and that you should have resources/procedures available to help meet these students' basic needs for nurturing.)

Some students may need gender specific nurturing. For example, a student whose mother is in the military and who has no other significant females (e.g., a grandmother) in her day-to-day life, may need a relationship with an adult female—even though she receives significant nurturing from her father.

Another thing to keep in mind is that when a student who comes from a non-nurturing home is chronically engaging in irresponsible behavior, the student's need for nurturing may be so great that he actually sabotages all the positive efforts to motivate him to behave responsibly (without even being aware of why). To help this student improve his behavior, you may need to find him an adult mentor with whom he can foster a positive relationship across a period of years.

The Need for Purpose

Note: As you read this section, be sure to have a copy of the Basic Needs Analysis Worksheet (at the end of this chapter) on hand.

Students need to feel that the time they spend in school has a reason. Every student needs to know that there is some purpose in working hard, in behaving in ways that do not interfere with the learning of others, in contributing something of themselves to the community called school. Without this sense of purpose, a student (and even the student's parent[s]) may view school as little more than killing time. For a student with a sense of purpose, however, daily actions and responsible choices assume greater importance because each action and each choice contributes to a bigger purpose.

Ideally, your school mission statement will clarify for students and parents, as well as staff, the school's overall purpose and each individual's purpose as part of the school. If one assumes that school is to students what jobs are to adults, then it is up to staff to help children engage in meaningful "careers"—not just endure boring, menial work. This includes making sure students (justifiably) view assignments as important steps in gaining important skills rather than as simply busywork. For middle school students, it may involve participating in some sort of community service that helps them begin to understand the purpose and benefits of altruism.

The Need for Stimulation/Change

Note: As you read this section, be sure to have a copy of the Basic Needs Analysis Worksheet (at the end of this chapter) on hand.

People need variety in their lives. This is true for students as well as adults. In order for school to be a place where students are excited about what they are doing, enthusiastic about growing, and interested in learning more about life and the world they live in, their classes must be stimulating. If classes are dull and predictable, no system of encouraging and motivating is likely to foster excitement, enthusiasm, or interest. As with the need for competence, meeting the need for stimulation/change is related, at least partially, to effective instructional practices. It also involves, in part, implementing positive policies/procedures that do not become overly routine.

For example, if you use monthly awards assemblies to acknowledge the accomplishments of individual students and/or staff, but all the assemblies are the same, it is likely that by Spring everyone will be bored by them. You need to plan ways of creating variety. When the awards assemblies at one elementary school start to feel dull, the principal (who is one of this book's authors) informs the student body that a substitute will be emceeing the next assembly. At the next assembly, she dresses in costume (for example, a cowboy outfit) and runs the entire assembly in character (with accent and everything!). The older students get a kick out of it because they realize it is the principal; the younger students aren't sure who it is but are excited about having a cowboy lead the assembly—and everyone enjoys themselves. Such a simple change keeps an important school ritual fun and exciting.

The "Encouragement Procedures" section of your SBP should include procedures and/or programs that ensure your students' basic needs will be met. If it does, there is a high probability that your students will be enthusiastic about coming to school and will strive to be successful. Section Four of this chapter contains numerous ideas for procedures/programs that you might want to include in your SBP.

section three
Using Schoolwide Reinforcement Systems

Occasionally it can be useful to implement a structured reinforcement system on a school-wide basis. If a school has a high percentage of students at risk for academic and/or behavioral problems, for example, it can be difficult for staff to meet students' basic needs (e.g., for acknowledgment, attention, etc.) through friendly interactions and positive feedback alone. Or, if a student body behaves responsibly on the whole but has problems with one particular inappropriate behavior (e.g., running in the halls) or in one particular part of the school (e.g., the cafeteria), a schoolwide structured reinforcement system may be helpful.

One thing to avoid is implementing a schoolwide system when the problem behavior actually involves only a small number of students (4%-5% of the student body). In this case, not only will a schoolwide system probably prove ineffective with the students for whom it is primarily intended (they will rarely earn rewards because the reinforcers are not likely to be powerful or immediate enough to get them to abandon their misbehavior), but it can also have a negative impact on the other 96% of the students. These students will start getting (and may eventually start expecting) "rewards" for the responsible behavior that they were exhibiting already. If you have only a small number of students who continually have trouble behaving responsibly, it makes much more sense to develop comprehensive individual plans for those students. See Volume II: Referrals and Solutions for information on setting up individualized plans.

When a schoolwide structured reinforcement system does seem appropriate, you want to make sure it allows a great deal of flexibility for staff to encourage positive behavior. Students' needs for acknowledgment vary, and systems that are designed to reward all students in exactly the same way tend to be problematic. In an effective system, staff will *occasionally* congratulate students who are consistently responsible, and *frequently* acknowledge the responsible behavior of those students with the greatest tendency to misbehave. (**Note:** see menu items: Golden Tickets, CARE, Goal Achieved! Book, Responsible student behavior system, Principal's Award, and Attendance/punctuality letter for examples of effective systems.)

There are a number of important considerations to keep in mind regarding schoolwide structured reinforcement systems. Foremost is that the system must be inclusionary. That is, it needs to be designed so that the students who generally get the least amount of positive recognition for their behavior (possibly because they do not demonstrate a lot of responsible behavior to recognize) have a good chance of earning rewards for improvements in their behavior. Other important considerations include the following:

1. **The system should reward** *the presence of positive behavior rather than the absence of negative behavior.*

    A system that rewards students for not misbehaving sends the wrong message. The purpose of a structured reinforcement system is to reward students for something that they accomplish—rather than for not misbehaving (or perhaps for not getting caught misbehaving). Remember, you want students to learn that you recognize when they behave responsibly, and that they will be acknowledged for their responsible behavior.

2. **The system should not require students to work for overly long periods of time in order to earn a reward.**

    When a structured reinforcement system is necessary, the chances are that at least some of the students involved will have trouble connecting their immediate behavior to an incentive that is too far into the future.

3. **The system should avoid an all-or-nothing type incentive structure (which can also be linked to time requirements).**

    A system in which students are rewarded for earning a certain number of points within a specific time period can actually work as a disincentive for students who have trouble meeting the criteria. For example, say a student who has a severe problem getting to school on time is placed on a system in which he can earn a privilege if he arrives at school on time every day for a week. Think about what happens if the student is tardy only on Friday morning. At the end of what may be the best week this particular student has ever had, he does not get rewarded. Or, consider what happens if the student is tardy on Tuesday. Since at that point the system has lost all its power to motivate (because the student already knows that he won't be getting his privilege that week), what's the incentive for trying to be on time the rest of the week. A better structure for this system would be to say that each day the student arrives on time, he earns one point. When he accumulates five points (which may take five days or 16 days), he earns the reward.

4. **The system should use reinforcers that are as close to intrinsic rewards as possible, yet will still serve to motivate students.**

    Intrinsic reward occurs when a person is inherently motivated by something about the task itself. For example, avid readers read because they enjoy stories and/or learning new information. Bicyclists cycle because they enjoy the feeling they get riding their bikes and/or like getting exercise and/or appreciate seeing the scenery, and so on. Extrinsic rewards, on the other hand, are things outside a task that motivate a person to engage in that task. Praise, award certificates, rewards, paychecks, and diplomas are all examples of extrinsic rewards. When an individual is motivated by intrinsic rewards to engage in a certain behavior, he or she is more likely to engage in that behavior even when there are no extrinsic rewards present.

    It is important to keep in mind that extrinsic rewards are not bad or wrong. In fact, they are part of how our society is organized, and most people do things because of a mix of intrinsic and extrinsic rewards. Consider, for example, people who work primarily to earn paychecks (an extrinsic reward), but go to their particular jobs because they find them challenging or fulfilling or interesting (all intrinsic rewards). Or, consider people who exercise only because their doctor said they needed to lose weight, but who choose a particular form of exercise because they enjoy it more than others.

5. **The system should use rewards that have as little monetary value and as much information value as possible.**

Using expensive rewards as incentives can be problematic. For example, there will be a tendency to require students to work for long periods of time to earn them. As noted earlier, the students who most need this type of system may be too immature to be sufficiently motivated to give up their irresponsible behavior for the possibility of a future reward. Another problem with rewards with high monetary value is they may increase negative traits (e.g., jealousy, excessive competitiveness, greed, lying to get the reward, and so on).

An example of a reinforcer with high monetary value would be giving out tickets for responsible hallway behavior that students can trade in on ice cream. To decrease the monetary value and increase the information value of this reinforcer, you could give students tickets for responsible hallway behavior that they take back to their classrooms, where they are then glued to a chart. When a classroom's chart is filled with 100 tickets, the principal could come in to congratulate the class on their responsible behavior. While both systems described would probably improve student awareness of and motivation to behave safely and responsibly in the halls, the latter system is preferable because it is more likely to lead to the students maintaining their appropriate hallway behavior when the system is removed.

6. **Make sure staff focus more on what the students accomplish than on what they earn.**

It can be easy, when implementing a reward system to acknowledge responsible behavior, for staff to fall into the habit of focusing on what students are getting rather than on what they are doing. "Allen, you have earned three 'Golden Tickets' this week. You have a great chance to win the drawing for the radio." In an effective structured reinforcement system, the adults act excited about and communicate to students precisely what the students did to earn the reward—in fact, the reward will almost seem like an afterthought. "Allen, you have been so responsible about completing and turning in your homework. Consistently being responsible for your work will really help you be successful in high school. By the way, here is a 'Golden Ticket' for making such good choices."

7. **The system should incorporate strategies that ensure that staff and students will maintain their levels of excitement and interest.**

An inherent problem with reinforcement systems is that they are, by definition, systematic. Consequently, they can have a tendency to become routine to the point of being boring. If staff implementation of a reinforcement system becomes pro forma (i.e., they just go through the motions), students soon lose interest in the system as well. This means, of course, that students also lose their motivation to try and earn the system's reward (and, consequently, their motivation to behave responsibly). One way to avoid this problem is to limit the length of time a system will run. An important feature of the CARE program is that it runs for only four weeks at a time—but is used two or three times during the year. This is done deliberately, to keep the system fresh and effective.

Another way of preventing boredom or disinterest is to build enough variety into the system that staff and students can stay at least somewhat excited about using it. For example, one elementary school has an "Awards Assembly" every month. But, each month the assembly has a different theme (e.g., Respect, Perseverance, Fitness) and is hosted by a different intermediate class. The hosting class is encouraged to be creative in designing and running the assembly.

Take Action!

1. Consider the following items related to schoolwide structured reinforcement systems. First, you will decide whether your school might benefit from such a system. Remember, you are best off using such a schoolwide structured reinforcement system only when behavioral problems involve a large percentage of your student body. If a structured system seems advisable (or if you already have a system in place), you can then work through the remaining items as a way of evaluating the features of your possible or current system. Please note that these items represent guidelines. They are considerations that can help make a system more effective, but they are not meant to be followed rigidly. For example, if your school has been borderline out of control and recently adopted a system in which every student who does not misbehave during a week gets to attend an ice-cream party on Friday—and things are improving—you should continue using your system as it is, and perhaps consider implementing our guidelines once the situation is under control.

Evaluation of Schoolwide Structured Reinforcement System	*Please circle yes or no.*	
Would your students benefit from a schoolwide structured reinforcement system? That is, do you have large numbers of students who are not now or are not likely to be encouraged or motivated to behave responsibly solely by general staff efforts to meet their basic needs?	Y	N
If **yes**, carefully consider the following guidelines in the design of the system (or the evaluation of the current system).		
• The system rewards the presence of positive behavior rather than the absence of negative behavior.	Y	N
• The system does not require students to work for long periods of time in order to earn a reward.	Y	N
• The system avoids an all-or-nothing incentive structure.	Y	N
• The system uses reinforcers that are as close to intrinsic rewards as possible.	Y	N
• The system uses rewards that have as little monetary value and as much information value as possible.	Y	N
• Staff have been/will be reminded to focus more on what the students have accomplished than on what they have earned.	Y	N
• The system incorporates strategies that ensure that staff and students will maintain reasonable levels of interest and excitement.	Y	N

2. After you have evaluated and modified (or designed from scratch) your schoolwide reinforcement system, prepare an implementation plan that addresses staff training.

Menu of Procedures/Programs to Encourage Responsible Behavior

This supplement consists of a comprehensive listing (i.e., a menu) of proven procedures and programs for encouraging students to behave responsibly. You should view it as you would a restaurant menu. That is, you selectively choose those procedures/programs that fit your needs and are most appropriate for your situation.

In addition to noting the basic need(s)—indicated in bold—that a particular procedure/program is intended to address, each item briefly describes what the procedure/program is, what its objective is, and how to implement it. For each item that you identify as potentially useful for your school, you can decide whether it can be used as described in the menu, or if (and how) you want to modify it. (**Note:** Most of the items would be appropriate for both elementary and middle schools. Those that seem to be primarily for one level or the other, as presented, should be evaluated to see whether they can be modified for the other level.)

1. Effective Instructional Practices

What is it?

Children thrive in environments in which they are actively engaged in meaningful, challenging, and interesting tasks and activities. If these tasks lead to mastery of important instructional objectives, students will experience increased competence in progressively more complex and useful tasks. On the other hand, exposing students to boring and/or meaningless tasks is very destructive to motivation. Given the ability and interest level differences in any group of students, though, the job of creating interesting, yet not frustrating, lessons, tasks, and activities is extremely difficult. Thus, implementing effective instructional practices is an ongoing challenge that requires a commitment to continual learning on the part of teachers.

What is its objective?

Effective instructional practices involve teachers creating lessons and activities to meet students' basic need for **stimulation** and striving to keep students actively engaged in mastering important objectives. They mean designing classroom expectations and activities so that every child experiences **competence**, a sense of **purpose** and of **stimulation/change** in the classroom. One of the goals of effective instructional practices is that staff work together so that each year students are fully prepared to meet the expectations and challenges of the next year.

How do you do it?

Every year certified staff need to make an effort to increase their skills in the immensely complex task of implementing effective instructional practices. Among other things, this can be done by employing long-range calendar planning, identifying important objectives for each instructional unit, providing direct instruction and practice for mastery of important objectives, adapting instruction to help low-performing students achieve mastery, designing lessons that create maximal interest and variety, and by presenting lessons and tasks in a manner that is interesting and fun.

2. Adult-Student Interactions

What is it?

One of the most important means of encouraging responsible behavior in students is for the adults in the school to instigate frequent, positive interactions with them. The nature of these positive interactions can include greeting students, talking to students, making eye contact with students, smiling at students, overtly praising students, and engaging in other forms of recognizing students.

What is its objective?

The goal with adult-student interactions is for students to have at least three times as many interactions with adults when they are behaving responsibly as they have when they are being corrected for some aspect of their behavior. These frequent, friendly interactions with adults will help meet students' needs for **recognition**, **acknowledgment**, **attention**, **belonging**, **nurturing**, and **competence**.

How do you do it?

Staff need to make a conscious effort to take every opportunity to interact with individual students in all school environments. They can greet students in the halls. In the cafeteria, they can talk to students as they are standing in line. Before class begins, they can ask individual students in their class(es) about their interests. All staff should look for opportunities to provide students with positive feedback about their academic and behavioral progress. When praising students, staff should provide specific information about which behaviors are contributing to their successes. "Alicia, you have been very responsible about remembering your homework on the day it is due." "Tyronne, I noticed you picking up litter in the hall. As custodian, I really appreciate your helping and taking pride in how this school looks."

3. Special Attention for Targeted Students

What is it?

When a student exhibits chronic misbehavior, it can be difficult for that student's classroom teacher to maintain a 3:1 ratio of positive to negative interactions—because so many of the student's behaviors need to be corrected. If other staff members make an overt effort to greet this student, talk to the student, and praise the student, as a staff you can increase the number of positive interactions the student has with adults—and make it easier to achieve the 3:1 goal.

What is its objective?

The goal of this procedure is to increase the number of staff who specifically seek and take the opportunity to have positive interactions with the student. This makes it more likely that the individual's needs for **attention**, **acknowledgment**, **belonging**, **nurturing**, and **competence** will be met, which very well may reduce the student's need to misbehave in order to get these needs met.

How do you do it?

Once it becomes obvious that a student has a pattern of misbehavior, that student's classroom teacher needs to discuss the problem with the principal. Together they can decide whether to ask all staff to make a conscious effort to interact positively with the student. As various staff members do this, the student's ratio of positive to negative interactions with adults will increase dramatically.

4. Positive Reports to Parents

What is it?

In addition to any regularly scheduled parent contacts (conferences and report cards), staff make a point of frequently reporting to parents the positive behavioral and academic accomplishments of their students. While some of the time, they simply make a phone call—other times they use the highly effective procedure of sending "Congratulations!" postcards (see the following figure) that specify the student's academic or behavioral accomplishment.

What is its objective?

The purpose of this program is to provide parents with information that allows them to give their children additional **recognition**, **attention**, **acknowledgment**, sense of **purpose**, and sense of **competence**. A simple communication device like a postcard can increase parents' perceptions that staff are trying to work with them as partners in creating a positive and productive school experience for their children.

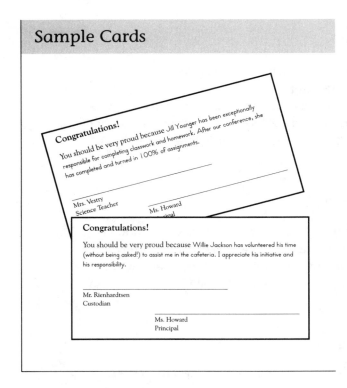

Sample Cards

Congratulations!
You should be very proud because Jill Younger has been exceptionally responsible for completing classwork and homework. After our conference, she has completed and turned in 100% of assignments.

_____

Mrs. Vestry
Science Teacher

Ms. Howard
Principal

Congratulations!
You should be very proud because Willie Jackson has volunteered his time (without being asked!) to assist me in the cafeteria. I appreciate his initiative and his responsibility.

_____

Mr. Rienhardtsen
Custodian

_____

Ms. Howard
Principal

How do you do it?

Every staff member should be given a supply of "Congratulations!" postcards. Then, when any individual staff member wishes to acknowledge the specific accomplishment of a particular student, the staff member simply fills out the informational side of the postcard, signs it, and turns it in to the office. Office staff have the principal sign the card, make a copy of it for the classroom teacher to keep on file, address it, and mail it.

If a card is filled out by someone other than the student's classroom/homeroom teacher (e.g., the custodian), the classroom teacher should be given a copy after the card has been sent and encouraged to verbally congratulate the student. In addition, classroom/homeroom teachers should keep track of which students have received cards so that as a term draws to a close, they can make an effort to find something relevant and send a "Congratulations!" card to any students who have not received at least one.

5. Mentorship

What is it?

Adult volunteers (e.g., from the staff, the school's business partners, the neighborhood retirement home, etc.) are paired with individual students who it has been determined would benefit from a friendly, nurturing, one-on-one relationship with an adult. Mentors meet with the students on school grounds and during school hours at least once a week. Activities can include, but are not limited to, having lunch together, playing a game, participating with the student in class activities or projects, or just taking a walk. Activities that will occur during class time must be approved by the classroom teacher. Mentor-student contact outside of school hours and/or off school grounds must be scheduled through the office and should involve at least two mentor/student pairs together (to reduce any potential for or appearance of impropriety).

What is its objective?

Mentorship is a way of providing one-to-one **nurturing** relationships to give students **acknowledgment** and **attention**. Students who do not have nurturing home situations, and even some students who do, often benefit from having a caring adult who consistently meets with and shows an interest in them. The one-on-one activities can be something a student eagerly anticipates and may help meet that student's need for **stimulation/change** and sense of **belonging**.

How do you do it?

Each year the counselor (or a Teacher Assistance Team, for example) identifies students who may benefit from a mentoring relationship. They will probably be students who have patterns of chronic misbehavior or absenteeism, chronically appear withdrawn or shy, and/or who have been recommended by their teachers. The counselor then seeks out volunteers from the staff, business partners, a nearby retirement home, and so on. Before being accepted as mentors, volunteers should be informed that the mentor relationships need to be maintained for at least one full school year. The counselor should also arrange for and conduct a training session with the mentors at the beginning of the school year and then again in January (as a follow-up).

Note: Be sure your mentorship program has some form of screening of mentors to ensure that no student could be paired with a mentor who might in any way harm the student.

6. Homework Room

Note: The following description, which is for a middle school, can be easily adapted for the elementary level.

What is it?

One classroom is opened for 30 minutes or so before school, during lunch, and after school for students who want a quiet place to work on their homework. It is a quiet, invitational environment to which students can choose to go. Teachers cannot assign students to go to the homework room (i.e., it is not to be used as a consequence for not completing work). The homework room is staffed with individuals (e.g., one or two paid paraprofessionals, student volunteers from a nearby high school, parent volunteers) who can answer students' questions and help them with their work.

What is its objective?

The major objective of this program is to increase rates of homework completion. Some students may have no quiet place to work on homework at home. Other students may struggle academically and have no one at home who can help them. Still other students may lack time-management skills, or have so many activities that they do not get their homework done at home. For all these students (who wish to take part), the homework room provides a place where they can focus on their work and get their questions answered quickly. As such, a homework room can increase students' sense of **competence**. In addition, it can help students feel a greater sense of **belonging** (because of the many caring people who are ready to help them) and provide **attention** and support.

How do you do it?

You need to identify a place that can house the homework room and then arrange for supervision by skilled paraprofessionals, students from the school (participating in a Meaningful Work Program), and/or high school students—who might get class credit for their time. A homework room program should be managed by a classroom teacher. The teacher would be responsible for training and monitoring an adequate number of supervisors (older students, parent volunteers, community volunteers) to ensure that students can quickly and easily get help when they need it. The supervisory training should include how to give positive reinforcement and how to correct errors and answer questions in an encouraging manner. The managing teacher should not be expected to be in the homework room during all the times it is open, but should go in intermittently to ensure that there is an adequate number of people to answer student questions and to see that the homework room is remaining an invitational environment where students want to come and spend their time. (**Note:** This teacher might have one less class to teach as compensation for assuming this responsibility).

7. Golden Tickets

What is it?

A Golden Ticket system is a structured reward system in which all staff members can recognize any student for any behavior or trait they wish. If they choose to, students who get Golden Tickets can put them in a jar in the office for a weekly drawing—and the person with the winning ticket gets an even more tangible reward.

What is its objective?

When a school has many at-risk students, staff may decide that recognizing student behavioral accomplishments with tangible rewards would be helpful in motivating students to behave responsibly. Because this program has a great degree of flexibility in the criteria for giving tickets, it is easier for staff to meet the **recognition** needs of all their students.

How do you do it?

At the beginning of each week, the principal gives every staff member, certified and noncertified, ten Golden Tickets. When a staff member wishes to acknowledge a significant accomplishment by any student, he/she writes the student's name on a ticket, along with a brief statement about what the student did to deserve it, and then signs it. Because students have been told about the program, they know that if they want to they can drop any tickets they receive into a jar in the office. Meanwhile, the principal arranges for a reward and a drawing each week. He/she should talk with various students about the types of things or activities they might want to earn—in order to come up with prizes that most students will value. (**Note:** The reward for each week can also be displayed in a locked case near the office so that students can determine whether they want to put their tickets in for the drawing.) At the end of each week, the principal has the drawing and announces the winner over the intercom.

8. Meaningful Work Program

Note: This program is covered in detail in Volume III: Meaningful Work—100 School-Based Jobs for Increasing Student Affiliation, Belonging, and Sense of Purpose.

What is it?

Recognizing that students thrive on feeling useful, needed, and important, a Meaningful Work program is designed to give students meaningful jobs around the school. In Volume III, we describe more than 100 different jobs, ranging from office helper to flag raiser to computer repair person. As many businesses do, a Meaningful Work Program might even have Employees of the Week to acknowledge individual student's outstanding work.

What is its objective?

A Meaningful Work program is specifically structured to meet individual students' **recognition**, **attention**, **acknowledgment**, **nurturing**, **belonging**, **purpose**, **stimulation/change**, and **competence** needs by engaging them in meaningful jobs that contribute to the school. Thus, a student who needs nurturing might be offered a job in which she works closely with a female staff member. Or, a student who needs lots of attention and a sense of purpose might be given a highly visible job that makes him feel important (e.g., cleaning the disk drives of the computers in each classroom).

How do you do it?

Identify students who might benefit from having a job—which could be almost all of your most needy students. Then identify jobs that truly need doing and that a student could do, and adults who would make good (and appropriate) job supervisors. Next, match the students who could use a job with an available job. Train supervisors to teach students how to perform the job, monitor the student's performance, provide positive and corrective feedback, communicate with the students' classroom teachers, and so on.

The program should be coordinated by a highly skilled paraprofessional. This person will be responsible for tracking who has what job, which adult supervises each job, what jobs are currently available, and who works with staff to identify additional job possibilities.

Note: Volume III is entirely about how to set up and implement a Meaningful Work program. This volume provides all the information you need to get started, and includes more than 100 written job descriptions.

9. Individualized Behavior Management Plans

What is it?

Individualized behavior management plans are comprehensive interventions that are designed specifically for those students who demonstrate overt signs of potential school failure (e.g., chronic absenteeism, excessive disciplinary referrals, failing grades) or are the subject of staff concern. They are the result of a team (of staff, a student, and the student's parents) working together to: clarify the nature and extent of a student's problem, set goals and identify strategies for improving the student's behavior, and determine an objective method for evaluating the student's progress in achieving the goals.

What is its objective?

When standard motivational and instructional procedures prove insufficient to prevent a student's continued behavioral (or social) failure, that student should become a target of staff concern and of an individualized plan to help him/her be more successful in school. Thus, tailored, individualized plans can be designed to meet individual students' needs for **recognition**, **attention**, **acknowledgment**, **nurturing**, **belonging**, **purpose**, **stimulation/change**, and/or **competence**.

How do you do it?

Any student who shows signs of school failure (for any reason) or is the subject of concern by a staff member is assigned a case manager. Case managers generally are the school counselor, the principal, the school psychologist, or a behavior management specialist. This individual is responsible for coordinating the development of and monitoring progress on an individualized plan for the student. This includes, but is not limited to, working with the student, the student's parent(s), and the student's teacher to clarify the nature of the student's problem, setting goals and identifying strategies for improving the student's behavior, and determining an objective way to evaluate the student's progress in achieving the goals. Strategies may involve having the student set goals, using a structured reinforcement system, giving the student a Meaningful Work job, pairing the student with a mentor, and so on. All case managers should meet as a group once a month to review the goals for and progress of identified students.

10. CARE

What is it?

CARE is a schoolwide structured reinforcement system designed to improve student behavior in a school's common areas (e.g., the hallways, playground, bus waiting area, etc.). The acronym stands for:

Careful commuting	Walking that follows bus and recess line rules.
Awesome attitude	Following school rules, being kind to others, continuing to walk and be a careful commuter.
Responsible leadership	Making good decisions, following school rules, continuing to commute carefully, and demonstrating an awesome attitude.
Exceptional empathy	Showing concern for others, following school rules, carefully commuting, demonstrating an awesome attitude, and exhibiting responsible leadership.

This program runs two to three times a year, for four weeks at a time. During the four-week period, one of the traits (e.g., careful commuting) is highlighted each week. Every staff member is given pads of tickets and asked to distribute them to any student seen exhibiting the highlighted trait in any common area. The actual tickets change each week—both in color and in terms of the trait written on them. Sample tickets are shown in this figure:

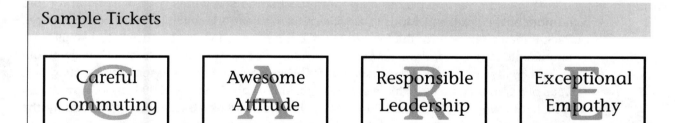

Sample Tickets

| Careful Commuting | Awesome Attitude | Responsible Leadership | Exceptional Empathy |

What is its objective?

This program is designed to improve student behavior in common areas by increasing the frequency of adult **recognition, acknowledgment,** and **attention** for students who behave responsibly. Because the program only occurs two or three times a year, it also meets students' needs for **stimulation/change.**

How do you do it?

To start the program, give several students the job of making pads of tickets (copying, cutting, and assembling with padding compound) for each trait. Then, at a short meeting with all staff who have contact with students in common areas (i.e., teachers, bus drivers, lunch servers, noon supervisors, office workers, and so on), explain the program and give out the pads of tickets. Encourage staff to give out the tickets quite freely and keep a ready supply of tickets in the office in case any staff person needs more.

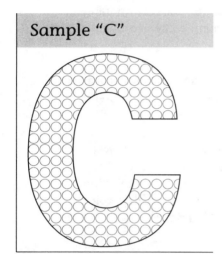

Sample "C"

Next, give each classroom teacher a set of large cards—each one with one of the letters of the acronym (i.e., C, A, R, or E) made up of 150 circles, and have each class set a goal for the number of tickets they hope to earn during a week. Each class, together with the teacher, should identify a small reward (e.g., a few minutes of extra recess, or a short game time) the class will earn if it reaches its goal. Then, whenever a student gets a ticket, he/she shows it to his/her teacher and initials one of the circles on that week's card—and the class is on its way.

In addition, after a student who has earned a ticket has shown it to his/her classroom teacher, he/she writes his/her name and room number on the ticket and deposits it in a large jar in a central location (e.g., the school library). Each Friday afternoon for the four weeks of the program, the principal selects a small team of students to help her draw names and give out prizes. The ten to fifteen prizes given out should be low- or no-cost items, such as fast-food coupons, free passes to the skating rink, bags of popcorn, pencils with the school logo, and so on. A school of 600 students may very well have over 10,000 tickets in the drawing each week—because students enjoy the suspense of having names drawn and announced over the intercom.

Note: Any acronym can be substituted for CARE. For example, you may want to use the name of your school mascot (e.g., EAGLES) or a word that is related to your mascot (e.g., SOAR). Staff should decide each year what acronym to use (based, in part, on what behaviors they want to emphasize).

11. Student of the Week

What is it?

In this program, a student from each classroom in the school is spotlighted each week. A picture of all the chosen students with the principal is posted on a main bulletin board, and each student's classroom teacher identifies ways to celebrate that individual's unique contribution to his/her classroom and the school. For example, a teacher might devote an entire bulletin board to the student—displaying the student's work, pictures of the student's family, baby pictures of the student, and/or any other items of importance to the student. (Teachers can contact parents to find out about special talents or interests the student might like to share.) Selected students might also be their class' designee for "Lunch With the Principal."

What is its objective?

By celebrating the unique contributions of every individual student to his/her classroom and the school, such a program increases students' sense of **purpose** and **belonging** at school. In addition, by recognizing every student for one week, staff are able to give all students **acknowledgment** and increase the amount of **attention** they receive.

How do you do it?

At the beginning of the year, every classroom teacher explains the Student of the Week program—its purpose and the activities (e.g., displays, lunch with the principal) that will be involved. Teachers need to make sure that students understand that every student will get a week and that the order is strictly random—that is, the student celebrated during the first week is neither more or less valuable than the student celebrated during the last week. To make sure this happens, each teacher can determine class order with a public name drawing. Then they can post the list of students' names, in the order in which they were drawn, so that all students can see it. Every Monday, teachers provide the name of the student from their classes (and a picture) to the office so the bulletin board can be prepared. (**Note:** If any class has more students than there are weeks in the school year, that class will have to have two students on some weeks. The weeks with more than one student of the week should occur in the middle of the school year.)

12. Lunch With the Principal

What is it?

Every Tuesday, the principal has lunch with a group of selected students—one from each classroom, and instead of eating in the cafeteria, this lunch occurs in a special room that has been arranged with tablecloths and so on (to give the appearance of a more formal dining experience). Participating students can be the designated "Students of the Week."

This luncheon provides a wonderful opportunity for primary students to get to know the principal in a relaxed setting. With the intermediate students, the luncheon can serve as a sort of informal student council meeting. Some weeks, the students and principal might discuss a particular issue (e.g., there has been too much litter in the halls so the principal asks the students to brainstorm ideas on solving this problem). Other weeks, the students might be asked to bring a question, suggestion, or concern that their classes have generated and would like to have discussed. They could then report back to their teachers (or, if the students are comfortable, to their entire classes) on the results of the discussion.

What is its objective?

For intermediate students, this procedure can give them a sense of **belonging** and of **purpose** for playing a role in the governance of the school. For both primary and intermediate students, it also provides **attention** (from the principal) and a way to meet their needs for **stimulation/change** because it is a break in students' routine.

How do you do it?

Each week the principal arranges for a room to be prepared. The selected students from each class go to the front of the line (if they are buying lunch), then proceed directly to the designated room. If an issue is to be discussed with intermediate students, the principal lets the teachers know in advance so that they can discuss the issue with their classes. If an issue is to be the subject of class discussions after the luncheon, the principal arranges for the students to take notes to share with their teachers and classmates.

13. Goal Achieved! Book

What is it?

A large book (22" x 22") with a fancy wooden cover and titled "Goal Achieved!" is kept in the office. Each day, any staff member can identify and give certificates to student(s) who have accomplished important academic or social goals. During the last ten minutes of the day, all students with certificates (whether 10 or 50) go to the office to tell the principal about the goal they achieved and sign their name in the book.

What is its objective?

The objective of this procedure is to **recognize** the academic and behavioral progress of individual students. Because staff can identify students for any reason, they should occasionally choose the students who are always responsible, as well as the more needy students who have a particularly good day. The procedure provides students with **attention** from the principal, office staff, and other students who get to sign the book that day. Getting to go to the office at the end of the day breaks up the daily routine, so it also helps meet students' needs for **stimulation/change**. Finally, if one of the school's goals is to foster student growth, acknowledging instances of growth helps meet students' sense of purpose.

How to do it?

Give all staff members blank "Certificates of Merit," each of which has a place to describe the goal the student achieved, and tell them that they are allowed to give up to five certificates a day. At the end of each day, every student who has a certificate gets to bring it to the office. The principal (or designee, if the principal is out of the building) meets with each student individually, asks the student about the goal he/she achieved, and has the student sign his/her name in the Goal Achieved! Book. The principal then signs the certificate and returns it to the student to take home. (Occasionally, the principal may choose to give the students juice or a small snack to add a sense of celebration to this end-of-the-day ritual.)

14. The RSB System

What is it?

A Responsible Student Behavior (RSB) program is a buildingwide structured program in which staff members reward students by giving them RSB slips. Each RSB slip includes a written description of the particular responsible behavior the student engaged in (or has engaged in across a period of time), and students who earn ten RSB slips can go to the office to be acknowledged by the principal and get his/her picture taken and put on a bulletin board, and to get a small reward.

Responsible Student Behavior!
RSB!

_____ demonstrated especially responsible behavior by
(Name of Student)

_____

_____

Staff Member Signature: _____

Once you have earned 10 RSB slips you can go to the office to receive your special privilege.

What is its objective?

An RSB program is designed to **recognize** students for responsible behavior and to give them additional staff **attention**.

How do you do it?

The principal supplies every staff member with RSB slips, and explains that whenever they want to acknowledge a student for responsible behavior, they should compliment the student, write a description of the behavior on the slip, and give the slip to the student.

Students need to be told (probably by their classroom teachers) that when they have collected ten slips, they are to show them to their classroom teacher and then report to the office. After the principal asks the students to identify their responsible behaviors that have been acknowledged and congratulates the students, he/she arranges for the students' pictures to be taken in the principal's chair and placed on a bulletin board near the office. For every ten slips a student receives after the first ten, he/she may also choose a small reward (erasers, bumper stickers, pens, buttons, or calendars).

15. Classwide Goal of the Month

What is it?

In this program, classroom teachers help their students choose a classwide goal for the upcoming month (e.g., "To increase classwide average rate of on-time assignment completion from 85%-95%"). Then, over the course of the month, the teachers use discussions and lessons to guide their classes in efforts to achieve the collective goal. At the end of each month, each class evaluates its progress—and determines whether it has met its goal. If so, the principal is notified and he/she gives the class a certificate that can be posted in the classroom.

What is its objective?

One purpose of this procedure is to give students a sense of **purpose**. Part of the school experience should be goal-directed growth. This activity models a process of goal setting, striving to achieve a goal, and evaluating whether the goal has been met. The procedure can also increase students' sense of **belonging**, because collective goals encourage a sense of collective responsibility for working to a specific goal.

How do you do it?

At the beginning of each month, the principal reminds teachers to review their previous month's goal with their students. If the class has met the goal, the students identify another. If they have not met it, students should determine whether the goal will remain the same, be modified, or set aside for a new goal. During the month, teachers should be reminded to provide feedback and conduct occasional classwide discussions to help their classes identify strategies that will help them achieve the goal. If appropriate, teachers can conduct lessons in which students role-play, use positive practice, read stories, and have writing assignments or art projects related to the goal. Goals might include:

- Increasing the amount of work handed in.

- Increasing the accuracy of work handed in.

- Improving note-taking skills.

- Being less critical and more respectful of others.

- Using work time more effectively.

- Taking better care of learning centers.

- Getting along better during games.

16. Principal's Award

What is it?

Each month, teachers identify two students from their classes (from one of their classes if it's a middle school) to receive the Principal's Award. One should be a student who is consistently responsible, and the other should be a student who has made significant improvements in academic or behavioral endeavors. The principal then sends the parents of these students letters and certificates describing the students' accomplishments and indicating the teachers who nominated the students.

What is its objective?

The objective of the Principal's Award program is to **recognize** improvements in behavioral or academic performance. The program also gives students **attention** from teachers, the principal, and (hopefully) their parents for behavioral or academic **competence**.

How do you do it?

At the beginning of each month, the principal distributes copies of a form similar to the one that follows to all teachers. The form asks teachers to identify two students from their classes (or from particular class periods) whom they want to nominate for the Principal's Award. They are then asked to turn the forms in to the office, where office staff, with the help of student office help workers, type the parent letters and make the certificates (e.g., using a computer program that generates certificates) for all identified students. (**Note:** The principal should periodically review lists of the recipients to ensure that there has been no gender bias. If it is found, for example, that significantly more males than females have been receiving the awards, the principal can recommend to teachers, in the next month's notice, that they choose female students to rectify the imbalance.)

In addition, occasionally when there is a particular trait that staff is trying to foster in students (e.g., treating others with respect), the principal can suggest that teachers target students who have demonstrated this trait for the Principal's Award.

Sample Letter

Dear Teachers:

It is once again time to identify students for the Principal's Award. This month, identify two students from your second period class. (If you have second period prep, disregard this notice.) Write the name of the student and a brief description (one or two sentences) of why that student deserves to be acknowledged.

The theme for this month is "Treating others with respect." If possible, identify students showing competence and improvement in this theme. However, if there is a student you wish to acknowledge for something other than this theme, do not be bound by the theme of respect.

1. Identify a student from your second period class who consistently behaves responsibly.

   _____

   Description of why you are recommending this student:

2. Identify a student from your second period class who has made significant improvement in academic progress or social behavior.

   _____

   Description of why you are recommending this student:

17. Calling Students With the Highest Score on Class Tests

What is it?

With this program, you encourage teachers to establish a class policy in which the male and female students from each class who score highest on important tests will be called at home and congratulated on their accomplishments.

What is the objective?

This procedure is designed to **recognize** academic excellence, and provide **attention** to those students who exhibit the highest levels of **competence**.

How do you do it?

Any teacher who wishes to participate should have class lists with home phone numbers. The evening after a test, the male and female from each class are called and informed that they are the "TOP GUN" (or any other suitable phrase) for the class on the recent test. If a student does not have a phone or no one answers, he/she could be given a note the next school day.

18. Honor Roll

What is it?

An honor roll system is a way to recognize outstanding student academic performance by identifying those students who achieve a specific grade point average for a term (e.g., 3.5 or higher), automatically placing them on the Honor Roll, and sending them written notification of their accomplishment with their report cards.

What is the objective:

An Honor Roll provides **recognition** for the intelligence, **competence**, hard work, and discipline required for a student to consistently maintain good grades.

How do you do it?

Office staff will prepare the Honor Roll listing and the letters to be sent as soon as all grades have been recorded in the computer.

Note: This procedure (along with the previous one) is somewhat exclusionary in that average- and low-performing students have less chance of receiving this recognition. Therefore, staff should make additional efforts to acknowledge any improved performance on the part of those students—by recognizing them in class and/or with notes on papers.

19. Grades

What is it?

Each classroom teacher should have grading polices that fit within the schoolwide guidelines for grading as stated in the student handbook.

What is the objective?

One of the major purposes of grading is to **recognize** successful completion of course requirements. Thus, a passing grade (or better) can be viewed as a reinforcing acknowledgment of adequate mastery of critical course content. Students, in turn, can feel proud of their accomplishments and their **competence**.

How to do it?

During the first week of the semester, teachers will give each student a course syllabus explaining grading practices. Students should be encouraged to keep accurate records of scores earned, so that at any time during the semester each student knows current grade status. Teachers should encourage students, if they are not satisfied with their current grades, to make appointments with the teacher to work out strategies for improving grades.

All staff should be careful to avoid implying that a grade of "C" is somehow a bad grade. When a student is capable of getting better than a "C," that student should be counseled privately—and perhaps a goal contract should be written.

If a student is consistently getting poor grades, it indicates that the student's academic or motivational needs are not being met, and therefore, staff should view this as "red flag" signals that the student may need an individualized plan to help him/her be more successful.

20. Attendance/Punctuality Letter

What is it?

With this program, students who have exemplary attendance for one year are eligible for letters that they can use when applying for part-time and/or summer jobs. The letter will specify that the student has an excellent attendance record and can be depended upon to arrive at work.

What it its objective?

The objective of this procedure is to motivate students to maintain good attendance/punctuality by **recognizing** these behaviors in a practical way that can help them get summer jobs.

How do you do it?

Any student who goes an entire year with no more than three excused absences and no unexcused absences will be eligible for a letter, signed by the principal, that notes the student's excellent attendance record and states that the student can be depended upon to arrive at work. If the student has no tardies, a punctuality clause can be added to the letter. A student with no unexcused absences, but more than three excused absences may be eligible for a similar letter, but one that specifies the number of excused absences the student had. This letter should not include an endorsement of the student's dependability.

Students should be informed of this policy at the orientation assembly at the beginning of each year. If possible, invite a businessperson from the community to speak to the student body about how important punctuality and attendance are to an employer. Encourage this person to tell students that a certificate of attendance and punctuality from the school could be of benefit when applying for after-school and/or summer jobs.

21. Problem-Solving Task Force

What is it?

This program is used when a schoolwide problem occurs (increased tardiness, vandalism, harassment, increased numbers of students not completing work, and so on). The principal and the counselor convene a task force of students to evaluate the problem, propose solutions, implement a plan, and evaluate the plan's effectiveness. In cases of severe problems (e.g., illegal activity), the task force should include staff and parent representatives as well.

What is its objective?

The objective of this procedure is to actively involve students in resolving school problems. This active participation it involves can give students a sense of **belonging** and of **purpose**, and increase their pride in and willingness to take care of their school. For the students on the task force, participation also provides **stimulation/change**.

How do you do it?

When a chronic and pervasive problem occurs, the principal and counselor should determine which students would be best to have on a task force for that issue. The idea is to include representatives from any major student factions who are part of or affected by the problem. This means that task forces will be different from student council, in that even some of the toughest or worst behaved students may be asked to participate on certain task forces. Once a list of recommended students has been developed, those students should be approached and asked if they would be willing to participate.

Schedule task force meeting times so that students miss relatively little class time. For example, a task force meeting on Mondays might meet during first period the first week, during second period the second week, and so on. Most task forces should last no more than two months.

Basic Needs Analysis Worksheet

Name of staff person: _____

Students I will think about while conducting the analysis:

	Academically High-Performing Students	Academically Average-Performing Students	Academically Low-Performing Students
Students who consistently behave responsibly	Male: Female:	Male: Female:	Male: Female:
Students who have trouble behaving responsibly	Male: Female:	Male: Female:	Male: Female:

Are we effectively meeting the need for **recognition** for all our students?

	If yes, how?	If no, what (if anything) do we recommend doing?
High academic performers who consistently behave responsibly		
Average academic performers who consistently behave responsibly		
Low academic performers who consistently behave responsibly		
High academic performers who have trouble behaving responsibly		
Average academic performers who have trouble behaving responsibly		
Low academic performers who have trouble behaving responsibly		

Menu Suggestions

2. Adult-student interactions
4. Positive reports to parents
7. Golden Tickets
8. Meaningful Work program
9. Individualized behavior management plans
10. CARE
13. Goal Achieved! Book

14. The RSB system
16. Principal's Award
17. Calling students with highest test scores
18. Honor Roll
19. Grades
20. Attendance/punctuality letter

Students I will think about while conducting the analysis:

	Academically High-Performing Students	Academically Average-Performing Students	Academically Low-Performing Students
Students who consistently behave responsibly	Male: Female:	Male: Female:	Male: Female:
Students who have trouble behaving responsibly	Male: Female:	Male: Female:	Male: Female:

Are we effectively meeting the need for **acknowledgment** for all our students?

	If yes, how?	If no, what (if anything) do we recommend doing?
High academic performers who consistently behave responsibly		
Average academic performers who consistently behave responsibly		
Low academic performers who consistently behave responsibly		
High academic performers who have trouble behaving responsibly		
Average academic performers who have trouble behaving responsibly		
Low academic performers who have trouble behaving responsibly		

Menu Suggestions

2. Adult-student attention
3. Special attention for targeted students
4. Positive reports to parents
5. Mentorship

8. Meaningful Work program
9. Individualized behavior management plans
10. CARE
11. Student of the Week

Students I will think about while conducting the analysis:

	Academically High-Performing Students	Academically Average-Performing Students	Academically Low-Performing Students
Students who consistently behave responsibly	Male: Female:	Male: Female:	Male: Female:
Students who have trouble behaving responsibly	Male: Female:	Male: Female:	Male: Female:

Are we effectively meeting the need for **attention** for all our students?

	If yes, how?	If no, what (if anything) do we recommend doing?
High academic performers who consistently behave responsibly		
Average academic performers who consistently behave responsibly		
Low academic performers who consistently behave responsibly		
High academic performers who have trouble behaving responsibly		
Average academic performers who have trouble behaving responsibly		
Low academic performers who have trouble behaving responsibly		

Menu Suggestions

2. Adult-student attention
3. Special attention for targeted students
4. Positive reports to parents
5. Mentorship
6. Homework Room
8. Meaningful Work program
9. Individualized behavior management plans
10. CARE
11. Student of the Week

12. Lunch with the principal
13. Goal Achieved! Book
14. The RSB system
16. Principal's Award
17. Calling students with the highest test scores
18. Honor Roll
19. Grades
20. Attendance/punctuality letter

Students I will think about while conducting the analysis:

	Academically High-Performing Students	Academically Average-Performing Students	Academically Low-Performing Students
Students who consistently behave responsibly	Male: Female:	Male: Female:	Male: Female:
Students who have trouble behaving responsibly	Male: Female:	Male: Female:	Male: Female:

Are we effectively meeting the need for **belonging** for all our students?

	If yes, how?	If no, what (if anything) do we recommend doing?
High academic performers who consistently behave responsibly		
Average academic performers who consistently behave responsibly		
Low academic performers who consistently behave responsibly		
High academic performers who have trouble behaving responsibly		
Average academic performers who have trouble behaving responsibly		
Low academic performers who have trouble behaving responsibly		

Menu Suggestions

2. Adult-student interactions
3. Special attention for targeted students
5. Mentorship
6. Homework Room
8. Meaningful Work program

9. Individualized behavior management plans
11. Student of the Week
12. Lunch with the principal
15. Classwide Goal of the Month
21. Problem-solving task force

Students I will think about while conducting the analysis:

	Academically High-Performing Students	Academically Average-Performing Students	Academically Low-Performing Students
Students who consistently behave responsibly	Male: Female:	Male: Female:	Male: Female:
Students who have trouble behaving responsibly	Male: Female:	Male: Female:	Male: Female:

Are we effectively meeting the need for **competence** for all our students?

	If yes, how?	If no, what (if anything) do we recommend doing?
High academic performers who consistently behave responsibly		
Average academic performers who consistently behave responsibly		
Low academic performers who consistently behave responsibly		
High academic performers who have trouble behaving responsibly		
Average academic performers who have trouble behaving responsibly		
Low academic performers who have trouble behaving responsibly		

Menu Suggestions

1. Effective instructional practice
2. Adult-student interactions
3. Special attention for targeted students
4. Positive reports to parents
6. Homework Room
8. Meaningful Work program

9. Individualized behavior management plans
16. Principal's Award
17. Calling students with the highest test scores
18. Honor Roll
19. Grades

Students I will think about while conducting the analysis:

	Academically High-Performing Students	Academically Average-Performing Students	Academically Low-Performing Students
Students who consistently behave responsibly	Male: Female:	Male: Female:	Male: Female:
Students who have trouble behaving responsibly	Male: Female:	Male: Female:	Male: Female:

Are we effectively meeting the need for **nurturing** for all our students?

	If yes, how?	If no, what (if anything) do we recommend doing?
High academic performers who consistently behave responsibly		
Average academic performers who consistently behave responsibly		
Low academic performers who consistently behave responsibly		
High academic performers who have trouble behaving responsibly		
Average academic performers who have trouble behaving responsibly		
Low academic performers who have trouble behaving responsibly		

Menu Suggestions

2. Adult-student interactions
3. Special attention for targeted students
5. Mentorship

8. Meaningful Work program
9. Individualized behavior management plans

Students I will think about while conducting the analysis:

	Academically High-Performing Students	Academically Average-Performing Students	Academically Low-Performing Students
Students who consistently behave responsibly	Male: Female:	Male: Female:	Male: Female:
Students who have trouble behaving responsibly	Male: Female:	Male: Female:	Male: Female:

Are we effectively meeting the need for **purpose** for all our students?

	If yes, how?	If no, what (if anything) do we recommend doing?
High academic performers who consistently behave responsibly		
Average academic performers who consistently behave responsibly		
Low academic performers who consistently behave responsibly		
High academic performers who have trouble behaving responsibly		
Average academic performers who have trouble behaving responsibly		
Low academic performers who have trouble behaving responsibly		

Menu Suggestions

1. Effective instructional practices
4. Positive reports to parents
8. Meaningful Work program
9. Individualized behavior management plans
11. Student of the Week

12. Lunch with the principal
13. Goal Achieved! Book
15. Classwide Goal of the Month
21. Problem-solving task force

Students I will think about while conducting the analysis:

	Academically High-Performing Students	Academically Average-Performing Students	Academically Low-Performing Students
Students who consistently behave responsibly	Male: Female:	Male: Female:	Male: Female:
Students who have trouble behaving responsibly	Male: Female:	Male: Female:	Male: Female:

Are we effectively meeting the need for **stimulation/change** for all our students?

	If yes, how?	If no, what (if anything) do we recommend doing?
High academic performers who consistently behave responsibly		
Average academic performers who consistently behave responsibly		
Low academic performers who consistently behave responsibly		
High academic performers who have trouble behaving responsibly		
Average academic performers who have trouble behaving responsibly		
Low academic performers who have trouble behaving responsibly		

Menu Suggestions

1. Effective instructional practices
5. Mentorship
8. Meaningful Work program
9. Individualized behavior management plans
10. CARE
12. Lunch with the principal
13. Goal Achieved! Book
21. Problem-solving task force

Disciplinary Procedures— Increasing Consistency and Effectiveness

This chapter contains information and suggestions for reviewing, revising, and/or developing content for that section of a School-wide Behavior Plan (SBP) that covers a school's disciplinary procedures, especially the use of disciplinary referrals (the authors' term for when staff refer a student to you [the principal] for disciplinary action). The procedures included in this section of an SBP should address two main issues: (1) How staff are to respond in the event of dangerous or emergency situations involving student misbehavior (to ensure the physical safety of both students and staff members); and (2) How staff will be supported in their efforts to deal with student misbehavior.

The chapter begins with a brief introduction that explains why it is important to have a section that specifically addresses disciplinary procedures in your SBP. Then, Section One offers suggestions for how to develop and what to include in plans for dealing with dangerous and/or emergency behavior situations (e.g., a student who is out of control, two students fighting, and so on). Section Two outlines six specific tasks that will help you to help your staff deal more effectively with student misbehavior— and keep you from getting buried in a daily avalanche of referrals. At the end of the chapter, there is a reproducible worksheet with structured items that parallel the chapter's contents. This worksheet can be copied and used for taking notes and/or as a Take Action! guide as you read through the chapter.

The goal of this chapter is to help you improve your school's disciplinary procedures. Because of a principal's prominent role in this area (i.e., in disciplinary referrals), with this section of the SBP, perhaps more than any other, you should make advance decisions on a number of the issues covered. For example, you should determine which of the decisions need to be made by you unilaterally and which can involve your staff and/or be consensual. Approach the task of improving this section of your SBP by reading through this entire chapter yourself first and then deciding when and how to best involve your staff.

This chapter does not cover how you should deal with students at the time of a referral (e.g., how to respond when two students have been referred for fighting). Information and suggestions on that topic are thoroughly addressed in Volume II: Dealing with Referrals—which includes general information on issues such as how to conduct a conference with a student, decide on appropriate consequences, and establish comprehensive intervention plans, as well as specific information on how to handle 32 common problem behaviors that you are likely to see in your office.

Note: If you get an excessive number of disciplinary referrals, and/or if staff have complained that you do not support them with severe and chronic behavior problems, and/or if staff have expressed concerns about how they are supposed to respond to fighting, aggressiveness, or other potentially dangerous problem behaviors, this section may be a logical starting point for improving your SBP. However, if none of these issues represent a large concern for you or your staff, it may be more productive to begin your SBP improvement efforts by working through the ideas and activities suggested in Chapter Six: Guiding Principles—The Core of Your SBP or Chapter Seven: Encouragement Procedures—Meeting Student's Basic Needs.

Introduction

Handling behavioral referrals has been a traditional part of an administrator's role. Unfortunately, this tradition has led some school staff to believe that it is the principal's job to "cure" all students who are sent to the office for disciplinary problems. These individuals may also feel that a principal is not doing his/her job if any of the students he/she sees misbehave again. Although having such power would be nice, the truth is that no administrator alone can magically make a student stop a negative behavior pattern. In fact, one of the major premises in this book is that helping students learn to behave appropriately must be a shared responsibility requiring the coordinated efforts of administrators, teachers, and paraprofessionals.

Thus, although the use of disciplinary referrals (i.e., administrative involvement) is a necessary and important part of any school's overall plan for a safe and productive environment, it should represent only one piece of that school's disciplinary procedures. It is essential—for several reasons—that staff do not overwhelm a principal with referrals. For one thing, when a principal is deluged with referrals for every little misbehavior, he/she is not likely to be able to adequately deal with the truly serious infractions that occur. In addition, when a principal has to spend all of his/her time responding to inappropriate student behavior, he/she will not have the time to work with staff on proactive and preventative efforts.

If you are constantly dealing with referrals, you need to help your staff learn to handle more of the misbehavior themselves, without involving you. One way to do this is to take a hard-line approach and inform staff members that they must handle all behavior situations themselves. We **do not** recommend this approach, though, because if staff are not allowed to refer any behavior problems at all to the principal, they are likely to feel unsure and helpless (and unsupported!) when incidents of severe misbehavior occur and/or when a student is violent or abusive.

We advocate a middle ground position—that is, as principal you should actively support staff by taking disciplinary referrals *for the most serious student behavior problems* and, at the same time, make sure staff have the structures, information, and resources necessary to help them handle the vast majority of misbehavior themselves. For example, we believe that in most cases when a student misbehaves in class, the teacher should implement a corrective consequence—in the classroom. Or, when a minor misbehavior occurs in the hall, an appropriate corrective consequence should be assigned right then by a staff person who has observed the infraction. On the other hand, if a student directly and repeatedly refuses to follow a reasonable staff direction, that staff member should have the option of sending the student to the office.

The suggestions in this chapter are designed to help you establish (or fine-tune) effective disciplinary procedures that will accomplish the following goals:

- Ensure the physical safety of students and staff in emergency situations involving misbehavior.

- Support staff in their efforts to deal with student misbehavior.

Note: Because this chapter deals with procedures and systems for responding to misbehavior, its focus is, by definition, reactive. We want to remind you that in addition to the strategies suggested here, you and your staff must also implement the kinds of proactive, positive, and preventative procedures suggested in Chapters Six through Nine—in order to reduce the probability that students will exhibit behaviors that require corrective consequences, including disciplinary referrals.

section one
Planning for Emergency Situations

One of the best ways to ensure the physical safety of your students and staff is to preplan for those situations involving student misbehavior that might threaten their safety. For the most part, this means specifying how staff should respond when students (individuals or a group) are out of control and/or engaged in behavior that is dangerous—to themselves or others (e.g., fighting). Obviously, students who are physically out of control or engaging in dangerous behavior should be referred to the principal (to the office). However, since there is a high probability that a student in a situation such as this will refuse to go to the office, you should have a preestablished plan (i.e., procedures) for how staff are to respond when this occurs. The following steps incorporate our recommendations on both how to develop such procedures and what they should include.

1. **Develop primary and back-up procedures by which all staff members can inform the office that an emergency involving student behavior exists and assistance is needed.**

   In general, we recommend using a school intercom system (when available) for classroom situations and a dependable walkie-talkie system for settings such as the cafeteria and playground. We also strongly recommend having some sort of nontechnology driven back-up system (like the "Red Card procedure") that can be used in case of problems with the primary system(s). With the Red Card procedure, all staff members are given several Red Cards, like the one shown in the following figure. Classroom teachers keep their cards on the opposite side of the room from the phone or intercom. If they are unable to get to the phone (e.g., the out-of-control student is near the phone), they can grab a Red Card, fill it out, and send it with a student to the office. Playground and cafeteria supervisors keep the Red Cards on their clipboards. If for any reason their primary communication system (e.g., walkie-talkie) fails during an emergency, a supervisor marks the relevant information on a card and gives it to a student to take to the office. For this system to work, all students in the school need to be taught that if they are ever given a Red Card they are to go immediately to the office and give the card to the secretary (or another adult staff member in the office). Office staff need to be trained that when a student comes into the office waving a Red Card, they are to drop whatever they are doing and attend immediately to the Red Card.

Red Card—This Is an Emergency

_____

Supervisor Name

❑ Fighting or out of control. Send help.

❑ Serious injury! Call 911.

❑ Student hurt. Send trained personnel.

❑ Stranger on the playground.

❑ Student left the grounds.

❑ Abduction. Call 911.

❑ Other:

_____

_____

---

2. **Develop procedures that ensure that when a staff member requests assistance, help will come immediately.**

   First, we recommend that you establish a chain of command of individuals who can cover emergency situations when you are out of the building or otherwise unavailable. This chain should be at least four people deep, so that if any one specified person is unavailable, the next person can be contacted and so on. Although many schools with only one identified designee haven't found it to be a problem, if there is even the remotest chance that both people could be unavailable at the time of a serious emergency, additional backups should be in place. We also recommend that all the individuals in your chain of command be trained in your school's procedures for dealing with emergency situations. An example of a chain of command might be:

Principal

Lead teacher, Ms. Arizmendi, Rm. 26

Mr. Goldhammer, Counselor

Ms. Tolson, Asst. Superintendent

Post or file the chain of command information in an easily accessible place in the office. That way, should the school secretary be out of the building at the same time as the principal, a replacement secretary could quickly determine who to contact in the event of an emergency. Office personnel, whether regular or temporary, should not be put in the position of having to make administrative decisions (e.g., whether to call the police about a child who is out of control).

Once you have a specified chain of command, the next task is to develop procedures for allowing whoever has responded to an emergency (you or a designee) to call for additional help should the circumstances warrant. For example, say you get an emergency call to go to the cafeteria, and upon arriving you see five or six eighth grade males in a *violent* fight. In this case, it might not be prudent for you and the lone cafeteria supervisor to try and intervene by yourselves. Therefore, you need a predetermined means of getting additional adults (preferably big strong adults) to converge at the scene of an emergency on a moment's notice. We suggest that you identify four or five adults who are willing (and generally available) to serve on a school "Emergency Team." These individuals should also be trained to deal with crisis situations—for suggestions on arranging such training, contact your local police, county educational agencies, or juvenile justice officials.

Finally, you need to come up with a specific message, that can be announced over the school intercom for example, to let your Emergency Team members know when and where they are needed (e.g., "Emergency Team report immediately to the cafeteria. Repeat. Emergency Team report immediately to the cafeteria."). In a scenario like the one described above, as soon as you saw what the situation was, you could contact the office (using a walkie-talkie or a Red Card) and request that someone make the Emergency Team announcement. Within a minute or two, you should have four or five more adults to help you handle the fighting students.

3. **Determine when staff should (and should not) use physical restraint and/or "room clears."**

Another important issue to consider with regard to emergency situations involving misbehaving students is if and when staff should use physical restraint. For several reasons, we generally recommend that staff be discouraged from this. First of all, restraint increases the possibility of physical injury to staff and/or students involved in a restraint situation. Second, because restraint itself can be a reinforcing event for some students, it may actually increase the likelihood that such students will get out of control and need to be restrained in the future. Another potential drawback is that often there is an audience (of other students) when a student is being restrained. In a worst case scenario, the misbehaving student may get reinforced by peers who later comment about how "bad" she is. Finally, restraint is undesirable because it communicates to the student being restrained that she cannot control her behavior on her own, but needs someone else to do it for her.

An alternative to physical restraint is the use of room (or area) clears. With this procedure, staff make no attempt to intervene or restrain an out-of-control student. Instead, all other students are removed from the room or area and one staff member stays nearby to ensure that the target student does not hurt himself. Room clears reduce the probability of anyone being inadvertently injured, remove audience attention from an out-of-control student, and give a student the message that he needs to, and is capable of, getting himself back under control.

If you decide that you will use room clears, there are several logistical issues that need to be decided in advance. First is how a staff member will contact the office to let them know that a room clear is taking place (e.g., you might use the same systems described in Step 1). Then, there has to be a way for office staff to immediately arrange for someone to supervise the students who have been removed. (One way to do this, in the school building, is to pair each teacher up with another nearby teacher. In the event one teacher has to use a room clear, he/she just sends his/her students to his/her partner's room.) In addition, there should be clear-cut guidelines about what is to be done if property or materials are being destroyed by the student(s). We suggest that students be held accountable for repairing or replacing any damage they cause during an incident of this nature—and that it is made clear to staff that they are not required or expected to intervene when a student is damaging materials.

The key to both of these procedures (i.e., physical restraint and room clears) is for staff to know exactly who does what in each type of situation. For example, staff should know ahead of time whether, in the case of a room clear, they are to go with the removed students and let an administrator supervise the student who is out of control, or vice versa. Similarly, if physical restraint is an option, staff need to know who (they? the administrator?) is supposed to do the restraining. There are no absolute answers to these questions. However, when a school's staff have discussed the issues and made decisions in advance, emergency situations will be handled more effectively.

At a minimum, staff should be given written guidelines on when to use physical restraint and when to use room clears. In addition, have something in writing that makes it clear to staff that if restraint is necessary, they are not required or expected to put themselves in physical danger. Finally, and perhaps most importantly, you need to make sure that all staff are aware of the lines of communication by which they can let the office know that help is needed for an emergency situation.

4. **Identify any other high-probability emergency events, and clarify the procedural responses staff are to use for those situations.**

A school's staff should have information on how to handle all serious problem situations that may occur at that school (e.g., an out-of-control parent who is making threats). What these situations might be will vary from school to school. To some extent, you can determine what situations your staff should be prepared for by considering your school's past history and the community you serve. For example, if you have never had an incident involving a gun being brought to school, it might not make a lot of sense to spend time developing and training staff on procedures for responding to weapons possession. However, if weapons in the school are a high (or even medium) probability event, then staff should have written guidelines for how they are to respond. (**Note:** In this case, it may be a good idea to involve police in the development of your guidelines.)

Again, once the procedures for these potential emergency situations have been developed, you need to make sure that all staff know what those procedures are. Among the ways to do this are walking staff step-by-step through the procedures and/or role playing "What if ..." scenarios. For example, you might describe a hypothetical situation and have staff explain exactly what they would do. You might ask questions like, "What would you do if you could not get to the intercom to call for help?"

Remember, you want to have your emergency procedures and back-up procedures in place before an emergency arises. It is too late to develop a plan when you are in the midst of an emergency. There is nothing worse than being in the middle of a terrible situation (e.g., the hypothetical cafeteria situation presented earlier) and thinking, "I should have developed a plan for getting additional help. What should I do now?"

Take Action!

Have a representative team (e.g., a leadership team or a special task force) examine all current policies and procedures regarding behavioral emergencies. Part of this process should involve finding out from staff their awareness of and comfort with current procedures. If it seems necessary, after the review, the team can develop proposals on this topic to present to the total staff for consideration and eventual adoption. In order to ensure that the proposed procedures not only fit your particular situation, but also meet school board guidelines and state statutes, it's probably a good idea to first get input from your central administration, local school board, local police, and/or state department of education about any expectations and/or liability issues related to room clears, physical restraint, and Emergency Teams.

Note: If your school has any sort of trained crisis intervention team, many of these recommendations may already be in place. In addition, *Managing Acting-Out Behavior* by Geoff Colvin is an excellent resource for training staff to deal with students who tend to get out of control.

section two
Supporting Staff Efforts to Deal With Student Misbehavior

Dealing with difficult students is frustrating for all school personnel. When a student says, "You can't make me," a staff member is often put in a somewhat helpless position. And, a chronically disruptive student can interrupt even the best teacher's effort to present effective instruction. Because a certain amount of irresponsible student behavior is inevitable, it's essential that your staff have effective procedures for responding to that misbehavior, and that you, as building leader, support your staff and help them deal effectively with behavioral challenges from students. The real issue is how you can and should best support them. That is, the most appropriate support may not always be exactly what a staff member wants. For example, there may be times when a staff member wants you to "Get this student out of my room—he needs to be expelled!" Since expelling the student is probably not in the student's best interest (or even legally possible), you have to carefully balance the needs (wants) of the staff member with the needs of the student. We believe that the following six specific tasks can help you help your staff to better deal with misbehaving students, yet still feel supported; ensure that your time is efficiently and effectively used; and ensure that the needs of misbehaving students are respected as well. Each of these tasks is explained in more detail following this list.

1. Clearly specify the types of misbehaviors for which disciplinary referrals (i.e., sending a student to the office to see you, the principal) can/should be used, and build a menu of administrator-assigned consequences.

2. Establish menus of recommended corrective consequences for staff to use. These consequences should fit a continuum of mild to severe misbehaviors (e.g., running in the hall to assaulting a teacher) and be appropriate for classrooms and common area situations.

3. Establish efficient and effective record-keeping materials related to disciplinary actions—for improving interstaff communication and monitoring your behavior management situation.

4. Set up well-defined procedures to be used when students report to the office at the time of a disciplinary referral.

5. Arrange for and make sure that staff are aware of an array of collaborative resources for dealing with and helping students who misbehave.

6. Establish "flagging" criteria to ensure that no students will "fall through the cracks" at your school.

1. Clearly specify the types of misbehaviors for which disciplinary referral can/should be used.

You need to work directly with your staff to establish guidelines that clarify those discipline situations for which it is appropriate (and acceptable) for staff to involve you (i.e., to make disciplinary referrals). This category of behaviors needs to be both limited and very well-defined. Without this level of precision about your role in disciplinary procedures, several problems can develop: (1) Some staff will refer students for all kinds of minor infractions, thus reducing your time and effectiveness to deal with more serious behaviors and/or to work on proactive aspects of behavior management (e.g., observing in classrooms, meeting with parents, etc.); (2) Staff who refer students for what you believe are minor offenses may feel unsupported because of the manner in which you interact with those students ("I send a student to the principal, and she just pats the student on the head and says to go back to class. I never get any support!"); and (3) Students are likely to get mixed messages about behavioral expectations—because, for example, some staff will refer students to you for using profanity but others will not.

You can avoid these problems by working with your staff to reach agreement on: the few, serious behaviors that ought to result in immediate office referral; and the fact that most misbehaviors ought to be handled by staff in the setting in which the infraction occurs (e.g., classroom, cafeteria, hall, and so on). We have identified three specific types of behavior that we believe are serious enough to warrant a disciplinary referral (i.e., administrative involvement).

- **Physically dangerous behavior** (assault, fighting, or any other behavior that has a high possibility for physical harm)

- **Illegal behavior** (possession of controlled substance, extortion, threats of violence, and so on)

- **Defiance** (overt and immediate refusal to follow a staff person's direction)

If you can think about student misbehavior in terms of the adult world of driving, disciplinary referrals would be a rough equivalent to DWIs (driving while intoxicated). These automobile-related infractions are serious enough that when individuals are caught, they are immediately removed from their vehicles and taken to another location—where additional corrective consequences are usually assigned. In addition, for this type of infraction, records of the incident are kept because if it should happen again, subsequent consequences may need to be more harsh and/or the person may be required to seek some form of treatment. Similarly, with disciplinary referrals, the infraction should be one that is serious enough that a student will be immediately removed from his/her current setting (classroom, playground, and so on) and sent to the office to see the principal and, when appropriate, receive additional consequences. Records need to be kept, so that if there are repeated infractions, the severity of the consequences can increase, and some form of proactive intervention (treatment) can be established.

Note: Although in general disciplinary referrals should be limited to a few, serious misbehaviors, we suggest that you make provisions for some exceptions. That is, we recommend establishing guidelines to permit staff members to use disciplinary referrals for less severe behaviors, as long as they discuss the problem with you in advance and together you agree that disciplinary referral will be part of a comprehensive plan to help the student. Your goal is to let staff know that when a student's behavior is a problem, they can come to you and together you will work out a plan.

Take Action!

Have a representative team (a leadership team or a special task force) work out a proposed description of disciplinary referral behaviors to present to the entire staff. It is particularly important that this team (and eventually the entire staff) discuss and agree on these specific behaviors and their definitions (and examples). Inconsistency in using disciplinary referral (whether because staff members don't know exactly when to use it and/or because they don't agree with how it is supposed to be used) can severely weaken the effectiveness of all your disciplinary procedures, and even your entire SBP. Consequently, we suggest that you not only develop clear guidelines related to disciplinary referral use, but also work to achieve staff consensus on those guidelines.

Once developed, have the team prepare a short inservice on the proposed guidelines for a staff meeting. Present the guidelines as a proposal—and get staff input (e.g., allow ten minutes for discussion). Then have a consensual vote to accept or reject the proposal. If rejected, the team should meet again to modify the proposal based on staff input.

Following is a sample of Disciplinary Referral guidelines that might be found in a written SBP. Although your guidelines should reflect the situation in your school and the collective opinion of your staff, you may wish to use this sample as a discussion starter—or even as a model.

Sample SBP Section on Disciplinary Referral

Three types of misbehavior are considered so serious that the student(s) will be sent immediately to the office and the administrator will become involved.

1. **Physically dangerous behavior** (fighting, assault, physical intimidation)

   Any physically dangerous actions should result in immediate disciplinary referral. If a student(s) is engaging in a dangerous activity, the staff member should firmly inform the student(s) to stop the physically dangerous behavior. If the behavior ceases, the student(s) should be given a disciplinary referral and sent immediately to the office. If the student(s) does not cease, the staff member should follow agreed upon emergency procedures for calling for assistance.

2. **Illegal acts** (possession of controlled substance, extortion, threats)

   If an adult is aware that a student has done or is doing something illegal, the staff member is obligated to refer the situation to the office. The principal must make all decisions regarding whether or not to contact any relevant authorities, contact parent(s), and so on.

3. **Defiance** (overt and immediate refusal to follow a staff member's directions)

   This behavior is defined as the direct and immediate refusal to comply with a reasonable adult direction within a specified period of time. First, the behavior must be an overt and observable direction: something you can see if the student carries it out ("Sit down and begin your assignment," is observable and "Change your attitude," is not).

Next, it must be immediate. Telling a student he must finish his work by the end of the period and not having him do so is not considered immediate. There can be in-class consequences for this problem, but the student should not be sent to the office as a disciplinary referral. "Allen, stop running in the hall and come here and speak to me," is an example of an immediate instruction. A student forgetting homework or being disruptive in class are not examples of defiant behavior.

The words "reasonable adult direction" are included in this definition so that as students are taught the definition they can be informed that if an adult suggests something unsafe (e.g., a stranger is telling them to get in a car), they can and should refuse to follow the instruction. Teach students that directions given by school personnel are to be considered reasonable unless the direction is unsafe.

Following is an example of how a staff member should handle a situation in which a student is refusing to follow direction.

Adult: Jason, you need to sit down and quit bothering people working on their lab activities.

Jason: Forget it. I don't have to do what you say!

Adult: Jason, You need to follow my instruction to go back to your seat. If you choose not to, it is called defiance and it is very serious.

Jason: I don't have to do what you say!

(continued)

Sample SBP Section on Disciplinary Referral (continued)

Adult: (Picks up a paper [referral form if immediately available] and pencil.) Jason, let me make sure I understand this. (While writing, the teacher says:) I said, "Go sit down." You are saying, "I don't have to do what you say." Do I understand this correctly?

If the student refuses to comply, he is defiant and should be referred immediately to the office. If the student refuses to go to the office, make no effort to coerce the student. Simply inform the office of the chain of events. If the student's name is unknown to you, describe the student to the office staff. There is an excellent chance that the office staff will be able to identify the student.

In the above scenario, if the student chooses to listen to and comply with the adult's instructions, a disciplinary referral would not result. Although, the adult should implement an appropriate classroom consequence and may even wish to fill out an administrator notification form regarding the student's disrespect.

Defiance is a breakdown of communication. When a student has been referred for defiance, the principal will arrange a conference between the student and staff member involved. The administrator may or may not include parents in this conference. The purpose of the conference will be to assign appropriate corrective consequences and to set up a plan that will help the student communicate more responsibly in the future.

Disciplinary referrals are to be reserved for the three types of behavior described above. The principal is unable to accept referrals for minor problems as students soon learn that receiving a disciplinary referral is no big deal. To maintain effectiveness, disciplinary referrals must be used only for these—the most severe of infractions.

Once you have defined your disciplinary referral guidelines, create a menu of "Administrator-Implemented Corrective Consequences" to include as part of your SBP. These will be consequences for severe misbehaviors that can only be assigned by you, the administrator (e.g., suspension, in-school suspension, etc.). The following sample menu lists and describes a variety of possible consequences. (**Note:** Other consequences for moderate to severe misbehavior that could be assigned by either you **or** by staff members (e.g., after-school detention, Administrator Notification Report, restitution, etc.) will be described later in this chapter.

Sample Menu (With Descriptions) of Administrator-Implemented Corrective Consequences

• **In-school suspension—ISS**

ISS programs have proven to be effective alternatives to out-of-school suspension. By removing students from their classrooms and interactions with their peers, but keeping them in school, you reduce the risk that a suspension will be perceived as a vacation (see Out-of-school suspension following). The goal of ISS is not to create an aversive setting, but to implement a more potent form of time-out, one in which the student is removed from all opportunities for positive reinforcement—instruction, visual and auditory stimulation, peer interactions, and so on.

There are two basic types of ISS. With the first type, you have a permanently designated ISS room in your building. It can be arranged to accommodate several students at a time by using study carrels or dividers—to ensure that the students cannot see or interact with each other, and it needs to be supervised at all times by either trained paraprofessionals or certified teachers (e.g., on a rotating duty schedule). The advantage of this type of ISS is that it is easier to make the experience very dull for the students. The disadvantage is that it uses up a classroom or other space and usurps the equivalent of a full-time staff person.

When a school does not have available space and/or personnel for a separate ISS room, an alternative is to put single carrels at the rear of several classrooms near the school office. When a student is assigned to ISS, that student is taken to one of these predesignated classrooms. The teacher in that room is not responsible for managing the student—and if there is any problem, whoever is overseeing ISS (e.g., the principal, the counselor) needs to remove the student and assign another type of consequence—probably out-of-school suspension. Enticing teachers to have an ISS carrel in their rooms may require some form of compensation—perhaps an increased materials budget or slightly smaller class loads than teachers with no ISS carrels.

Whatever type of ISS is used, the following implementation guidelines should be kept in mind:

1. Students should be taught some ISS rules before they begin their time in ISS. Rules might include:

   - Remain quiet

   - Stay seated

   - Restroom use is limited and will not be allowed between classes or during lunch

   - No sleeping

   - Work on your assigned work

2. ISS supervisors should receive training in how to interact with students. For example, they might be asked to:

   - Review with each student the infraction for which he has been assigned to ISS

   - Take a few minutes to help each student explore alternative behaviors that will reduce likelihood of a future infraction leading to ISS

   - Not counsel students during ISS

   - Keep interactions with students to a minimum—adult attention is potentially highly reinforcing

   - Assign additional ISS time for infractions of the ISS rules (e.g., each infraction adds an additional class period to the ISS assignment)

   - Notify the principal or assistant principal in case of severe ISS rule infractions (refusal to follow directions, disrespect toward supervisor, etc.)

   - When more than one student is in the ISS room, separate them as much as possible and do not allow them to interact with each other

(**Note:** Many of these guidelines would not apply to teachers who have carrels in their rooms, as they are not expected to deal with the students.)

3. An assignment to ISS should be made for the school day following an infraction. (Lengthy delays between the infraction and assignment to ISS will reduce effectiveness.)

4. Students who have been assigned more than an hour of ISS should be required to spend a full day, and should have school work to complete. (**Note:** Students should not be allowed to go around to classrooms to collect their schoolwork; the attention from many different adults is potentially highly reinforcing.)

5. Students in ISS should be as isolated from their peers as possible. For example, they should not be allowed to eat lunch with other students in the cafeteria—they should get their lunches before the official lunch period begins and then return to the ISS setting.

6. ISS assignments can/should range in severity. For example, one might assign:

    •   An hour of ISS, with work to do

    •   Three days of ISS during a particular period (e.g., if the misbehavior occurred 2nd period, the student could have ISS for three days during 2nd period—doing work from 2nd period class)

    •   One full day of ISS, doing work from all classes

    •   Three full days of ISS, doing work from all classes

    For a more detailed treatment of the pros and cons of and implementation guidelines for ISS programs, see:

    •   Kerr, M.M., Nelson, C.M., & Lamber, D.L. (1987). *Helping adolescents with learning and behavior problems*. Columbus, OH: Merril.

    •   Reavis, H.K. (1996). *BEST practices: Behavioral and educational strategies for teachers*. Longmont, CO: Sopris West.

•   **Saturday school**

Saturday school requires students to report to school for a few hours on Saturday. They may be assigned to do schoolwork or to work on the school grounds, depending on the nature of the infraction (e.g., someone who sprayed graffiti might be assigned to repaint walls).

When Saturday school is a corrective consequences option, there should be written guidelines (e.g., in a student handbook) delineating the types of offenses that may result in assignment to Saturday school. This consequence should be monitored by an administrator, as students must be directly and closely supervised during their time in Saturday school. Do not overuse this consequence—if too many students are in Saturday school on a given day, it may seem more like a party than a corrective consequence.

- **Filing criminal charges**

If a student breaks the law, you will have to decide whether or not to contact the police and/or file charges. These decisions are legally and politically volatile, and should be made with care. Before filing charges, consider getting input from your school district's attorney and the superintendent or assistant superintendent of your district. (**Note:** When one student has harmed another student, you should inform the parent[s] of the injured student about the incident. You may or may not need to inform them that they can explore filing charges against the offending student if they so desire.)

- **Out-of-school suspension**

Out-of-school suspension is a corrective consequence that should be used only as a last resort, when everything else has failed or when school board policy requires it. The rationale behind out-of-school suspension is that students who are excluded from school will discover that they miss being in school and therefore will change their behavior. This assumption might be reasonable if parents and guardians could be counted on to ensure that the time spent at home was not enjoyable. We know, however, that many students who are suspended spend their time at the mall, on the streets, or watching TV. Since schools cannot know for sure that suspension will be an aversive experience for a student, using it is somewhat risky. If a student decides that it is more fun to be out of school than in school, then you have lost that student.

If a suspension is necessary, try to make it very clear to the parent or guardian that the student must be confined to his/her room during school hours, and not allowed to watch TV, play video games, go to the mall, or engage in any other recreational activity. Explain that the goal of suspension is to demonstrate to the student that school (i.e., being with friends and participating in meaningful instruction) is better than being bored at home.

Note: Make sure your staff understand that because suspension is not viewed as aversive by some students, you will not use it indiscriminately. If some staff think you are not sufficiently tough because you do not implement enough suspensions, remind them that when a student enjoys being out of school, suspension is not tough, it is simply giving the student what he/she wants.

- **Expulsion**

Expulsion, which should only be implemented when school board policy or state law requires it, represents an admission on the part of the school that it has given up on a student and/or that the student's troubles are so severe that school can be of no help. Therefore, you should never willingly choose to implement an expulsion.

2. Establish menus of recommended corrective consequences for staff use that fit a continuum of mild to severe misbehaviors and that are appropriate for classrooms and common areas.

When disciplinary referrals are limited to only the most serious infractions, it's important for staff to have and be comfortable with other corrective consequences they can implement when students misbehave. We advocate that you and your staff create two additional corrective consequences menus—one with suggestions that are appropriate for classrooms and one for common areas. Each menu should include consequences designed to fit a range of misbehavior (mild to severe). Consequences at the *mild* end would be for misbehaviors that staff should handle right in the setting where the behavior occurred. For example, if a staff member observes a student running in the hall, he/she might have the student go back and walk, or stop the student and discuss school safety, or even just delay the student. The *middle* consequences would be for slightly more serious misbehaviors and could include the staff member assigning the student to a schoolwide consequence such as after-school detention. Finally, at the extreme other end of the continuum, the consequence available for *severe* misbehaviors (those that staff have agreed on) would be a disciplinary referral. (**Note:** Any additional consequences for severe misbehaviors will, by necessity, need to be implemented by you rather than by staff. That is, only you should make decisions about when and how to assign suspension, file criminal charges, and institute expulsion proceedings.)

Giving staff menus such as these is a good way to help them effectively respond to behaviors that do not warrant disciplinary referral. Without such a menu, they can end up feeling helpless and alone when faced with a student's misbehavior. "What should I do to correct this misbehavior? Does the principal think I should keep students in from recess or not?"

Following are two sample corrective consequences menus. (**Note:** These menus are just lists; they do not include explanations.) The first is a menu of *classroom-based* corrective consequences, which has procedures that are appropriate for use by a teacher in his/her own classroom. The second menu—of common area–based corrective consequences—consists of procedures that are appropriate for misbehavior in hallways, playgrounds, the cafeteria, and so on. Details, including how-to information, on the consequences indicated with an * on these menus can be found in Chapter Nine: Common Areas—Improving Behavior in Halls, Cafeteria, Playground, and Other Areas.

Sample Menus

Classroom-Based Consequences

- Give a gentle verbal reprimand*
- Use a proximity correction*
- Keep a record of the behavior*
- Contact parent(s)*
- Use planned ignoring*
- Reduce points (for teachers with a point system)*
- Implement a response cost lottery*
- Assign time owed off of recess or after class*
- Assign time-owed after school*
- Assign a time-out at the student's desk (e.g., head down)*
- Assign a time-out within the classroom*
- Assign an interclass time-out
- Issue demerits (e.g., three demerits equals an after-school detention)
- Have student fill out a behavior improvement form*
- Order restitution (restore/repair damage done, e.g., wash desks, write apology)*
- Implement one of the schoolwide consequences (**Note:** These will vary from school to school, but may include the following)
  - Send student to problem-solving room
  - Assign an after-school detention
  - File an administrator notification report
  - Use disciplinary referral—**only for**:
    1. Illegal acts
    2. Physically dangerous behavior
    3. Overt and immediate refusals to follow a reasonable direction

Common Area–Based Consequences

- Give a gentle verbal reprimand*
- Use a proximity correction*
- Keep a record of the behavior*
- Provide positive practice (e.g., walk in the hall, go around a game)*
- Assign time-out where infraction occurred (stand in one place for one minute)*
- Assign time-out in a set location* (e.g., against the wall at recess, at a special table in the cafeteria)
- Prepare a written report to classroom teacher*
- Have student fill out a behavior improvement form*
- Implement a schoolwide consequence (**Note:** These will vary from school to school, but may include the following)
  - Send student to problem-solving room
  - Assign an after-school detention
  - File an administrator notification report
  - Use disciplinary referral—**only for**:
    1. Illegal acts
    2. Physically dangerous behavior
    3. The overt and immediate refusal to follow a staff member's direction

- **Behavior conference with administrator (Must be prearranged with the principal)**

  For some students in some situations, simply being assigned to meet with you and discuss their behavior problems (and perhaps make plans for improving) may be a sufficient corrective consequence. If you decide, after meeting with a student, that no other corrective consequence is necessary in a particular instance, be sure to let the student know that you expect him/her to behave more responsibly in the future and that if he/she is referred again, he/she will not get off so lightly—that there will be an additional consequence next time.

- **Restitution (May be assigned by any staff member, but if for an illegal behavior [e.g., vandalism] it can only be assigned by the administrator)**

  In some cases, a student's misbehavior may cause some level of damage. When damage has been done, a logical corrective consequence is to make the student repair what was damaged. If the damage is to the building (e.g., littering, vandalism, or theft), the student might be required to do some kind of building improvement work, such as picking up litter, painting walls, or other custodial work to "pay back" the school.

  If the damage is to other people (e.g., disrespect toward a staff member, name-calling, bullying, and so on), the student might be required to do something that will "restore" the situation. Recent studies in the field of juvenile justice have yielded some very exciting results on the use of restorative consequences with youth offenders. An example of a restorative consequence for a student who has bullied other students might involve requiring the student to listen to the perspectives of those whom he has bullied (a victim's participation, however, must be strictly voluntary), come up with a plan to make it up to the victims, and prepare lessons for younger offenders on the results of bullying behavior. This type of corrective consequence will probably mean more work for you than simply assigning detention, but it just may have a greater impact on the lifelong behavior of the student.

Take Action!

Have a representative team (a leadership team or a special task force) work out menus and descriptions of those consequences that can be assigned only by the administrator and those consequences that can be assigned directly by an individual staff member.

Note: Corrective consequences included on the classroom or common-area menus that will involve more than one staff member should be described within your SBP. For example, if staff have the option of assigning a student to a lunch-time detention that is supervised by a paraprofessional, your SBP should provide information on what types of behaviors might be appropriately corrected using detention, how detention referrals should be assigned, and how the detention supervisors should conduct the detention. On the following pages are descriptions of several possible consequences that could be assigned by any staff member, but that require schoolwide consistency to implement effectively.

Options for Schoolwide Corrective Consequences
(For Moderate to Severe Misbehaviors)

- **Administrator Notification Report**

Administrator notification involves having staff provide a written notice of a particular incident of misbehavior, that they have handled, to the administrator. It is a similar concept to the procedure used when a person gets caught speeding. That is, there is not only an immediate corrective consequence (the cost of a speeding ticket), but the incident is recorded so that should the driver have more moving violations in the future, the consequences for each violation will increase (e.g., the person's insurance rates go up and she may lose her license). The idea behind having an administrator notification consequence is that while any one infraction by a student may not be severe enough to warrant a disciplinary referral, a pattern of such misbehavior could indicate a serious behavior problem (requiring more severe corrective consequences and/or a comprehensive intervention plan). But, without some kind of record, a behavior pattern might not be recognized. For example, a student who is disrespectful to supervisors on the playground might also be exhibiting this behavior in the halls and cafeteria. However, since these settings are supervised by different adults, all of whom respond to individual incidents on their own, no one may realize how pervasive this problem is. When these kinds of behavior problems generate an Administrator Notification Report though, the administrator who is reviewing and filing these reports will get a sense of how widespread an individual student's problem is, and can determine whether a more comprehensive intervention approach is necessary.

Administrator notification can also be used by a staff member who is not sure whether he/she has handled a situation correctly. For example, if a group of second grade boys have been teasing the girls on the playground, a playground supervisor may correct it immediately by informing the boys such behavior is not acceptable and by applying a reasonable corrective consequence (e.g., time-out). However, if he/she has questions about whether or not the behavior constitutes sexual harassment, the adult could also fill out an Administrator Notification Report. This report would make the administrator aware of the situation and allow him/her to decide whether further action is necessary. If the administrator believes the behavior could indeed be considered harassment, he/she might meet with the offending students and/or prepare a presentation to staff about the importance of teaching all students the line between appropriate teasing and harassment. The Administrator Notification Report then provides a record of the incidents and can provide a summary of any actions taken.

Note: You should work it out so that you personally get all the Administrator Notification Reports that have been filled out each day. Review the reports daily and decide whether any require your immediate action (e.g., parental contact, meeting with the student, and so on). In addition, have the secretary send copies of the reports to the students' classroom teachers (advisory teachers). Either you or the secretary should file the reports in the students' individual files—and check to see if there are any other Administrator Notification Reports in any student's file. If there are, you will again have to make a decision about whether additional action on your part is necessary. For example, say the custodian submits an Administrator Notification Report on a student who treated him disrespectfully. You determine that the custodian handled the situation well, and that no further action from you is required. However, upon filing the report, you see that a playground supervisor had submitted a report earlier in the year, for the same behavior. With this information, you may want to reevaluate your decision to take no immediate action.

A staff member who uses an Administrator Notification Report should let the student involved know that he/she is filling out a form about the incident for the administrator. The student should also be told that the principal will keep the report on file and that if the problem happens again, the student (and perhaps his/her parent[s]) may be called in to discuss the problem. The staff member may also choose, at his option, to have the student sign the report form.

• **Problem-solving room**

A problem-solving room, which is a variation of time-out, involves removing a student from his class for a short period of time, and requiring the student to think about the inappropriate behavior and develop a plan for avoiding future problems. The setting of a problem-solving room needs to be supervised and should not be an overly stimulating environment (such as a front office).

One school with an effective problem-solving room uses a small room just off the front office (reducing the stimulation somewhat). When a student is assigned to the problem-solving room, he is seated in the room next to the office and given a problem-solving form (see sample that follows), which he is instructed to complete. The school counselor, the principal, and the school secretary (a highly trained and experienced individual) share the responsibility for dealing with students sent to the problem-solving room. Thus, whoever has the most time flexibility when a student arrives, meets with the student, discusses the problem with him, reviews the student's plan, helps the student develop or fine-tune that plan as necessary, and then sends the student back to class. Students usually spend about 10-15 minutes in the problem-solving room.

Problem-Solving Form

Name:_____

Date:_____

School Rules:

- Be respectful of others, yourself, and things.
- Be ready to learn.
- Be responsible for your own behavior.

1. What did I do that led to my being sent to the problem-solving room?

2. Why should I NOT do what I did?

3. What will I do next time, instead of (#1)?

4. So, my plan for improving my school life (and not being sent to the problem-solving room) is that ...

   I'll stop _____

   _____

   and I'll start _____

   _____

_____
Student Signature

Adapted (with permission) from the staff of East Elementary School in Knoxville, IA.

- **Detention**

Detention, which can occur before school, after school, during lunch, or any combination, requires a supervised room. Supervision of after-school detention is commonly provided by teachers, who rotate the duty on a weekly basis. Lunch detention, on the other hand, is often supervised by a skilled paraprofessional. Some schools have both after-school detention (supervised by teachers) and lunch detention (supervised by a paraprofessional)—which gives staff the option of assigning a student to whichever time will serve as the most effective deterrent to future misbehavior.

Detention can be assigned by any staff member. The assigning staff member should then contact the student's parent and inform him/her that the student has been assigned detention for the next school day. Although the one-day delay (between assignment and implementation) weakens this procedure slightly, it is necessary to give the parent a chance to arrange alternative transportation if the student will be missing the bus due to the detention.

A detention room should have posted rules, and the supervisor should remind students of the rules at the start of the detention period. Rules might include:

- Remain quiet

- Stay seated

- No sleeping

- Work on your assigned work

During the detention period, students should be required to do school work. If they do not have any assigned work, the detention supervisor should have some sort of task or worksheet to give them.

Once you work out the details of your detention (time, location, and supervision logistics), you need to determine what behaviors will warrant assignment to detention—and then let students and parents know about the detention plan. (**Note:** You may want to consider a notification letter like the one that follows.)

Letter to Parent(s)

Dear Parent(s),

In our continuing effort to provide an enriching learning atmosphere, the staff of _____ is implementing a new discipline procedure. We will be keeping students after school for any of the following infractions:

- Wasting class time

- Being disrespectful in class

- Not completing homework

- Repeated tardiness

- Misbehavior in the cafeteria, halls, or on the bus

Each of these problems interferes with the process of learning. If a student exhibits any of these behaviors, a teacher may keep the student after school. We recognize that this may cause transportation problems; therefore, we will notify you one day in advance of the detention. If a problem occurs on Tuesday, we will notify you that the student will stay after school on Wednesday.

If your child has to stay after school, the teacher will try to reach you between 3:00 PM and 3:30 PM. This will give you 24 hours to arrange transportation. Please return this form with three telephone numbers where the teacher can reach you or get a message to you.

These procedures have been discussed with all students. However, please go over them with your son or daughter. We appreciate your support in this matter.

Sincerely,

The staff of _____

Phone numbers where I can be reached (or left a message between 3:00 PM and 3:30 PM)

_____   _____   _____

_____   _____
Student signature   Parent signature

Adapted (with permission) from Sprick, R. (1985). *Discipline in the Secondary Classroom: A Problem-by-Problem Survival Guide*. West Nyack, NY: Center for Applied Research.

3.   Establish efficient and effective record-keeping materials related to disciplinary actions.

You cannot support staff in their efforts to deal with misbehavior if you do not have accurate information about the misbehavior that occurs. Although no one likes unnecessary paperwork, certain misbehaviors (e.g., those that warrant a disciplinary referral and those for which staff give an administrator notification) should be documented in writing, using standardized forms. A written document not only provides you with the referring staff member's perspective on the student's behavior, but also allows you to record the student's action and the school's response. Your goal should not be to eliminate all paperwork, but to develop efficient and effective forms that provide essential information for making good decisions about behavioral incidents and for keeping accurate records. If possible, have your forms printed on multicopy paper. This will make it easier for all relevant and concerned parties (e.g., referring staff person, student's parent[s], student's classroom advisory/homeroom teacher, the administrator) to be given information on each and every incident.

Copies of both Disciplinary Referral and Administrator Notification Report forms should be kept in individual students' files in the office. That way, when a particular student gets in trouble, you can easily determine any past misbehavior(s) the student has been involved in, what action was taken in response to the past misbehavior(s), and what the student was told would occur in the event of another behavioral problem.

The use of forms also serves to support staff. When a referring staff person receives a copy of the Disciplinary Referral or Administrator Notification Report with a record of the action taken, it reduces the chances that he/she will feel that "Whenever I send a student to the office, I have no idea if the principal even does anything. If she does, I certainly never hear anything about it."

Disciplinary Referral forms should include on them a list of the infractions for which disciplinary referrals are allowed, as well as a place for the referring staff member to indicate the type of infraction that has led to the current referral. This provides a reminder to staff that only certain types of problems may be referred.

On the following pages you will find sample Disciplinary Referral and Administrator Notification Report forms. You might want to compare them with any forms currently in use in your school.

Disciplinary Referral

Student _____ Date _____ Time _____

Referring staff member _____

Category of Behavior:

❑ Illegal behavior
❑ Physically dangerous behavior
❑ Defiance—The overt and immediate refusal to follow a staff member's direction
❑ Other:

_____

(Note: This category requires prior approval from Principal)

Staff member's description of incident:

Note: Shaded area to be filled out by principal or counselor.

Follow-up action:

Parent contacted: ❑ Yes ❑ No

Notes on parental contact:

Action to be taken if problem recurs:

_____   _____
Signature of principal or designee   Student signature

Administrator Notification Report

Name of referring staff person _____

Location of the incident _____

Name of student(s) _____

Date _____   Time _____

Description of the incident:

Check the action(s) taken at the time of the incident:

❏ Discussion

❏ Time-out

❏ Loss of privilege

❏ Assigned after-school detention

❏ Other:

_____

_____   _____
Student signature   Staff signature

Develop Written Forms for Referrals to Other Schoolwide Consequences

When staff can assign schoolwide consequences other than Disciplinary Referrals or Administrator Notification Reports (e.g., after-school detention or a problem-solving room), there should be standardized written forms for each additional option. The forms provide the supervisors of those settings with information about why a student is there, as well as giving you summary records that allow you to analyze the effectiveness of the settings. For example, written documentation lets you determine whether there have been more students in detention in a current year than there were in previous years. Written forms also make it easier for you to determine how frequently any individual student has been assigned to detention and which staff members assign detention most frequently (which will help you make judgments about whether or not they may need additional help with behavior management). Without adequate and cumulative records, a consequence such as detention can become a "black hole" to which students are continually sent, with no appreciable improvement in their behavior. Section Two in Chapter Five contains suggestions on how to lay out a computerized database for recording and analyzing this type of information.

These referral forms, like your others, should be run on multiple-copy paper (or copies made of the filled out form) so that the referring staff member, the student, the detention supervisor, the parent(s) can each be given a copy. In middle school, you may also want a copy for the student's advisory teacher.

The sample After-School Detention Referral form that follows could be adapted to fit any type of schoolwide, nonadministrative referral consequence.

After-School Detention Referral

Name _____   Date of Infraction _____

Parental notification: ❏ Phone call   ❏ Written

Date of the detention _____

Reason for the referral:

Note to detention supervisor:

❏ Have the student work on his assignment.

❏ Have the student develop a written plan for ensuring the above problem does not recur.

❏ Have the student write an apology to _____ for the above problem; have his parent sign, and return to me tomorrow.

Take Action!

Compare any referral forms currently in use at your school with the samples provided in this chapter. Make sure your forms provide a place for the staff member's perspective on the student's misbehavior, all the information needed for adequate record keeping, and a way to ensure that all concerned parties will get a copy. In addition, Disciplinary Referral forms should be set up to allow the referring staff member to receive feedback from the administrator about what action was taken. Revise your forms as needed.

4. Specify roles and procedures office staff are to use when students report to the office for disciplinary referrals.

Establishing clear and efficient office procedures for dealing with disciplinary referrals is an essential part of supporting staff because it lets everyone know exactly who does what in these situations. If their roles are not specified, office staff may be nervous and unsure when a student arrives at the office for disciplinary reasons. It is unreasonable to expect office staff to make spur-of-the-moment decisions about what to do. Or you may have teachers who resent a secretary they think is "too nice" to students who are sent to the office or whom they believe assumes too much responsibility for interacting with referred students in harsh or corrective ways. Clearly defining the roles of office staff and the procedures they should use in disciplinary referral situations will increase consistency and help everyone feel more supported.

The more office procedures can be preestablished, the easier it will be on the office staff. We have identified several issues that should be addressed. If your school secretary is experienced, there is an excellent chance that he/she has, at some point, considered many of these issues. Consequently, you should involve him/her in the development of your procedures. There is also the possibility that if you and your secretary already have well-established procedures for disciplinary referrals, you might consider it somewhat unnecessary to actually document them. Written procedures are important though. If either of you should change jobs, written procedures will make it much easier for a new person to know how things have been handled in the past.

As with much of what we have covered in this chapter, there are no right or wrong ways to deal with office roles and procedures for disciplinary referrals, and every school will have its own unique considerations to address. However, the following suggestions reflect general concepts that we recommend you keep in mind when designing your logistic procedures.

Ensure that students will be adequately supervised at all times during the referral process.

It's important to preclude the possibility that when a staff member sends a student to the office for a disciplinary referral, the student could leave the building without any staff member knowing. That is, once a staff member sends a student to the office, he/she turns responsibility for that child's immediate supervision over to the office staff. Therefore, you need an established way for a referring staff member to let office personnel know that a student is on the way and that they (office personnel) now have supervisory responsibility for that child. Then, if the student does not show up at the office within a reasonable period of time (e.g., five minutes), office personnel can arrange for someone to look for him/her. There should also be predetermined procedures for office staff to follow in case the child is not found. In all probability, this will involve informing an administrator—who, in turn, can arrange for the grounds to be searched and, if the child is still not found, for the parents and the police to be contacted.

Identify where students (one and more than one) should wait for the administrator.

A referred student who has to wait for the principal should be in as uninteresting a place as possible. Because the typical school office is a bustling environment (with phones ringing, equipment running, and people coming and going), some students may find that sitting in the front office is the most interesting place in the school to be. Therefore, if possible, you want to avoid having the waiting area be right in the office or in full view of all the office activity. At the same time, however, the waiting area must be a supervised environment.

From the no-interest standpoint, a small room off the office may be the ideal location, but unless the room is in easy view of the secretary and can be supervised, this is too risky. Students referred to the office may be very troubled, and waiting in an unsupervised place could be an invitation to vandalism (or, in extreme circumstances, even a suicide attempt). Unfortunately, finding a waiting area in the office that has adult supervision and is isolated from office activity can be very difficult. If your only options are the front office (in full view of all activity) or an unsupervised place, your choice must be the office.

If students will have to wait in the front office, try to arrange it so that the actual waiting area is away from the reception area—where everyone, including possibly friends of theirs (e.g., a student who is delivering attendance slips) enters the office. The waiting area should also be away from staff mailboxes (where every few minutes a teacher checking his/her box might talk to the student). You don't want students who are in trouble to get more adult attention in the office than they do in any other school setting. The goal is to have students in a supervised environment where they will get as little attention as possible.

If you and your staff successfully reduce the overall number of referrals, there should be only a few occasions when more than one student is waiting to see an administrator at the same time. As unlikely as this is, though, it is possible. Therefore, you should be prepared with two appropriate waiting places—both supervised, but separated from each other.

Identify exactly what office personnel should do if you are out of the building or are otherwise occupied when a referred student arrives at the office.

You need to let office personnel know when a referred student should wait for you and when a designee (the next person in your chain of command) should be contacted to handle the referral. You also need to identify what office personnel should do if you are on the phone or in a conference. Should the student wait or do you want to be interrupted?

For a couple of reasons, the shorter wait time a referred student has, the better. First, when the time between an infraction and the assignment of a consequence is too long, younger students may actually forget what it was they did to warrant the consequence. Second, the closer in time that a consequence follows an infraction, the more likely it is that the consequence will deter the student from the misbehavior in the future. From the student's perspective, when the time is too great, the consequence may seem more like something the principal is doing because she does not like the student or is angry with him/her. And last but not least, when staff are making the effort to send only the most severe problems, you need to support them by seeing those referred students as quickly as possible.

Identify what a referred student(s) should
do while waiting for you.

When a referred student's wait time is only a couple of minutes, then having him/her sit and do nothing is fine. However, if the wait will be longer than about five minutes, asking a student to sit and do nothing can be a recipe for trouble. The student may become restless, start fidgeting, wander around, and/or play with nearby objects. Office personnel are then put in the position of having to reprimand the student and make him stop misbehaving. Given the many tasks that these individuals have to do as part of their regular job responsibilities, it is not reasonable to expect them to manage the behavior of referred students who have nothing to do.

One possible solution is for office staff to give a referred student a behavior improvement form (see the following figure) to complete.

Behavior Improvement Form

Name _____ Date _____

What did you do?

Why did you do it?

What should you have done instead?

What should you do when you go back to class?

Can you do what you need to do when you go back to class?

This form is adapted from Colvin, G. & Sugai, G. (1989).
Managing escalating behavior. Eugene, OR: Behavior Associates.

For times when a student is too young to complete the form or completes it but still has to wait, you might consider having office personnel give the student a book to look at—from a set of books (appropriate for different age and ability levels) that are kept in the office. (**Note:** If staff complain that giving a referred student a book is like entertaining a student who has misbehaved, try to get them to consider the situation from the point of view of office staff. That is, help them understand that making a student sit and wait for you with nothing to do is almost certain to lead to more problems [because the student is more likely to engage in behaviors that office staff will have to try to stop] and that giving the student a book to keep him/her occupied is not an unreasonable solution.)

Train office personnel in how to interact with students at the time of a disciplinary referral.

In general, adults in the office should give referred students as little attention as possible. A referred student who is given too much sympathy may find that he/she likes the attention he/she gets in the office, which could result in the student misbehaving more frequently in the future—in order to get sympathy, support, and attention from the office staff. While you want your office staff to be warm, caring people who like children, too much attention right after a student has engaged in a serious misbehavior can reinforce that misbehavior. Remind your office staff that the time to give students support and attention is when the students are in the office for reasons other than misbehavior. At the same time, you do not want office personnel to be negative, hostile, judgmental, or disapproving to students who have been referred for disciplinary reasons. The best approach is a neutral demeanor that gives relatively little attention to the student.

If a student is very angry and using bad language, office personnel should tell the student, one time in a firm voice, that sort of language is unacceptable. If the student continues with the inappropriate language, office staff should make no further attempts to control it. When a student has a tendency to get out of control, he/she is more likely to do so if someone tries to make him/her stop doing what he/she is doing—and an emotional response from an adult will likely feed this student's emotional response.

If a student continues to exhibit severe misbehavior in the office and/or appears to be on the edge of losing control, office personnel should immediately get an administrator or a designee. As stated before, office staff should not have to interact with an out-of-control student. They need to know that they have permission, and in fact are expected, to turn a situation in which a student is out of control over to the administrator immediately.

Determine how a referring staff member will be informed of your response to a disciplinary referral, and how referred students will be expected to reenter class.

Decide how the referring staff member or the student's classroom or advisory teacher will get feedback on the results of the referral. One way is to have the student hand deliver a copy of the referral form (which you have completed during your meeting with the student) to the "referring staff person." Thus, if the referral came from the classroom teacher, the student would have to return to class, give the teacher the form, and ask the teacher what he (the student) is expected to do next. This way the teacher sees immediately what action you have taken. It also has the advantage of forcing the student to reestablish his relationship with the referring staff member. At the conclusion of your meeting with the student, you can prompt him to return quietly to class, give the teacher the form, and politely ask what he is required to do next. You might even have the student practice this behavior before leaving your office.

Take Action!

Arrange a time (i.e., get someone to cover the phones and man the counter for an hour) for you and your office staff to discuss the preceding recommendations and develop the procedures that will be used in your school. You should use the opportunity to resolve issues like the following:

- How will staff ensure adequate supervision of students at the time of a referral?

- Where is a referred student supposed to wait for the administrator?

- What happens when two or more students have been referred at the same time?

- What happens if the administrator is out of the building when a student is sent to the office? Should the student wait for the administrator to return or should a designee be contacted? What if the designee is in class?

- What happens when the administrator is in a conference with parents or on the phone? Is the student to wait or is the administrator to be interrupted?

- What should referred students do while waiting?

- What should be done if the student is upset and crying?

- What should be done if the student is angry and is using foul language?

- What should be done if the student is out of control or appears likely to become out of control?

5.　Arrange for and make sure that staff are aware of an array of collaborative resources for dealing with and helping students who misbehave.

If, as recommended, you limit the use of disciplinary referrals to the most severe behavioral infractions, it is essential that your staff know that they are "not alone" when they have to deal with other misbehaviors. Your goal should be to see that no staff member ever feels as if he/she has to "sink or swim" when it comes to handling problem behaviors. Even relatively minor misbehavior can leave a staff member feeling frustrated and angry, particularly if it continues over a period of days or weeks.

One way to do this is to make sure all staff have access to a variety of resources for getting intervention ideas. For example, you might give each teacher or each grade level team a copy of *The Teacher's Encyclopedia of Behavior Management: 100 Problems/500 Plans* by R. Sprick and L. Howard. Or you might place that book, along with other behavior management materials, in a professional library in the staff lounge. Another excellent resource that has specific behavior management and instructional intervention ideas is *Project RIDE* (see Resources/References). This computer and video program allows a person to look up a specific problem, get a printout of intervention suggestions, and watch a video that models how to implement the intervention.

In addition to making reference and training materials available, you want to encourage your staff to collaborate with each other and other professionals when trying to solve students' behavior and/or motivation problems. The old adage that two heads are better than one is particularly true when it comes to designing interventions for modifying stubborn or chronic behavior problems, and you play a key role in creating a climate that is conducive to collaboration. That is, your staff need to know that you, as well as others (e.g., counselor, school psychologist, district behavior specialist, and so on), are there to help them should they need assistance with difficult behavioral situations. Unfortunately, in some schools teachers may avoid asking for assistance because they fear it will reflect badly on them as professionals or even affect their formal evaluations.

To reduce staff anxiety about asking for assistance you can clarify for them the relationship between their requests for voluntary collaboration and their performance evaluations. Thus, along with letting staff know the individuals and/or groups that are available to provide ideas and assistance, you also want to let them know whether collaborating with any of those persons or groups could in any way affect their evaluations. You might consider developing a chart similar to the one in the following figure. Start by listing all the resources for help in developing an intervention plan to which staff have access. Then, for each resource listed, note whether the person (or group) is expected to report requests for assistance (and their specific nature) to you and whether you can or do consider that in your formal evaluations of staff.

Relationship Between Collaboration Requests and Performance Evaluations

Collaborative Services Available	Reports on Collaborative Relationship Given to Administrators?	Relationship to Staff Evaluation
Peer Coaches	No	None
Coteaching	No	None
Consultation With Special Ed. Staff	Only as related to placement decisions for identified special education students	Administrators may use information from mentor as part of evaluation
Mentors for New Staff	Mentor provides progress reports to administrator twice during probationary year	None
District Behavior Specialist	Yes	None
School Counselor	No	Administrator may use information from counselor as part of evaluation
School Psychologist	Only as related to placement decisions for identified special education students	Administrator may use information from school psychologist as part of evaluation
School Nurse	No—unless a student has a health issue that must be reported	None
Lead Teacher	No	None
Grade Level Staffings	No	None
Intervention Planning Team (IPT) Meetings	Administrator may take part in the meeting	None
Multidisciplinary Team Meetings (MDT)/IEP Meetings	Administrator may take part in the meeting	None
Administrative Coaching	Observations and consultation conducted directly by administrative staff	None—unless related to identified goal for that staff person
Formal Teacher Evaluation	Administrator conducts the evaluation	Yes—make up the sum total of formal evaluation unless the staff member has been otherwise notified

A teacher who asks the counselor for assistance on how to deal with a disruptive student, for example, should know beforehand whether you expect the counselor to inform you of the request and how this information will be used by you. (**Note:** It should be made clear that if a request for assistance has to do with anything illegal a staff member may have done [e.g., physically abusing students], it has to be reported to you.) If a teacher is afraid of the formal evaluation process and thinks that the counselor will inform you of his/her request for assistance, he/she may be unwilling to voluntarily work with the counselor. However, the more you can clarify the resources that are available for staff and the logistics of using those resources, the greater the probability that your staff will seek collaborative assistance when they need it.

Be sure to include yourself as one of the resources available to staff. Principals who aren't terribly confident in their own behavior management abilities may be somewhat uncomfortable doing this—for fear that they will not have "all the answers" to a particular problem. However, nothing will build your credibility as a valued resource more than being willing to admit that you are unsure of the "right" intervention for a problem. Being able to say something like, "Ruth, that is really a difficult situation. In fact, I am completely baffled about how you might proceed. Let's explore some different options for getting more information," communicates that it is all right to be unsure about what to do—and may actually make the staff person feel more supported. Practical information on handling a number of common problems is presented in Volume II: Referrals and Solutions.

Finally, besides identifying available resources for staff, consider actively "marketing" those resources. When staff get busy (and what school employee does not?), they are likely to slip into "survival mode"—just working to get through each day. They may very well need occasional reminders that there are resources in the building for helping them solve problems. The kinds of reminders you might use include:

- A two-minute "commercial" from the school counselor about the help he can provide staff regarding difficult students.

- A brief testimonial, given by a classroom teacher during a faculty meeting, about the assistance she received from the district's behavioral specialist.

- A poster in the faculty room that lets staff know that you are available and willing to be a resource for any staff person in need of solutions to problematic behaviors (see accompanying figure).

Notice: Job Wanted

Principal seeks work as a resource for teachers or paraprofessionals who have a student they would like to see "walk the plank" or be "lashed to the yardarm." If a student (or group of students) is getting you down, let's get together and design a plan. I may not have all the answers, but two heads are better than one—and we can probably come up with a pretty good plan for solving your problem.

Let me know how I can help!

- A memo in the staff bulletin, or placed in staff boxes, or sent by e-mail to each staff member that reminds them about the collaborative resources available (see the following figure).

Memo to Staff

Date: March 1

To: All Staff

From: Intervention Planning Team

Re: Those pesky middle school kids

> Spring is here …
> The flowers bloom.
> The birds return.
> **The adolescents turn weird!**

Last year about this time, we started having a significant increase in the number of discipline referrals and administrator notifications. Don't forget about us. We'd love to help you with those challenging behavioral and motivational problems. Just drop one of us a note and we can meet to knock around a few ideas (more legal and more effective than knocking around a few heads).

Sincerely,

Ms. Aliquots, Vice Principal
Mr. Welsh, Resource Teacher
Miss Saito, Counselor
Ms. Young, School Psychologist
The Grade Level Assistance Teams
The Schoolwide Assistance Team

Adapted with permission from Sprick, R.S., Sprick, M.S., & Garrison, M., (1993).
Interventions: Collaborative planning for at-risk students. Longmont, CO: Sopris West.
A book of detailed suggestions on collaborative planning in designing behavioral and academic interventions.

Another possibility for encouraging collaboration is to consider some form of teacher-to-teacher collaborative team that meets on a regular basis and is trained to help teachers design intervention plans. These kinds of teams go by a variety of names—Teacher Assistance Teams (TAT), Schoolwide Assistance Teams (SWAT), Staff/Student Support Teams (SST), Intervention Planning Teams (IPT), and so on. For more information on establishing and implementing a collaborative problem-solving team, you might consult *Interventions: Collaborative Planning for High-Risk Students* or the *Project RIDE* program cited earlier in this chapter. In addition *SST: Student/Staff Support Teams* by Phillips, V. & McCullough, L. provides excellent information and training suggestions for how such teams can function.

Take Action!

Using the chart on page 244 as a starting place, build a chart that shows the collaborative personnel available to staff and their relationship to evaluation. Ask each person or group represented on the chart to come up with a "marketing idea." Use these marketing ideas periodically throughout the year so that staff get ongoing information about who is available to help and brief, but steady, reminders about the importance of collaboration.

---

6. Establish "flagging" criteria to ensure that no students will "fall through the cracks" at your school.

A final task in your efforts to support staff involves identifying conditions that will automatically result in collaborative planning to provide help for a student regardless of whether any staff member has initiated a request for assistance with the student. This procedure may not seem, at first glance, to be a procedure to support staff. Establishing flagging procedures may even result in a staff member having to participate in designing a collaborative plan for a student who the staff member had no significant concerns about. However, any procedures that result in increased success for students represent powerful ways to support staff. Therefore, designing early identification procedures to establish collaborative problem solving does provide support for staff. Sample "flagging" criteria might include any time a student accumulates:

> 3 disciplinary referrals
> 5 Administrative Notification Reports
> 4 unexcused absences
> 10 excused absences
> 8 after-school detention referrals

When a student is flagged by one or more of the criteria above, some form of collaborative problem solving (e.g., TAT) should occur to help the student be more successful.

Conclusion

Disciplinary referrals (i.e., disciplinary action involving the principal) are a necessary and important part of a Schoolwide Behavior Plan—so that staff know they have administrative support for severe and/or chronic student behavior problems and so that students who exhibit severe misbehavior learn there are serious consequences for their actions. In addition, a Schoolwide Behavior Plan should include policies and procedures designed to help staff handle less severe behavior problems themselves and respond to emergency situations involving student misbehaviors in a safe and productive way. For this to happen, you need to work closely with your staff to develop appropriate procedures.

As suggested, start by working with your staff to identify those misbehaviors that will warrant disciplinary referral. It's important that these behaviors be few in number and specifically defined because without guidelines, some staff may overuse referral to the point that you are so deluged with referrals that you have little time for anything else, and students become inured to being sent to the office. On the other hand, when referrals are reduced to a reasonable level, you will have time to deal more effectively with the truly severe behavior problems and to work proactively to help troubled students behave more responsibly. You will also have more time to get into classrooms, work with parents, and engage in long-range planning and other tasks that benefit the entire school.

Effective discipline involves more than just specifying what misbehaviors will warrant disciplinary referral. You (and your staff) need to develop "menus" of corrective consequences, appropriate for situations ranging from mild to severe misbehaviors, that can be used by staff in classrooms and in common areas. You also need to develop efficient and adequate forms for three major categories of disciplinary actions (i.e., disciplinary referrals, administrator notification, and other schoolwide disciplinary systems such as after-school detention), clearly identify the roles and procedures to be used by office staff when students are sent to the office for disciplinary referrals, and ensure that staff have (and know about) a variety of available collaborative resources for helping them deal with student misbehavior.

This chapter has explained why and how your disciplinary procedures should provide efficient and effective responses to emergency situations involving behavior and support staff in their efforts to deal with student misbehavior. Ideally, you and your staff will work closely together regarding your disciplinary procedures so that misbehaving students will sense staff's unified approach in helping them learn to behave more responsibly in the future.

Take Action!

Check staff perceptions about the degree to which they feel supported by you in matters of behavior and discipline. For example, you might consider giving staff an open-ended survey like the one that follows. A survey like this provides an opportunity for staff to express what they appreciate and do not appreciate about your role in behavior management and discipline issues. Notice that the instructions direct staff to return their completed surveys to a staff member other than you (e.g., a secretary) who will compile and type up their responses, ensuring complete confidentiality.

An effort like this may feel somewhat threatening, but it is well worth doing. Just your willingness to solicit this kind of evaluation of your efforts communicates to staff that you want to support them and are willing to examine their input.

If you find that staff express some level of dissatisfaction with one or more aspects of the disciplinary procedures within the school, have your SBP team or a special task force work through all of the issues and tasks suggested within this chapter. This group can design recommendations to present to the entire staff that will improve the levels of consistency, support, and cooperation in dealing with disciplinary problems.

Staff Survey Example

Dear Staff:

We all play a part in our efforts to teach students to behave responsibly. One of the most difficult aspects of effective discipline is the coordination between all the different adults in the school. I want to improve my efforts to support you in the area of discipline and classroom management. To assist me in those efforts, please take a few moments to respond to the questions below and return the form to Lisa Allen's box by April 30. Lisa will type a summary of the responses to give to me, and I will share the summary with the Leadership Team, so we can discuss and consider changes based on what we learn from your responses. You do not need to put your name on the completed questionnaire. Thank you for your time and effort in providing me with this information.

1. One aspect of our school's policies for discipline and behavior management that I feel is working well and should not be changed is …

2. One aspect of our school's policies for discipline and behavior management that I feel is not working well and should be changed is …

3. I feel supported by our principal with discipline because …

4. I sometimes feel that I could be supported more effectively by the principal if …

5. When a student is sent to the office with a disciplinary referral, I think that the principal should …

6. Do you feel we have adequately prepared and trained staff in dealing with emergency situations, such as fighting or an angry and out-of-control student? If not, for what situations would you like more training?

7. Please list any other ideas that you feel should be considered by the principal regarding behavior, discipline, disciplinary referral, the principal's role, etc.

8. I would like the principal to come to my classroom:

   ❏ more   ❏ less   ❏ about the same

Name (optional)

Worksheet for Disciplinary Procedures

1. **Emergency procedures:**

   • Do we have primary and back-up procedures by which all staff members can inform the office that an emergency involving student behavior exists and assistance is needed?

      – If no, how and when do you plan to develop such procedures?

      – If yes, do all school staff have the information and do they consistently have the materials they might need (e.g., Do cafeteria supervisors have a walkie-talkie and the "Red Card?")? If no, what is your plan to get the information and material to those staff?

   • Do we have procedures (like the following) that ensure that help will be immediately available when a staff member requests assistance?

      – A clearly established "line of command" for dealing with disciplinary and emergency issues when you are not available?

      – All office staff are aware of that "line of command"?

      – Procedures for getting additional adult help when needed (e.g., an "Emergency Team")?

   If you answered "no" to any of the three questions above, what is your plan for developing such procedures?

   • Are staff aware of and comfortable with procedures having to do with when (and when not) to use "room clears" and "physical restraint"?

      – If yes, are they consistent in implementation or do they need additional training?

      – If no, identify your plan for arranging training in the use of these procedures.

   • Have you developed a plan for dealing with any high-probability events that should be addressed in more detail regarding dangerous or other emergency situations?

      – If yes, is staff ready to implement the agreed upon procedures or is additional training required?

      – If no, identify your plan for preparing inservice to make staff aware of and trained in the use of the agreed upon emergency procedures.

2. **Do we provide adequate support for staff in dealing with chronic and severe misbehavior? Specifically:**

   • Have we worked as a staff to clarify and provide guidance regarding when to use "disciplinary referral" (i.e., involving you, the principal) as opposed to when staff should handle misbehavior on their own?

   • Have we established a menu of appropriate consequences to fit the continuum of mild to severe misbehavior (e.g., from running in the hall to assaulting a teacher)?

   • Do we have established record-keeping procedures related to severe and chronic misbehavior that provide clear communication and essential information in the event of a repeat offense?

   • Have we designed consistent office procedures for dealing with a student at the time of a disciplinary referral?

   • Do staff have access to an array of collaborative resources for developing plans for severe and chronic misbehavior, and do we "market" those services to staff?

   • Have we identified "flagging" criteria that ensure that no students will "fall through the cracks" at our school?

If the answer to any of the above questions is "No," identify your plan for addressing that topic:

Common Areas—Improving Behavior in Halls, Cafeteria, Playgrounds, and Other Areas

This chapter contains information and suggestions for reviewing, revising, and/or developing content for that section of a School-wide Behavior Plan (SBP) that addresses the school's common areas—those nonclassroom settings or contexts such as playgrounds, hallways, or assemblies where students frequently tend to have behavior problems. In this section of an SBP, you should address each of your common area settings and contexts individually, and you should document, in detail, what everyone is expected to do to ensure that every common area setting and context is safe and productive.

The chapter begins with a brief introduction that explains some of the reasons for misbehavior in common areas and why each setting/context should, at some point, be a focus of your SBP improvement efforts. The main part of the chapter fully explains seven strategies for improving any common area. These strategies include: (1) Developing a goal statement describing what you want the setting/context to be like; (2) Making any necessary modifications on the structural and organizational features of the setting/context to increase the likelihood of achieving your goal; (3) Clarifying behavioral expectations for students; (4) Identifying the teaching responsibilities; (5) Delineating the supervision responsibilities/techniques; (6) Ensuring that responsible behavior is encouraged; and (7) Ensuring that misbehavior is responded to affectively. This main body of the chapter concludes with a structured checklist that can be reproduced and used by those responsible for developing proposals for the common areas section of your SBP.

The chapter also has two supplements. Supplement One consists of sample tools designed to gather *in-depth* information about a cafeteria setting. They include a systematic form for analyzing the structural and organizational features of a cafeteria, as well as surveys and interview protocols for finding out how various members of the school community feel about the cafeteria. Although these specific tools pertain to a cafeteria, they can easily be adapted for any common area setting or context. (**Note:** You may or may not need this much detail for your improvement efforts—however, the greater the extent of problems in a given setting/context, the more information you should have before developing/revising procedures for it.) In Supplement Two, we provide sample written SBP documents for the following common area settings and contexts: playground, cafeteria, halls, restrooms, assemblies, commons/outside area (e.g., in a middle school), before/after campus behavior, and times when a substitute teacher is present. These sample documents are intended to be models for and/or to stimulate discussion and ideas about this section of your SBP.

Note: If you find, in your general review, that there are excessive disciplinary referrals from student injuries, student or parental concerns, or staff complaints related to one or more of your common areas, this section of your SBP may represent a logical starting point for your improvement efforts. If only one common area is causing concern, you might want to work on that area at the same time as you are working through the ideas and activities suggested in one or more of the other SBP content chapters (i.e., Chapters Six, Seven, Nine, and Ten).

If you have many problematic common areas you could schedule "improvement" of one common area per year until you have done them all. Or you might have multiple task forces—each working on a different common area—so that you address most or all of your common areas during a single year. As with all other decisions with respect to your SBP improvement efforts, there is no right or wrong order or time line for proceeding.

Introduction

Common areas are those school settings and contexts that have many different supervisors (e.g., halls, bus waiting areas), or have paraprofessionals as supervisors (e.g., cafeteria, busses, playgrounds), or have large numbers of students (e.g., assemblies). Part of what makes common areas problematic in terms of behavior management is that it is often unclear who (among the adults) is supposed to do what. For example, paraprofessionals may be unsure about whether they should intervene with misbehavior in the halls, or classroom teachers may not know if they are supposed to supervise restrooms, and so on. Staff members who are not certain about their roles and responsibilities with regard to various common area settings and contexts often end up doing nothing at all. Another problem stems from the fact that while classroom teachers are probably the most appropriate staff members to teach students the behavioral expectations, common area supervisors probably have the most direct knowledge about what aspects of a setting/context tend to be the most problematic (e.g., playground supervisors will know which areas of the playground have the most student misbehavior, or which games result in more fighting). This is why we recommend that both certified and classified staff have input on this section of your SBP—particularly on the behavioral expectations, supervision responsibilities, and management procedures.

When there are behavior problems in common areas, often the first instinct is to consider harsher consequences for the misbehavior. However, when many students are exhibiting problem behaviors in a setting, there are probably a number of contributing factors. If you have found significant problems or concerns about any of your common areas, carefully consider whether one or more of the following issues could be part of the problem. (**Note:** Specific strategies and detailed suggestions for dealing with each of these issues comprise the remainder of this chapter.)

First, organizational and/or structural features of a setting/context can set students up for behavioral problems. For example, overcrowding on a playground, having to wait too long in lunch lines, or dismissing all the classes in a large school to the bus waiting area at the same time may increase the probability of behavior problems in those areas. Second, when the behavioral expectations for students in a common area are not clear—to students and/or to staff—the students are more likely to misbehave. Further, even if staff know what the expectations are, unless those expectations have been taught *directly* to students, it is unlikely that students will follow them.

A third issue affecting behavior in a common area involves insufficient and/or inconsistent supervision. If there are never any adults present in the hallways, for example, or if only some of the adults present bother to stop students when they run in the hallways, running in the halls will probably be a problem. Finally, unless students receive adequate and appropriate information about their actual behavior from the supervisors in a common area setting/context (i.e., both positive feedback about responsible behavior and corrective consequences for misbehavior), there is a high probability of ongoing misbehavior in that common area.

When considering behavior management in your school's common areas, you need to take each of these issues into account. The seven strategies explained in this chapter are designed to help you do this—and even if you have no immediate problems, consider each of your common area settings/contexts in terms of these seven strategies every three to five years. As you (or a task force or team) start looking at a particular common area, you may decide that more information about that setting/context is needed before procedures can be developed/revised.

Seven Strategies for Improving a Common Area

The following strategies are applicable for improving SBP practices related to any specific common area setting (cafeteria, restrooms, computer room, and so on) or any particular common area context (assemblies, before/after school, days when a substitute teacher is present in a classroom). (**Note:** There is a reproducible checklist on page 276 that you might want to use to take notes while reading this chapter and/or as a guiding structure when developing/revising the common areas section of your SBP.)

Strategy 1:
Establish a goal statement for the setting/context.

Having a stated purpose or goal for each of your common area settings (and contexts) will make it much easier to come up with appropriate behavioral expectations and effective management procedures for those settings—that is, expectations and procedures that focus less on restraining students, and more on achieving the goal for the area. Having a goal statement can also make it easier for you to determine whether (and even how) a setting needs to be improved. For example, if the goal for your cafeteria states that it will be a setting in which students can "eat and quietly converse in a calm, relaxed atmosphere," but it is in fact a loud and chaotic setting, you will know that something must be done. Without a goal statement, there may be a tendency to think that loud and noisy is just the way school cafeterias are—"it may be unpleasant, but that is the way they are." As a staff (or team or task force), you need to think through what you want your various common area settings/contexts to be like and then set goals for them that reflect your vision. Following are sample goal statements for different common areas:

- The Jackson Elementary cafeteria will be a place where students can eat and quietly converse in a calm, relaxed atmosphere.

- The playground of Jackson Elementary will be a place where students interact and play safely in all games and on all equipment.

- Assemblies at Franklin Middle School will be respectful and enhance school pride as students participate, listen, and follow directions.

- The hallways and restrooms of Franklin Middle School will be safe settings where people interact with courtesy and respect.

Strategy 2:
Evaluate and, as necessary, revise the structural and organizational features of the setting/context to prompt more responsible student behavior.

The way a setting is organized has a big impact on how people behave in that setting. When little thought has been given to structural and organizational variables in a common area, it's possible that students are actually being prompted to behave irresponsibly. For example, if students have to wait too long in lunch lines every day (e.g., more than two or three minutes), there is an increased probability of impatient student behavior: pushing, cutting in line, arguing, and so on. Modifying the schedule and/or the procedures for collecting lunch tickets to reduce the length of time in lines may very well reduce the impatience and horseplay—and result in a more calm, relaxed atmosphere for students. By making a setting or context more "user-friendly" for students, many of the behavioral problems will simply disappear.

It's easy to underestimate just how much the organizational and structural features of a given setting affect student behavior. For example, many middle schools schedule lunch periods to be the same length as their standard class periods. This can mean that students have to sit in a lunchroom for 45 minutes, even though most finish their lunch within 15 minutes. It can also mean that, at the end of the first lunch period, 200 sixth graders are trying to leave the cafeteria at the same time as 350 seventh and eighth graders are trying to get into the cafeteria (creating a "fish-swimming-upstream" phenomenon). Modifying the schedule so that each lunch period is 30 minutes long and the sixth grade students are through with lunch and back in their classrooms before the seventh/eighth grade lunch begins just may avert many behavior problems and increase the likelihood of achieving a "calm, relaxed" atmosphere in the cafeteria.

Unfortunately, in schools (as in many institutions) there is a tendency for procedures to become ritualized. Thus, a school's lunch routine may be done a certain way simply because that's how it has always been done. If you have found that there are an unusual number of behavioral problems in or concerns about a particular setting/context, one of the first things you should do is to look at that common area with the eyes of an outsider and ask questions about its organizational and structural features. The types of questions you might ask about a cafeteria setting, for example, include:

- Could class dismissals be staggered so there are not so many students arriving at once?

- Could the way tickets are taken be modified and/or could there be two serving lines rather than one, so that the amount of time students have to spend in lines is reduced?

- Could procedures be modified so that the confidentiality of students on free/reduced lunch is respected?

- Could the salad bar be moved to a different location so that there isn't so much congestion in the center of the cafeteria?

- Could the physical setting of the cafeteria be modified to create better traffic patterns?

- Could the daily schedule be modified so that the students' lunch period is not quite so long?

- Is there a way to create more supervised physical activities for students who have finished lunch, so that they are not just sitting and waiting to be dismissed?

When evaluating a common area's structural and organizational features, be careful not to unconsciously resist change. This happens more often than one might think. For example, after a group of middle school students and staff did an observation of their cafeteria, one of the students suggested that the location of the salad bar be moved. Several staff members immediately responded, "But it is built into the floor!" Fortunately, the custodian was a member of this committee and he explained that while moving the salad bar would involve about four hours of work, it could be done. When considering potential modifications to a given setting/context, you need to be prepared to ask the "big" questions about how things are currently structured.

Strategy 3:
Define precisely how students are expected to behave (i.e., behavioral expectations or rules) in the setting/context.

There are two primary reasons to take the time to clearly define what you think responsible and irresponsible student behavior should look like—for all your common area settings and contexts. First, if your classroom teachers are not clear about exactly what the behavioral expectations (rules) for a particular setting or context are, they won't be able to teach students what those rules are or how to meet them. And if students haven't been taught (directly and operationally) what it means to "behave responsibly at an assembly," for example, one student might think it means reading a book while the guest speaker is talking (as long as he's quiet), another might think it means clapping after the speaker says something, and yet another might think that talking quietly is okay as long as the speaker can't hear him. Not all of your students will have had direct experience assembling with 500 other people to function in unison as an audience, and therefore it is unreasonable to expect them to behave responsibly unless you have clearly defined for them what "responsible" is.

The second reason for clearly defining your expectations for each common area setting and context is so that the supervision of students will be more consistent. Without clearly defined expectations, the staff members supervising an assembly might have different ideas about what responsible student behavior is—and therefore deal with students differently. One supervisor might ignore the student who is reading while the speaker is presenting, while another will give that student (or another book-reading student) a reprimand. It's important that all staff at an assembly know what is OK and what is not OK for students to be doing during the assembly.

Going through a process of clarifying expectations for common area settings/contexts can actually increase the likelihood that staff will be consistent in responding to student misbehavior. (**Note:** When behavioral expectations have been clearly defined and taught, it's also more likely that students will realize that supervisors are not "out to get them," but that they are just following through on the established expectations.)

Whatever the setting or context, you want to have as few expectations as possible (for ease of understanding), but as many as necessary to ensure the setting is safe and productive. To the extent you can, frame your rules or expectations as positive rather than negative statements. For complex settings like playgrounds, it may be necessary to have several expectations (in order to ensure safety for one thing); however, keep in mind that the more complex (or numerous) the behavioral expectations are, the greater the need is for comprehensive classroom lessons.

Having written lists of expectations for each common area will increase the consistency with which your classroom teachers present the expectations for these settings and contexts. If they are given a written list of rules, for example, you can be more certain that all your primary teachers will teach their students the same set of rules for behavior during recess. If you do not have written lists of your expectations concerning student behavior in all common area settings and contexts, they should be developed. And, if you have written rules for common areas, but it has been more than a year since you have reviewed and revised them, they should be updated. Schools continually and gradually evolve so that once appropriate rules for a particular setting or context eventually become outdated. For example, changes in where parents pick up students after school may mean that the rules for the bus loading areas (i.e., where students line up for busses and so on) need to be changed too. When rules are outdated, even if only in part, both students and staff will be more inclined not to pay attention to them.

Following is a sample set of rules that might be applicable for elementary school restrooms:

1.   Use restrooms on your way out to recess.

2.   If restrooms must be used during class or recess, students must have a restroom pass.

3.   Use restrooms appropriately and leave them clean.

4.   Put toilet paper in the toilet. Put all other paper in the garbage can.

5.   Flush the toilet after use.

6.   Wash your hands with soap and water after using the toilet.

Note: At first glance, it may seem silly to have a rule about "flushing the toilet after use." However, at one school that was having ongoing problems with unflushed toilets, staff learned that many of their students—who had moved from a country with severe water shortages—had been trained not to flush toilets because it was an adult responsibility and only occurred once or twice a day. Further proof that each school's rules need to reflect its unique circumstances!

Strategy 4:
Determine how and ensure that students will be taught what the behavioral expectations are and how to meet them.

Whenever you expect students to behave responsibly, you must make sure they have been taught what constitutes responsible behavior and, when necessary, how to meet those expectations. As part of this section of your SBP, therefore, you should specify how, when, and by whom these lessons will be taught to students. Without direct teaching of expectations for a given setting, it is unreasonable to expect students to behave responsibly in that setting. For example, unless students have been taught how to come into the school at the conclusion of recess, they may not do so in a prompt and orderly fashion. After all, where else are they expected to stop playing and converge with 200 other people through one doorway. The expected behavior is unique and idiosyncratic to this one situation. Thus, for every common area setting and context, both what the expectations are and how to meet them need to be specifically taught and practiced until students fully understand them.

Lessons on behavioral expectations for all common areas should take place during the first week of school. In most cases, it makes sense for these lessons to be taught by classroom teachers. For variety, however, you may want to use an assembly with the whole student body to present a lesson on hallway and cafeteria behavior, for example. Keep in mind that the goal of these lessons (whether in class or in an assembly) is not for students to memorize the behavioral expectations word for word. The point is for them to get enough specific information to be clear about how they are expected to behave so that the goal of the particular setting will be achieved.

The amount of detail, modeling, and practice included in the lessons should be higher for younger students and students who are new to the school. For example, playground lessons with intermediate students (most of whom have been at the school for several years) can consist of a quick review of playground rules and a more detailed discussion of rules for common games played by the older students—taking about five minutes each day for two or three days. For primary students, playground lessons should consist of a walking tour of the playground, identifying on- and off-limits areas, and modeling and practicing the safe use of each piece of playground equipment—a lesson of 15-30 minutes each day for three to five days. With eighth grade students in middle school, a cafeteria lesson can consist of a quick review of the rules lasting three to four minutes. With sixth grade students, the lesson should include showing them where the cafeteria is, where lines form, how to deal with trays and clean up messes, as well as the specific behavioral rules. A lesson like this, to really orient students, would probably take 10-15 minutes.

For students just entering middle school (i.e., sixth graders), you might want to use an assembly situation to teach them behavioral expectations in a controlled setting without older students present. A good general rule to remember is that it is much easier to teach and expect appropriate behavior from the very beginning than to correct misbehavior after the fact. In fact, in a middle school with history of out-of-control behavior, you might want to start the year with a series of grade level assemblies to teach required behaviors. Then, when the whole school comes together for the first time (e.g., at an assembly), the behaviors can be reinforced by all staff.

Some behaviors are best taught in a group setting such as school assembly. For example, school assemblies can be very effective forums for teaching schoolwide manners—such as how to behave in a school assembly or in the lunchroom. For a school behavior assembly to be successful and memorable, it should be well planned and creatively presented. The tradition of bringing the whole school into the gymnasium the first day of school and reading a series of rules needs to be abandoned. Students learn from a very early age to tune out nagging, preaching, and rule stating. Your goal is to get your point across while keeping the students' interest and creating a strong memory of the rules. This can be achieved by reducing the rules to a concise number that can be presented by students or staff in both oral and visual formats, and made real through modeling and even role playing.

Side Note

Students should be taught how to express their enthusiasm in different types of assembly situations. That is, while it might be perfectly appropriate to hoot and call out support in a donkey basketball game, this would not be an acceptable way to show appreciation to a singing group. For some students, a school assembly may be the only cultural event they have ever been exposed to, and therefore cultural conventions must be taught and reinforced.

If you do use a rules assembly format, separate students into age level groupings—so that you can gear the presentations to the age level, sophistication, and knowledge level of each group. While it is important to very clearly describe the simplest of rules to very young children, older children generally know the rules but need to be reminded to follow them. Likewise, younger children may enjoy a dramatic enactment of examples and nonexamples of rule following, while the drama may need to be toned down and a bit more sophisticated for the older students.

Behavioral expectations for common areas should be reinforced consistently. As students are called to an assembly, for example, the principal might remind them that they need to move through the halls quietly and enter the assembly area using a minimum of noise.

The following pages contain model lesson plans for teaching behavioral expectations for different common area settings/contexts. The first describes an assembly lesson regarding playground behavior for primary students. The second is a lesson plan classroom teachers could use to teach cafeteria behavior. The last one is a lesson plan that can be used by teachers to prepare students for substitute teachers. These model lesson plans may be useful as you design lessons to teach specific expectations for the various common area settings in your school.

Model Lesson Plan: Assembly to Teach Primary Students Playground Expectations

Jenne-Wright School is a primary school of 600 kindergarten and first grade students. The staff of Jenne-Wright have agreed upon a few key rules that need to be presented to students in a schoolwide assembly. After the assembly teachers will return to the classroom to discuss the rules and practice them. Over the next few weeks, all staff will make a conscious effort to compliment students on following rules, clearly stating what the rule is and why following it makes the school a safer place to be.

The assembly begins with the principal announcing there will be two visitors to the school. Their names are Jenny Right and Jenny Wrong. Jenny Right and Jenny Wrong enter the gym as the principal narrates, "Jenny Right is playing with a playground ball the right way. She is bouncing it and sharing with others. She isn't kicking the ball, and notice that she keeps it in her hands until she gets out to the playground. Now Jenny Wrong has decided that she wants to play with the ball. Let's see if she knows the right way to share." Jenny Wrong goes up to Jenny Right and shouts, "I want that ball!"; then takes it from Jenny Right and runs away. The principal asks the student body, "Is that the right way to share?" The students chorus "No!" The principal then states, "I am looking for someone in the audience who will show Jenny Wrong the right way to share. I'll know who to pick because he/she will have his/her hand up, be sitting flat on the floor, and will be quiet." The principal then has a student demonstrate the right way to ask to share.

The assembly proceeds with demonstrations of a few more playground rules, then a demonstration to students of the correct way to clean up after themselves in the lunchroom. In every case an example and nonexample are shown, and students from the audience are used to demonstrate the correct behavior. Students visibly enjoy the assembly, and before they are excused they are asked to reflect for a moment on three rules they remember from the assembly. They are told they will be asked to share with a neighbor. Students are then excused to go back to class. Each classroom teacher conducts a follow-up discussion in which students discuss rules with another student and then with the entire class.

Model Lesson Plan: Cafeteria Behavior

Overall Goal of Lessons

The lunch area will be a safe and clean environment where all people interact with courtesy and respect.

Specific Objectives (Target Skills) of Sample Lesson

Identify two to three critical behaviors on which the particular lesson will focus. For example:
- How one finds a place to sit in the cafeteria
- How one sits at the lunch table

Structure of the Lesson

Individual lessons will vary in time, depending upon the specific skills addressed and the age of the students; however, you may want to keep each lesson to somewhere between five and fifteen minutes. The following outline is one way to effectively structure your lessons.

- **Introduction**—Explain to the students the purpose of the lesson and identify the specific behaviors that will be addressed. "This morning we are going to continue our lessons on appropriate behavior in the cafeteria. Today we are going to concentrate on …."

- **Tell Phase**—Talk about WHY it is important to behave appropriately in the cafeteria and why these particular skills are necessary. Encourage student input and participation in this discussion.

- **Show Phase**—For each target behavior, first define the difference between appropriate and inappropriate behavior. You may wish to use something like a T-chart to help the students recognize the "lines" between acceptable and unacceptable behavior. The following T-chart has been designed to define "how one finds a place to sit in the cafeteria."

T-Chart: How One Finds a Place to Sit in the Cafeteria

Responsible Ways to Find a Place to Sit	Irresponsible Ways to Find a Place to Sit
(Below are some examples that could be generated by students.)	(Below are some examples that could be generated by students.)
– Look for an empty seat. – Ask if you can sit down. – Ask, "Is this seat taken?" – Sit down carefully. – Don't bump into people. – Don't push someone's tray out of the way. – If a seat is taken, go find a different seat.	– Push into a tight space. – Shove a tray out of the way. – Sit down without asking. – Bump or push people as you sit down. – Sit down even though someone said the seat was taken.

(continued)

Next, model the appropriate behavior—clearly identifying any major steps that comprise it. For example, when modeling the appropriate way one sits at the lunch table, you can specifically identify that one:

- keeps one's rear on the bench/chair at all times
- faces the table
- keeps both feet on the ground
- keeps hands within one's own space

Note: If you choose to model examples of inappropriate behavior as well, demonstrate the inappropriate behavior once, first—then follow with one or two examples of appropriate behavior. You want the students to focus on and remember the appropriate behavior, not the inappropriate behavior.

- **Do Phase**—The purpose of this phase is to have students practice the appropriate behavior in the actual setting. (**Note:** You will need to make arrangements in advance to use the cafeteria.) Once you get the students to the cafeteria, take a few minutes to review. That is, define the appropriate behavior, provide a rationale for using it, list the major steps of the behavior, and model it yourself.

Then have several different students practice the behavior. Ask the onlookers to identify potentially inappropriate ways of behaving and how the students could respond to such inappropriate behavior. If possible, provide the students with strategies on how they can maintain appropriate behavior during challenging situations.

Use feedback and praise during the practice sessions. You should give the students honest and specific feedback (including praise) on their efforts, and you can have the students give each other praise and feedback.

Assigning additional practice can be a very effective way of reinforcing both the actual target behavior and the fact that you consider it important. Possible practice ideas include having the students complete a journal entry in which they describe the behavioral expectation and why it is important, asking students to identify other settings in which these skills would apply, and/or periodically having the students report back about their use of the target skills.

- **Conclusion**—Summarize the lesson.

Follow-Up Lessons

Subsequent lessons should emphasize the following topics:

- Entering the cafeteria appropriately
- Waiting in line
- Making menu choices quickly
- Treating supervisors and servers with respect

- Cleaning up your own mess
- Appropriate noise level
- Procedures for recycling and waste disposal

Model Lesson Plan: Having a Substitute Teacher in the Classroom

Introduction

Identify the purpose of the lesson: To prepare for those times when the regular classroom teacher is absent, so that:

- The students will be comfortable and will behave appropriately.
- The substitute teacher will be treated well.
- Learning can continue.

Tell Phase

- Provide students with information on why a substitute may be needed (e.g., the teacher is ill, at a workshop, etc.).
- Explain the designation that will be used to refer to substitutes (e.g., "guest teacher").
- Describe what would contribute to an effective day with a substitute (e.g., everyone is treated respectfully, work gets done, etc.).
- Create a partially completed T-chart that includes positive and negative examples of how to treat a substitute respectfully. Have students brainstorm additional examples for both sides.

Behavior Toward a Guest Teacher

Respectful	Disrespectful
– Raise hand; wait to be called on. Tell guest teacher where math books are located. – Listen quietly while guest teacher gives directions.	– Shout out to guest teacher, "Are you a real teacher?" – Talk with a friend while guest teacher is giving directions.

Show/Practice Phase

- Describe a scenario that might occur (e.g., the substitute does not know how to fill out the attendance forms) and model appropriate ways students could respond.
- Role-play a couple of other situations and have the students describe what they might do and/or how they could respond to help the substitute.
- Have the students practice the expected behaviors. (**Note:** This can be done by setting aside one day in which the teacher acts the part of a substitute all day.)

Conclusion

Review the highlights of the material covered in the lesson.

Follow-Up

Review the contents of this lesson for at least five minutes each month and immediately before any prearranged teacher absences.

Strategy 5:

Ensure adequate and consistent
adult supervision for the setting/context.

In an unsupervised (or an inadequately supervised) setting/context there is a much greater likelihood of behavioral problems and/or potentially dangerous situations occurring. After all, the reason for highway patrols is that people, even responsible, law-abiding citizens in every other respect, are more likely to speed when they know that no one in authority will be around to catch them doing so. In the same way, a hallway where no adults patrol during passing periods is more likely to have behavior problems, and a restroom where students know adults never enter has a greater probability of illegal and/or potentially dangerous activity than it would if students knew that an adult was likely to enter at any time.

One of the most important strategies for all common areas is to make sure that every setting/context has enough adult supervisors. Because conditions vary so widely among schools (and even among various settings/contexts in a single school), there are no firm guidelines about what constitutes "adequate" supervision. On some elementary play-grounds with 250 students, two supervisors may be sufficient. However, if the playing area is large and/or if there are many obstacles to efficient visual scanning and/or if there is a high percentage of risk factors in the student body (e.g., poverty, high transience rate, many angry students, and so on), five or six supervisors may be necessary for adequate supervision. One of the best ways to determine how many supervisors you need for each of your common areas is to watch the current supervisors. If they appear flustered or seem to be continually running from one crisis to the next, the number probably needs to be increased.

We recommend that you use twice as many supervisors per common area setting during the first week of school (which is also the week when students are getting instruction on expectations) as you expect to use during the rest of the year. For example, if you plan to have two supervisors in your cafeteria, use four during the first week of school. This not only tends to "prompt" students to behave more responsibly, but also doubles the probability that an infraction will be observed, and corrected, by an adult. In addition, it increases the amount of friendly adult-to-student interactions taking place, which is a great way to start the year.

Another important way to ensure adequate supervision is to make sure that your common area supervisors know exactly what their supervisory responsibilities entail (i.e., *how* they are to supervise). In the same way that you cannot expect students to meet your behavioral expectations if they do not know what they are, you can't expect common area supervisors to meet your supervisory expectations if they do not know what they are. We have identified some key "supervision behaviors" that improve supervisor effectiveness and consis-tency—and that increase the chances of having safe and productive environments.

One of the features of effective supervision is continual visual scanning of the area being supervised. This significantly increases the probability of seeing misbehavior—and lets students know that there is a reasonable chance they will be caught if they misbehave. Supervisors should also be reminded that since it is very difficult for supervision to be continual (i.e., for a supervisor to be in all places all the time), it will be more effective if it is unpredictable. If students know that the only time an adult ever enters a particular restroom is between third and fourth periods (when the principal sometimes checks in), it is quite likely that smoking or other illegal behavior will take place in that restroom at all times except between third and fourth periods. Playground supervisors, for example, should be expected to continually move around the playground area, and when there is more than one supervisor, they should be in different places—not standing talking to each other. Teachers in a middle school should know if they are expected to assume some responsibility for supervising halls between class periods. (**Note:** Even if there are no actual duty schedules, they might be informed that "In the north wing, at least two staff members should be patrolling the halls [and occasionally dropping in on a same-sex restroom] before school, after school, and between every class period. The staff of the north wing will work together to determine how this coverage will be arranged.")

Supervisors also need to have very specific information about and guidelines for dealing with emergency situations. What should be done if a student collapses? What if there is a fight? (Suggestions for creating plans regarding incidents such as these are offered in Chapter Eight: Disciplinary Procedures.) The point is that as you define your expectations for supervisors, you need to include the procedures they are to follow for high-probability emergency situations.

Note: Clearly specifying supervisory responsibilities, including emergency procedures, is also important for reducing school liability. In the event of an injury and a negligence suit, for example, you want to be able to point to the fact that an organized plan for providing supervision has been developed and implemented. Plans should be reviewed and revised on a yearly basis, and records of this review/revision process should be kept because it documents that you are paying active and ongoing attention to ensuring that every setting is as safe as possible.

Strategy 6:

Give all common area supervisors information on appropriate and accepted procedures for encouraging responsible student behavior in the setting/context they supervise.

Without positive feedback on their appropriate behavior in common areas, students are unlikely to develop a sense of pride in and ownership for these settings and contexts. Unfortunately, in many schools no effort is made to acknowledge students, individually or collectively, for behaving responsibly in common areas. Common area supervisors in particular may need reminders that they are as responsible for encouraging responsible behavior as they are for responding to misbehavior. You can increase the likelihood of this happening by giving supervisors suggestions (e.g., a menu of ideas) on how to do it.

Perhaps the most important form of positive feedback is praise and attention from the supervisors in each of the common areas. That is, you want supervisors to be interacting frequently with students in positive ways—saying hello, asking students how they are, and just generally showing an interest. In addition, they should provide occasional specific positive feedback to students regarding their responsible behavior.

You can also make schoolwide efforts to acknowledge responsible behavior in common areas. At the simplest level, this might entail making an occasional announcement over the intercom, thanking the entire student body for their responsible behavior. This kind of action helps students to learn to take pride in their collective responsibility to the school. "Students of Franklin Middle School, NOW HEAR THIS! NOW HEAR THIS! THIS IS THE PRINCIPAL! I have had several compliments from visitors to our school that students in the halls are friendly, polite, and have made our visitors feel welcome. We should all be proud of the responsible behavior in the halls and our friendly treatment toward guests. Thank you for your attention."

Occasionally, you may find it useful to implement a short-term structured reinforcement system to reward positive behavior in common areas. The advantage of a short-term system (e.g., lasting one to four weeks) over a long-term system is that staff and students are less likely to get complacent and bored with the system. When reinforcement systems continue indefinitely (e.g., everyday the staff is supposed to award "Caught you being good!" tickets to individuals exhibiting responsible behavior in common areas), the likelihood is that after a couple of months, no one will be excited about or interested in the system anymore (so it won't be effective).

What follows are some examples of short-term systems that you might find useful for your school. Additional examples of reinforcement systems can be found in Section Four of Chapter Seven: Encouragement Procedures.

- **CARE** (**Note:** Complete details for setting up and running this program can be found in Section Four of Chapter Seven.)

  The point of a four-week long CARE program (which would be most appropriate for an elementary school) is for staff to "catch" students behaving responsibly—as they move about the hallways, playground, lunchroom, bus, and other common area settings—and give them tickets that can be used to generate individual and/or whole class rewards. The acronym CARE stands for:

Careful Commuting	walking, following "line rules" at lunch, recess, and for getting on busses.
Awesome attitude	following school rules, being kind to others, continuing to be a "careful commuter."
Responsible Leadership	making good decisions and continuing to demonstrate "Awesome Attitude and Careful Commuting."
Exceptional Empathy	showing caring for others while continuing to practice "Responsible Leadership, Awesome Attitude, and Careful Commuting."

- **Activity Day**

  With this program, middle school students are issued tickets by staff (as in the CARE program) for responsible behavior in common area settings. The students then give the tickets they receive to their advisory teachers, who record how many tickets have been earned by each student. At the end of a four-week period, the school holds an activity day, which includes a wide variety of activities such as inline skating, bowling, bicycling, craft classes, and so on. Although everyone gets to participate, students sign up for specific activities based on the number of tickets they earned (i.e., those with the greatest number of tickets get to sign up first—and generally get the most highly desired activities). As with CARE, there can also be a weekly drawing from all that week's tickets (with one or two highly valuable prizes) to increase student interest in the program.

- **Walking to Disneyland**

  In this program, staff members again give out tickets to students who are behaving responsibly in a common area. Each ticket equals 1/10th of a mile toward a destination (in this particular case, Disneyland, but it could be anywhere) about 1,800 miles away. Each time a student earns a ticket, they get to put the ticket in for a weekly drawing (just as in the CARE program), and get to fill in a 1/10th-mile space on a chart in the main hall that shows the "1,800 miles" to the destination. When the chart is all filled in, the entire student body gets to have a special activity such as a parade or a movie.

- **Other rewards that can be given to the entire student body include:**

  - Staff set up a carnival and kids use the tickets they have earned to play the games and buy snacks.

  - The principal arranges to have a helicopter land on the school grounds (contact state patrol, coast guard, or local news agency to see if they would do this for the kids).

  - Teachers put on a talent show.

  - Staff do video broadcasts of funny skits.

  - A high school gymnastics team is invited to perform at an assembly.

  - You hold a school sleepover. (This sounds scary, but with enough adult supervision it is a lot of fun, especially if you can arrange to do it at a local high school and have access to its gym and pool. High school kids can be recruited to help with supervision.)

  - Hold a teacher versus student sports event or an all-school talent show.

- **The Bathroom Fairy**

One of the authors (Kim Marcum) established this system for improving messy bathrooms in her elementary school. Each bathroom has a chart outside the door. After school, the "bathroom fairy" comes around and puts a star on the chart if that bathroom is neat and clean. After the student body receives a certain number of stars, the "bathroom fairy" arranges a treat for all students. Once, Kim even dressed up as the Bathroom Fairy, complete with a toilet plunger on her head, and gave out the treats to each classroom. This is a good example of how a principal can be creative and have fun while motivating students to behave responsibly in common areas.

Strategy 7:
Give all common areas information on appropriate and accepted procedures for responding to irresponsible student behavior in the setting/context they supervise.

No matter how well you implement the other six strategies described in this chapter, there will be instances of student misbehavior in your common area settings and contexts. And supervisors must be prepared to respond consistently and appropriately to that misbehavior. They will be more effective in their efforts if they have been given suggestions and parameters for how to respond. For each common area setting/context, therefore, provide supervisors with a menu of appropriate and acceptable corrective consequences to use. That way, when a supervisor observes an infraction, he/she can simply choose a consequence that "best fits" the particular infraction.

You want the menus to include a variety of items that a supervisor can easily implement, even if more than one student misbehaves. Suppose, for example, a playground supervisor assigns a student to a short time-out against a wall. If more than a couple of students get "timed out," there will soon be so many students in proximity to each other that the consequence no longer serves as a time-out (i.e., a quiet, boring place with nothing much going on). With a list of reasonable options, however, a playground supervisor with two students on time-outs could choose to tell the next student who misbehaves to "Stay where you are and think about what you should have done instead. I'll be back to excuse you in about a minute." Another student who misbehaves might be told to "Walk with me for a couple of minutes until you are ready to play safely."

Be sure to create a range of appropriate corrective consequences for each common area. If the only corrective consequences a supervisor uses are verbal reminders or warnings ("Paula, I have told you before, stop running in the halls," or "Jerome, I'm through warning you about running through other people's games"), some students may learn that misbehaving doesn't really have a cost. Similarly, if the only corrective consequence supervisors have is to send students to the office, they may feel "forced" into giving repeated warnings so as not to deluge the office with trivial referrals. To effectively correct misbehavior, staff need a range of consequences that they can implement easily and reasonably when an infraction occurs. Thus, a student might get a warning the first time he/she misbehaves and a brief time-out for subsequent infractions. If the student's pattern of misbehavior continues over time, a supervisor should report the situation to the office so that the administrator can decide about setting up a special plan, contacting parents, and so on.

Sample Menu of Corrective Consequences for Halls

- Verbal reprimand
- Positive practice—have the student go back and walk
- Briefly delay the student
- Have the student walk with you for a while
- Administrator Notification Report
- Use disciplinary referral only for illegal actions, physically dangerous behavior, and the overt and immediate refusal to follow directions

As you develop a menu of corrective consequences for your common areas, it can be useful to work through several "What if …" scenarios. What if a student is running in the hall? What if you do not know that student's name? What if the student is rude to you when you tell him to go back and walk? What if he refuses? When you have considered high probability scenarios in advance and given supervisors recommended response options, they are more likely to be confident when correcting misbehavior in the setting/context. Remember to emphasize that the key to effectively correcting misbehavior is for supervisors to be calm and consistent in the application of appropriate corrective consequences.

This is important because consistent instructional corrections are major factors in responsible student behavior. In fact, even when you have an adequate number of supervisors, if they intervene inconsistently or inappropriately, that setting or context is going to have problems. For example, a middle school may have enough adults in the halls during passing periods, but if not all of the adults are stopping students from running or engaging in inappropriate intimacy, these behaviors will be more of a problem than if staff were consistent. As stated before, inconsistency may occur because staff are not clear about the expectations. However, it can also occur because some staff just don't care about particular infractions. Unless all staff are committed to enforcing a particular rule, there might as well not be a rule.

Supervisors who intervene with rule infractions in a calm manner will be more effective in changing behavior and in setting a positive school climate than supervisors who are angry and harsh. Supervisors who enforce rules in a negative and hostile manner tend to create power struggles with students that actually increase misbehavior. In fact, negative supervision can prompt some students to misbehave in order to get the adults mad and can prompt others to misbehave to see if they can "get away with it." Effective supervision requires the adults to interact with students in friendly and supportive ways that provide lots of adult attention, acknowledgment, and support. When misbehavior occurs, a supervisor should calmly correct the misbehavior and then continue giving positive attention to students as they are behaving responsibly.

Below are samples of written expectations for playground supervision:

1. During the first week of the new procedures and during the first week of each new school year, there will be four staff supervising the playground—one assistant and three certified teachers.

2. For subsequent weeks there will be two supervisors—one assistant and one teacher.

3. All supervisors will circulate about the playground and avoid standing in one place.

4. Supervisors will be visible and interact positively with as many students as possible by greeting them and engaging in short and friendly conversations.

5. When a student violates a rule, a supervisor will give a gentle verbal reprimand first, using a firm but respectful voice, such as, "Jessica, get off the monkey bars. You can get on the monkey bars after the first bell, when the younger students have gone in."

6. For subsequent infractions, implement as mild a consequence as reasonably fits the infraction.

7. Use disciplinary referrals only for illegal behavior, physically dangerous behavior, or overt and immediate refusal to follow directions.

8. Crisis procedures: Call on the walkie-talkie or send a responsible student to the office with the Red Card (see the following figure) when any of the following occurs:

   - Severe injury/medical crisis

   - Fights, physically dangerous acts, illegal acts, insubordination

   - Student leaves site without permission

   - Unidentified person on site

9. Report to duty on time with walkie-talkie, whistle, Red Card, pen, clipboard, and behavior improvement forms.

   The Red Card is to be run off on bright red paper and should be kept on a clipboard in the possession of anyone involved with playground supervision. In the event of a malfunction of the walkie-talkie system during an emergency, the supervisor should check off the nature of the emergency and give a responsible student the Red Card to take to the office. Office personnel should be trained to drop everything and deal with the emergencies if and when they arise.

Red Card—This Is an Emergency

_____

Supervisor Name

o Fighting or out of control. Send help.

o Serious injury! Call 911.

o Student hurt. Send trained personnel.

o Stranger on the playground.

o Student left the grounds.

o Abduction. Call 911.

o Other: _____

_____

Special Note—The Principal's Role in Common Areas: We noted in Chapter One that, as building leader, it is your responsibility to ensure that every school setting is safe and productive. To accomplish this, plan to guide staff in the development and implementation of the seven strategies just discussed for each common area. In addition, you need to be highly visible in the common areas (e.g., out in the halls, walking through the cafeteria, out meeting busses, and so on). This high visibility gives you a great opportunity to interact with students, parents, and staff. In addition, it allows you to observe staff and students. As you observe, remember to ask yourself the key questions about all school settings summarized in the visual following:

Is the Setting Safe and Productive?

Is student behavior:

Responsible?

Are students behaving in a manner you would want the school superintendent to see?

❏ Yes   ❏ No

Engaged?

Are students actively involved in a meaningful activity?

❏ Yes   ❏ No

Motivated?

Are students interested and enthusiastic about the activities they are engaged in?

❏ Yes   ❏ No

If "Yes" to **all** of the questions:

> If it isn't broken don't fix it!

If "No" to any of the questions, analyze if staff is:

Proactive?   Are staff preventing problems by scanning the setting and circulating among students. Has the setting been structured to prompt active, safe, and productive behavior?

Positive?   Are staff interacting often and in a friendly manner with all students?

Instructional?   Have expectations been taught? Are staff providing age-appropriate positive feedback and correcting behavioral errors calmly and consistently?

Continue to analyze and modify these three staff variables until student behavior is responsible, engaged, and motivated.

Note: If the behavior of a small number of students (e.g., five percent) is irresponsible, it may be necessary to set up individualized plans for these

When you visit a common area (e.g., the bus loading area), you want to look first at students' behavior (to see if it is responsible, engaged, and motivated), but then to consider staff behavior as well. Ask yourself whether the supervisors are supervising in a basically proactive and positive manner. In addition, observe how they correct misbehavior. The goal should be calm and consistent corrections of student rule infractions (i.e., an instructional approach). If you find that students (or staff) are not meeting their responsibilities, provide staff with suggestions for how to improve students' behavior in that setting. For example, you might suggest that teachers reteach expectations to students or that supervisors spend more time in a particularly problematic part of that setting. If there are a significant number of problems in the setting you observe, arrange for a representative team (or a special task force) from your staff to gather more information about that setting and to work through the seven strategies presented in this chapter to develop a revision plan to present to the entire faculty.

If you want more detailed information, the following is a list of inservice programs that can be used for staff inservice and to guide staff in conducting an analysis of specific settings.

- Sprick, R.S. (1990). *Playground discipline: Positive techniques for recess supervision*. Eugene, OR: Teaching Strategies.

- Sprick, R.S. & Colvin, G. (1992). *Bus discipline: A positive approach*. Eugene, OR: Teaching Strategies.

- Sprick, R.S. (1995). *Cafeteria discipline: Positive techniques for lunchroom supervision*. Eugene, OR: Teaching Strategies.

- Sprick, R.S. (1995). *STP: Stop/think/plan—A school-wide strategy for teaching conflict resolution skills*. Eugene, OR: Teaching Strategies.

- Sprick, R.S. & Howard, L. (1996). *Substitutes: Planning for productivity and consistency*. Longmont, CO: Sopris West.

Conclusion

In summary, using the seven strategies described in this chapter, you can significantly improve student behavior in your common areas. Misbehavior in common areas is usually the result of one or more factors, including but not limited to:

- Poorly designed structure or organization

- Unclear expectations

- Expectations have not been taught

- Inadequate and/or ineffective supervision

By defining and teaching expectations, structuring and organizing for success and by ensuring adequate supervision, every common area setting in your school can become a safe and productive part of your school. The following "Checklist for Common Area Settings" is designed to help you do a quick analysis of how well you are implementing the seven strategies in your common areas. Complete one copy of the checklist for each of your common area settings and contents.

Checklist for Common Area Settings

Setting or context (e.g., hallways, assemblies, and so on): _____

STRATEGY 1. Do we have a written goal that describes what we want this setting to be like? ❏ Yes ❏ No

If no, plan to develop one, but in the interim, assume that the goal is for the setting to be "safe and productive."

Overall Rating (based on preliminary observations)

Student behavior consistently matches the goal.	A small percentage of students (2-5%) are frequently not behaving in a manner that meets the goal.		Many students are frequently not behaving in a manner that meets the goal. This setting is bordering on crisis.	
1	2	3	4	5

If the rating above is in the three to five range, plan to analyze and revise policies and procedures for that setting.

If the rating is one to two, plan to write a description of that setting for each of the headings on the grid below (including the goal statement), and place that information in your written SBP to maintain effective practices.

STRATEGY 2: What organizational or structural factors could be modified to improve student behavior (including facilities, scheduling, crowding, and so on)? Be creative and THINK BIG!

	Do we have a written document for this setting that includes:		Do staff know what is written?		Do staff follow the written policies and procedures?	
	Yes	No	Yes	No	Yes	No
Expectations (rules) **STRATEGY 3**	❏	❏	❏	❏	❏	❏
Teaching responsibilities **STRATEGY 4**	❏	❏	❏	❏	❏	❏
Supervision responsibilities **STRATEGY 5**	❏	❏	❏	❏	❏	❏
Encouragement procedures **STRATEGY 6**	❏	❏	❏	❏	❏	❏
Corrective consequences **STRATEGY 7**	❏	❏	❏	❏	❏	❏

Any **"No"** response on the above grid is an indication of work that needs to be done—either revising and writing new procedures or increasing staff knowledge and their abilities.

If the answers are all **"Yes"** on the above grid, but there are still problems, conduct a more thorough analysis of that setting (see the supplement at the end of this chapter) and modify procedures until student behavior is consistently safe and productive.

supplement one
Evaluating the School Cafeteria Environment

Note the following materials are used with permission from:

- Sprick, R.S. (1995). *Cafeteria discipline: Positive techniques for lunchroom supervision*. Eugene, OR: Teaching Strategies.

Although these tools focus on gathering useful information about a cafeteria setting, they can be easily adapted to playgrounds, busses, substitutes, and so on.

The following pages contain suggestions about what kinds of information may be useful to a planning team evaluating the school's cafeteria environment, as well as ideas on how to collect information. Also included are black-line master copies of student and parent surveys, student and parent interview protocols, and a staff interview protocol. These documents may be used as models for developing your own evaluation instruments, or may be reproduced and used without permission from the publisher.

Collecting General Information on the Cafeteria Environment

The following logistical information should be assembled before you begin your evaluation of the cafeteria:

- Numerical information
  - How many students use the cafeteria
  - How many students buy lunch
  - How many students bring lunch
  - How many students get free/reduced lunch
  - How many adults in the cafeteria per shift
- Schedule information
  - How are shifts currently arranged (and numbers of adults per shift)
  - How is cafeteria used both immediately before and immediately after each shift
- Facilities information
  - What is the diagram of the physical layout of cafeteria (i.e., a blank, to-scale drawing)
  - What is the number of tables available
  - What is the number of chairs available
  - What is the number of garbage cans available

Actually "documenting" various aspects of the cafeteria environment (e.g., how noisy it is, how messy it is) can help you prioritize your efforts. For example, you may wish to:

- Audiotape the noise level in the cafeteria
- Videotape the lunchroom (record both noise and activity levels)
- Time how long different lunchtime activities take
  - How long it takes individual students to get from their classroom to the cafeteria
  - How long it takes individual classes to get from their classroom to the cafeteria
  - How long it takes individual students to go through the lunch line (i.e., get their food)
  - How long it takes individual students to go through the checkout line (i.e., pay for their food)
  - How long it takes individual students to eat lunch and get outside (**Note:** When collecting this information, be sure to include students from different grades, classrooms from different parts of the school, and the differences among hot lunches, salad bars, snack lines, etc.)
- "Measure" the amount of food thrown away each day (e.g., weigh the food, use a metric such as number of garbage cans)
- Record (either with videotape or a photograph) what the cafeteria looks like before lunch and after lunch, before it has been cleaned up

Note: The goal here is to get a sense of the cafeteria environment on average. Therefore, you might use a particular technique every day for one week or on random days over, for example, a two- or three-week period.

(continued)

Collecting General Information on the Cafeteria Environment (continued)

General Suggestions for Collecting Information From Individuals

- You can use surveys, interviews, or both to collect information (i.e., perceptions of and concerns) about the cafeteria from individuals. In general, surveys allow you to get less detailed information from more people, while interviews are better for getting more detailed information from a few individuals. The optimum situation is to use a combination of both (e.g., survey all/most students about a number of general issues, and interview a small subset from each grade to get detailed information on specific problem areas), however either alone can provide useful information.

- Do not make this part of the information-gathering process too time-consuming or unwieldy—for yourselves, the classroom teachers, the parents, or the cafeteria workers. Whatever process you choose (surveys or interviews or both), keep it reasonable. That is, cover only important issues and be as brief as possible. In general, neither an interview nor a survey should take longer than 15 minutes.

- Be sure to address the issue of confidentiality—no one should have to worry about being identified. With surveys this is easy; just include a note that no names are required. With interviews, it's a little more complicated. The interviewer will have to assure the respondent that his/her name will not be included on the interview protocol.

- When constructing surveys, keep the following hints in mind:

  - An even number of response choices eliminates the tendency many people have to choose "the middle" or neutral response. With four choices, for example, you have two choices that are negative and two that are affirmative.

  - Framing your statements so that you can use the same response choices for each item makes it easier for respondents (especially children) to understand.

Specific Suggestions for Collecting Information From Students

- When using student surveys, administer them all on the same day or within a two- or three-day period. Have the classroom teachers introduce and explain the surveys. Let them know how important it is for them to ensure that their students understand both the statements and the response choices on the survey. What this entails will vary depending on the grade level of the students. For example, a middle school teacher may only have to clarify the difference between "strongly agree" and "agree," whereas a primary teacher will probably need to read the items and teach the students the difference between "agree" and "disagree."

- Make sure your data collection instruments are appropriate for their audiences. For example, you would not be able to use the same survey with first graders and sixth graders. The vocabulary (and perhaps the length) will need to be adjusted.

(continued)

Specific Suggestions for Collecting Information From Parents

- If you plan to solicit information from parents, don't "surprise" them. Particularly if you will be doing phone interviews (but also if you are sending out surveys), let parents know in advance that they will be receiving a phone call and/or a survey regarding the cafeteria.

- Parents need to know that this (survey and or interview) is something that is sanctioned by and important for the school. The advance notice might include a cover letter on school letterhead from the principal that explains how you intend to use the information and why it is important (some type of cover letter should also accompany the survey itself).

- Parent surveys can either be mailed or attached to a school newsletter. It may be taken more seriously if it is mailed; however, mailing costs certainly must be considered.

- Facilitate survey response by making it easy for the parents to return the surveys (e.g., provide stamped envelopes) and/or by using incentives (e.g., each class that has a 75% return rate gets rewarded).

- Anytime you ask the parents for information, be sure to include some way for them to follow up if they choose to (e.g., provide the name and phone number of a contact person).

Specific Suggestions for Collecting Information From Staff

- Because there are generally few cafeteria staff and because you want detailed information from them, it probably makes most sense to use interviews rather than surveys (i.e., food service personnel, supervisors, and custodians). Keep in mind that these people are busy professionals and arrange the interviews in advance and at their convenience. Let them know when you schedule the interviews what the purpose is (to gather information to help improve the cafeteria environment) and about how long it will take (10 minutes).

- You may or may not find the following questions to be appropriate or useful in your situation. They are more directed at "job satisfaction" types of issues—which can, in fact, have a significant impact on the overall atmosphere in the cafeteria.

  - Do you have sufficient supplies/support to do your job in the cafeteria as you believe it should be done?

  - Who is responsible for making the decisions that affect your job (self, principal, district person)?

  - Are changes to your "area" discussed with you before they are implemented?

  - Do you feel as if you have an avenue for sharing ideas/concerns about the cafeteria? Who do you go to with concerns/suggestions?

On the next 12 pages you will find six sample data collection instruments for gathering information from students, parents, and staff. These instruments may be reproduced and used as is, or they can serve as models for creating your own surveys and/or interview protocols. The sample instruments include:

- Cafeteria Survey for Students

- Cafeteria Survey for Primary Students

- Cafeteria Interview Protocol for Students

- Cafeteria Survey for Parents

- Cafeteria Interview Protocol for Parents

- Cafeteria Interview Protocol for Staff

Cafeteria Survey for Students

(**Note**: Do not put your name on this survey.)

Grade _____   Lunch Shift _____

We want to make our school's cafeteria better. You can help us by answering the following questions as honestly as you can. For each of the following statements, think about what it is like when you eat your lunch in the cafeteria and decide how much you agree with each statement. When you **really don't** agree with a statement, circle the 1. If you don't agree with the statement, but don't feel strongly about it, circle the 2. If you agree with the statement, but don't feel strongly about it, then circle the 3. Finally, if you **really agree** with the statement, circle the 4.

		Strongly Disagree	Disagree	Agree	Strongly Agree
1.	The adults working in the cafeteria are friendly and helpful to me.	1	2	3	4
2.	I like eating my lunch in the cafeteria.	1	2	3	4
3.	The lines in the cafeteria are too long.	1	2	3	4
4.	It is too noisy in the cafeteria during lunch.	1	2	3	4
5.	Messiness is a problem in the cafeteria during lunch.	1	2	3	4
6.	Sometimes other students pick on me when I am in the cafeteria.	1	2	3	4
7.	I know that there is someone who will help me if I have a problem in the cafeteria.	1	2	3	4
8.	I know the rules for behaving in the cafeteria.	1	2	3	4
9.	I know exactly what will happen if I misbehave in the cafeteria.	1	2	3	4
10.	The cafeteria rules are enforced consistently and fairly.	1	2	3	4

Thank you for your help!

Cafeteria Survey for Students (Primary Grades)

(**Note**: Teacher, please read this information to the whole class.)

Grade _____   Lunch Shift _____

Teacher Introduction: We are trying to make our school's cafeteria better. You can help us by answering the ten questions on this survey as honestly as you can. I will read each statement out loud, and while I am reading, I want you to think about what it is like when you eat your lunch in the cafeteria. Then decide whether you think the statement is true for you. If it is true for you, that means you agree with the statement and so you should color/mark the smiley face. If the statement is not true for you, then it means that you don't agree with the statement and you need to color/mark the frowny face.

		Agree	Disagree
1.	The adults working in the cafeteria are friendly and helpful to me.	☺	☹
2.	I like eating my lunch in the cafeteria.	☺	☹
3.	The lines in the cafeteria are too long.	☺	☹
4.	It is too noisy in the cafeteria during lunch.	☺	☹
5.	Messiness is a problem in the cafeteria during lunch.	☺	☹
6.	Sometimes other students pick on me when I am in the cafeteria.	☺	☹
7.	I know that there is someone who will help me if I have a problem in the cafeteria.	☺	☹
8.	I know the rules for behaving in the cafeteria.	☺	☹
9.	I know exactly what will happen if I misbehave in the cafeteria.	☺	☹
10.	The cafeteria rules are enforced consistently and fairly.	☺	☹

Thank you!

Cafeteria Interview Protocol for Students

(**Note**: Interviewer should fill in this form.)

Date _____   Student's Grade _____

Interviewer Initials _____   Student's Lunch Shift _____

Introduction: Hi (*student's name*), my name is _____. I am part of the team that is working to make the school cafeteria better. I think (*teacher's name*) told your class that we would be asking some students to help us, right? Well, you are one of the ones we picked. If it's okay with you, I'd like to spend about 10 minutes asking you some questions about the cafeteria. Please be as honest as you can when you answer these questions. I am not putting your name on this, so no one besides me will know that these are your answers. Are you willing to help us? Great, let's get started.

1. For you, what is the best part about eating lunch in the cafeteria?
    (If necessary, prompt—spending time with friends, food, break from class, etc.)

    _____

    _____

2. Do you think that any of these things is a problem in the cafeteria?

    ❑ Yes   ❑ No . . . . Noise
    ❑ Yes   ❑ No . . . . Messiness
    ❑ Yes   ❑ No . . . . Students being mean
    ❑ Yes   ❑ No . . . . Students stealing
    ❑ Yes   ❑ No . . . . Not having enough time to eat
    (If the student answers yes to any of the above, probe for details.)

3. For you, what is the worst part about eating lunch in the cafeteria?

    _____

    _____

4. Do the adults who work in the cafeteria treat you the way you want them to?   ❑ Yes   ❑ No
    (If the student answers no, probe for details.)

5. What do you do when you have a problem in the cafeteria?

    _____

    _____

(continued)

6. Can you tell me what the cafeteria rules are?
   (Probe for details.)

   _____

   _____

7. What happens if someone _____ (fill in some inappropriate
   behavior, such as "running in the cafeteria")?

   _____

   _____

8. Okay, this is the last question. What suggestions do you have to make the cafeteria better?

   _____

   _____

(*Student's name*), thank you for helping us with this project.
You are really being a responsible member of our school.

Cafeteria Survey for Parents

The cafeteria planning team at _____ is currently working on improving the environment in our cafeteria. We strongly feel that we need parental, as well as staff and student, input on this subject. Therefore, we are asking you to take five minutes or so to answer the following questions about your experiences with and/or perceptions of the cafeteria. Thank you for helping us with this important task.

1. What grade(s) is your child(ren) in (list all that apply)? _____

2. Have you ever visited our cafeteria during lunch?   ❏ Yes   ❏ No
    If "Yes," when (check all that apply)?

    ❏ Within the last month   ❏ This school year   ❏ Last school year   ❏ Several years ago

    Briefly describe your overall impression of the cafeteria.

    _____

    _____

3. In general, which of the following phrases do you think best describes how your child feels about eating lunch in the cafeteria?

    ❏ He/she hates it   ❏ He/she thinks it's okay   ❏ He/she enjoys it

4. Has your child mentioned any specific problems or complaints involving the cafeteria this year (for example, waiting in lines, not enough food, being picked on)?   ❏ Yes   ❏ No

    Please briefly describe these problems.

    _____

    _____

5. Do you know what behavioral expectations are for your child in the cafeteria?   ❏ Yes   ❏ No

    Are you aware of how discipline is administered in the cafeteria?   ❏ Yes   ❏ No

    Please briefly describe your understanding of these issues and how you learned about them.

    _____

    _____

(continued)

6. Are you concerned about your child eating all of his/her lunch?   ❑ Yes   ❑ No

    Please describe the arrangements, if any, you have with your child about finishing all of his/her lunch?

    _____

    _____

7. If we had an "invite a parent to lunch program" would you be interested in and able
    to participate?   ❑ Yes   ❑ No

    Please briefly explain why or why not?

    _____

    _____

8. Are there any other issues related to our school's cafeteria that you think the planning team ought
    to address? Please briefly describe.

    _____

    _____

Thank you for your help!

If you think of anything else you want to add and/or if you would like to follow up on our progress, please
feel free to contact us.

Cafeteria Interview Protocol for Parents

Date _____   Interviewer _____

Introduction: Hello, my name is _____, and I am a member of the cafeteria planning team at *(school's name)*. As part of our efforts to improve the cafeteria environment, we are seeking input from parents, as well as school personnel and students. Therefore, we are calling a number of parents of students in each grade. Do you have about five minutes to answer some questions for me about your experiences/perceptions of the cafeteria? *(If parent indicates that it isn't a good time, ask whether there is some other time that might be more convenient.)* Great, thanks a lot.

1. What grade is your child in? _____
   (**Note:** If individual has children in more than one grade, list all and follow up on subsequent questions with probes on each student's experience.)

2. Have you ever visited our cafeteria during lunch?   ❑ Yes   ❑ No

   If "Yes," when was the visit (check all that apply)?

   ❑ Within the last month   ❑ This school year   ❑ Last school year   ❑ Several years ago

   What was your overall impression (probe for details)?

   _____

   _____

3. In general, which of the following phrases would you say best describes how your child feels about eating lunch in the cafeteria (check one)?

   ❑ He/she hates it   ❑ He/she thinks it's okay   ❑ He/she enjoys it

   Note any comments:

   _____

   _____

(continued)

Cafeteria Interview Protocol for Parents (continued)

4. Has your child mentioned any specific problems or complaints (for example, waiting too long in lines, being picked on, etc.) involving the cafeteria this year?　❑ Yes　❑ No

   If "Yes," probe for details.

   _____

   _____

5. Do you know what the behavioral expectations are for your child in the cafeteria?　❑ Yes　❑ No
   Are you aware of how discipline is administered in the cafeteria?　❑ Yes　❑ No

   If "Yes," probe for details—what are the expectations and how did they learn of them.

   _____

   _____

6. Are you concerned about your child eating all of his/her lunch?　❑ Yes　❑ No

   What kind of arrangements, if any, do you have with your child about finishing all of his/her lunch?

   _____

   _____

7. If we implemented an "invite a parent to lunch" program, would you be likely to participate?　❑ Yes　❑ No

   Why or why not?

   _____

   _____

8. Are there any other issues related to our cafeteria that you would like the planning team to address?
   ❑ Yes　❑ No

   If "Yes," get details.

   _____

   _____

Thank you very much for taking the time to talk with me about these issues.
Please feel free to contact the planning team with additional concerns and/or suggestions.

Cafeteria Interview Protocol for Staff

Date _____   Interviewer _____

Cafeteria role of person being interviewed (check all that apply).

❑ Food service worker   ❑ Cafeteria supervisor   ❑ Custodian

Introduction: As you know, we are trying to improve the cafeteria environment. Your input is very important in helping us to do that. I know how busy you are, and I want to thank you for taking the time to do this.

1. In general, which of the following phrases best describes how you feel about the time you spend working in the cafeteria?

    ❑ I hate it   ❑ I think it's okay   ❑ I enjoy it

2. What would you identify as the most positive aspects about the cafeteria?

3. I'm going to name several different "cafeteria issues." For each one, I'd like you to rate how much of a problem it is on a one to four scale, with 1 indicating that it's not a problem at all and 4 indicating that it is a very serious problem.

	Not a Problem		A Serious Problem	
Students being disrespectful to adults	1	2	3	4
The amount of food wasted	1	2	3	4
Messiness	1	2	3	4
Noise	1	2	3	4
The procedures for students getting food	1	2	3	4
The procedures for students paying for food	1	2	3	4
Students stealing food from food service	1	2	3	4
Students stealing food from each other	1	2	3	4
Students mistreating other students	1	2	3	4
Students not following the rules	1	2	3	4
Other adults not doing their part	1	2	3	4

(continued)

Cafeteria Interview Protocol for Staff (continued)

4. In your opinion, what is the **biggest** problem (or problems) with the cafeteria? What do you think needs to be done to remedy the problem(s)?

_____

_____

5. Do you get the respect and support you need from other staff members?   ❑ Yes   ❑ No
Probe for details—examples.

If "No," do you have any suggestions for improving this?

_____

_____

6. Do you know what the designated school policy is for the various misbehaviors and/or special circumstances that might occur in the cafeteria? (Possible probes include stealing, fighting, drug/alcohol use, medical emergency.)

_____

_____

7. When students misbehave in the cafeteria, do you usually attempt to correct or discipline them, or do you tend to ignore it? Why?

_____

_____

8. When an individual student misbehaves in the cafeteria, are you more likely to talk to an administrator or the student's classroom teacher (probe for details)?

_____

_____

9. Are there any specific issues related to the cafeteria that you would like the planning team to address (probe for details)?

_____

_____

supplement two
*M*odel Procedures for Common Areas

The following pages contain samples of written documents developed by school staff (actually these are composites from many schools). Use these models to generate ideas that are tailored to fit the unique needs of your school. When you and your staff agree to accept a written description of the procedures for a common area, include it in a staff handbook.

- Playground (Elementary)

- Restrooms (Elementary)

- Halls, Restrooms, Passing Periods (Middle School)

- Common and Outside Areas (Middle School)

- Assemblies (Middle School)

- Before and After School (Elementary)

- Cafeteria (Middle School)

- Substitutes (Elementary or Middle School)

- Busses

Responsibility in Common Areas

A school's common areas include such places as the playground, hallways, restrooms, and the cafeteria. With different staff supervising these areas, it is important to share consistent expectations for responsible behavior. Without consistency from staff, there will be continued testing of limits by students. With clarification of expectations, the staff at Lincoln Elementary can focus on encouraging student responsibility and reduce the need to correct misbehavior.

Because each common area is unique, a separate document has been developed for each so that staff and students will have a clear understanding of appropriate behavior in each area. Important expectations that students must understand from the first day of school are marked with "**."

Each classroom teacher will use the information on the following pages to teach students what constitutes responsible behavior on the playground, in the hallways, restrooms, and cafeteria. Expectations will be taught and retaught. The younger the students, the more time teachers will spend discussing, modeling, practicing, and role-playing. If problems occur in any area, staff will resume lessons on responsible behavior in that setting. All students will receive positive instruction and information on how to behave responsibly in different settings. A copy of the rules and expectations for common areas should be placed in an information folder for substitute teachers.

Playground

Goal

Students will play safely in all games and on all equipment.

Responsible Playground Behavior

Note: The following list of expectations is designed to help staff increase consistency while supervising common areas, and to provide teachers with a basis for teaching and reteaching responsible behavior. Given the complexity of these expectations, students should not be asked to memorize or recite them verbatim.

Items that are marked with "**" indicate expectations that students must understand fully and immediately.

1. Rough play is not allowed on the playground.

**2. When the bell rings, students are to stop what they are doing and line up quickly.

**3. Students will settle differences peacefully using the STP (Stop, Think, Plan) method.

**4. Students will show respect for others and follow instructions given by staff.

5. Students will stay outside in the morning before school and during all recesses, unless they have a "pass."

6. Students will stay out of ditches, off hills, and away from puddles and mud.

(continued)

Responsibility in Common Areas—Playground (continued)

7. Students will leave rocks, bark, sticks, and other dangerous objects alone.

8. Students will play only on playground areas, not in the courtyard, grassy areas, or bushes.

9. Students will show pride in their school by keeping the building and grounds free of litter.

10. Students will take turns on equipment.

11. Students will not chew gum or eat candy on the playground.

12. Students will leave knives and other unsafe objects at home. This applies to radios, tape players, hard balls, and toys as well.

13. Students in grades Kindergarten through third will stay off the monkey bars until the first bell during the lunch hour.

14. Students will leave the playground immediately after school and not return until after 3:00 PM.

15. During school, students will not leave the playground for any reason without a note signed by their parents, their teachers, or the principal. The note must be shown to the supervisor on duty.

Consequences for Infractions

When a student misbehaves, the supervisor will calmly and consistently implement the mildest consequence that might be appropriate.

1. Give a verbal reprimand.

2. Use positive practice (have the student do it the right way).

3. Have students involved in a hassle use the STP (Stop, Think, Plan) method.

4. Have the student stay with you for two minutes.

5. Impose a time-out against the wall for one minute or a time-out for five minutes.

6. Have the student write a description of the misbehavior and sign it (see sample Playground Behavior Improvement Form).

7. Submit an incident report to the administrator.

8. Make an office referral.

Playground Behavior Improvement Form

Name _____   Date _____

1. Describe the problem that just happened.

2. What could you have done differently?

3. If the problem happens again, your parents will be contacted. Do you understand?   Y   N

_____

Student's Signature   Supervisor's Signature

The Behavior Improvement Form is a tool for helping students think about their own behavior. After a student has engaged in a misbehavior, a staff member may give the student a Behavior Improvement Form as an assignment. The supervisor should give the student the form on a clipboard with a pencil or pen and have the student fill out the form right then—on the playground. When the form has been completed by the student, the supervisor should discuss the student's responses with the student. The goal is to help the student see that there are more responsible ways to handle the problem situation. A further purpose is to help orient the student to the next activity that he/she should engage in.

(continued)

Responsibility in Common Areas—Playground (continued)

Encouragement Procedures

Staff will consistently encourage responsible behavior through positive interactions.

1. There will be friendly interactions from playground supervisors.

2. There will be schoolwide compliments over the intercom after especially good recesses.

3. Principal may award one minute of extra recess for the entire school.

4. Two or three times a year, the entire school will be given an extra ten-minute recess at the end of the day.

5. Visits will be made to particular classrooms by the playground supervisor and the principal to compliment a class.

6. Twice a year the CARE program will be implemented.

Supervision Responsibilities

1. During the first week of the new procedures and during the first week of each new school year, there will be four staff supervising the playground—one assistant and three certificated teachers.

2. For subsequent weeks there will be two supervisors—one assistant and one teacher.

3. All supervisors will circulate about the playground and avoid standing in one place.

4. Supervisors will be visible and interact positively with as many students as possible by greeting them and engaging in short and friendly conversation.

5. When a student violates a rule, a supervisor will give a gentle, verbal reprimand first, using a firm but respectful voice. For example, "Jessica, get off the monkey bars. You can get on the monkey bars after the first bell, when the younger students have gone in."

6. For subsequent infractions, supervisor will implement as mild a consequence as reasonably fits the infraction.

7. Supervisors will use office referrals only for illegal behavior, physically dangerous behavior, or overt and immediate refusal to follow directions.

(continued)

Responsibility in Common Areas—Playground (continued)

8. **Crisis Procedures**: Supervisors will call on the walkie-talkie or send a responsible student to the office with the Red Card (see figure) when any of the following occurs:
   - Severe injury/medical crisis
   - Fights, physically dangerous acts, illegal acts, insubordination
   - Student leaves school site without permission
   - Unidentified person on site

9. Supervisors will report to duty on time with walkie-talkie, whistle, Red Card, pen, clipboard, and behavior improvement forms.

Teaching Responsibilities

During the first week of each new school year and for the first week that a new procedure is implemented, each classroom teacher will conduct a lesson on playground behavior. These lessons will consist of a discussion of the rules. For younger students, the teacher should actually take the students on a tour of the playground to discuss off-limits areas. With older students, the teacher may want to go through the rules quickly and then spend time teaching and role-playing STP (Stop, Think, Plan)—our school's conflict resolution method.

If problems recur, teachers will be asked to resume conducting short lessons on playground rules and conduct.

Student teachers and aides will be taught playground rules, expectations, consequences, and reinforcers by the principal or another designated staff member.

Note: Training in this method of conflict resolution is available from *STP: Stop, Think, Plan: A School-Wide Strategy for Teaching Conflict Resolution Skills* by Randall Sprick.

Red Card

❑ Fighting or out of control. Send help.

❑ Serious injury! Call 911.

❑ Student hurt. Send trained personnel.

❑ Stranger on the playground.

❑ Student left the grounds.

❑ Abduction! Call 911.

❑ Other

_____

Supervisor's Name

The Red Card is to be run off on bright red paper and should be kept on a clipboard in the possession of anyone involved with playground supervision. In the event of a malfunction of the walkie-talkie during an emergency, the supervisor should check off the nature of the emergency and give a responsible student the Red Card to take to the office. Office personnel should be trained to drop everything and deal with the Red Card emergencies if and when they arise.

The Red Card and techniques for its use are included in the video inservice program:
Playground Discipline
Teaching Strategies, Inc.
P.O. Box 5205
Eugene, OR 97405

Restrooms

Goal

The restrooms at Lincoln Elementary will be clean and safe.

Responsible Restroom Behavior

Note: The following list of expectations is designed to help staff increase consistency while supervising common areas, and to provide teachers with a basis for teaching and reteaching responsible behavior. Given the complexity of expectations, students should not be asked to memorize or recite these expectations verbatim.

Items that are marked with "**" indicate expectations that students must understand fully and immediately.

**1. Use restrooms only on your way out to recess.

**2. If restrooms must be used during class or recess, students must have a restroom pass.

**3. Use restrooms appropriately and leave them clean.

4. Put toilet paper in the toilet. Put all other paper in the garbage can.

5. Flush the toilet after use.

6. Leave stalls unlocked after use.

7. Wash your hands.

8. Leave the restroom as soon as you finish.

Consequences for Infractions

When a student misbehaves, the supervisor will calmly and consistently implement the mildest consequence that might be appropriate.

1. Give a verbal reprimand.

2. Inform the student's classroom teacher.

3. Issue a detention to clean the restroom.

4. Notify the student's parent/guardian.

5. Directly supervise every restroom visit for one week.

6. Submit an incident report to the administrator.

7. Refer student to the principal for insubordination, dangerous behavior, or destructive acts.

(continued)

Responsibility in Common Areas—Restrooms (continued)

Encouragement Procedures

1. Teachers will periodically discuss the importance of responsible behavior and will encourage students to continue to be responsible in managing their own behavior in restrooms.

2. Several times per year the custodian and the principal will send a memo for teachers to read to students providing positive feedback to students for keeping the restrooms neat.

3. Twice a year the CARE program will be implemented.

Supervision Responsibilities

1. When dismissing students for recess, teachers will have them go to the restroom first. Teachers will remind students that "Restrooms will be clean and safe."

2. If a student violates a rule, a supervisor will use a respectful but firm voice to inform the student of what he/she should be doing.

3. For any repeated infractions, a supervisor will have the student call a parent to notify him/her that the student will be staying after school to assist in cleaning the restroom.

4. If a student refuses to follow a direction or argues, a supervisor will calmly inform the student that he/she can choose to follow the direction or be sent to the office.

5. If the student refuses to accompany the supervisor, he/she should make no attempt to physically move the student. Inform the principal or designee of the incident.

6. During the first week of each new school year, teachers should walk students to restrooms at the beginning of each recess and state the restroom goal before students enter. They will stand outside restroom doorways during their class' use. In addition, teachers should plan to enter the restroom at least once each day. Note positive things to reinforce and areas to be improved. Discuss this information with the class.

Teaching Responsibilities

At the beginning of each new school year and after each long vacation, there will be a short lesson on proper use of restrooms. The rules specified above can serve as the basis for this short lesson. Teachers will be responsible for teaching any new students the rules and expectations.

Hallways/Restrooms/Passing Periods

Goal

The hallways and restrooms of Franklin Middle School will be safe environments where people interact with courtesy and respect.

Responsible Hallways/Restrooms/Passing Periods Behavior

Note: The following list of expectations is designed to help staff increase consistency while supervising common areas and to provide teachers with a basis for teaching and reteaching responsible behavior. Given the complexity of expectations, students should not be asked to memorize or recite these expectations verbatim.

1. When moving from one class to the next, students will move safely through the hallways.

2. With 1,100 people in the hallways at the same time, there is going to be noise. However, each individual should try to keep the noise down. Use a normal speaking voice. If you want to talk to someone down the hall, go to them rather than shouting at them. Close lockers quietly.

3. During class time, you must have a signed pass to be in the hallways.

4. Treat everyone with dignity and respect.

5. If a staff member asks to speak with you, stop and talk with that person.

6. If a staff member requests that you correct a behavior, do what the staff member asks you to do. If you feel you have been treated unfairly, make an appointment to discuss the situation with that staff member. If you still feel you are being treated unfairly, you may make an appointment to see the assistant principal to discuss the situation.

Consequences for Infractions

When a student misbehaves, staff will calmly and consistently implement the mildest consequence that is appropriate.

1. Give a verbal reprimand.

2. Use positive practice—for example, have the student go back and walk.

3. Briefly delay the student.

4. Submit an incident report to the administrator.

5. Use office referral only for insubordination or for dangerous or illegal situations.

(continued)

Responsibility in Common Areas—Hallways/Restrooms/Passing Periods (continued)

Supervision Responsibilities

1. Each teacher is responsible for being in the hallways and supervising restrooms during one passing period each day. During at least two other passing periods, teachers should be in the hallways or in their doorways. The staff of each wing will be responsible for establishing their own supervision routine for hallways and restrooms. The schedule will be arranged so that one male and one female teacher are available to do a quick walk through student restrooms to make sure there are no major problems.

2. While in the hallways or classroom doorways, staff will interact positively with students as they pass by. The goal is for staff to supervise in a warm and friendly way rather than in a cold and hostile way.

3. If a student violates a rule, staff will use a respectful but firm voice to inform the student of what he/she should be doing. Staff will point out the appropriate behavior the student needs to exhibit.

4. For repeated infractions, staff will have the student go back and walk, or delay the student for a short period of time.

5. If a student refuses to follow instructions, staff will inform the student that he/she can choose to follow the instruction or be referred to the office for insubordination.

6. If the student refuses to accompany a staff member to the office, the staff member should make no attempt to physically take the student. The staff member will simply inform the assistant principal of the incident.

Teaching Responsibilities

At the beginning of each school year, there will be a short lesson on hallway expectations. To vary the process, on even-numbered years, this will take place during the first period class on the first two days of school. On odd-numbered years, this will be part of the beginning-of-the-year orientation assembly. (This is just one method of diversity to maintain the effect of the lesson from year to year.)

The lessons should be conducted in a way that informs students of the rationale for the procedures (i.e., safety, respect, setting a calm tone for entering class, etc.), and should be presented in a way that implies faculty and students will work together.

If there are recurring problems in the hallways exhibited by a large number of students, a group of students and faculty will attempt to work out new procedures for improving the situation.

Common and Outside Areas

Goal

To allow a safe, supervised outdoor environment for students to congregate during morning break and lunch break.

Responsible Common and Outside Area Behavior

Note: The following list of expectations is designed to help staff increase consistency while supervising common areas, and to provide teachers with a basis for teaching and reteaching responsible behavior. Given the complexity of expectations, students should not be asked to memorize or recite these expectations verbatim.

1. Students will congregate in common areas only during morning break and lunch break.

2. Garbage cans will be provided in each area, and students will be expected to use them for all trash and litter.

3. Everyone will treat others with dignity and respect.

4. A three-minute warning bell will sound to signal that the break period will be over in three minutes. When this bell sounds, students should leave the areas and go to their next class.

5. Twice a year, an "Activity Day" program will be implemented.

Consequences for Infractions

When a student misbehaves, staff will calmly and consistently implement the mildest consequence that is appropriate.

1. Give a verbal reprimand.

2. Remove student from the area for the remainder of that break period.

3. Assign student to clean up an outside area.

4. Submit an incident report to the administrator.

5. Use office referrals only for physically dangerous acts, illegal acts, and insubordination.

(continued)

Responsibility in Common Areas—Common and Outside Areas (continued)

Encouragement Procedures

Staff will consistently encourage responsible behavior through positive interactions.

1. Staff supervising and passing through these areas are expected to interact positively with students.

2. When appropriate, staff will provide positive feedback to students behaving responsibly.

3. Several times a year the assistant principal and custodian will make an announcement over the intercom to congratulate the student body on responsible behavior and for keeping the common areas clean.

Supervision Responsibilities

1. These areas will be supervised during breaks by support staff and the assistant principal. The assistant principal will arrange the supervision schedule for each area.

2. Teaching staff are encouraged to walk through these areas on their way to and from their lunch breaks.

3. During nonbreak passing periods, teachers supervising the hallways should periodically monitor these areas to see if students are congregating in ways that may make them late to class. If so, the staff member should instruct the students to move on.

4. When supervising or passing through these areas, staff should interact with students in a relaxed, friendly manner.

5. If an area appears messy, staff should instruct the students in the area to assist in picking up some litter.

Teaching Responsibilities

At the beginning of the year, all classroom teachers will identify where the common and outside areas are and will discuss the rules for those areas. If there are significant problems in any particular area, the assistant principal will provide a memo to teachers. Teachers will then be expected to discuss this problem with the students. The memo will indicate that if the problem is not solved within one week, that particular area will become off-limits for a week. Problems might include excessive litter or noise, students congregating too long and being late to class, or fighting.

Assemblies

Goal

Franklin Middle School students will demonstrate respectful behavior during assemblies by listening, participating, and following directions.

Responsible Assembly Behavior

Note: The following list of expectations is designed to help staff increase consistency while supervising common areas, and to provide teachers with a basis for teaching and reteaching responsible behavior. Given the complexity of expectations, students should not be asked to memorize or recite these expectations verbatim.

Items that are marked with "**" indicate expectations that students must understand fully and immediately.

**1. When the leader goes to the microphone and says, "May I have your attention please," students are to stop talking and look at the person at the microphone.

**2. Students are to listen carefully.

3. Students will follow their teacher's directions regarding where to sit.

4. Everyone will wait quietly for the program to begin. Quiet talking will be allowed until the program is ready to begin.

5. Students will communicate with the performers with their eyes and ears.

6. Students will never boo, whistle, yell, or put someone down.

7. At the end of the program, the leader will conclude the assembly by thanking the performers.

8. Students will remain seated until the teacher gives them the signal to stand and follow the teacher from the assembly area.

Consequences for Infractions

When a student misbehaves, staff will calmly and consistently implement the mildest consequence that is appropriate.

1. Give a nonverbal warning.

2. Move close to the student and give a quiet verbal warning.

3. Quietly remove the student from the assembly.

(continued)

Encouragement Procedures

1. If the student body was respectful and followed the rules, the assistant principal or other leader will verbally praise the appropriate assembly behavior during the closing comments.

2. Compliments given to the student body by a performer will be shared with the school via the intercom.

3. Teachers will discuss the assembly behavior shortly after each assembly and will congratulate students on their maturity if the assembly went well.

Supervision Responsibilities

1. All teachers should attend every assembly and should place themselves throughout the audience to assist with supervision. If the assembly occurs during a duty-free preparation period, staff members are not required to attend.

2. Staff members will model appropriate behavior for students—no talking while the assembly is in progress, clapping at appropriate times, and so on.

3. If a student is misbehaving, staff will give the student a nonverbal signal to stop.

4. If necessary, staff will go to the student and give a verbal warning—as unobtrusively as possible.

5. If a student needs to be removed, staff will escort the student to the office.

6. The assistant principal will introduce and close each assembly. In the event the assistant principal cannot attend, he/she will arrange for an alternate leader to serve this function.

Teaching Responsibilities

1. Teachers will be given a handout the day before each assembly. This handout will include the following:
   - Style of assembly—entertainment or content focused;
   - Agenda—times, objectives, etc.; and
   - Learning activities to use before or after the assembly (when appropriate).

2. Prior to each assembly, teachers will discuss the agenda and review the assembly rules as specified above. If appropriate, teachers will have students practice how to show appreciation.

3. All teachers will have a follow-up lesson shortly after the assembly to discuss the content of the assembly.

4. After each assembly, teachers will discuss student behavior at the assembly with their classes.

Before and After School

Goal

Students will arrive and depart school in a safe and orderly manner.

Responsible Before- and After-School Behavior

Note: The following list of expectations is designed to help staff increase consistency while supervising common areas, and to provide teachers with a basis for teaching and reteaching responsible behavior. Given the complexity of expectations, students should not be asked to memorize or recite these expectations verbatim.

Items that are marked "**" indicate expectations that students must understand fully and immediately.

1. No students should be in front of the school building in the morning.

2. Staff must provide a hall pass or note to any student who is to be in the building prior to 7:45 AM or after 3:10 PM.

3. At the 7:45 AM bell, students should enter the building in an orderly manner.

**4. While waiting for busses, students should maintain orderly lines behind the yellow line.

**5. Students being picked up by parents must use the crosswalk by the front door. No students are allowed to cut between parked busses to cross the driveway.

Consequences for Infractions

When a student misbehaves, staff will calmly and consistently implement the mildest consequence that is appropriate.

1. Give a verbal reprimand.

2. Use positive practice—have the student do it the right way.

3. Notify the student's teacher.

4. Contact the student's parent(s).

5. For repeated infractions, staff will talk to the assistant principal. The assistant principal may then make parental contacts.

Encouragement Procedures

1. Encouragement will consist of attention and praise from supervising staff members. Students should be congratulated on their ability to be responsible.

2. If deemed appropriate, the assistant principal may provide positive feedback to the entire student body on responsibility before and after school.

(continued)

Responsibility in Common Areas—Before and After School (continued)

Supervision Responsibilities

1. Teachers will be in the hallways or their classroom doorways as students enter the building.

2. Supervisors of the bus area will move up and down the length of the waiting area.

3. When excusing their classes at the end of the day, teachers should periodically monitor to see that their students are being reasonably quiet and orderly.

Teaching Responsibilities

During the first week of each school year, teachers will conduct a lesson on before- and after-school behavior. The lesson will consist of a discussion of the rules. If problems begin to escalate, teachers will be asked to resume these lessons.

Cafeteria

Goal

The cafeteria of Franklin Middle School will be a safe and clean environment where all people interact with courtesy and respect.

Rules for Responsible Cafeteria Behavior

The following list represents the expected behaviors of students related to cafeteria use. These expectations are intended to provide teachers with the basis for classroom instruction in responsible cafeteria behavior, and to help staff increase supervision consistency as well as encourage positive behavior.

1. Students will use quiet voices in the cafeteria.

2. Students will keep their hands and feet and objects to themselves.

3. Students will walk in the cafeteria.

4. Students will eat quietly and use good manners.

5. Students will stay in their seats until dismissed. (To get help, students will raise their hands.)

6. Everyone will treat others with dignity and respect.

Encouragement Procedures

The following list represents various ways in which the staff can consistently use positive interactions to encourage responsible cafeteria behavior.

1. Initiate positive attention and friendly interactions.

2. Provide verbal praise to students who are following cafeteria rules and expectations.

3. Have the assistant principal make a schoolwide announcement over the intercom congratulating the entire student body when cafeteria behavior has been especially good.

4. Have the administration provide a special treat (e.g., ice cream) for all students when cafeteria behavior has been good over a long period of time.

5. Twice each year, implement the CARE program.

(continued)

Consequences for Inappropriate Behavior in the Cafeteria

The following list identifies how infractions of the cafeteria rules will be handled. When a student misbehaves, a responsible adult should calmly and consistently implement the mildest consequence that is appropriate for the particular incident. Possibilities include:

1. Issue a verbal reprimand.

2. Provide positive practice—have the student try it again.

3. Have the student go to the end of the line.

4. Assign the student to a seat at the designated "overflow" table.

5. Have the student walk with the supervisor for two minutes.

6. Remove the student from the cafeteria.

7. Report the situation to the classroom teacher (if an entire class fails to behave appropriately).

8. Submit an incident report to the administrator.

9. Refer the student to the office (use ONLY for physically dangerous or illegal behavior, or for overt insubordination).

Teaching Responsibilities

The following list identifies basic guidelines for teaching students the behavioral expectations and procedures related to the cafeteria.

1. Classroom teachers will be responsible for teaching their students the rules, expectations, and consequences for appropriate behavior in the cafeteria at the beginning of each school year and after any extended vacations (i.e., longer than five school days).

2. Classroom teachers are encouraged to eat lunch with their classes at least twice during the first week of the year in order to reinforce appropriate cafeteria behavior.

3. The assistant principal will be responsible for reviewing cafeteria rules, expectations, and consequences with all new staff members (e.g., student teachers, instructional aides, etc.).

(continued)

Responsibility in Common Areas—Cafeteria (continued)

Supervision Procedures

The following list specifies the logistics of cafeteria supervision, including specific recommendations for supervisor behavior.

1. There will be two supervisors per lunchroom shift. These supervisors will be trained by the assistant principal.

2. The assistant principal will assist with cafeteria supervision at least two days per week.

3. During the first week of school, there will be four supervisors in the cafeteria. The assistant principal will make the arrangements for and train these additional supervisors.

4. While on duty, cafeteria supervisors will:

   - Circulate through the cafeteria, interacting with students in a friendly manner;

   - Use a firm, respectful voice to tell a student who has violated a rule what he/she should be doing instead;

   - Implement a mild consequence (e.g., positive practice) for repeat infractions;

   - Calmly explain to a student who refuses to follow directions or who argues that he/she can choose to follow directions or be referred to the office for insubordination; and

   - Inform the assistant principal if a student refuses to go to the office (i.e., the supervisor should not attempt to physically force the student).

Substitutes

Goal

Students will work productively on days with a guest teacher and the guest teacher will be consistently treated with respect.

Expectations for Student Behavior

1. Follow directions.

2. Work hard and stay focused.

3. Raise your hand and wait to be called on when you have something to say.

4. Give your full attention to the guest teacher when she or he is talking to the class.

5. Accept that the guest teacher will do some things differently than your regular teacher.

Consequences for Infractions

These are to be implemented by the guest teacher:

1. Give a verbal reminder.

2. Use positive practice (have the student do it the right way).

3. Assign the student one minute off recess time per infraction.

4. In middle school, keep student 30 seconds after class.

5. Have student complete a behavior improvement form (see page 240 for a sample).

6. Report the infraction to the classroom teacher.

7. Send student to the office.

These should be implemented by the regular teacher upon his/her return:

1. Contact parent.

2. Give extra lessons to class on treating guests with respect.

3. File an Administrator Notification Report form with the administrator (see page 235).

(continued)

Encouragement Procedures

These should be implemented by the guest teacher.

1. Give verbal praise focusing on respect, productivity, and following directions.

2. Intermittently reward activities—at discretion of guest teacher.

3. Give a positive report (when appropriate) to the classroom teacher.

These should be implemented by the regular teacher upon his/her return.

1. Give verbal congratulations.

2. Plan a special activity for the class (e.g., extra recess time, reduction of homework).

Teaching Responsibilities

Within the first two weeks of school, all classroom teachers will conduct a short lesson on the expectations for student behavior when a guest teacher is present. This lesson can consist of discussing the rules and role-playing some common scenarios where the guest may do things differently. With older students, teachers may wish to increase student empathy toward the guest teacher by using the assignments on page 265.

Within one week of conducting this lesson, each teacher is encouraged to "role-play" as a guest teacher for the day. Whether he/she will tell the class in advance or just begin the role play without advance notice is up to the discretion of each teacher. This "role play" gives the teacher a chance to demonstrate to students the types of things a guest teacher may do differently and the types of information the guest may need from students. This activity also demonstrates to students that the regular teacher understands that things will be different on a day the guest is present.

Supervision Responsibilities

All teachers are assigned a coteacher with the same scheduled lunch period. When one teacher is absent, the coteacher is responsible for making contact with the guest teacher, answering any questions, making himself/herself available should the guest need assistance, and generally making the guest feel welcome. Coteachers will also invite the guest to lunch in the faculty room and will introduce that person to other staff members.

The principal will make an effort to meet the guest teacher in the morning before the students arrive. In addition, the principal will drop in during the day and ask if the guest needs anything.

Busses

Note: We have not included a document on busses because many states and many individual transportation departments have specific rules that students are expected to follow. If this is not the case in your district, work with a team of drivers, transportation supervisors, principal, and a couple of teachers to develop a written document about bus rides that addresses each of the items on the checklist below. This checklist is copied with permission from *Bus discipline: A positive approach* by R.S. Sprick and G. Colvin.

Checklist and Implementation Plan for School Transportation Policy and Procedures Manual

This checklist is designed to determine whether a given item is written or clearly expressed in the school transportation manual.

_____ 1. **Statement of philosophy or rationale**
_____ Transportation is part of the school day (beginning and end).
_____ Bus expectations have the same status as expectations for any school setting.
_____ The bus driver has the same authority as other school staff.

_____ 2. **Goals**
_____ Goals are consistent with schoolwide goals.
_____ Safety is the major goal.
_____ Good behavior is necessary for safety.

_____ 3. **Expected behaviors**
_____ Expected behaviors are directly related to goals.
_____ Expected behaviors are stated in positive terms.
_____ Expectations are expressed as observable behaviors.
_____ Expected behaviors are explained in terms that are easy for children to understand.

_____ 4. **Consequences (positive and negative)**
_____ Ways to acknowledge positive behavior are included.
_____ Consequences to address problem behaviors are presented as a hierarchy.

_____ 5. **Crisis or life-threatening behaviors**
_____ Behaviors are identified.
_____ Procedures to begin immediately are clearly specified.
_____ Follow-up procedures are specified.
_____ Procedures are coordinated with law enforcement (as appropriate).

_____ 6. **Dissemination and implementation**
_____ Procedures are included to communicate the plan to others.
_____ All parties to receive the plan are identified.
_____ Provisions for ongoing training are included.

(continued)

**Responsibility in Common Areas—Busses (continued)**

_____ 7. **Monitoring or tracking system**

_____ Data to be collected is specified.

_____ A system for collecting and recording data is specified.

_____ A system for signaling or "red-flagging" problems is included.

_____ 8. **Structure to review policy and procedures**

_____ Procedures for establishing a review team are identified.

_____ Provision for input and feedback from all parties is included.

_____ Review and revision procedures are specified.

Classrooms—Assisting Teachers With Behavior and Discipline

This chapter contains information and suggestions for reviewing, revising, and/or developing content for that section of a School-wide Behavior Plan (SBP) that addresses student motivation and behavior in classrooms. The purpose of this section of an SBP is twofold: (1) To provide a broad description of what teachers are expected to do to keep their classroom safe and productive, along with general guidelines about how they are to do this; and (2) To make it clear that there is plenty of room for professional judgment in exactly what behavior management procedures can be used to achieve those expectations and meet those guidelines. Therefore, this section of an SBP should be a written document that both specifies the basic principles of classroom management that staff have agreed will guide their efforts (including the idea that every teacher will have a classroom behavior plan [CBP]) and presents a template or basic structural outline for teachers to use when developing their own CBPs. Section Two of this chapter is geared specifically to you as principal and has information on how you can help your teachers, as needed, improve their classroom management skills.

The suggestions in this chapter involve the content of and a process for developing an agreed upon statement of the staff's overall approach to classroom-based management and a CBP template. It begins with a discussion of why we believe each classroom needs a behavior plan, and why those plans should be structured for a certain level of continuity, while still leaving room for differences in teacher styles. Section One includes models of materials that might be given to teachers to help them plan and implement their own CBPs and samples of written SBP sections that focus on classroom teachers. These materials and samples can be used by you and/or the team that is developing proposals for the "classroom" portion of your SBP.

Section Two starts with suggestions (and a simple form) for observing in classrooms as part of your efforts to help teachers implement the agreed upon principles for classroom management. It also includes detailed suggestions that you can use to help an individual teacher who is having difficulty with student behavior (e.g., the classroom is out of control)—in the form of four written intervention plans that you can give directly to a teacher or that you work through together with the teacher.

Note: If you get an excessive number of disciplinary referrals from classrooms and/or if a significant number of teachers complain about student behavior in their classes, the tasks described in this chapter should be an important part of your SBP improvement efforts. However, because the "Classrooms" section of an SBP involves what individual teachers do in their own classrooms, it tends to be very politically sensitive and consequently needs to be handled very carefully. When developing or revising this section of your SBP, staff need to be as actively involved as possible, and you should work for true consensus before any portions of this section are formally adopted.

This section is often not the best place to start SBP improvement efforts. In fact, tackling the classroom portion of an SBP can be easier and more fruitful once guiding principles have been clarified and/or the section on common areas has been updated. Whether or not it is the logical starting place for your SBP improvement efforts, the "Classrooms" section is an essential area to address at some point. The suggestions in Section Two—on observing in classrooms and helping teachers who are having trouble with behavior management in their classrooms—can and should be implemented by you, the principal, at any point.

Introduction

Because students spend about 80% of their time in school in classrooms, addressing classroom teachers' behavior management practices is an essential part of an effective Schoolwide Behavior Plan (SBP). For example, in a school where all the classroom teachers are proactive, positive, and instructional in their approach to behavior management, the school climate is more likely to be positive and supportive, and students and parents are more likely to feel pride at being affiliated with the school. Students in such a school are more likely to understand that behaving responsibly will help them grow and thrive—personally and academically. And such a school will be one where staff, students, and parents feel joy in the learning process, and where positive energy fuels everyone's behavior. On the other hand, imagine a school were 10% or 20% of the teachers are not effective in managing behavior. Some of these teachers may be highly negative, some may be very disorganized, and some may just let their class run wild. This small minority of teachers will not only have a deleterious effect on the overall school climate, but will also have a disastrous effect on the students who are in their classrooms for a full year.

The "Classroom" section of your SBP needs two major components. The first should be a brief summary of the basic behavior management principles that will guide teachers in their efforts to create a safe and productive classroom. To assist your teachers in developing these basic principles, you should provide them with information (in writing or via inservice) that will better enable them to set up classroom plans that are compatible with both the teacher-effectiveness literature and with the other aspects of your SBP. The second component in this section of an SBP should be a template (i.e., an organizational structure) for the individual Classroom Behavior Plans (CBPs) required of all teachers. This outline should provide the overall parameters (and required categories) for teachers' plans, but be designed so that each individual teacher's CBP can fit his/her style and preferences. The goal of this "Classrooms" section of your SBP is to provide teachers with enough guidance that it is not likely that any individual teacher will implement an ineffective management plan, yet allow enough latitude for the professional judgment and individual styles of your teachers. What follows is a more detailed explanation of the two components, along with model materials and sample documents.

---

section one
*G*uiding Principles of Classroom Management

The first component of the "Classroom" section of an SBP should be a summary statement of an overall approach to classroom management to which all your teachers have agreed. Thus, if your school has adopted a particular classroom management model (such as Cooperative Discipline, Discipline with Dignity, or Assertive Discipline), your summary statement should briefly describe the major tenets of that model. The statement in the following figure is a summary of our model—that is, one that reflects a proactive, positive, and instructional approach. If your school does not currently have a model for classroom management, or if you are dissatisfied with the model you have, you may wish to use this sample as a starting point for discussions with your staff.

Sample Summary Statement for the **Classrooms** Section of an SBP

The classroom teacher is the center of our school responsibility and discipline policy. Teachers will strive to ensure that classrooms are safe and productive and will continually emphasize to students the importance of being responsible, engaged, and motivated. Teachers will focus on teaching and encouraging responsible behavior, rather than trying to "control" irresponsible behavior. This will be accomplished by helping students see how their behavior relates to our schoolwide guidelines for success; emphasizing responsibility, trying, doing one's best, cooperating with others, and treating everyone with respect. Three basic principles of behavior management will be implemented by all teachers.

1. **Proactive**—Classrooms will be structured for academic success, which means having efficient routines, focused instruction, clear rules and expectations, direct teaching of expectations, and frequent monitoring.

2. **Positive**—Classroom teachers will strive to interact frequently with each of their students, providing noncontingent attention/acknowledgment ("Good morning, Tyson. How are you feeling Alicia?") as well as positive recognition when students are behaving appropriately ("Group 4, you are doing a great job of keeping your discussion focused on the original question").

3. **Instructional**—Classroom teachers will view incidents of misbehavior as teaching opportunities and will calmly and consistently implement appropriate corrective consequences.

Note: Though these principles will guide teachers in their classroom management, each teacher, each student, and each situation is unique. Therefore, the specific procedures that will be used by any individual teacher will be determined by that teacher and will be based on the teacher's professional judgment of student needs and specific situations, along with the principles described above.

Provide Information/Inservice to Assist in Implementation

Along with working with your staff to develop a statement summarizing the classroom aspects of your SBP, you also need to give them guidance (in writing or via inservice) on how they can implement the kind of classroom management plan that has been described. The following material, which you are welcome to use, represents "inservice" information on implementing a management plan that is proactive, positive, and instructional. If your overall classroom approach is fundamentally different from this, you can tailor the material to fit your approach and the CBP template that you develop.

An effective CBP will help teachers to be:

1. **Proactive**—organizing their classrooms and clarifying expectations, teaching the expectations to students, and monitoring student behavior;

2. **Positive**—providing frequent positive attention (i.e., noncontingent acknowledgment such as greetings, showing an interest, etc.) and positive recognition; and

3. **Instructional**—responding calmly and consistently to misbehavior so that students learn from these situations.

Specific implementation suggestions for each of these components follow.

1. Proactive

Classrooms will be structured for academic success, which means having efficient routines, focused instruction, clear rules and expectations, direct teaching of expectations, and frequent monitoring.

As you design your CBP, give careful thought to your classroom organization, your classroom rules, and your school's guidelines for success. These proactive procedures can help you orient students to your classroom and increase the probability that your students will behave responsibly.

Develop and teach classroom routines for attendance, tardiness, heading papers, homework, completing work, transitions, in-class movement, getting help from the teacher, and so on. These routines should be designed to maximize instructional time, minimize time spent on administrative and housekeeping details, and facilitate active student involvement in important instructional tasks.

Your CBP should include three to six classroom rules, framed as observable statements of positive expectations, that address the most common misbehaviors you anticipate may occur. Plan on posting these rules, teaching them to students at the beginning of the year, and reviewing them periodically. In addition, be prepared to consistently implement appropriate corrective consequences when a student breaks a rule. Your classroom rules can be developed by you alone or can be the result of a joint teacher/student discussion process that occurs at the beginning of the school year. Sample rules might include the following:

*   Keep hands, feet, and objects to yourself.

*   Arrive on time, ready to learn, with all your materials.

*   Follow directions.

*   Keep your attention focused during instruction and work periods.

In addition to your own classroom rules, you may wish to post your school's Guidelines for Success. When developed as part of a Schoolwide Behavior Plan, both classroom rules and the Guidelines for Success should serve as the basis for lessons throughout the year (see

Chapter Six: Guiding Principles for more information). That is, when encouraging responsible behavior and correcting irresponsible behavior, you want to explain to students how their behavior relates to one or more of the rules or guidelines.

- "Bobby, you were very helpful. You carefully followed our rule, 'Follow directions.'"

- "Sam, I'd like you to finish your assignment. You forgot to finish problems 2 and 5. Remember our rule, 'Always do your best.' It might help for you to go back and check to see that you have a complete answer for every problem before you turn it in."

It is not enough to simply develop and post rules or Guidelines for Success. If you actually want students to meet your classroom expectations, you also need to directly teach these expectations to students. Therefore, another section of your CBP should specify how you will teach your expectations to students. Identify lessons that might be conducted to help students manage situations that cause difficulties—and for each lesson, include the teaching procedures you will use and how you will provide positive practice and feedback. Examples of wording that might be found in this section of your CBP include:

- Teaching students how to handle transitions between activities and lessons

- Teaching students how rules relate to each different type of classroom activity

- Working with the class on conflict resolution strategies

- Conducting lessons on social skills

- Conducting lessons on study strategies

- Teaching and reviewing grading procedures with a course syllabus

In addition to clarifying expectations and teaching those expectations to students, effective classroom management requires you to monitor student behavior frequently, praising positive behaviors whenever possible and correcting negative behaviors as necessary. Systematic monitoring will increase the consistency with which you implement corrective consequences and will allow you to more effectively provide recognition and attention to students who are being responsible. That is why a CBP should specify how student behavior will be monitored. Examples of monitoring procedures include:

1. **Scanning the room frequently.**

   Visually scanning a room provides information and many opportunities to acknowledge responsible behavior. Whether you are teaching the class, helping individual students, or participating with a cooperative group, periodically look around to all parts of the classroom. Stay in touch with what is going on in the room.

2. **Moving about the room during independent work periods and during cooperative groups.**

   Physical proximity not only provides unique opportunities to acknowledge appropriate behavior with a smile, a nod, or a hand on the shoulder, but also increases the likelihood that student behavior will be responsible and engaged—especially if you move frequently and unpredictably throughout the classroom.

3. **Making notes throughout the day on a daily record form.**

   Anecdotal records are another way of monitoring student behavior. The following sample daily record form is an easy-to-use way of collecting useful information on students, without having to write lengthy reports each day.

This type of form can be used for keeping notes on one student, five students, or even the whole class. You might want to consider using this form or designing a record-keeping form that is more tailored to your needs and style. An advantage to an open-ended form such as the one above is that it allows you to record information about students who deserve recognition for special or sustained efforts as well as those who have problems you wish to address. A form like this can also be used to keep organized records of other corrective consequences—for example, you might note students who owe time off of recess or after school, or even things such as the number of times during the day a particular student needed to be sent to in-class time-out. A variation of this form, which can be used for whole classes by middle school teachers or elementary specialists, is a weekly record form as shown following.

Sample Daily Record Form

Name	Comments
Alijan, Tim	Time-owed off recess = AM ////// PM ////
Anderson, Tyronne	Had a great morning—call his mom. Afternoon went pretty well, but he got "wound up" during science labs.
Eichman, Hallie	Time-owed off recess = AM / PM First day with only one minute owed—praise her first thing tomorrow.
Simons, Cheryl	Came to me and asked for help when she got teased—progress!

Weekly Record Form

Student Name	Mon.	Tues.	Wed.	Thur.	Fri.
Adams, Jake	00		000		
Albrecht, Brianna					
Belcher, Tanis			D		DD
Broughton, Emily					
Burris, Adam		A			

Code: 0 = off task   D = disruptive   A = argumentative

What the Research Says—Teachers Who Establish Smooth, Efficient Classroom Routines:

1. Plan rules and procedures before the school year begins and present them to students during the first few days of school.

2. Begin class quickly and purposefully, with assignments, activities, materials, and supplies ready for students when they arrive.

3. Require students to bring the materials they need to class each day and assign storage space as needed.

4. Establish routines for handling administrative matters quickly and efficiently, with minimum disruption of instructional time.

5. Make smooth, rapid transitions between activities throughout the class period or school day.

6. Circulate around the room during seat-work activities, keeping students on task and providing help as needed.

7. Conduct periodic review of classroom routines and revise them as needed.

Allen (1986); Anderson et al. (1980); Armor et al. (1976); Bain, Lintz, and Word (1989); Bielefeldt (1990); Brophy (1979, 1983, 1986); Brophy and Good (1986); Brown, McIntyre, and McAlpine (1988); Doyle (1986a); Edmonds (1979a); Emmer et al. (1980, 1982); Evertson (1982, 1985); Evertson and Harris (1992); Evertson et al. (1985); Gersten and Carnine (1986); Good and Brophy (1986); Hawkins, Doueck, and Lishner (1988); Hawley et al. (1984); Kounin (1977); Leinhardt, Weidman, and Hammond (1987); Medley (1978); Rosenshine (1983); Rosenshine and Stevens (1986); Sanford, Emmer, and Clements (1983); Sanford and Evertson (1981); Wang, Haertel, and Walberg (1993-1994).

The above material is reprinted with permission from *Effective Schooling Practices: A Research Synthesis, 1995 Update*. This excellent summary of school and teacher effectiveness literature was compiled by Kathleen Cotton. To order copies of this resource, call or write:

Document Reproduction Service
Northwest Regional Educational Laboratory
101 S.W. Main Street, Suite 500
Portland, Oregon 97204
503-275-9519

2. Positive

Classroom teachers will strive to interact frequently with each of their students—providing noncontingent attention/acknowledgment ("Good morning, Tyson. How are you feeling, Alicia?") and positive recognition when students are behaving appropriately ("Group 4, you are doing a great job of keeping your discussion focused on the original question").

As part of your CBP, identify two separate (but related) categories of positive procedures. The first category should consist of ways to demonstrate noncontingent interest in and acknowledgment of every student—and can include things such as simple greetings, friendly interactions, active listening, and so on. Saying hello to students as they enter the classroom, chatting with students in the halls, talking quietly with a few students on the way to the cafeteria, showing interest in the individual work of students, stopping by a student's desk to see how work is progressing, discussing projects with students, asking how the recess soccer game went, and otherwise engaging students in a moment of conversation here and there will help you establish rapport with your students. Students should not have to behave in a certain way or achieve at a certain level to be the recipient of this sort of acknowledgment and attention. These interactions communicate to a student that he/she is a valuable member of the classroom and is accepted with warmth and positive regard by you—and may be the most powerful strategy you have for creating a warm, inviting classroom atmosphere.

To increase your use of positive acknowledgment, it may help to identify specific instances during the day that will provide you with opportunities for interacting positively and personally with individual students. Possibilities include:

- Greeting all students as they enter the room.

- Talking quietly with one or two students as they walk to the cafeteria.

- Occasionally, escorting a few students to the bus.

- Discussing work with individuals during independent work times.

- Inviting students to help put up a bulletin board during recess, lunch, or after school.

What the Research Says—Teachers Who Interact with Students in Positive, Caring Ways:

1. Pay attention to student interests, problems, and accomplishments in social interactions both in and out of the classroom.

2. Encourage student effort, focusing on the positive aspects of students' answers, products, and behavior.

3. Communicate interest and caring to students both verbally and through such nonverbal means as giving undivided attention, maintaining eye contact, smiling, and nodding.

4. Encourage students to develop a sense of responsibility and self-reliance. They give older students, in particular, opportunities to take responsibility for school-related activities and to participate in making decisions about important school issues.

5. Share anecdotes and incidents from their experiences appropriate to build rapport and understanding with students.

Agne, Greenwood, and Miller (1994); Allen (1986); Anderson, C.S. (1985); Bain, Linz, and Word (1989); Bain and Jacobs (1990); Cooper and Good (1983); Cooper and Tom (1984); Cotton (1992); Doyle (1986a); Edmonds (1979a,b); Emmer and Evertson (1980, 1981a); Glatthorn (1989);Good (1987); Good and Brophy (1984); Gottfried and Gottfried (1991); Hawkins, Doueck, and Lishner (1988); Kearns (1988); Marshal and Weinstein (1985); McDevitt, Lennon, and Kopriva (1991); Midgley, Feldlaufer, and Eccles (1989); Mills (1989); Mortimore and Sammons (1987); Mortimore et al. (1988); Pecukonis (1990); Rutter et al. (1979); Taylor, S.E. (1986-87); Teddlie, Kirby, and Stringfield (1989); Wang, Haertel, and Walberg (1993-1994); Weinstein and Marshall (1984); Woolfolk and Brooks (1985).

The above material is reprinted with permission from *Effective Schooling Practices: A Research Synthesis, 1995 Update*, cited earlier in this chapter.

The second category of positive procedures involves ways of providing positive feedback and contingent recognition to individuals and groups in order to reinforce their responsible behaviors. The word "contingent" here simply means that this form of attention and recognition is given in response to the specific behavioral and/or academic progress by students. That is, every student should receive recognition for behaving responsibly and making progress, but not receive this form of attention when he/she is not behaving responsibly. This category should include a range of encouragement procedures such as: verbal praise, positive notes on papers, celebrations of progress, celebrations of achievement, symbolic rewards, and (when useful) tangible rewards.

In addition to providing frequent recognition for appropriate behavior, teachers may also wish to acknowledge a student or group in a more structured manner. However, infrequent, major rewards given to a few students tend to be less effective than frequent recognition of daily efforts.

Some suggestions for ways to provide recognition include the following:

1. **Verbal praise for successful and mature behavior.**

    When positive comments are relatively brief, age-appropriate, and frequent, students are generally not embarrassed by recognition. Rather, teacher praise becomes a positive and appreciated part of the daily rhythm of the classroom.

    Examples of age-appropriate positive statements:

    *   *For a first grader:* "Kevin, you are being responsible for your behavior. I can see that you are listening and watching."

    *   *For an eighth grader:* "Whitney, your contributions to our discussion really added to our understanding of the issues."

2. **Written feedback to a student.**

    Special notes to students usurp very little time and often have a special significance to the student.

    Special Note From the Teacher's Desk

    Dear Jenny:
    Thanks for the great day. You are a very responsible and hardworking student.

    Your teacher,
    Ms. Simms

    ---

3. **Written feedback to parent(s) or guardian(s).**

    Outside of report card time, parents rarely hear from the school unless there is a problem. A note to parents regarding responsible behavior, a job well done, or general appreciation helps students feel valued. Parents feel proud, and the positive bond between parents and their children is reinforced as both take a moment to recognize accomplishments. Recognition for improvement is especially important if the student has a problem that he is working to resolve.

    A Note From the Teacher's Desk

    Dear Mr. and Mrs. Polansky:
    Just a note to let you know that Martin has been working hard on getting along with other kids at recess. He should be proud of his efforts. Thank you for your assistance.

    Sincerely,
    Mr. Bender

    ---

4. **Calling the parent(s) or guardian(s).**

    A positive phone call to a parent works much like a positive note. Though phone calls are more time-consuming, a positive phone call tends to take much less time than a call regarding problems.

5. **Certificates of Merit.**

    Certificates of merit for special efforts tend to be highly valued by students. Certificates are more public and formal than notes to students, but provide another way to let students know that their efforts have been acknowledged. Some teachers give certificates of merit intermittently through the year and others give certificates to a few individuals each week in a regularly scheduled five-minute ceremony.

    Certificate of Merit

    This certificate is awarded to _____

    on the _____ day of _____, _____

    in recognition of _____

    Your efforts are appreciated!

    Signed

    ---

6. **Give students additional responsibility.**

    Unfortunately, students who have behavior difficulties are seldom given classroom responsibilities. Yet successfully meeting a responsibility breeds a greater sense of responsibility. As students demonstrate mature choices, their efforts can be acknowledged by earning the right to have special jobs, privileges, or responsibilities.

    From Ms. Feldman

    Letty, you have turned in your homework three days in a row. How would you like to be my homework checker this week? During attendance and lunch count, you would collect papers and check them off.

    ---

7. **Other options.**

The following list of ways to acknowledge student responsibility is not exhaustive. You should add to these ideas for your own CBP.

- Let the class have five minutes of free time.

- Allow music to be played during seat-work time.

- Compliment a student in front of another staff member.

- Ask the principal or another staff member to acknowledge student accomplishments.

- Publicly post a student's work.

- Read a student's work to the class.

- Allow the students to take their work to show the principal.

- Shake a student's hand.

- Award computer time.

- Let a student teach a portion of a lesson.

- Let the class have a few extra minutes of recess.

- Give a student extra adult time.

- Conduct class outside.

- Give a short class party.

In summary, the section of your CBP on positive procedures should consist of two categories: ways of providing noncontingent acknowledgment for all students and procedures for recognizing positive behavior (e.g., praise, notes, incentives, and rewards). Your goal should be that every student receives three times more combined positive attention (contingent and noncontingent) than negative interactions/corrective consequences. Thus, every student should be getting at least three times as much attention when behaving responsibly as when engaged in misbehavior.

What the Research Says—Teachers Who Provide Incentives, Recognition, and Rewards to Promote Excellence:

1. Define excellence by objective standards, not by peer comparison. They establish systems for consistent recognition of students for academic achievement and excellent behavior.

2. Relate recognition and rewards to specific student achievements and use them judiciously. As with praise, teachers are careful not to use unmerited or random rewards in an attempt to control students' behavior.

3. Provide incentives and rewards appropriate to the developmental level of students, including symbolic, token, tangible, or activity rewards.

4. Make certain that all students know what they need to do to earn recognition and rewards. Rewards should be appealing to students, while remaining commensurate with their achievements, i.e., not too lavish.

5. Present some rewards publicly and others privately; present some immediately and some delayed to teach persistence.

6. Make some rewards available to students on an individual basis, while allowing others to be earned by groups of students—as in some cooperative learning structures.

Bain, Lintz, and Word (1989); Brophy (1980, 1986a, b, 1987, 1988b); Brophy and Good (1986); Cameron and Pierce (1994); Cannella (1986); Emmer and Everston (1980, 1981a); Evertson (1981); Evertson, Anderson, and Anderson (1980); Gettinger (1983); Good (1984b); Rosenshine and Stevens (1986); Rosswork (1977); Rutter et al. (1979); Slavin (1980, 1984,1988, 1989, 1991, 1994).

Reprinted with permission from *Effective Schooling Practices: A Research Synthesis, 1995 Update*, cited earlier in this chapter.

3. Instructional

Classroom teachers will view incidents of misbehavior as teaching opportunities and will calmly and consistently implement appropriate corrective consequences. In this section of your CBP you want to identify your responses to misbehavior. As you develop it, keep in mind that your goal with corrective consequences is to reduce the probability of continued misbehavior by teaching alternative behaviors and implementing appropriate and effective consequences.

Using corrective consequences for inappropriate behavior is an inevitable part of teaching. To ensure that corrective consequences will be effective, you must implement the procedures consistently, fairly, and calmly. Students should be informed in advance that certain behaviors are unacceptable and will lead to predetermined consequences. The following information may be useful in determining effective ways to deal with misbehavior.

Misbehavior can be thought of as mistakes—like arithmetic errors. When handled appropriately, students come to understand that their mistakes are actually learning opportunities. Each classroom management plan should therefore include a series of consequences that will be applied consistently to any student who exhibits misbehaviors. You want to have four categories of corrections: (1) Those designed to provide information; (2) Those that involve ignoring; (3) Those that are implemented as in-class consequences; and (4) Those that are implemented as out-of-class consequences.

1. **Corrections that provide information**

   When a student does not know that a behavior is unacceptable and/or does not know *how* to behave responsibly, the most appropriate correction will be one that involves teaching the student. When a student makes math mistakes, you do not "punish" the student, but provide him/her with more information so that he/she can perform the operation successfully—that is, you teach. This is the rationale behind corrections that provide information. Below are brief descriptions of correction procedures that provide information.

   • Verbal reprimands

     Students require corrective feedback or verbal reprimands when they do not know that a behavior is inappropriate or when they are unaware that they are engaging in inappropriate behaviors.

     Cora is a very sarcastic student. Other students find her comments offensive and choose not to be around her. Cora's teacher feels that corrective feedback is an appropriate response to her sarcasm as Cora doesn't seem to know when she is hurting others. Instead, she thinks her comments are teasing. Cora's teacher responds to her behavior by saying, "Cora, when Ben's mom brought in the treats, your comment about not liking that kind of treat was hurtful. It would be better to tell Ben thank you for the birthday treat, or not to say anything."

     Verbal reprimands should also be linked to the class rules when appropriate. This helps students understand the practical implications of how class expectations can guide their behavior. For example: "Andrea, you need to watch the film. Remember our rule, 'Keep your attention focused.'"

   • Proximity management

     When students know how they should behave, but forget briefly, they can often be reminded of what they know without your saying a word. Simply moving toward a student(s) engaged in irresponsible behavior may be a sufficient reminder. An advantage is that you can continue teaching (e.g., presenting the lesson or helping students with a lab exercise) without having to say anything directly to the student(s) engaged in the misbehavior.

- Positive practice

  When a student(s) is having repeated difficulty with a particular behavior, you might want to structure opportunities for the student to "practice" the responsible way to behave. This can be as simple as having a student who runs in the hall go back and walk, or as involved as arranging for a student to receive daily lessons from the school counselor on "following directions."

- Keep a record of a behavior

  This procedure can involve counting the frequency of a particular behavior or writing anecdotal notes on a problem situation. Counting a behavior involves recording the number of times the behavior occurs within a given span of time. For example, an elementary teacher might count how often a student asks seemingly unnecessary questions each day, or a middle school teacher might count the number of times that students in third period make cutting and hurtful comments to one another. By making your counting actions overt, you may increase student awareness about the nature and magnitude of the problem—which, in turn, may be sufficient to change the behavior. This kind of information (e.g., frequency counts) can also easily be charted and used to discuss goals with students.

  Anecdotal notes can be used to describe a particularly troublesome behavior. When the problem behavior occurs, simply write a brief description of the student's behavior. For example, if a student is making inappropriate jokes during class, you could write exactly what the student said. As with counting a behavior, it can be effective as an intervention for the student to be aware of the types of notes you are making. In the hypothetical situation described above, for example, after having a talk with the student about the inappropriate use of humor, you might make notes on the student's subsequent comments during class. Although you don't want to embarrass or humiliate the student, there is nothing wrong with the student realizing that his actions are serious enough to warrant keeping a record. This procedure has the further advantage of providing a detailed account should the problem continue and require that you contact the parent(s).

- Awareness discussion

  Awareness discussions should be a part of every intervention for misbehavior. By themselves, they function as "preliminary" interventions because they let the student(s) know that you have concerns and may motivate the student to improve. For more involved problems, an awareness discussion serves to orient a student to the type of intervention plan that you are considering and gives the student an opportunity to suggest alternative plans or modifications to your proposal. One objective of awareness discussions is to preclude the sense that you are doing something "to" the student, and instead promote the idea that you are inviting the student to work with you to achieve some common goals.

2. **Planned ignoring**

When students engage in misbehavior because they need attention, any interactive correction—from a mild verbal reprimand to a more severe consequence—may actually fuel their misbehavior. That is, these students will be reinforced for their misbehavior when you correct them. If you notice that the frequency of a student's misbehavior increases after using verbal reprimands, you should consider ignoring the behavior. Behaviors that can be ignored are those that do not get in the way of teaching, or in the way of students' learning. Though ignoring is sometimes hard to do, misbehavior is less likely to interrupt instruction when the teacher keeps teaching. Ignoring is the only response to misbehavior that does not require teacher time.

3. **In-class consequences**

When a student understands your expectations and his/her misbehavior interferes with learning, mild classroom consequences should be implemented calmly and consistently. When possible, use a consequence that has some logical association with the inappropriate behavior. Consequences that can be used by teachers in the classroom include the following:

• Contact parent(s)

When contacting parents about problem behavior, treat the parent as an ally—that is, someone who, like you, wants the student to be successful in school. Be descriptive, not judgmental. Tell the parent exactly what the student did, and encourage the parent to talk to the student about how he/she might behave more responsibly in the future. Do not imply that the parent is supposed to "punish" the student for the infraction. Let the parent know that you will keep him/her informed about whether or not the student's behavior improves.

• Reduction of points (for teachers with a point system)

Reducing points is like assigning the student a fine for exhibiting a misbehavior. Therefore, it requires that you have some form of token- or point-based reinforcement system, and that you determine how much each infraction will cost. Be careful of fines that are too expensive. If you have a system in which every student can earn ten points each day, and each incidence of disruptive behavior will cost five points, you need to plan ahead about what you will do if a student misbehaves more than twice. One way to do this is to think about how many times some of the students are currently misbehaving. Then set it up so that the cost of the fine and the number of points the student begins the day (or period) with on a bad day are more than the student might lose, and on a good day the student would have quite a few points left. If one or more students are disruptive 10-20 times a day, design a system that starts each day with 20 points (or one where students can earn 20 each day) and for each disruptive act, the student loses one point.

A variation of point reduction is a Response Cost Lottery described in *The Tough Kid Book* by Rhode, Jenson, and Reavis. This technique involves giving each student a set number of tickets at the start of the day. The students write their names on each of those tickets. Then, any student who commits an infraction has a ticket taken away. All tickets left at the end of the day go into a drawing for a prize. The more tickets a student has left at the end of the day, the greater his/her chances of "winning the lottery."

Another form of Response Cost Lottery is to assign the students to teams. Each of the classroom teams gets an equal number of tickets to start the day. If a student engages in misbehaviors that have been previously discussed, his/her team loses a ticket. At the end of the day, teams place their remaining tickets in a lottery drawing and the winning team receives a reinforcer for every member of that team.

A Response Cost Lottery system can also be used with an individual student. Give the student a predetermined number of tickets (e.g., ten) each day. Each ticket should have a positive reinforcer the student would like to receive written on the ticket. One of the tickets should have a reinforcer the student highly values (e.g., a free homework pass). Two or three of the tickets should name or describe a reinforcer that would be valuable to the student but slightly less so (e.g., 15 minutes of computer time). The remaining tickets should have reinforcers the student would find moderately valuable (e.g., a certificate of merit, getting to choose a class job, getting to go to recess one minute early). The student should know what is on the tickets at the start of the morning. When an infraction occurs, a ticket is withdrawn. The student should not get to see what is written on the ticket or look at the remaining tickets. With each subsequent infraction, the student loses another ticket. At the end of the day, the student gets to draw one ticket from those that remain and this will be the reinforcer he earns. If there are no tickets remaining, there is no reinforcer. The more tickets the student has at the end of the day, the greater the chance that the big prize will still be there to be drawn.

- Time-owed off of recess or after class or after school

Time-owed is a consequence in which each time an infraction occurs, the student loses some time from recess, free time, or after school. Time-owed is especially useful for disruptive and acting-out behaviors. One form of time-owed involves recording the length of time it takes a student (or students) to comply with an instruction. "Class, it should not take longer than two minutes to get our things put away and ready for math. If we are not ready at the end of two minutes, I will start the stop watch. However long it takes until we are ready, the class will owe off the next recess."

To implement this consequence, you need to make a decision about how the time will be paid back. As a general rule, plan to have the student(s) sit and do nothing with the time-owed. In some cases you may wish to use the time to instruct the student in alternative behaviors, but there is a slight risk that the student will find the one-to-one time with you to be reinforcing.

- Time-out (at desk, in room, in another classroom)

  Time-out consists of removing the student from the chance to earn positive reinforcement for a short period of time. Essentially it communicates, "You don't get to play." Determine the length of time that the student should be in time-out (usually not more than five minutes) and identify any other criteria for ending the time-out period. The time should be short so the student has a chance to join class activities and experience the interaction and positive reinforcement that should be an inherent part of instructional activities. Choose a type of time-out procedure that is mild and fits the infraction, then use it consistently. Below are four different types of time-out procedures.

  (1) Head down time-out—When the student misbehaves, he is instructed to put his head down on his desk for the length of the time-out period.

  (2) Sit and watch time-out—In this form of time-out, a chair is placed to the side of the classroom. When the misbehavior occurs, the student is instructed to go to the time-out area and watch to see what the rest of the class is doing, but the student himself does not get to participate.

  (3) Nonobservational time-out—A chair is placed in the classroom facing a wall or corner. The student does not get to observe what is going on in the classroom.

  (4) Interclass time-out—When the misbehavior occurs, the student goes to a prearranged spot in a nearby classroom. This can be especially effective if the student is being sent to a class one or two grade levels different from his own so he does not have his peer group as his audience. Thus a fourth grade student might have a prearranged time-out in a fifth grade room.

- Demerits (e.g., three demerits equals an after-school detention)

  Demerits are most frequently used in middle school when the teacher has a class for only one period each day. For relatively minor misbehavior (e.g., being off task), you can set up a system in which the student only receives an actual consequence (e.g., staying after school) if he/she accumulates three reminders (demerits).

- Restitution (repair damage that was done, e.g., wash desks or write apology)

  This is basically self-explanatory. Just be sure the student knows that when damage is done, the damage needs to be repaired.

- Have student fill out a "behavior improvement form"

  When you want a student to think about what he/she has done, have him/her fill out a form like the one below and sign it. This procedure has the dual advantage of getting the student to think about the problem and providing you with a written record of the problem behavior. This can often be used in conjunction with in-class time-out.

  Behavior Improvement Form

  Name _____   Date _____

  Describe your behavior:

  What could you do differently?

  What do you need to do next?

  Will you be able to do it?   ❏ Yes   ❏ No

- File an Administrator Notification Report

  When a behavior is serious enough that you want the principal to know about it, but not so serious that it warrants immediate disciplinary referral, let the student know that you are notifying the principal about the problem. This procedure can be used in addition to an in-class consequence such as time-owed or time-out. Following is a sample of a Administrator Notification Report.

  Administrator Notification Report

  Name of Referring Staff Person _____

  Location of the Incident _____

  Name of Student(s) _____

  Date _____   Time _____

  Description of the Incident:

  Check the Action(s) Taken at the Time of the Incident:
  - ❏ Discussion
  - ❏ Time-Out
  - ❏ Loss of Privilege
  - ❏ Assigned After-School Detention
  - ❏ Other _____

  _____   _____
  Student Signature   Staff Signature

  ---

4. **Out-of-class consequences**

Occasionally, misbehaviors are so severe that they should not be handled with in-class consequences. However, when a classroom behavior plan is carefully implemented, out-of-class consequences will only be needed when a student engages in physically dangerous behavior, illegal acts, or the overt and immediate refusal to follow adult directions. For information on out-of-class consequences, see Chapter Eight: Disciplinary Procedures.

• Determine which behaviors warrant which type of correction procedure.

Once you have established a "menu" of correction procedures, determine which common misbehaviors should be handled using corrective information, which should be ignored, and which will generate corrective consequences. That is, predetermine how you want to respond to various misbehaviors. When you have determined correction procedures in advance, you will find it easier to respond to an incident of misbehavior calmly and appropriately. For misbehaviors that will require consequences, identify which consequences might be appropriate. Then categorize the various misbehaviors using a chart similar to the sample that follows. By predetermining a menu of correction procedures and categorizing misbehavior, you create an effective plan for responding consistently.

Categorizing Misbehaviors for Correction

Behaviors Requiring Information	Behaviors to Ignore	Behaviors Requiring In-Class Consequences	Behaviors Requiring Out-of-Class Consequences

Teasing
Off task
Bad habits
Sarcasm
	Blurting out answers
	Smart comments
	Minor disruptions
	  – Chair noise
	  – Brief pencil tapping
	Asking silly questions
	Tattling
		Pushing, poking, other minor hitting—
		  Time-out.
		Disruptive behavior—
		  – Pounding on the desk
		  – Shouting in class
		Disrespectful to teacher
			Physically dangerous behavior
			Illegal behavior
			Overt and immediate refusal to follow directions

What the Research Says—Teachers Who Set Clear Standards for Classroom Behavior and Apply Them Fairly and Consistently:

1. Set standards which are consistent with or identical to the building code of conduct.

2. Let students know that there are high standards for behavior in the classroom and clearly explain rules, discipline procedures, and consequences.

3. Provide written behavior standards and teach and review them from the beginning of the year or the start of new courses.

4. Establish rules that are clear and specific; they avoid vague or unenforceable rules such as "be in the right place at the right time."

5. Provide considerable reteaching and practice of classroom rules and procedures for children in grades K-3.

6. Involve older students in helping to establish standards and sanctions.

7. Apply consistent, equitable discipline for all students, making certain that sanctions are clearly linked to students' inappropriate behavior.

8. Teach and reinforce positive, prosocial behaviors and skills, including self-control skills, especially with students who have a history of behavior problems.

9. Stop disruptions quickly, taking care to avoid disrupting the whole class.

10. Focus on students' inappropriate behavior when taking disciplinary action—not on their personalities or histories.

11. Handle most disciplinary matters in the classroom, keeping referrals to administrators to a minimum.

12. Participate in training activities to improve classroom management skills.

Allen (1986); Anderson (1980); Bain, Lintz, and Word (1989); Bielefeldt (1990); Brophy (1979, 1983a, 1986); Brophy and Good (1986); Cotton (1990b); Doyle (1986b); Emmer and Evertson (1981a, b); Emmer and Aussiker (1989); Emmer (1982); Evertson (1985,1989); Evertson and Harris (1992); Gettinger (1988); Good and Brophy (1986); Gottfredson, Gottfredson, and Hybl (1993); Hawkins, Doeck, and Lishner (1988); Kounin (1977); Leming (1993); Mayer (1993); Medley (1978); Render, Padilla, and Krank (1989); Rutter et al. (1979); Sanford and Evertson (1981); Solomon et al. (1988); Teddlie, Kirby, and Stringfield (1989); Vincenzi and Ayrer (1985).

Reprinted with permission from *Effective Schooling Practices: A Research Synthesis, 1995 Update*, cited earlier in this chapter.

Take Action!

In addition to summarizing your basic principles of classroom management in this section of your SBP, you and your staff should develop a template (i.e., a structural organization of major headings) that can be used by all classroom teachers to develop their own CBPs. A template will help you ensure that the plans of all teachers address the essential features of classroom management agreed to by staff (which will increase consistency across teachers and between the various CBPs and your SBP) and yet allow all teachers to complete the details of their plans to fit their own teaching styles. The following two sample are for your information. The first, which is blank, represents a sample template that all teachers would fill out. The second is a sample CBP that has been filled out by an individual teacher.

Classroom Behavior Plan

Teacher _____

Rules

Guidelines for Success

1. _____

2. _____

3. _____

4. _____

5. _____

Teaching Responsibilities

Monitoring

Encouragement Procedures

    Class

    Individual

Possible Corrective Consequences

Classroom Behavior Plan

Teacher __Mr. Kuske__

Rules	**Guidelines for Success**

Rules

1. __Arrive on time with all materials.__

2. __Keep hands, feet, and objects to yourself.__

3. __Follow directions.__

4. __Stay on-task during work times.__

5. _____

Guidelines for Success

Be responsible.

Always try.

Do your best.

Cooperate.

Treat everyone with dignity and respect.

Teaching Responsibilities

- Teaching students how to handle transitions between activities and lessons.
- Teaching students how rules relate to each different type of classroom activity.
- Conducting lessons on study strategies.
- Teaching and reviewing grading procedures with a course syllabus.

Monitoring

1. Frequent scanning and use of proximity management to keep "in touch" with what the students are doing.
2. Weekly printout to each student on current grades and missing assignments—conference with students as necessary.
3. Use of the Weekly Record form to keep track of misbehavior.

Encouragement Procedures

Class

Verbal feedback
Group activities (e.g., game time or time outside)
Cooperative groupings—train to encourage each other

Individual

Verbal feedback
Frequent noncontingent
  acknowledgment
Written feedback—notes on papers,
  certificates, thank-you notes.

Lottery tickets toward drawing (only
  some weeks—to maintain variety)
Parental contacts
Free "Homework" pass
Call on "Top Guns" at home—highest
  male and female on each test
Individualized contracts as necessary

Possible Corrective Consequences

Verbal reprimand
Proximity management
Keep a record of the behavior
Time-owed after class

In-class time-out
Parental contacts
Restitution
Administrator Notification Form

Disciplinary Referral

section two
$\mathcal{G}$uiding Staff in Effective Classroom Management

As principal, one of your most important tasks is to spend time in classrooms guiding teachers in the use of effective classroom management practices. When you see examples of effective practices, you can reinforce those practices by providing positive feedback. And when you see areas in which improvements are needed, you can help the teacher set goals and provide information and/or coaching to assist that teacher in implementing those goals. In the first part of this section, you will find suggestions on how to observe in classrooms with brief "drop-in" visits (to get a sense of which teachers are doing well and which might need assistance), as well as how to do more lengthy observations, as necessary (to get detailed information about what specifically might need to be improved). In the second part of the section, there are four problem-solving plans that you might either copy and give to a teacher who needs assistance or, if you and the teacher prefer, use as a basis for your coaching the teacher in classroom management skills.

Observing in Classrooms

Classrooms are the settings in which your students spend the vast majority of their school time. In fact, the purpose of all other school settings is really to support what goes on in classrooms. Therefore, addressing classroom behavior management issues is of paramount importance. Even a small number of ineffective classroom behavior managers can have a negative effect on overall school climate—which in turn can reduce the degree to which student behavior is responsible, motivated, and engaged. The old adage "one bad apple spoils the bunch" is a very real factor when it comes to school climate. For example, even a school environment where most teachers are outstanding motivators, but where two or three are *highly* reactive, negative, and punitive in their approach to behavior management, will not be as safe and productive as it could be. As the instructional leader of your building, it is essential that you know what is going on in classrooms, and that you be prepared to "coach" (i.e., assist some teachers in their efforts to implement effective classroom behavior techniques).

One of the first things you must do is to establish the expectation that effective behavior management practices will be implemented in every classroom. You cannot do this by merely talking about effective classroom management, or even by seeing to the development of a comprehensive SBP. You must be willing to get into classrooms to find out what is going on, to reinforce effective practices, and to help teachers learn new skills (as necessary). If you are unwilling to do this, some teachers will stagnate, implementing the same ineffective management techniques year after year. And, as stated earlier, even if this involves only a handful of teachers, it can have a detrimental effect on the entire school. The following information describes two major tasks you can use to help teachers improve their skills in managing classroom behavior: conduct frequent "drop-in" classroom visits and schedule longer observations for teachers who need assistance.

Conduct Frequent "Drop-in Visits"

As principal, you should conduct frequent drop-in visits to all classrooms. These visits can help you begin to identify which teachers manage their classrooms well and which are experiencing difficulty. Think of these visits as a way of demonstrating interest and support to teachers and students, as well as an informal screening technique.

You want your presence to be as nonthreatening as possible. Thus, these visits should last for no more than about five minutes, and you should not plan on taking any kind of data or notes. Frequent drop-in visits will help both students and teachers get used to your being in classrooms and will reduce any "threat" that your authority may carry with some staff. However, while in any classroom, you should ask yourself the basic questions that have been suggested throughout this book (and which are summarized on the following graphic).

Is the Setting Safe and Productive?

Is student behavior:

Responsible?

Are students behaving in a manner you would want the school superintendent to see?

❑ Yes   ❑ No

Engaged?

Are students actively involved in a meaningful activity?

❑ Yes   ❑ No

Motivated?

Are students interested and enthusiastic about the activities they are engaged in?

❑ Yes   ❑ No

If "Yes" to **all** of the questions:

If it isn't broken don't fix it!

If "No" to any of the questions, analyze if staff is:

Proactive?

Are staff preventing problems by scanning the setting and circulating among students. Has the setting been structured to prompt active, safe, and productive behavior?

Positive?

Are staff interacting often and in a friendly manner with all students?

Instructional?

Have expectations been taught? Are staff providing age-appropriate, positive feedback and correcting behavioral errors calmly and consistently?

Continue to analyze and modify these three staff variables until student behavior is responsible, engaged, and motivated.

Note: If the behavior of a small number of students (e.g., five percent) is irresponsible, it may be necessary to set up individualized plans for these

During these spot checks, you should mainly be watching behavior of the students, not the teacher. As the graphic indicates, when student behavior in a given setting is predominately responsible, motivated, and engaged, the setting is probably safe and productive, and you do not want to suggest that the teacher do anything different. Therefore, as you watch students, the most fundamental questions you should ask are:

- Is student behavior responsible?

- Are students engaged in important activities?

- Do students seem to be motivated?

These questions are important because your answers will indicate whether students are behaving in ways that demonstrate that class time is being used well, that they are engaged and enthused about what they are doing, that they know what is expected of them, and so on. If your answers to all of these questions are yes, then you should make a point of commenting to the teacher, within the next day or so, about the positive student behavior you observed. If the answer to any of these questions is no, plan to meet with the teacher briefly within a day or two and present your concerns. Be sure to let the teacher know that what you saw in five minutes in no way affects his/her evaluation, but that you have specific concerns about student behavior and that you do want to conduct a more lengthy observation at a later time. If during this conversation you arrange a more lengthy observation, then this contact with the teacher serves as a preconference for the observation (see information that follows). (**Note:** This may be based on one five-minute spot check, or a combination of several spot checks across days or weeks.)

If your staff is not used to having you make these sorts of drop-in visits, inform them at a faculty meeting that you want to spend more time in classrooms. Let them know that you will be doing five-minute drop-in visits more frequently, but that the visits will not have anything to do with the formal evaluation processes adopted by your district. Also inform them that unless you have arranged with them in advance to do a more formal observation, you will not spend more than two to five minutes in a classroom and that you are not looking for or evaluating anything in particular; the purpose is to maintain visibility and to have a sense of what is going on in all parts of the school.

Coaching Staff Who Need Assistance

If you find that a staff member is struggling with classroom management (or with the behavior of one or two individual students), remember that one of your roles is as a coach—observing, making suggestions, occasionally modeling, then observing again, and giving more feedback.

If you determine that it is necessary to do a longer (and slightly more formal) observation of a teacher's implementation of his/her classroom behavior plan, it's important to keep the following three steps in mind.

1. **Arrange a preconference.**

   Meet with the teacher to prearrange an observation. The teacher should know approximately when you will be coming in and what things you plan to observe. In addition, if you will be taking notes, be sure to let the teacher know that and show him/her copies of any forms you might use (e.g., the observation form shown in the "Conduct the observation" section that follows). Give the teacher an overview of the types of things you will be writing. If you plan to observe the behavior of an individual student, show the teacher the types of notes you plan to take. If you have not already done so, inform the teacher whether or not the observation will have any bearing on his/her formal teacher evaluation. Informing a teacher about your observations ahead of time decreases the chance that he will perceive that you are trying to catch him at his worst.

   Find out from the teacher the nature of the lesson you will be observing, and discuss where you should be during the observation. You want to be in a place where you can easily observe both student behavior and teacher behavior. With the spot checks, you mainly observe student behavior, but for a longer observation you also want to watch the teacher to determine the degree to which the teacher is being proactive, positive, and instructional. You might also wish to inform the teacher how you will handle student questions about why you are there. (Give a fairly neutral response, such as, "I am just visiting. I like to see what is going on in every part of the school.")

   End the preconference by arranging a time and place for a postconference. You should allow plenty of time for the postconference (e.g., between 15-30 minutes for every 30 minutes of observation).

   Note: These preconferences are not necessary for the kind of "drop-in" visits discussed earlier. For those, you simply need to let all staff know that you will be dropping into all classrooms frequently, that you will have no specific purpose for observing, and that you will not be looking for anything in particular. Therefore, unless they have had a preconference with you, teachers can assume that a classroom visit will not last more than five minutes.

2. **Conduct the observation.**

When a classroom visit is specifically designed to help a teacher with behavior manage-ment, you want to observe in as nonjudgmental a manner as possible. The following form provides an easy way to "script" notes on what occurs. That is, you note what the teacher does and says, along with corresponding information about what students are doing. Using a format like this will allow you to discuss what you observed with the teacher in a reasonably objective way. What follows is a reproducible blank copy of the form, followed by a sample that shows how the "script" for a 30-minute observation might look.

Observation Form

Teacher _____   Activity _____

Date _____   Time _____

Observer _____

Teacher Behavior	Student Behavior

Sample 30-Minute Observation Form

Teacher _____Mr. Kuske_____   Activity _____Lesson on Westward Expansion_____

Date _____October 21_____   Time _____2:15–2:45_____

Observer _____Ms. Miser_____

Teacher Behavior	**Student Behavior**
2:15 Class attendance/announcements	Most listening, four students in back of room playing hockey on desk with pencils.
2:17 Review via a Q&A format	Students listening and answering. Four students still playing hockey.
"You four—stop playing desk hockey and listen"	Four students continue playing and do not respond to reprimand. Most students are paying attention and taking notes.
2:20 Continues Q&A format. As other students join in, teacher sighs and says, "I wish you students would listen to me. You are more engrossed in that game than you are in getting ready for Friday's test."	Four students continue playing and two others move their desks over to join them.
	Three or four others begin paying attention to the hockey game.
"I told you yesterday. If you people would be polite and listen for a change, we would not have these problems."	Two students shout out "A test on Friday? You never told us about any test."
	Another student shouts, "What is the test going to cover?"
"Paul, I am glad that you are interested in the content of the test. It will cover the material I am reviewing right now, and the new content I want to present today on the Oregon Trail."	About half the students are trying to pay attention to Mr. Kuske, but the others are now watching and cheering the hockey game.
"Charlotte, I think if you and the sports fans in the back of the room are going to pass Friday's test you had better pay	A students calls out, "I have a computer game on the Oregon Trail, so I don't need to listen to what is going on today."

Sample 30-Minute Observation Form (continued)

Teacher ___Mr. Kuske (page 2)___   Activity _____

Date _____   Time _____

Observer _____

Teacher Behavior	Student Behavior
"Well, Zach, that can certainly be your choice."	Zach, one of the hockey players, shouts, "On the last test, I tried to listen and study, but I failed anyway; so I might just as well play hockey."
2:22 "Let's get back to this review. Who can tell the class about …"	As the questions are presented, more of the students begin paying more attention to the lesson and less to the hockey game.
Teacher then asked a series of about ten questions in quick succession, and responded with positive and corrective feedback.	By the end of the review, the teacher has just about everyone with him but the original four hockey players.
2:29 "Okay class, the new content of today's lesson involves…"	During the first part of the lecture, most of the students are paying attention.
"I hope you four in the back can get on a professional hockey team because you are sure not going to succeed in school or a job with that kind of behavior."	The four students just keep playing but laugh loudly.
Teacher presented information for 15 minutes, without clarifying expectations regarding what students should be doing (e.g., taking notes, asking questions).	By the end of the 15-minute lecture, most of the students seem to have ceased paying attention to the lesson and are watching the hockey game, looking at magazines, filing nails, and so on.
2:44 "Okay class, let's get into our cooperative groups and work on your projects for the last 15 minutes of the period."	As I left the room some of the students were moving their desks together, but many just stayed where they were.

During an observation, always be as unobtrusive as possible. Operate from the assumption that in the classroom, the teacher is the boss, and that you do not want to do anything that might lessen the teacher's authority in any manner. For example, never take over the class unless the teacher asks you to do so. Never intervene with a student's misbehavior unless you ask the teacher or he/she asks you to do so. If students ask why you are there, give the type of response suggested earlier—just inform them that you like to observe in all parts of the school.

3. **Have a postobservation conference.**

At the time and the place arranged during the preobservation conference, start the postobservation conference by sharing the information from your scripted observation form. Present this information as an objective description of what you saw and heard, without making judgments. If student behavior was responsible, engaged, and motivated, congratulate the teacher on the behavior of the students. If you choose, you can point out specific things the teacher did that impressed you. Provide specific and descriptive positive feedback. For example, from the hypothetical observation above, the principal could point out that when the teacher kept a fast pace during the Q &A review, most students kept their attention focused on the lesson—and comment that it is because the teacher is so knowledgeable in the subject area that he can present a brisk and interesting interactive portion of the lesson.

If only one or two students demonstrated problematic behavior while the rest of the students were behaving responsibly, you might ask the teacher if he/she would like help setting up an individualized plan for those one or two students. If so, consider one or more of the plans suggested in Sprick, R.S. & Howard, L.M. *Teacher's Encyclopedia of Behavior Management: 100 Problems/ 500 Plans*. If the teacher prefers to build a plan for the student(s) without your assistance, allow the teacher to do so, but make it clear what behaviors the teacher's plan should attempt to address.

If the behavior of many students was problematic, discuss the concerns you have. Identify the aspects of student behavior that did not seem to be responsible, motivated, or engaged. Your goal is not to directly criticize the teacher's behavior, but merely to point out that the teacher's current efforts do not seem to be facilitating responsible, engaged, and motivated student behavior.

Work with the teacher to come up with specific goals for improving student behavior. That is, together try to identify exactly what the teacher should be striving to achieve (e.g., increased on-task behavior or decreased disruptive behavior). Again, in the hypothetical sample above, the principal might suggest that the teacher strive to improve levels of on-task behavior from the majority of the class, make fewer call outs, and make fewer requests for compliance with ineffective instructions to cease misbehavior ("You four, stop playing desk hockey and listen").

After initially discussing student behavior, consider bringing up issues such as the ones following. Keep in mind that because these questions tend to focus more closely on the teacher's behavior they may be somewhat more threatening.

- Did students seem to know what the teacher expected of them?

- Were the teacher's reactions to misbehavior consistent?

- Were corrective consequences appropriate to the misbehavior?

- Was the teacher calm in correcting misbehavior?

- Did the teacher provide age-appropriate positive feedback?

- Was the positive feedback specific and descriptive?

- Did the teacher pay more attention to positive behavior than to negative?

If the teacher wants assistance and ideas for addressing questions like the ones above and for achieving the goals for student behavior, you could work with the teacher to implement one or more of the specific plans (Plans A–D) that follow in this section. For example, the teacher in the observation above and the principal might work together to implement Plan A. If the teacher wants to make improvements in student behavior without your assistance, remind him that his efforts must fit within your school's overall SBP.

End the postconference by arranging a date and time for a follow-up observation. If your schedule permits, set the next observation for approximately one week (sooner if the teacher wants). This will give the teacher enough time to experiment with strategies to achieve the desired student behavior, but not so much time that the teacher will be likely to ignore the suggestions you have provided. The end of this postobservation conference functions as the preobservation conference for the next observation. Invite the teacher to come see you at any point before the next observation to discuss difficulties or questions he has with the agreed upon intervention plan. This cycle of observations and conferences should continue until the goals for student behavior are consistently being achieved by this teacher.

Depending on the severity of the teacher's problem, the suggestions in Plans A–D and your observation/conference process with the teacher may not be sufficient. If these plans do not provide enough detail, or if you try them and find them ineffective, you and the teacher may want to engage in joint study of a good book on behavior management. Some suggestions follow:

- Emmer, E.T., Evertson, C.M., & Clements, B.S. (1994). *Classroom management for secondary teachers*. Englewood Cliffs, NJ: Prentice Hall.

- Evertson, C.M., Emmer, E.T., Clements, B.S., & Worsham, M.E. (1994). *Classroom management for elementary teachers*. Englewood Cliffs, NJ: Prentice Hall.

- Jones, V.F. & Jones, L.S. (1986). *Comprehensive classroom management*. Boston: Allyn and Bacon.

- Kameenui, E.J. & Simmons, D.C. (1990). *Designing instructional strategies: The prevention of academic learning problems*. Columbus, OH: Merrill/ Macmillan.

- Morgan, D.P. & Jenson, W.R. (1988). *Teaching behaviorally disordered students*. Columbus, OH: Merrill.

- Paine, S.C., Radicchi, J., Deutchman, L., Rosellini, L.C., & Darch, C.B. (1983). *Structuring your classroom for academic success*. Champaign, IL: Research Press.

- Sprick, R.S. (1985). *Discipline in the secondary classroom: A problem by problem survival guide*. Englewood Cliffs, NJ: Prentice Hall.

- Sprick, R.S. (1981). *The solution book: A guide to classroom discipline*. Chicago: Science Research Associates.

- Sprick, R.S., Garrison, M., & Howard, L.M. (In press). *Prevention: Building a classroom behavior plan*. Longmont, CO: Sopris West.

- Sprick, R.S. & Howard, L.M. (1995). *Teacher's encyclopedia of behavior management: 100 problems/500 plans*. Longmont, CO: Sopris West.

- Wong, H.K. & Wong, R.T. (1991). *The first days of school: How to start school successfully*. Sunnyvale, CA: Harry K. Wong.

Helping Individual Teachers Implement an Effective Classroom Behavior Plan

In your role as the instructional leader of your school, one of your most important—and potentially most difficult—tasks is to help any teacher who is struggling with classroom management. You can become aware that a teacher needs assistance in a variety of ways. The teacher may make an excessive number of disciplinary referrals (or otherwise indicate frustration with student behavior). You may notice the teacher's trouble during your spot checks and observations. In some cases, you may learn about the teacher's difficulty because of student and/or parental complaints. Regardless of how you become aware of the problem, it is part of your responsibility as principal to help that teacher. If the problem is with a specific student, you may want to involve the school counselor (or a school psychologist or district behavior specialist) to work with you and the teacher to design an individualized behavior management plan. However, when many different students in a teacher's class are misbehaving, consider using the material on the following pages (which can be reproduced) to help the teacher improve overall classroom management. This material has been adapted and is used with permission from the "Classroom Chaos" section of:

- Sprick, R.S. & Howard, L.M. (1995). *Teacher's encyclopedia of behavior management: 100 problems/500 plans*. Longmont, CO: Sopris West.

Overview of the Intervention Plans

Plan A—For a situation in which it appears that revising classroom organization might result in more responsible student behavior.

Plan B—For a situation in which it appears that the students do not know how to behave responsibly and meet classroom expectations.

Plan C—For a situation in which it appears that the students do not realize how often they engage in irresponsible behavior.

Plan D—For a situation in which it appears that the students are not motivated to behave responsibly and follow the rules.

Reproduce one of the following plans and give it to the teacher and/or work through the procedures with the teacher, providing guidance in the form of discussion, modeling, or even role playing. You may wish to provide classroom demonstrations for the teacher as well.

Plan A

If it is early in the school year and/or it has been sometime since you have reviewed and revised your classroom management and organization procedures, the following actions may be sufficient to resolve the situation. Even if they are not effective, however, "preventative management" is a prerequisite for the success of any of the other plans.

1. **Post three to six positively stated classroom rules.**

    Clear, concise, posted classroom rules should be the basis of behavior management and discipline. Whenever you have discussions with the class or with individuals about behavior or motivation issues, the rules should be a focal point. When you correct misbehavior, your corrections and consequences should be based on your rules. Even when you provide positive feedback to students, relate your feedback to the rules. "Holly, you consistently arrive on time with all of your materials. Nice job of following Rule #2." Plan B provides suggestions for involving the students in the process of developing or revising classroom rules, if this seems necessary.

2. **Keep your attention focused on positive behavior.**

    Whatever you pay the most attention to will tend to occur more frequently. Many teachers inadvertently reinforce inappropriate behavior by giving it too much attention. Interact frequently with students who are behaving well. Call on them. Praise them. Comment on their work. Catch those students who have the greatest tendency to misbehave when they are not misbehaving, and let them know how responsible they are being. With every student, try to interact more frequently when he/she is behaving well than when he/she is misbehaving. Your goal should be three positive interactions for every negative interaction.

Monitor your interactions by periodically audiotaping yourself while teaching. As you listen to the tape, tally the ratios of positive to negative interactions on a sheet of paper. Count each interaction you have with students as either positive or negative by putting a "+" or a "–," respectively. To determine whether an interaction is positive or negative, ask yourself whether the student was breaking a rule (or otherwise misbehaving) at the time. Any interaction that stems from inappropriate behavior is negative, while all interactions that occur while the student is meeting classroom expectations are positive. Thus, stating warnings or issuing consequences are both negative interactions, but praising an individual or the group is positive. Greeting the students as they enter the room or asking a student if she has any questions during independent work are also considered positive interactions. (**Note:** Ignoring a student's inappropriate behavior is not recorded at all because it is not an interaction.)

If you find that you are not giving the class three times as much positive as negative attention, try to increase the number of positive interactions you have with students. Sometimes prompts can help. For example, you might decide that each time any student enters the classroom you will say hello to him or her, that you will try and praise at least ten different students each half hour, or that whenever someone uses the drinking fountain you will check the class and praise one individual or group who is following the rules. You can also increase the ratio of positive to negative attention by ignoring more of the students' mild inappropriate behaviors (e.g., a student makes a smart aleck remark).

3. **Adjust instructional techniques.**

If you find that student behavior is worse during particular instructional activities, modify those activities. For example, if you lecture, modify your instructional style to keep students more actively involved in the lessons. If you are trying to have students work a lot in cooperative groups but frequent off-task behavior or arguing takes place, reduce the amount of time each day in cooperative learning until students demonstrate they have the skills to work cooperatively. If students are assigned to work independently, but are frequently off task, increase the amount of interactive, teacher-directed instruction.

4. **Examine the schedule of activities for a typical day and revise it to ensure a fast pace that keeps students academically engaged.**

If students are given long periods of time for independent seat work, revise the schedule so there is greater variety. For example, if students are typically given 30 minutes to work on math assignments, consider breaking the time up by having five minutes of guided practice, five minutes of independent work, five minutes of teacher-directed work to correct what they have done so far and guide them through more of the assignment, and then 15 minutes to complete the assignment. An effective schedule has daily consistency, but a wide variety of activity.

5. **Increase the efficiency of transitions.**

Define for students exactly how long transitions should take place, providing feedback on their efficiency and, if necessary, practicing that transition until students are able to handle the transition efficiently. "Class, I need your attention. It is time for our spelling test. Take out a sheet of lined paper, put on the heading, and number the paper from 1-20. In one minute I will begin the test, so get ready quickly and quietly."

6. **Increase the amount of supervision by being out among the students as much as possible and by visually scanning all parts of the room.**

To use an adult example, a freeway with visible and numerous police cars will have more people driving the legal limit than a freeway with no police presence. Whether the activity is teacher-directed instruction, small group work, or independent work, your presence will prompt more responsible behavior, so move around in unpredictable patterns. Regardless of what you are doing, frequently scan all parts of the classroom. You should know what is going on at all times. Even when you are sitting in with a cooperative learning group, you should periodically stand up and scan what is taking place in the other groups.

7. **Modify the physical setting to prompt appropriate behavior.**

Make sure that desks are arranged so that you can move throughout the classroom easily. Separate students who have trouble if they sit together. Recognize that with very social groups of children, a U-shape arrangement (or even a double U-shape as long as you can easily get back to the second tier) will be less conducive to off-task talking than having students in rows, and rows will be less conducive than groups or clusters. If you have students in clusters, avoid having more that four students clustered together—groups of six or eight will be more problematic.

Plan B

Sometimes students may be unclear about the expectations for their behavior and/or may be rebelling against procedures they feel no allegiance to. If either or both of these conditions exist, you and your students should collaboratively develop clear rules, expectations for student behavior, consequences for infractions, and rewards and incentives.

1. **Have the students revise classroom rules and develop a realistic list of corresponding consequences. Examine your classroom rules.**

   • If you do not have rules, or you have rules but the students do not take them seriously, schedule a discussion to develop new rules. Have the class brainstorm a set of possible rules. In setting this up, cover some rules for brainstorming. For example:

     – Any idea is okay (but no obscenity).

     – Ideas will not be evaluated initially (i.e., no approval, "Good idea," or disapproval, "What a stupid idea," or "We couldn't do that").

   – All ideas will be written down and discussed at the conclusion of brainstorming.

- After brainstorming, lead the class through a discussion. Evaluate each idea and guide the group in narrowing the list to three to six statements of positive expectations. Once developed, use these as a basis for correcting irresponsible behavior and for providing positive feedback.

- If you anticipate that students may be out of control during a discussion of this type, ask the building administrator to join you and assist in conducting this discussion. This will also demonstrate to students that you and the administrator are equally concerned about the problem and want them to take ownership for defining rules for the classroom.

- Have the class brainstorm consequences for rule violations. After brainstorming, lead the class through a discussion to evaluate the ideas. Have the class select several consequences (voting is one strategy that could be used) ranging from mild (e.g., one minute owed from recess, or a short time-out) to severe (parental contact, after-school detention, office referral).

- Lead the class through a "If a student breaks rule #2 by ____, what should I implement as a consequence? And what if he argues about it?" discussion. If students suggest something unrealistic, tell them why and have them identify another possible consequence. "No, I don't think that would work. If I had to call parents whenever someone blurted out without raising his/her hand, I would have to spend all evening on the phone. What is something milder and more immediate?" Continue this process until you have a written list of consequences.

2. **Respond calmly and consistently to each instance of misbehavior.**

   Follow through on the consequences that have been established by you and the class. When a rule violation happens, do not argue or negotiate. Be emotionally neutral and avoid talking too much while giving the correction—your goal is to let the student know the consequence for that action. "Jared, that was disrespectful. As you know, the consequence for disrespect is to write an apology. It needs to be done before you can go out to recess."

3. **Teach students how the new rules relate to each type of classroom activity.**

   After school on the day that the new rules are developed, spend some time thinking and visualizing **exactly** how, given the new rules, you expect students to behave during each activity. Think about the school day, and take one activity at a time. Begin with students entering the room before school begins. Answer all of the following questions for this particular activity:

   - What should they be doing?

   - Where should they be?

- Are they talking to each other? about what? how loud? for how long?

- Are they talking to you?

- How will you get the attention of the class, if necessary?

- What are common misbehaviors that occur and what should students be doing instead?

Make notes on your expectations, then go on to the next activity—beginning class with attendance and other housekeeping. Continue this exercise for every activity throughout the day. Even include things such as going down the hall to the lunchroom.

- The day after conducting this exercise, share the expectations you developed with your students, immediately before each activity. "Class I am about to take attendance, and while I am taking attendance what you should be doing is ..." With primary students, take the time to demonstrate, have a few students demonstrate, and then ask students questions to verify that they understand the expectations. With intermediate students, explain how the expectations fit in with the rules the class developed. Give students an opportunity to ask questions, express concerns, even suggest alternatives. If students have reasonable suggestions, incorporate the suggestions into your expectations. If students have unreasonable suggestions (e.g., "Let us sleep instead of answering questions and taking notes"), inform them that you care too much about their education to allow that. If possible, use the rules the class developed to inform students why you cannot accept a particular suggestion. "Lyle, I can't let you sleep; one of the rules the class developed is 'Do your best—participate!' I care too much about the rules the class developed and too much about everyone's education to allow sleeping when you need to be participating." Do not begin any activity until students understand your expectations.

- Continue this every day until a particular activity has gone well for at least a week. By day two or three, do not allow students to negotiate alternative expectations, and do not continue to provide rationale for procedures you have previously explained. If students continue to make the same suggestions or ask questions, let them know that you will ignore those suggestions in the future. ("Lyle, you know why I can't let you sleep, and from now on, I am not going to respond to that suggestion. However, if you want to talk to me after school about your suggestion, feel free to come see me.") With any activities that are not yet going well, continue to introduce the activity by reviewing the expectations for responsible behavior.

- End each activity by telling the group how well the activity went. If it went perfectly, tell the students. "During our cooperative learning groups, every group used the time wisely and stayed on task. The noise level in each group was very respectful of the other groups. And each group that I listened to was doing a great job of giving each person in the group a chance to participate." If the activity did not go perfectly, set goals for the next day. "During our cooperative learning groups, every group used the time wisely and stayed on task. However, tomorrow let's work harder on managing the noise level. Several of the groups got so into the lesson that people got too loud and I had to come over and remind them to be more quiet.

Tomorrow let's see if each group can manage their own noise level without needing me to give reminders."

4. **Use positive recognition to encourage appropriate behavior.**

   - Praise individual students for following rules and procedures agreed on by the class. Keep a special eye on those students who have had the greatest tendency to engage in misbehavior. Whenever one of these students is not misbehaving, praise him/her for demonstrating the ability to follow the rules the class developed. If the student would be embarrassed by public praise, do it privately or even give the student a note.

   - In addition, occasionally praise those students who rarely or never have a problem with misbehaving. Because these students have already mastered the positive expectations, they do not need positive feedback as often as the students who have had difficulty. However, you do not want them to feel that you take their positive behavior for granted. "Libby, Greg, and Akeem, you are all very responsible. I didn't want to embarrass you in front of the others, but you should each be very proud. I appreciate the effort you put into making this a good class."

   - Finally, when there has been a significant improvement in the behavior of the entire group, praise the class. Remember that anytime the students are refraining from misbehaving, you can praise them for being responsible and following the rules.

Plan C

Sometimes students do not seem to realize when and/or how much they are misbehaving. In this case, the intervention should include some way of helping the students become more aware of their own behavior.

1. **Have the students revise classroom rules and develop a realistic list of corresponding consequences (see Plan B).**

2. **Respond consistently to each instance of misbehavior.**

   - Whenever an individual student engages in misbehavior, follow through on procedures you and the class developed (see Plan B).

   - In addition, whenever you correct any student's behavior make sure the incident is recorded (step 3 below).

3. **Publicly monitor how often incidents of misbehavior occur.**

   - To help the students become more aware of their own behavior, create a wall chart to record the daily frequency of rule violations. Post the chart in a visible spot in the room. If you are a middle school teacher, put the chart on a transparency and show the chart at the end of the class period.

Since you do not want to give too much peer attention to an individual student who misbehaves, correct the individual and state the consequence. Record the incident on a record sheet like the one below, but do not make the entire class aware of who engaged in the behavior. The idea is to have a total count of rule violations at the end of the day, without publicly identifying how many incidents any particular individuals were responsible for.

Tally of Rule Violations						
Week of _____						
Name	Mon	Tue	Wed	Thu	Fri	Total
Akajima, Linda						
Bessom, Jim						
Carter, Todd	**d**					
...						
Ziminski, Brett	**oo**					
Code a = Arguing d = Disruptive o = Off Task						

A form of this type allows you to figure a class total at the end of the day, has records of individual misbehaviors that are useful for keeping track of consequences, and is extremely useful for conferences with individual students and parents. For example, if a student is having ongoing difficulties, you might invite the parent(s) and student in for a planning conference. If you had been using and saving the record sheet, you could easily show the student and his parent(s) the number of problems that have occurred over the past several weeks. Notice on the sample above that the information is coded by type of infraction. If you wanted to, you could put a "+" next to the names of students you praise. This could be useful for monitoring your own ratios of interactions with the group as a whole, and with each individual student.

- Every day conduct a short class meeting to review that day's record. Have someone record the information on the chart (or do it yourself), and discuss whether the day was better, worse, or about the same as previous days. If the day did not go well, encourage the students to talk about why and have them identify what they can do the next day to help in remembering to follow the classroom rules. If the students act inappropriately during the meeting, keep the review session very short. Just let the class know that you are sure tomorrow will be a better day.

4. **Use positive recognition to encourage appropriate behavior.**

- Praise individual students for meeting expectations and praise the entire class when improvement takes place (see Plan B).

- During the review meetings, praise students for being willing to look seriously at the cumulative record for the day. Even on a bad day, if the students are willing to discuss why it was a bad day, praise them. "Class, you are really handling this responsibly. Even though it was a rough day, you are willing to talk about things you might do differently tomorrow. That is a real sign that we are making progress." Regardless of how the day went, try to make the end-of-day meeting upbeat and encouraging—you want the students to look forward to the review at the end of the day.

- You may also wish to use intermittent rewards to acknowledge the class' success. Occasional, and unexpected, rewards can motivate students to demonstrate responsible behavior more often. The idea is to provide a reward when the entire class has had a particularly good period of following the rules. For this particular situation, appropriate rewards might include an extra recess, a special treat for all students at lunch (e.g., an ice cream), or having the principal come and congratulate the class and lead the class in a fun activity. If you use intermittent rewards, do so more frequently at the beginning of the intervention to encourage the student, and then less often as the student's behavior improves. Do not give rewards indiscriminately. There must be a significant improvement before providing a reward to the entire group.

Plan D

Sometimes, an entire classroom will fall into a pattern of misbehaving. This can happen when a particular behavior has become habitual and/or when a majority of students try to emulate a few influential students who are misbehaving to look "cool" or "tough." In these cases it can be very difficult to change student behavior, and you may need to use some kind of structured reinforcement system that creates mild peer pressure to motivate students to behave appropriately. A basic system will be suggested and then several alternative systems will be briefly described. Feel free to combine two or more of these alternatives to create even stronger incentives to encourage appropriate behavior.

1. **Publicly monitor the frequency of misbehaving (see Plan C).**

2. **Encourage the class to set daily performance goals.**

   Some students want to set a very challenging goal, such as reducing the number of incidents from 40 per day to zero per day. Suggest that students set a more realistic goal such as reducing from 40 to 32. Let them know that if the goal is no more than 32, they can always get less than that, but by making the goal attainable, they increase their chances of success. As the class experiences success, the goal should become progressively lower until there are no more incidents on most days.

3. **Establish a group reinforcement system.**

   - Have the class brainstorm reinforcement ideas for the entire class. After brainstorming, eliminate any items from the list that are not possible (i.e., the suggestion is too expensive or could not be provided to all the students in the class).

   - Assign prices to the remaining items on the list. (**Note:** The prices should be based on the instructional, personnel and/or monetary costs of the items. Monetary cost is clear—the more expensive the item, the more points required to earn it. Instructional cost refers to the amount of instructional time lost or interfered with by a particular reward. Thus, an activity that causes the class to miss part of math instruction should require more points than one the class can do during recess time. Personnel cost involves the time required by you and/or other staff to fulfill the reinforcer. Getting an extra recess period with extra supervision would cost more than playing music in class for 15 minutes.)

   - Have the class vote on the reinforcers. The reinforcer that gets the most votes is the one they will work for first, and the items that come in second (and third) will be the next ones worked for.

   - On days when the group is successful in keeping the number of misbehaviors under the identified goal, the group earns a point toward a reward that the group agreed to work toward. Establish a sliding scale so the group earns additional points for keeping the number even lower than the performance goal. For example:

More than 32 incidents	0 points
22–32	1 point
15–21	2 points
7–14	3 points
3–6	4 points
1–2	5 points
0	6 points

Alternative Systems

1. **If a classwide system seems unlikely to be effective, set up a team competition and response cost lottery.**

   In this type of system, the class would be divided into four to six teams. Design the makeup of teams to be as equitable as possible. Each team starts the day with a certain number of tickets on which they would write the name of their team. Every time someone misbehaves, that person's team loses a ticket. At the end of the day, each team puts its remaining tickets in a hat for a lottery drawing. The winning ticket has the name of the team that will earn the reward for that day.

2. **Reward individuals for responsible behavior.**

   One relatively simple and high-powered plan is to have small tickets like the sample below.

Date _____   _____ has been especially responsible. This ticket is worth one chance in the lottery drawing on Friday.

   One of these tickets can be given to any individual for any instance of following the rules. The student can write his/her name on the ticket and put it in a box for a drawing at the end of the week. The prize can be an individual reward from a list generated by the class. Give tickets when you see instances of positive behavior you are trying to encourage.

   If you use a system of this type, be careful to avoid being discriminatory. For example, there may be particular individuals who have been especially troublesome in the past, and you may inadvertently harbor a grudge, and therefore, you may not notice positive behavior of these students. Or, some teachers work so hard to notice the small improvements of the troubled students and the great leaps of the academically high achievers, they do not notice the regular ongoing sustained effort of average students.

3. **Perform intermittent spot checks.**

   Let students know that you are going to set a timer for anywhere from 10 minutes to 120 minutes. If everyone in the class is behaving responsibly at the instant the timer goes off, someone in the group will roll a pair of dice. The number that comes up will determine a reward given to the entire group as indicated on a chart posted in the room. The chart might look something like this:

1	(Something must be wrong with these dice)
2, 3, or 4	Better luck next time. (But nice job anyway!)
5 or 6	Five minutes at end of day for choice time
7 or 8	Reduce math homework by half
9 or 10	Music played during study time
11	Five bonus points on group system
12	Extra ten minutes of recess

   Once the timer goes off, determine whether everyone was behaving responsibly. If so, ask a student to roll the dice. Once the reward has been determined, reset the timer.

   Note: By creating a reinforcement plan using two or three of the above systems, the hope is that there will be gentle peer pressure to behave appropriately. Let students know that if someone is forgetting to behave responsibly, a quiet reminder to behave might help. Also let them know that yelling at another student to behave would not be responsible and therefore would be just as much of a problem as any other misbehavior.

4. **While implementing any of the above reinforcement systems, keep students' attention focused on the fact that they are behaving responsibly.**

   "Class, you earned seven points for the day, but more importantly, you are all helping this class be a place that we all will enjoy. Room 14 is a place we can all be proud of."

Conclusion

As the person with ultimate responsibility for the development of a safe and productive school, you as principal need to be in classrooms to identify which teachers might need help implementing effective classroom behavior procedures. As you identify one or more teachers needing assistance, you can provide them support by helping them work through one of the "remedial" management plans provided in the last section of this chapter.

In addition, as part of your overall SBP improvement efforts, you should guide staff in the development of a "Classrooms" section for that document: Although this section of an SBP is one of the most difficult and politically charged tasks, it is vitally important. Actively involving staff in development of this material results in their agreement and participation regarding what effective classroom behavior plans should consist of. These plans should allow flexibility for each teacher, but should all fit within the parameters defined by the school effectiveness literature.

resources / references

Agne, J.K., Greenwood, G.E., & Miller, L.D. (1994). Relationships between teacher belief systems and teacher effectiveness. *Journal of Research and Development in Education*, *27*(3), 141-152.

Albert, L. (1995). *Cooperative discipline: Classroom management that promotes self-esteem*. Circle Pines, MN: American Guidance Services.

Allen, J.D. (1986, Fall). Classroom management: Students' perspectives, goals, and strategies. *American Educational Research Journal*, *23*(3), 437-459.

Amabile, T.M., Hennessey, B.A., & Grossman, B.S. (1987, April). *Immunizing children against the negative effects of reward*. Paper presented at the Biennial Meeting of the Society for Research in Child Development, Baltimore, MD (ERIC Document Reproduction Service No. 285 655).

Anderson, C.S. (1985). The investigation of school climate. In G.R. Austin & H. Garber (Eds.) *Research on exemplary schools* (pp 97-126). Orlando, FL: Academic Press.

Anderson, L.M., Evertson, C.M., & Emmer, E. (1980). Dimensions in classroom management derived from recent research. *Journal of Curriculum Studies*, *12*(4), 343-362.

Anderson, L.W. (1980, December). Learning time and educational effectiveness. *NASSP Curriculum Report*, *10*(2) (ERIC Document Reproduction Service No. 210 780).

Andrews, R.L. & Soder, R. (1987, March). Principal leadership and student achievement. *Educational Leadership*, *44*(6), 9-11.

Armor, D., Conry-Oseguera, P., Cox, M., King, N., McDonnell, L., Pascal, A., Pauly, E., & Zellman, G. (1976). *Analysis of the school preferred reading program in selected Los Angeles minority schools*. Santa Monica, CA: Rand Corporation (ERIC Document Reproduction Service No. 130 243).

Arterbury, E. & Hord, S.M. (1991). Site-based decision making: Its potential for enhancing learner outcomes. *Issues about Change*, *1*(4).

Bachus, G. (1992, Fall). School-based management: Do teachers want more involvement in decision making? *Rural Educator*, *14*(1), 1-4.

Bain, H., Lintz, N., & Word, E. (1989). *A study of first grade effective teaching practices* from the Project STAR class size research (ERIC Document Reproduction Service No. 321 887).

Bain, H.P. & Jacobs, R. (1990). *The case for smaller classes and better teachers*. Alexandria, VA: National Association of Elementary School Principals (ERIC Document Reproduction Service No. 322 632).

Bamburg, J.D. & Andrews, R.L. (1991). School goals, principals and achievement. *School Effectiveness and School Improvement*, *2*(3), 175-191.

Berman, P. & McLaughlin, M. (1979). *An exploratory study of school district adaptation*. Santa Monica, CA: Rand Corporation.

Bielefeldt, T. (1990, February). Classroom discipline. *Research Roundup*, *5*(2) (ERIC Document Reproduction Service No. 318 133).

Biester, T.W., Kruss, J., Meyer, F., & Heller, B. (1984). *Effects of administrative leadership on student achievement*. Philadelphia, PA: Research for Better Schools (ERIC Document Reproduction Service No. 244 348).

Block, A.W. (1983). *Effective schools: A summary of research* (Research Brief). Arlington, VA: Educational Research Service (ERIC Document Reproduction Service No. 240 736).

Block, P. (1987). *The empowered manager: Positive political skills at work*. San Francisco, CA: Jossey Bass.

Bossert, S.T. (1988). School effects. In N.J. Boyan (Ed.), *Handbook of research on educational administration* (pp. 341-352). New York: Longman.

Boyd, V. (1992, Spring). Creating a context for change. *Issues about Change*, *2*(2).

Brookover, W.B. (1979). *School social systems and student achievement: Schools can make a difference*. New York: Praeger Publishers.

Brookover, W.B. & Lezotte, L.W. (1979). *Changes in school characteristics coincident with changes in student achievement*. East Lansing, MI: Michigan State University, College of Urban Development (ERIC Document Reproduction Service No. 181 005).

Brookover, W.B. (1981). *Effective secondary schools*. Philadelphia, PA: Research for Better Schools (ERIC Document Reproduction Service No. 231 088).

Brophy, J.E. (1979, December). Teacher behavior and its effects. *Journal of Educational Psychology*, *71*(6), 733-750 (ERIC Document Reproduction Service No. 181 014).

Brophy, J.E. (1980). *Teacher praise: A functional analysis*. East Lansing, MI: The Institute for Research on Teaching (ERIC Document Reproduction Service No. 181 013).

Brophy, J.E. (1982, April). Successful teaching strategies for the inner-city child. *Phi Delta Kappan*, *63*(8), 627-630.

Brophy, J.E. (1983, March). Classroom organization and management. *The Elementary School Journal, 83*(4), 265-285.

Brophy, J.E. (1986, February). Classroom management techniques. *Education and Urban Society*, 18(2), 182-194.

Brophy, J.E. (1986, October). Teacher influences on student achievement. *American Psychologist, 4*(10), 1069-1077.

Brophy, J.E. (1987, October). Synthesis of research on strategies for motivating students to learn. *Educational Leadership, 45*(2), 40-48.

Brophy, J.E. (1988). Educating teachers about managing classrooms and students. *Teaching and Teacher Education, 4*(1), 1-18.

Brophy, J.E. (1988, Summer). Research linking teacher behavior to student achievement: Potential implications for instruction of Chapter 1 students. *Educational Psychologist, 23*(3), 235-286 (ERIC Document Reproduction Service No. 293 914).

Brophy, J.E. & Good, T.L. (1986). Teacher behavior and student achievement. In M.C. Wittrock (Ed.), *Handbook of research on teaching* (3rd ed.). New York: Macmillan.

Brown, S., McIntyre, D., & McAlpine, A. (1988, April). *The knowledge which underpins the craft of teaching*. Paper presented at the Annual Meeting of the American Education Research Association, New Orleans, LA (ERIC Document Reproduction Service No. 294-873).

Brundage, D. (Ed.). (1979). *The journalism research fellows report: What makes an effective school?* Washington, DC: George Washington University (ERIC Document Reproduction Service No. 226 606).

Caldwell, S.D. & Wood, F.H. (1988, October). School based improvement—Are we ready? *Educational Leadership, 42*(2), 50-53.

Cameron, J. & Pierce, W.D. (1994, Fall). Reinforcement, reward, and intrinsic motivation: A meta-analysis. *Review of Educational Research, 64*(3), 363-423.

Cannella, G.S. (1986, March/April). Praise and concrete rewards: Concerns for childhood education. *Childhood Education, 62*(4), 297-301.

Canter, L. & Canter, M. (1976). *Assertive discipline: A take charge approach for today's educator.* Los Angeles, CA: Canter & Associates.

Cantrell, R.P. & Cantrell, M.L. (1993, November). Countering gang violence in American schools. *Principal, 72*(3), 6-9.

Cawelti, G. (1987, February). *How effective instructional leaders get results*. Paper presented at the Annual Meeting of the American Association of School Administrators, New Orleans, LA (ERIC Document Reproduction Service No. 328 935).

Center on Evaluation, Development and Research/Phi Delta Kappa. (1985). *Effective classroom management* (1984-85 Hot Topic Series). Bloomington, IN: Phi Delta Kappa (ERIC Document Reproduction Service No. 329 935).

Cistone, P.J., Fernandez, J.A., & Tornillo, P.L., Jr. (1989, August). School-based management/Shared decision making in Dade County (Miami). *Education and Urban Society, 21*(4), 393-402.

Cohen, D.L. (1989, March 15). Joining forces: An alliance of sectors envisioned to aid the most troubled young. *Education Week, 8*(25), 7-14.

Cohen, S.A. (1994). Instructional alignment. In T. Husen & T.N. Postlethwaite (Eds.), *International encyclopedia of education: Research and studies* (2nd ed., Vol. 5), (pp. 2852-2856) London: Pergamon Press.

Colvin, G. (1992). *Managing acting-out behavior*. Eugene, OR: Behavior Associates.

Colvin, G. & Sugai, G. (1989). *Managing escalating behavior*. Eugene, OR: Behavior Associates.

Conley, S.C. & Bacharach, S.B. (1990, March). From school-site management to participatory school-site management. *Phi Delta Kappan, 71*(7), 539-544.

Cooper, H.M. & Good, T.L. (1983). *Pygmalion grows up: Studies in the expectation communication process*. New York: Longman Press.

Cooper, H.M. & Tom, D.Y.H. (1984, September). Teacher expectation research: A review with implications for classroom instruction. *The Elementary School Journal, 85*(1), 77-89.

Corbett, H.D., Dawson, J.A., & Firestone, W.A. (1984). *School context and school change: Implications for effective planning*. New York: Teachers College Press.

Corbett, H.D. & Wilson, B.L. (1992, January). The central office role in instructional improvement. *School Effectiveness and School Improvement, 3*(1), 45-68.

Corcoran, T.B. (1985, May). Effective secondary schools. In *Reaching for excellence: An effective schools sourcebook* (pp. 71-97). Washington, DC: National Institute of Education.

Cotton, K. (1989). *Expectations and student outcomes* (Close Up #7). Portland, OR: Northwest Regional Educational Laboratory.

Cotton, K. (1990). *Preventing and treating alcohol, drug, and smoking addiction: Research on effective practices*. Portland, OR: Northwest Regional Educational Laboratory.

Cotton, K. (1990). *Schoolwide and classroom discipline* (Close-Up #9). Portland, OR: Northwest Regional Educational Laboratory.

Cotton, K. (1991). *Educating urban minority youth: Research on effective practices* (Topical Synthesis #4). Portland, OR: Northwest Regional Educational Laboratory.

Cotton, K. (1992). *Developing empathy in children and youth* (Close-Up #13). Portland, OR: Northwest Regional Educational Laboratory (ERIC Document Reproduction Service No. 361 876).

Cotton, K. (1995). *Effective schooling practices: A research synthesis, 1995 update*. Portland,OR: Northwest Regional Educational Laboratory.

Crisci, P.E., March, J.K., Peters, K.H., & Orrach. L.P. (1988). *Results of the two-year pilot of the achievement formula that applies the correlates of effective schools and recommendations of the "excellence" reports to predict, monitor, and enhance student achievement*. Paper presented at the Annual Meeting of the American Educational Research Association, New Orleans, LA (ERIC Document Reproduction Service No. 302 923).

Curwin, R.L. & Mendler, A.N. (1988). *Discipline with dignity*. Reston, VA: Association for Supervision and Curriculum Development.

David, J.L. (1989, May). Synthesis of research on school-based management. *Educational Leadership*, *46*(8), 46-63.

DeBevoise, W. (1984, February). Synthesis of research on the principal as instructional leader. *Educational Leadership*, *41*(6), 14-20.

Doyle, W. (1986). Classroom organization and management. In M.C. Wittrock (Ed.), *Handbook of research on teaching* (3rd ed.), (pp. 392-431). New York: Macmillan.

Doyle, W. (1986, May). Effective secondary classroom practices. In *Reaching for excellence: An effective schools sourcebook*. Washington, DC: National Institute of Education.

Doyle, W. (1989). Classroom management techniques. In O.C. Moles (Ed.), *Strategies to reduce student misbehavior* (pp. 11-31). Washington, DC: Office of Educational Research and Improvement, U.S. Department of Education (ERIC Document Reproduction Service No. 311 608).

Druian, G. & Butler, J.A. (1987). *Effective schooling practices and at-risk youth: What the research shows* (Topical Synthesis #1). Portland, OR: Northwest Regional Educational Laboratory (ERIC Document Reproduction Service No. 291 146).

Dryfoos, J.G. (1990). *Adolescents at risk: Prevalence and prevention*. New York: Oxford University Press.

Duke, D.L. (1989). School organization, leadership, and student behavior. In O.C. Moles (Ed.), *Strategies to reduce student misbehavior* (pp. 31-62). Washington, DC: Office of Educational Research and Improvement (ERIC Document Reproduction Service No. 311 608).

Eberts, R.W. & Stone, J.A. (1988). Student achievement in public schools: Do principals make a difference? *Economics of Education Review*, *7*(3), 291-299.

Edmonds, R.R. (1979). Some schools work and more can. *Social Policy*, *9*, 28-32.

Edmonds, R.R. (1979, October). Effective schools for the urban poor. *Educational Leadership*, *37*(1), 16-24.

Edmonds, R.R. (1982, December). Programs of school improvement: An overview. *Educational Leadership*, *40*(3), 4-11 (ERIC Document Reproduction Service No. 221 636).

Edmonds, R.R. & Frederiksen, J.R. (1979). *Search for effective schools: The identification and analysis of city schools that are instructionally effective for poor children*. (ERIC Document Reproduction Service No. 170 396).

Emmer, E.T. (1982). *Management strategies in elementary school classrooms*. Austin, TX: Research and Development Center for Teacher Education (ERIC Document Reproduction Service No. 251 432).

Emmer, E.T. & Aussiker, A. (1989). School and classroom discipline programs: How well do they work? In O.C. Moles (Ed.), *Strategies to reduce student misbehavior* (pp. 105-142). Washington, DC: Office of Educational Research and Improvement, U.S. Department of Education (ERIC Document Reproduction Service No. 311 608).

Emmer, E.T. & Evertson, C.M. (1980). *Effective management at the beginning of the school year in junior high classes* (Report No. 6107). Austin, TX: Research and Development Center for Teacher Education, University of Texas (ERIC Document Reproduction Service No. 241 499).

Emmer, E.T. & Evertson, C.M. (1981, January). Synthesis of research on classroom management. *Educational Leadership*, *38*(4), 342-347.

Emmer, E.T. & Evertson, C.M. (1981). *Teacher's manual for the junior high classroom management improvement study*. Austin, TX: Research and Development Center for Teacher Education, University of Texas.

Emmer, E.T., Evertson, C.M., & Clements B.S. (1994). *Classroom management for secondary teachers*. Boston: Allyn & Bacon (ERIC Document Reproduction Service No. 369 781).

Emrick, J.A. (1977). *Evaluation of the national diffusion network* (Vol. I). Stanford, CA: The Stanford Research Institute.

Evertson, C.M . (1981). *Organizing and managing the elementary school classroom*. Austin, TX: Research and Development Center for Teacher Education, University of Texas (ERIC Document Reproduction Service No. 223 570).

Evertson, C.M. (1982). Differences in instructional activities in higher and lower achieving junior high English and math classes. *Elementary School Journal*, *82*(4), 329-351.

Evertson, C.M. (1985, September/October). Training teachers in classroom management: An experimental study in secondary school classrooms. *Journal of Educational Research*, *79*(1), 51-58.

Evertson, C.M. (1986, February). Do teachers make a difference? *Education and Urban Society*, *18*(2), 195-210.

Evertson, C.M. (1989, November/December). Improving elementary classroom management: A school-based training program for beginning the year. *Journal of Educational Research*, *83*(2), 82-90.

Evertson, C.M., Anderson, C., & Anderson, L. (1980, Spring). Relationship between classroom behavior and student outcomes in junior high mathematics and English classes. *American Elementary Research Journal*, *17*(1), 43-60.

Evertson, C.M., Emmer, E.T., Clements, B.S., & Worsham, M.E. (1994). *Classroom management for elementary teachers*. Boston: Allyn & Bacon (ERIC Document Reproduction Service No. 369 782).

Evertson, C.M. & Harris, A.L. (1992). What we know about managing classrooms. *Educational Leadership*, *49*(7), 74-78.

Evertson, C.M., Weade, R., Green, J.L., & Crawford, J. *Effective classroom management and instruction: An exploration of models*. Washington, D.C.: National Institute of Education (ERIC Document Reproduction Service No. 271 423).

Fenley, M.A., Gaiter, J.L., Hammett, M., Liburd, L.C., Mercy, J.A., O'Carroll, P.W., Onwuachi-Saunders, C., Powell, K.E., & Thornton, T.N. (1993). *The prevention of youth violence: A framework for community action*. Atlanta, GA: Centers for Disease Control and Prevention (ERIC Document Reproduction Service No. 360 610).

Fortune, J.C., Williams, J., & White, W. (1992). *Help instructional growth to happen*. Final Evaluation Report, Chapter 2 Competitive Grant Program. Palmyra, VA: Fluvanna County Public Schools (ERIC Document Reproduction Service No. 344 313).

Fullan, M. (1990). Staff development, innovation, and instructional development. In B. Joyce (Ed.). *Changing school culture through staff development* (pp. 3-25). Alexandria, VA: Association for Supervision and Curriculum Development.

Fullan, M. (1993). Coordinating school and district development in restructuring. In J. Murphy & P. Hallinger (Eds.), *Restructuring schooling: Learning from ongoing efforts* (pp. 143-164). Newbury Park, CA: Corwin Press.

Fullan, M. & Shegelbauer, S. (1991). *The new meaning of educational change*. New York: Teachers College Press (ERIC Document Reproduction Service No. 354 588).

Gaddy, G.D. (1988, August). High school order and academic achievement. *American Journal of Education, 96*(4), 496-518 (ERIC Document Reproduction Service No. 303 434).

Gall, M.D. & Renchler, R.S. (1985). *Effective staff development for teachers: A research-based model*. Eugene, OR: University of Oregon, College of Education. (ERIC Document Reproduction Service No. 256 009).

Gersten, R. & Carnine, D. (1986). Direct instruction in reading comprehension. *Educational Leadership, 43*(7), 70-78.

Gettinger, M. (1983, October). Student behaviors, teacher reinforcement, student ability, and learning. *Contemporary Educational Psychology, 8*(4), 391-402.

Gettinger, M. (1988). Methods of proactive classroom management. *School Psychology Review, 17*(2), 227-242.

Glasman, N.S. (1984). Student achievement and the school principal. *Educational Evaluation and Policy Analysis, 7*(2), 283-296.

Glatthorn, A.A. (1989). *Secondary English classroom environments*. Greenville, NC: North Carolina State University and East Carolina University.

Good, T.L. (1984). Teacher effects. In *Making our schools more effective: Proceedings of three state conferences*. Columbia, MO: University of Missouri.

Good, T.L. (1987, July/August). Two decades of research on teacher expectations: Findings and future directions. *Journal of Teacher Education, 38*(4), 32-47.

Good, T.L. & Brophy, J.E. (1984). *Looking in classrooms* (3rd ed.). New York: Harper & Row.

Good, T.L. & Brophy, J.E. (1986). School effects. In M.C. Wittrock (Ed.), *Handbook of research on teaching* (3rd ed.), (pp. 570-602). New York: Macmillan.

Gottfredson, D.C. (1987, December). An evaluation of an organization development approach to reducing school disorder. *Evaluation Review, 11*(6), 739-763.

Gottfredson, D.C., Gottfredson, G.D., & Hybl, L.G. (1993, Spring). Managing adolescent behavior: A multiyear, multischool study. *American Educational Research Journal, 30*(1), 179-215 (ERIC Document Reproduction Service No. 333 549).

Gottfredson, G.D. & Gottfredson, D.C. (1989). *School climate, academic performance, attendance, and dropout*. Baltimore, MD: Center for Social Organization of Schools, Johns Hopkins University/Institute of Criminal Justice and Criminology, University of Maryland, College Park (ERIC Document Reproduction Service No. 308 225).

Gottfried, A.E. & Gottfried, A.W. (1991, April). *Parents reward strategies and children's academic intrinsic motivation and school performance*. Paper presented at the Biennial Meeting of the Society for Research in Child Development, Seattle, WA (ERIC Document Reproduction Service No. 335 144).

Great Falls Public Schools (1996). *Project RIDE: Responding to individual differences in education* (8th ed.). Longmont, CO: Sopris West.

Hallinger, P., Bickman, L., & Davis, K. (1989, March). *What makes a difference? School context, principal leadership, and student achievement*. Paper presented at the Annual Meeting of the American Educational Research Association, San Francisco, CA (ERIC Document Reproduction Service No. 332 341; ERIC Document Reproduction Service No. 308 578).

Hallinger, P. & Murphy, J. (1985, February). Characteristics of highly effective elementary school reading programs. *Educational Leadership*, *52*(5), 39-42.

Hawkins, J.D., Doueck, H.J., & Lishner, D.M. (1988, Spring). Changing teaching practices in mainstream classrooms to improve bonding and behavior of low achievers. *American Educational Research Journal*, *25*(1), 31-50.

Hawley, W.D., Rosenholtz, S.J., Goodstein, H., & Hasselbring, T. (1984, Summer). Good schools: What research says about improving student achievement. *Peabody Journal of Education*, *61*(4).

Heck, R.H. (1992, Spring). Principals' instructional leadership and school performance: Implications for policy development. *Educational Evaluation and Policy Analysis*, *14*(1), 21-34.

High, R.M. & Achilles, C.M. (1986, April). *Principal influence in instructionally effective schools*. Paper presented at the Annual Meeting of the American Educational Research Association, San Francisco, CA (ERIC Document Reproduction Service No. 277 115).

Hord, S.M. (1992). *Facilitative leadership: The imperative for change*. Austin, TX: Southwest Educational Development Laboratory (ERIC Document Reproduction Service No. 370 217).

Hord, S.M. (1992). The new alliance of superintendents and principals: Applying the research to site-based decision making. *Issues about Change*, *2*(1).

Jackson, R.M. & Crawford, G.J. (1991, April). *The superintendent and school improvement: Antecedents, actions and outcomes*. Paper presented at the Annual Meeting of the American Educational Research Association, Chicago, IL (ERIC Document Reproduction Service No. 333 538).

James, W. (1992). *The principles of psychology*. Boston: Harvard University Press.

Jones, V.F. & Jones, L.S. (1986). *Comprehensive classroom management*. Boston: Allyn and Bacon.

Kameenui, E.J. & Simmons, D.C. (1990). *Designing instructional strategies: The prevention of academic learning problems*. Englewood Cliffs, NJ: Prentice Hall.

Kearns, J. (1988, April). *The impact of systematic feedback on student self-esteem*. Paper presented at the Annual Meeting of the American Educational Research Association, New Orleans, LA (ERIC Document Reproduction Service No. 293 897).

Keedy, J.L. (1992, March). *Translating a school improvement agenda into practice: A social interaction perspective to the principalship*. Paper presented at the Annual Meeting of the Eastern Educational Research Association, Hilton Head, SC (ERIC Document Reproduction Service No. 348 766).

Kerr, M.M. & Nelson, C.M. (1989). *Strategies for Managing Behavior Problems in the Classroom* (2nd ed.). New York: Macmillan.

Kounin, J.S. (1977). *Discipline and group management in classrooms*. Huntington, NY: Krieger Publishing.

Krug, S.E. (1992). *Instructional leadership, school instructional climate, and student learning outcomes*. (Research Tech. Rep. No. 143). Urbana, IL: University of Illinois at Urbana-Champaign (ERIC Document Reproduction Service No. 359 668).

Larsen, R.J. (1987). *Identification of instructional leadership behaviors and the impact of their implementation on academic achievement*. Paper presented at the Annual Meeting of the American Educational Research Association, Washington, DC (ERIC Document Reproduction Service No. 281 286).

Lasley, T.J. & Wayson, W.W. (1982, December). Characteristics of schools with good discipline. *Educational Leadership*, *40*(3), 28-31.

Leach, D.J. & Byrne, M.K. (1986). Some "spillover" effects of a home-based reinforcement program in a secondary school. *Educational Psychology*, *6*(3), 265-276.

Lee, V.E. & Smith, J.B. (1993, July). Effects of school restructuring on the achievement and engagement of middle-grade students. *Sociology of Education*, *66*(3), 164-187.

Leinhardt, G., Weidman, C., & Hammond, K.M. (1987). Introduction and integration of classroom routines by expert teachers. *Curriculum Inquiry*, *17*(2), 135-176.

Leithwood, K. (1994, November). Leadership for school restructuring. *Educational Administration Quarterly*, *30*(4), 498-518.

Leithwood, K.A. & Montgomery, D.J. (1982, Fall). The role of the elementary school principal in program improvement. *Review of Educational Research*, *52*(3), 309-339.

Leithwood, K.A. & Montgomery, D.J. (1985). The role of the principal in school improvement. In G.R. Austin & H. Garber (Eds.), *Research on exemplary schools* (pp. 155-177). Orlando, FL: Academic Press.

Leming, T.J. (1993, November). In search of effective character education. *Educational Leadership*, *51*(3), 63-71.

Levine, D. (1982, April). Successful approaches for improving academic achievement in inner city elementary schools. *Phi Delta Kappan*, *63*(8), 523-526.

Levine, D.U. (1990, Fall). Update on effective schools: Findings and implications from research and practice. *Journal of Negro Education*, *59*(4), 577-684.

Levine, D. & Eubanks, E.E. (1989). Organizational arrangements at effective secondary schools. In H.J. Walberg & J.J. Lane (Eds.), *Organizing for learning: Toward the 21st century* (pp. 41-49). Reston, VA: National Association of Secondary School Principals.

Levine, D.U. & Eubanks, E.E. (1992). Site-based management: Engine for reform or pipedream? Problems, prospects, pitfalls, and prerequisites for success. In J.J. Lane & E.G. Epps (Eds.), *Restructuring the schools: Problems and prospects* (pp. 61-82). Berkeley, CA: McCutchan.

Levine, D.U. & Lezotte, L.W. (1990). *Unusually effective schools: A review and analysis of research and practice*. Madison,WI: The National Center for Effective Schools Research and Development (ERIC Document Reproduction Service No. 330 032).

Lewis, A. (1989). *Restructuring America's schools*. Arlington, VA: American Association of School Administrators.

Little, J.W. (1982, Fall). Norms of collegiality and experimentation: Workplace conditions and school success. *American Educational Research Journal*, *19*(2), 325-340.

Louis, K.S. & King, J.A. (1993). Professional cultures and performing schools: Does the myth of Sisyphus apply? In J. Murphy & P. Hallinger (Eds.), *Restructuring schooling: Learning from ongoing efforts* (pp. 216-250). Newbury Park, CA: Corwin Press.

Louis, K.S. & Miles, M.B. (1990). *Improving the urban high school: What works and why*. New York: Teachers College Press (ERIC Document Reproduction Service No. 327 623).

Madden, J.V., Lawson, D.R., & Sweet, D. (1976). *School effectiveness study*. Sacramento, CA: State of California Department of Education.

Malen, B., Ogawa, R.T., & Kranz, J. (1990). What do we know about school-based management? A case study of the literature—A call for research. In *Choice and control in American education* (Vol 2). New York: Falmer Press.

Malen, B., Ogawa, R.T., & Kranz, J. (1990, February). Site-based management: Unfulfilled promises. *The School Administrator*, *47*(2), pp. 30, 32, 53-56, 59.

Marshall, H.H. & Weinstein, R.S. (1985, April). *It's not how much brains you've got, it's how you use it: A comparison of classrooms expected to enhance or undermine students' self- evaluations*. Paper presented at the Annual Meeting of the American Educational Research Association, 69th, Chicago, IL (ERIC Document Reproduction Service No. 259 027).

Mayer, G.R. (1993, May). A dropout prevention program for at-risk high school students: Emphasizing consulting to promote positive classroom climates. *Education and Treatment of Children*, *16*(22), 135-146.

McCarthy, J. & Still, S. (1993). Hollibrook accelerated elementary school. In J. Murphy & P. Hallinger (Eds.), *Restructuring schooling: Learning from ongoing efforts* (pp. 63-83). Newbury Park, CA: Corwin Press.

McDevitt, T.M., Lennon, R., & Kopriva, R.J. (1991, March). Adolescents' perceptions of mothers' and fathers' prosocial actions and empathic responses. *Youth and Society*, *22*(3), 387-409.

Medley, D.M. (1978). *Teacher competence and teacher effectiveness: A review of process product research*. Washington, DC: American Association of Colleges for Teacher Education.

Midgley, C., Feldlaufer, H., & Eccles, J.S. (1989, August). Student/teacher relations and attitudes toward mathematics before and after the transition to junior high school. *Child Development*, *60*(4), 981-992.

Mills, R.S. & Grusec, J.E. (1989, July). Cognitive, affective, and behavioral consequences of praising altruism. *Merrill-Palmer Quarterly*, *35*(3), 299-326.

Mojkowski, C. & Fleming, D. (1988). *School-site management: Concepts and approaches*. Andover, MA: The Regional Laboratory for Educational Improvement of the Northeast and Islands (ERIC Document Reproduction Service No. 307 660).

Morgan, D.P. & Jenson, W.R. (1988). *Teaching behaviorally disordered students*. Columbus, OH: Merrill.

Mortimore, P. & Sammons, P. (1987, September). New evidence on effective elementary schools. *Educational Leadership*, *45*(1), 4-8.

Mortimore, P., Sammons, P., Stoll, L., Lewis, D., & Ecob, R. (1988). *School matters*. Berkeley, CA: University of California Press.

Murphy, J. & Hallinger, P. (1985, January). Effective high schools—What are the common characteristics? *NASSP Bulletin, 69*(477), 18-22.

Murphy, J. & Hallinger, P. (1988, January/February). Characteristics of instructionally effective school districts. *Journal of Educational Research, 81*(3), 175-181.

Murphy, J. & Hallinger, P. (Eds.). (1993). *Restructuring schooling: Learning from ongoing efforts*. Newbury Park, CA: Corwin Press.

Nanus, B. (1992). *Visionary leadership*. San Francisco, CA: Jossey Bass.

Oakes, J. (1989, Summer). What educational indicators? The case for assessing the school context. *Educational Evaluation and Policy Analysis, 11*(2), 181-199.

Odden, E.R. & Wohlstetter, P. (1995, February). Making school-based management work. *Educational Leadership, 52*(5), 32-36.

Ogawa, R.T. & Hart, A.W. (1985, Winter). The effect of principals on the instructional performance of schools. *The Journal of Educational Administration, 23*(1), 59-72.

Paine, S.C., Radicchi, J., Deutchman, L., Rosellini, L.C., & Darch, C.B. (1983). *Structuring your classroom for academic success*. Champaign, IL: Research Press.

Paredes, V. & Frazer, L. (1992, September). *School climate in the Austin Independent School District*. Austin, TX: Austin Independent School District, Office of Research and Evaluation (ERIC Document Reproduction Service No. 353 677).

Pavan, B.N. & Reid, N.A. (1991, April). *Espoused theoretical frameworks and the leadership behaviors of principals in achieving urban elementary schools*. Paper presented at the Annual Meeting of the American Educational Research Association, Chicago, IL (ERIC Document Reproduction Service No. 337 533).

Pavan, B.N. & Reid, N.A. (1994, January). Effective urban elementary schools and their women administrators. *Urban Education, 28*(4), 425-438.

Pecukonis, E.V. (1990, Spring). A cognitive/affective empathy training program as a function of ego development in aggressive adolescent females. *Adolescence, 25*(97), 59-76.

Phillips, V. & McCullough, L. (1992). *SST: Student/staff support teams*. Longmont, CO: Sopris West.

Porter, A.C. & Brophy, J. (1988, May). Synthesis of research on good teaching: Insights from the work of the institute for research on teaching. *Educational Leadership, 45*(8), 74-85.

Prestine, N.A. (1993). Feeding the ripples, riding the waves. In J. Murphy & P. Hallinger (Eds.), *Restructuring schooling: Learning from ongoing efforts* (pp. 32-62). Newbury Park, CA: Corwin Press.

Prestine, N.A. & Bowen, C. (1993, Fall). Benchmarks of change: Assessing essential school restructuring efforts. *Educational Evaluation and Policy Analysis*, *15*(3), 298-319.

Purkey, S.C. & Smith, M.S. (1983, March). Effective schools—a review. *Elementary School Journal*, *83*(4), 427-452 (ERIC Document Reproduction Service No. 221 534).

Render, G.F., Padilla, J.N.M., & Krank, H.M. (1989, Summer). Assertive discipline: A critical review and analysis. *Teachers College Record*, *90*(4), 607-630.

Rhode, G.R., Jenson, W.R., & Reavis, H.K. (1992). *The tough kid book: Practical classroom management strategies*. Longmont, CO: Sopris West.

Rosenholtz, S.J. (1985, May). School success and the organizational conditions of teaching. *American Journal of Education*, *93*(3), 352-387.

Rosenholtz, S.J. (1989). *Teachers' workplace: The social organization of schools*. New York: Longman.

Rosenholtz, S.J. (1989, March). Workplace conditions that affect teacher quality and commitment: Implications for teacher induction programs. *The Elementary School Journal*, *89*(4), 421-439.

Rosenshine, B. (1983). Teaching functions in instructional programs. *Elementary School Journal*, *83*(4), 335-351.

Rosenshine, B. & Stevens, R. (1986). Teaching functions. In M.C. Wittrock (Ed.), *Handbook of Research on Teaching* (3rd ed.), (pp. 376-391). New York: Macmillan.

Rosswork, S. (1977, December). Goal-setting: The effects on an academic task with varying magnitudes of incentive. *Journal of Educational Psychology*, *69*(6), 710-715.

Rutter, M., Maughan, B., Mortimore, P., & Ouston, J. (1979). *Fifteen thousand hours: Secondary schools and their effects on children*. Cambridge, MA: Harvard University Press.

Sammons, P., Hillman, J., & Mortimore, P. (1994, November). *Key characteristics of effective schools: A review of school effectiveness research*. London: International School Effectiveness & Improvement Centre, University of London.

Sanford, J.P., Emmer, E.T., & Clements, B.S. (1983). Improving classroom management. *Educational Leadership*, *40*(7), 56-60.

Sanford, J.P. & Evertson, C.M. (1981, January/February). Classroom management in a low SES junior high: Three case studies. *Journal of Teacher Education*, *32*(1), 34-38.

Schmitt, D.R. (1990, September). *The effect a principal has on the effective school program*. Paper presented at the Annual Meeting of the Association of Louisiana Evaluators, New Orleans, LA (ERIC Document Reproduction Service No. 330 089).

Shann, M.H. (1990). *Making schools more effective: Indicators for improvement*. Boston, MA: Boston University, School of Education (ERIC Document Reproduction Service No. 327 559).

Short, P.M. (1988, January). Effectively disciplined schools: Three themes from research. *NASSP Bulletin*, *72*(504), 1-3.

Short, P.M. & Greer, J.T. (1993). Restructuring schools through empowerment. In J. Murphy & P. Hallinger (Eds.), *Restructuring schooling: Learning from ongoing efforts* (pp. 165-187). Newbury Park, CA: Corwin Press.

Slavin, R.E. (1980, Summer). Cooperative learning. *Review of Educational Research*, *50*(2), 315-342.

Slavin, R.E. (1984, September). Students motivating students to excel: Cooperative incentives, cooperative tasks, and student achievement. *The Elementary School Journal*, *85*(1), 53-63.

Slavin, R.E. (1988, October). Cooperative learning and student achievement. *Educational Leadership*, *46*(2), 31-33.

Slavin, R.E. (1989). Cooperative learning and student achievement. In R.E. Slavin (Ed.), *School and classroom organization*. Hillsdale, NJ: Erlbaum.

Slavin, R.E. (1991, February). Group rewards make groupwork work. *Educational Leadership*, *48*(5), 89-91.

Slavin, R.E. (1994). Quality, appropriateness, incentive, and time: A model of instructional effectiveness. *International Journal of Educational Research*, *21*, 141-157.

Solomon, D., Watson, M.S., Delucchi, K.L., Schaps, E., & Battistich, V. (1988, Winter). Enhancing children's prosocial behavior in the classroom. *American Educational Research Journal*, *25*(4), 527-554.

Sparks, G.M. (1983, November). Synthesis of research on staff development for effective teaching. *Educational Leadership*, *41*(3), 65-72.

Sparks, G.M. (1986, Summer). The effectiveness of alternative training activities in changing teaching practices. *American Educational Research Journal*, *23*(2), 217-225.

Sprick, R.S. (1985). *Discipline in the secondary classroom: A problem by problem survival guide*. Englewood Cliffs, NJ: Prentice Hall.

Sprick, R.S. (1990). *Playground discipline: Positive techniques for recess supervision*. Eugene, OR: Teaching Strategies.

Sprick, R.S. (1995). Cafeteria discipline: Positive techniques for lunchroom supervision [video program]. Eugene, OR: Teaching Strategies.

Sprick, R.S. (1995). School-wide discipline and policies: An instructional classroom management approach. In E. Kameenui & C.B. Darch (Eds.), *Instructional classroom management: A proactive approach to management behavior* (pp. 234-267). White Plains, NY: Longman Press.

Sprick, R.S. (1995). *STP: Stop, think, plan: A school-wide strategy for teaching conflict resolution skills*. Eugene, OR: Teaching Strategies.

Sprick, R.S. & Colvin, G. (1992). *Bus discipline: A positive approach*. Eugene, OR: Teaching Strategies.

Sprick, R.S., Garrison, M., & Howard, L.M. (1998). *CHAMPS: A proactive approach to classroom management and discipline*. Longmont, CO: Sopris West.

Sprick, R.S. & Howard, L.M. (1995). *Teacher's encyclopedia of behavior management: 100 problems/500 plans*. Longmont, CO: Sopris West.

Sprick, R.S. & Howard, L.M. (1996). *Substitutes: Planning for productivity and consistency*. Longmont, CO: Sopris West.

Sprick, R.S., Sprick, M.S., & Garrison, M. (1993). *Foundations: Establishing positive discipline policies*. Longmont, CO: Sopris West.

Sprick, R.S., Sprick, M.S., & Garrison, M. (1993). *Interventions: Collaborative planning for students at-risk*. Longmont, CO: Sopris West.

Staub, R.W. (1990, August). The effects of publicly posted feedback on middle school students' disruptive hallway behavior. *Education and Treatment of Children*, *13*(3), 249-257.

Stevens, B. (Ed.). (1985). *School effectiveness: Eight variables that make a difference*. Lansing, MI: Michigan State Board of Education (ERIC Document Reproduction Service No. 257 218).

Stiggins, R.J. (1990). *Classroom assessment training program*. Portland, OR: Northwest Regional Educational Laboratory.

Stiller, J.D. & Ryan, R.M. (1992, April). *Teachers, parents, and student motivation: The effects of involvement and autonomy support*. Paper presented at the Annual Meeting of the American Educational Research Association, San Francisco, CA (ERIC Document Reproduction Service No. 348 759).

Stringfield, S. & Teddlie, C. (1988, October). A time to summarize: The Louisiana school effectiveness study. *Educational Leadership*, *46*(2), 43-49.

Taylor, B.O. & Levine, D.U. (1991, January). Effective schools projects and school-based management. *Phi Delta Kappan*, *72*(5), 394-397.

Taylor, S.E. (1986-87). The impact of an alternative high school program on students labeled "deviant." *Educational Research Quarterly*, *11*(1), 8-12.

Teddlie, C., Kirby, P.C., & Stringfield, S. (1989, May). Effective versus ineffective schools: Observable differences in the classroom. *American Journal of Education*, *97*(3), 221-236.

Tracz, S.M. & Gibson, S. (1986, November). *Effects of efficacy on academic achievement*. Paper presented at the Annual Meeting of the California Educational Research Association, Marina Del Ray, CA (ERIC Document Reproduction Service No. 281 853).

Venezky, R.L. & Winfield, L.F. (1979). Schools that succeed beyond expectations in reading. *Studies in Education*. Newark, DE: University of Delaware (ERIC Document Reproduction Service No. 177 484).

Vincenzi, H. & Ayrer, J.G. (1985, July). Determining effective schools. *Urban Education*, *20*(2), 123-132.

Wade, R.K. (1985, December/January). What makes a difference in inservice teacher education? A metaanalysis of research. *Educational Leadership*, *42*(4), 48-54.

Wang, M.C., Haertel, G.D., & Walberg, H.J. (1993, December–1994, January). What helps students learn? *Educational Leadership*, *51*(4), 74-79.

Wayson, W.W. & Lasley, T.J. (1984, February). Climates for excellence: Schools that foster self-discipline. *Phi Delta Kappan 65*(6), 419-421.

Weber, G. (1971). *Inner city children can be taught to read: Four successful schools* (Occasional Paper No. 18). Washington, DC: Council for Basic Education (ERIC Document Reproduction Service No. 057 125).

Weinstein, R.S. & Marshall, H.H. (1984). *Ecology of students' achievement expectations* (Executive Summary). Berkeley, CA: California University/Washington, DC: National Institute of Education (ERIC Document Reproduction Service No. 257 806).

White, P.A. (1989, September). An overview of school-based management: What does the research say? *NASSP Bulletin*, *73*(518), 1-8.

Wilson, B.L. & Corcoran, T.B. (1988). *Successful secondary schools: Visions of excellence in American public education*. New York: Falmer Press.

Wilson-Brewer, R., Cohen, S., O'Donnell, L., & Goodman, I.F. (1991, September). *Violence prevention for young adolescents: A survey of the state of the art*. Cambridge, MA: Education Development Center (ERIC Document Reproduction Service No. 356 442).

Wohlstetter, P., Smyer, R., & Mohrman, S.A. (1994, Fall). New boundaries for school-based management: The high involvement model. *Educational Evaluation and Policy Analysis, 16*(3), 268-286.

Wolery, M.R., Bailey, D.B., Jr., & Sugai, G.M. (1988). *Effective teaching: Principles and procedures of applied behavior analysis*. Boston: Allyn and Bacon.

Wong, H.K. & Wong, R.T. (1991). The first days of school: How to start school successfully. Sunnyvale, CA: Harry K. Wong Publications.

Woods, E.G. (1995, March). *Reducing the dropout rate* (Close-Up #17). Portland, OR: Northwest Regional Educational Laboratory.

Woolfolk, A.E. & Brooks, D.M. (1985, March). The influence of teachers' nonverbal behaviors on students' perceptions and performance. *The Elementary School Journal, 85*(4), 513-528.